The TINI™ Specification and Developer's Guide

Don Loomis

ADDISON-WESLEY

Boston • San Francisco • New York • Toronto • Montreal
London • Munich • Paris • Madrid
Capetown • Sydney • Tokyo • Singapore • Mexico City

The publisher offers discounts on this book when ordered in quantity for special sales. For more information, please contact:

Pearson Education Corporate Sales Division
One Lake Street
Upper Saddle River, NJ 07458
(800) 382-3419
corpsales@pearsontechgroup.com

Visit us on the Web at www.awl.com/cseng/

Library of Congress Cataloging-in-Publication Data
Loomis, Don.
    The TINI™ specification and developer's guide / Don Loomis.
        p. cm.
    Includes index.
    ISBN 0-201-72218-6
        1. Telecommunication systems--Design and construction--Data
    processing. 2. TINI. I. Title

TK5101 .L66 2001
621.382--dc.21

                                                              2001022528

ISBN 0-201-72218-6

Text printed on recycled paper
123456789—CRS—05 04 03 02 01
First printing, June 2001

To my family:
Judy, Jamie, and Nathan

Contents

Foreword

"Prediction is very difficult, especially about the future."
—Niels Bohr

Despite this authoritative caveat, here is a threefold prediction for this decade:

1. Demand for embedded software will grow significantly.
2. Java will be the language of choice for writing much of this new software.
3. Engines like TINI will host much of this Java code.

The ever-broadening reach of the Internet will motivate much of the increasing demand for embedded systems. Existing devices that have hitherto been driven by isolated controllers will become part of the network. New devices and new applications will exploit the opportunities of ubiquitous communications. These new (or newly connected) systems will appear in factories, offices, and homes. Some may radically affect the way we live; many will squeeze higher productivity from existing activities; some will be short-lived novelties. The obvious industrial applications include networked process control, networked power management, networked security, and so on. But the full extent of the network's reach isn't clear. Will networked process control allow a consumer to interact with a manufacturing system that's assembling a custom product? Will network power management enable your dishwasher to negotiate with a power utility to decide when to wash the dishes? Will networked security include regulated webcams in day-care facilities?

Can we afford to write the software for these new systems without Java? Traditionally, embedded software has been written in assembler, C, and some C++. Although these languages were undoubtedly the right choice to date, Moore's Law compels us to reevaluate that decision. As the relative cost of the programming rises against that of the hardware being programmed, we must move to languages that make better use of programmers, at the expense of cycles executed by our microprocessors. Java is the single best candidate to meet this need today.

Java is a higher-level language than C and C++. For example, Java's model of memory provides garbage-collected objects, whereas C's has little more than raw bytes. Java's higher-level abstractions, combined with its libraries, offer the programmer a tool that's portable, robust and network-ready. Although some hard real-time requirements may exceed Java's current reach, the language amply meets the needs of a wide range of embedded systems.

Java's suitability for embedded programming is no surprise. Java's roots are in embedded systems. James Gosling and his team at Sun created OAK—Java's precursor—almost a decade ago to meet their needs for coding a variety of networked consumer devices. Java blossomed on the desktop and in servers, but it still meets its original design constraints for portable, network-enabled, embedded software.

The TINI's microcontroller realizes the software benefits of Java in a cheap-hardware package that can be easily interfaced into a wide variety of systems. Its designers have selected and constructed an impressive balance of base components: hardware, firmware, and application libraries. The resulting platform is remarkable for its ease of use and flexibility. It is well positioned to play a significant role in the wave of network embedded systems that I anticipate.

Although I believe this formal rationale, it's only half the story. Just as important, the TINI is fun. The technology surprises and delights; it challenges our traditional thinking about how and where to apply computers. You'll be amazed when you first see a Web server running on a computer that's little bigger than a stick of chewing gum. Join the fun, and discover what you can build!

Tom Cargill
Boulder, Colorado
http://www.profcon.com/cargill

Preface

The earliest implementation of TINI actually dates back to late 1998 when a handful of engineers at Dallas Semiconductor, working with engineers at Sun Labs, demonstrated a very small, Java programmable device that was capable of controlling household electrical appliances. The prototype modules were crammed into light switch housings, coffee pots, HVAC systems, and fans. The appliances communicated with one another and with a central server, using a crude form of power line networking. The main idea was to provide not only local control of the appliance but also network connectivity to allow for remote control and monitoring. This increased the flexibility as well as the ease of use of the appliance. While none of the engineering work of this ancient version of the technology remains, the concept of a Java programmable runtime environment used to create embedded network applications is still the cornerstone of the TINI platform.

Over the past two years, the power line has given way to Ethernet, and the network programming interface has transitioned from an application specific interface to a standards-based TCP/IP protocol stack. The device I/O capabilities have also been greatly extended. Today, TINI is a broad platform that includes both hardware and software used to create intelligent network devices. These are often devices that require a small footprint, have low power consumption, and are cost sensitive. A few examples include industrial automation equipment, access control, vending machines, remote meters, and environmental sensors.

The TINI development project is a first for Dallas Semiconductor in that its design has been open to public scrutiny. The networking portion of the runtime environment along with the core Java APIs are of course well defined and well understood by a large development community. However, several new APIs have been created to expose the rich I/O capabilities of the technology. Major contributions to the definition of these new APIs have been made by the TINI SIG (special interest group). The result of this cooperative effort is a feature-rich platform. This work is an attempt at presenting a reasonably complete specification of the platform with plenty of examples to help clarify important topics. The book focuses on the following three areas.

- Platform definition
- Local device I/O APIs
- TCP/IP networking capabilities

Several of the chapters describe the APIs that expose the various forms of device I/O. Some of these may not be required by developers with specific applications in mind. However, the reader is encouraged to read at least the first and last chapters in addition to the chapters that expose capabilities relevant to his or her particular application. The first chapter provides a thorough definition of the platform, while the final chapter focuses on performance improvements and application hardening—two important topics for anyone writing serious applications targeted for the TINI runtime environment. Chapter 7, Building a Remote Data Logger, is also quite useful as it details a large example that brings together several of the concepts presented to that point in the book, including serial communication, 1-Wire networking, and TCP/IP networking over both Ethernet and serial interfaces.

The best way to become familiar with this technology is, of course, to use it. For this reason, every attempt has been made to create examples that are easily run on the most commonly available hardware. Some of the larger examples require additional hardware, but any additional hardware should be relatively inexpensive and easy to attain.

A strong familiarity with the Java programming language and some experience with network programming concepts is assumed. While a comfort level with hardware-related topics is helpful, it is not a requirement for understanding the bulk of the contents of this book. It is my hope that "pure programmers" can start with the code examples and gradually become more comfortable with the hardware-oriented concepts presented here.

ACKNOWLEDGMENTS

I would like to thank the many people who have contributed to the TINI project and this book. First and foremost I would like to thank the talented engineers who contributed so much to this long and intense development effort for their hard work and dedication: Kris Ardis, Bryan Armstrong, Tom Chenot, Chris Fox, Stephen Hess, Nicolas Kral, Yolanda Lei, Jesse Marroquin, Caroline McLean, Jeff Owens, David Smiczek, Lorne Smith, Stephen Umfleet, and Clayton Ware. I would also like to thank my management, Steve Curry and Michael Bolan, for their support and encouragement while I was writing this book. I am grateful for the volunteer efforts of many on the TINI SIG, who not only provide fantastic support to new developers but also contribute to the quality and definition of the platform.

Thorough and insightful technical reviews of early drafts were provided by Tom Cargill, Steve Curry, Peter Haggar, Judy Loomis, Robert Muchsel, and John Wilson. I appreciate all of the excellent feedback.

I am also grateful to Mike Hendrickson and Heather Olszyk at Addison-Wesley, who patiently guided me through the writing process. I would also like to thank the copy editor, Debbie Prato, who did a terrific job.

Finally, many thanks to the folks at Sun Microsystems who allowed me to use their excellent MIF Doclet tool to create the Almanac. The legend page of the Almanac is also the result of blatant thievery from the Java Real-Time specification.

CHAPTER 1   The TINI Platform

1.1   DESCRIPTION

Tiny InterNet Interface (TINI) is a platform developed by Dallas Semiconductor to provide system designers and software developers with a simple, flexible, and cost-effective means to design a wide variety of hardware devices that can connect directly to corporate and home networks. The platform is a combination of a small but powerful chip-set and a Java programmable runtime environment. The chip-set provides processing, control, device-level communication and networking capabilities. The features of the underlying hardware are exposed to the software developer through a set of Java application programming interfaces.

The primary goal of the platform is to provide a voice on the network to everything from small sensors and actuators to factory automation equipment and legacy hardware. The combination of broad-based I/O capability, a TCP/IP network protocol stack, and a Java programming environment empowers programmers to quickly create applications that provide not only local control of but also global access to TINI-based devices. TINI's networking capability extends the connectivity of any attached device by allowing interaction with remote systems and users through standard network applications such as Web browsers.

This chapter examines a few applications of the technology, followed by a high-level description of both the hardware and software components of the platform. The chapters that follow will focus on TINI's capabilities and features in much more detail.

1.2   APPLICATIONS

TINI is designed to meet the functional requirements for commercial and industrial embedded network applications. However, because of its low-cost hardware and the availability of free software development tools, it is beginning to find a home in the educational and hobbyist arenas as well.

TINI can be used for traditional stand-alone embedded tasks such as monitoring and controlling a local device or system, but the majority of applications utilize TINI's networking capabilities. A few applications of the technology include the following.

- *Industrial controls.* TINI's integrated Controller Area Network (CAN) support is instrumental in implementing factory automation equipment, networked switches, and actuators.
- *Web-based equipment monitoring and control.* It can be used for communication with equipment to provide remote diagnostics and data collection for purposes such as monitoring device utilization.
- *Protocol Conversion.* TINI-based systems can be used to connect legacy devices to Ethernet networks. Depending on the I/O capabilities of the legacy system, this may be a job that can be done with a PC or workstation as well. However, TINI can do the job at a fraction of the cost and size.
- *Environmental monitors.*[1] Using TINI's built-in support for 1-Wire networking, an application can query sensors and report the results to remote hosts.

Figure 1.1 shows a use model in which TINI is employed as a protocol converter (or link) between a legacy embedded device and an Ethernet network. The legacy device may communicate with the outside world using an RS232 serial port, Controller Area Network (CAN), or perhaps some type of parallel interface. The Java application running on TINI performs the task of communicating with the attached device in its native language (using a device-specific communication protocol) and presents the results to remote systems reachable via a TCP/IP network. The link provided by TINI is bidirectional, allowing a remote system to control as well as monitor the device.

Figure 1.1 focuses on an embedded system that controls and provides network connectivity to a single device. However, TINI can also serve to interconnect var-

---

1.   Chapter 7 presents a remote climate monitor application using TINI and a 1-Wire humidity sensor.

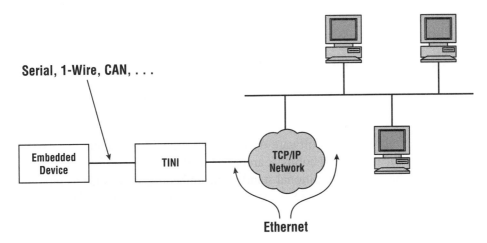

Figure 1.1 Protocol conversion

ious types of networks by bridging the gap between smaller, localized networks of inexpensive and lightweight devices and a "big world" TCP/IP network such as the Internet.

In general, TINI applications interface to other equipment and networks as opposed to humans. Due to the embedded control and I/O-centric nature of most embedded network applications, there is no built-in hardware or API support for a human interface. TINI-based systems often provide a remote display by implementing a network server, such as an HTTP server, allowing the user to interact with the system using a network client such as a Web browser. Local display and data entry can be obtained by interfacing to a PDA over a wireless link such as infrared (IR) or a hard-wired serial link. TINI systems requiring dedicated human interfacing capability can be implemented using liquid crystal displays (LCDs) and keypads.

1.3   TINI HARDWARE

This section presents a broad overview of TINI hardware and examines the major components as a chip-set. This includes primarily the large-scale integration (LSI) chips. Other small chips and miscellaneous discreet components, such as resistors, capacitors, and crystals, are of course required by any design. While every attempt has been made to keep the hardware description at a high level, parts of this section assume a comfort level with hardware-oriented concepts. However, complete comprehension of this section is not required for programmers wanting only to create Java applications for "off the shelf" TINI hardware. We will return to our regularly scheduled programming topics in the next section.

At the very minimum the TINI hardware consists of the following LSI chips.

- Microcontroller
- Flash ROM
- Static RAM

A block diagram of a minimal TINI hardware implementation is shown in Figure 1.2. The microcontroller is the heart of any TINI hardware design and directly executes the native code portion of the runtime environment. The microcontroller used in current TINI hardware implementations is the DS80C390. It is a small microcontroller with built-in support for several distinct forms of I/O, including serial and CAN. It also provides several general purpose port pins that can be used to perform simple control tasks such as driving relays and status LEDs.

The flash memory stores TINI's runtime environment and satisfies the following two important requirements.

1. The memory contents are maintained even in the absence of system power.
2. The memory is reprogrammable.

EEPROM[2] also meets both of the preceding criteria, but rapidly growing demand for flash memory has driven equally rapid advancement of flash technology, yielding faster and higher density memories.

The static RAM contains the system data area as well as the garbage collected heap from which all Java objects are allocated. It also stores all file system data. Whether the file system data persists in the absence of power depends on whether the static RAM is battery-backed (nonvolatized). This is discussed in more detail later in this section.

Peripheral devices, other than memory, can also be interfaced directly to the microcontroller's address and data buses (labeled "Parallel I/O expansion" in Figure 1.2). Two such peripherals that are commonly used in TINI-based systems are an Ethernet controller and a real-time clock. This configuration, shown in Figure 1.3, extends the reach of embedded devices to Ethernet networks. It also provides an accurate time reference for time-stamping purposes. Without the clock, commonly used Java methods such as `java.lang.System.currentTimeMillis` and `java.util.Date` methods that use `currentTimeMillis` return constant, and therefore useless, values. Section 1.3.1 discusses where peripheral devices such as the Ethernet controller and clock are included into the system's memory map.

---

2. EEPROM stands for electrically erasable programmable read-only memory.

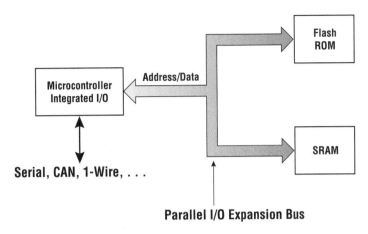

Figure 1.2 Minimal TINI Block Diagram

Another addition that is shown in Figure 1.3 is the battery-back circuity. The battery is a very small, single-cell lithium battery. Both the SRAM and clock used in TINI designs have very low stand-by power requirements, which means that an appropriately chosen lithium cell will keep the clock running and the SRAM data persistent for over 10 years.

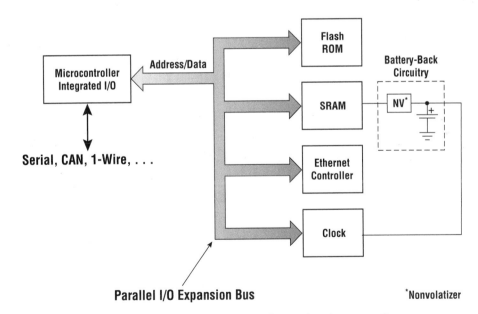

Figure 1.3 A more full-featured TINI hardware implementation

This circuitry performs two functions. First, it keeps the clock running in the absence of main power (V_{cc}), ensuring that an accurate time can always be read from the clock. The lithium cell alone performs this task. Also, the lithium cell, in conjunction with a small chip known as an SRAM nonvolatizer, maintains the contents of the static RAM in the absence of main power. The primary reason to nonvolatize the SRAM is to allow file system data to persist even when power is removed from the system.

1.3.1   The Memory Map

A memory map specifies where memory and other peripheral devices are decoded in the microcontroller's address space. The memory map used by TINI, shown in Figure 1.4, consists of the following three distinct segments.

- Code
- Data
- Peripheral

The segment sizes shown in the figure are maximums and are all multiples of 1 megabyte. If, for example, only 512 kilobytes of flash ROM exists in the code segment, the starting address of the data segment remains 0×100000. In other words, the starting addresses of the different segments are always as shown in Figure 1.4. But the ending address may be less than those indicated, depending on how much of the space is actually occupied by the memory chips. The minimum memory requirement for the code and data segments is 512 kilobytes each.

The code and data segments are occupied by memory chips, and the peripheral segment is occupied by other types of hardware components such as the Ethernet controller and real-time clock shown in Figure 1.3. Other peripheral devices that support a parallel bus interface compatible with the microcontroller's bus can also be mapped into the peripheral segment. A word of caution: Adding hardware in this fashion also adds capacitive loading to either or both the data and address busses (depending on the device). The system designer must be aware of this loading to ensure reliable system operation.

The Ethernet controller and real-time clock occupy these address ranges:

- Ethernet controller - [0x300000 - 0x0x307FFF]
- Real-Time clock - 0x310000

System designers must avoid these ranges for interfacing any device other than an Ethernet controller or real-time clock. The rest of this address range is available for adding other peripheral devices.

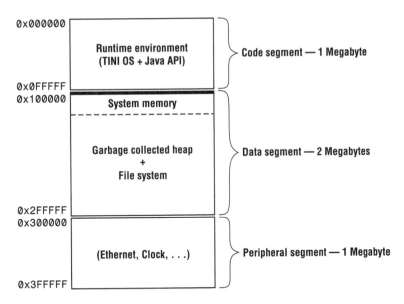

Figure 1.4 Memory map

There is also a separate 4-megabyte peripheral area, known as peripheral chip enable (PCE) space, that can be used to interface large (up to four 1-megabyte) external memory chips or other hardware devices directly to the microcontroller's address and data busses. However most hardware is mapped in the peripheral segment, shown in Figure 1.4, because it can be accessed more efficiently by the controller. The microcontroller uses four pins to control the PCE space. If no devices are mapped into this space, the microcontroller pins can be dedicated for use as general purpose port pins. The system designer is free to use the peripheral area either for interfacing hardware directly to the controller's address and data busses or general purpose TTL I/O, but not both. The topics of interfacing devices to the parallel expansion bus are discussed in Chapter 8, and accessing microcontroller port pins is covered in Chapter 9.

1.3.2 Integrated I/O

The peripheral devices described in the previous section are all interfaced to the microcontroller's address and data busses. However, a broad range of devices that are interesting to network-enable with TINI don't have support to interface to a full parallel bus. Often these devices have some form of serial interface. This usually results in a lower communication bandwidth. But a serial interface also reduces the required pin count, simplifies communication, and often lowers cost when compared with devices that have parallel bus-type interfaces. Serial interrupts also have the advantage of adding no load to either of the microcontroller's busses. Support for the following low-level serial communication protocols has been integrated onto the microcontroller.

- *Serial communication.* Synchronous serial protocols, using a 2-wire interface, and asynchronous serial communication, based on the RS232-C standard, are supported. TINI's controller provides two integrated UART (Universal Asynchronous Receiver Transmitter) circuits to facilitate serial communication. Asynchronous serial ports are extremely common in legacy devices. Asynchronous serial communication is the subject of Chapter 3.
- *Controller Area Network (CAN).* Originally developed at Bosch-Siemens, CAN is now described in two ISO standards.[3] It provides a reliable serial communications bus that is commonly used in automotive and industrial control applications. TINI's microcontroller provides two integrated CAN controllers. The application programming interface for communicating with CAN devices is shown in the appendix.
- *1-Wire net.* Developed by Dallas Semiconductor, the 1-Wire net is a network of small sensors, actuators, and memory elements that all share the same conductor for both communication and power. Programming for the 1-Wire net is the subject of Chapter 4.
- *TTL I/O.* These general purpose, bidirectional microcontroller port pins may be used for various control tasks and are not necessarily tied to any type of serial communication device. Both bit and byte-wide TTL I/O are covered in Chapter 9.

Utilizing the microcontroller's integrated I/O capabilities instead of the memory-mapped I/O, reduces both total device count and the cost of communicating with an external device because it burdens the CPU less than communicating with devices interfaced to the microcontroller's busses. For example, the microcontroller's CPU core runs at full speed, executing the runtime environment, while the UART is simultaneously sending and receiving serial characters. Communicating with bus interfaced peripherals, on the other hand, requires the CPU to stop what it's doing and execute instructions to read data from or write data to the device.

1.3.3   A Hardware Reference Design

Not requiring a single hardware design or form-factor provides system designers with the flexibility needed to design the TINI chip-set into custom products. But without a concrete and commercially available reference implementation of TINI hardware, each new design would have to begin with the rather painful process of

---

3.   ISO 11898 is for high-speed applications, and ISO 11519-2 is for low-speed applications.

designing and debugging new hardware. The TINI Board Model 390 (TBM390) has been developed to solve this problem. It allows both hardware and software designers to begin prototyping and development work without a large up-front investment of either money or time.

The TBM390 serves the following purposes.

- *Reference implementation.* All of the details of its design are public. Hardware developers are free to use information gleaned from the TBM390 when designing the chip-set into their own TINI-based systems.
- *Development tool.* It provides easy access to much of the platform's I/O capability, allowing designers to quickly interface custom external hardware and develop their applications. It has also been used internally by the TINI engineering team to develop and test the runtime environment.
- System component. The TBM390 is a fully specified[4] design. It has been heavily tested and functionally characterized over voltage and temperature and is therefore well suited for use as a core component for deployment in commercial and industrial embedded network applications.

The TBM390 is a compact (31.8 mm × 102.9 mm) 72-pin SIMM board. It is an Ethernet-ready hardware implementation and supports all of the functionality shown in Figure 1.3. It includes these important features.

- 512 kilobytes of flash memory for critical system code
- 512 kilobytes nonvolatile (that is, persistent) SRAM, expandable to 1 megabyte
- 10Base-T Ethernet controller
- Real-time clock
- Dual 1-Wire net interface
- Dual CAN controllers
- Dual serial port (one RS-232 level and one +5V level)
- 2-wire synchronous serial port
- Exposes the microcontroller's address and data busses for parallel I/O expansion
- Requires only a single +5V power supply

We'll meet the TBM390 again in the next chapter when we begin to work in a more hands-on fashion with TINI technology. A complete schematic and pin description is included in the CD provided with this book.

---

4. The specification for the TINI board model 390 can be found online at *http://www.ibutton.com/TINI/dstini1.pdf* and is also included in the accompanying CD.

1.4   TINI RUNTIME ENVIRONMENT

Providing hardware essential for developing embedded network devices is only half of the job. A large amount of software is also required to free application developers from having to worry about the details of creating layers of infrastructure to provide support for executing multiple tasks, network protocol stacks, and an application programming interface. A well-defined runtime environment that provides all of these features allows the developer to focus primarily on the details of the application. For this reason a runtime environment was developed from the beginning as an integral part of the overall platform.

The software that comprises TINI's runtime environment can be divided into two categories: native code executed directly by the microcontroller and an API interpreted as bytecodes by the Java Virtual Machine. Application code is written in Java and utilizes the API to exploit the capabilities of the native runtime and the underlying hardware resources. It is also possible to write native libraries that can be loaded from within an application to meet strict real-time requirements. A graphical representation of the runtime environment is shown in Figure 1.5.

Java programs running on TINI are most definitely applications and not applets. They are stand-alone programs that begin execution from a "main" method with the following signature.

```
public static void main(String[] args)
```

Also, unlike applets, they have no "sandbox" restrictions. On TINI, Java applications have full privileges and access to all system resources, even more so than on other platforms that support a Java runtime environment. This is particularly important for embedded applications because they are closely coupled with physical devices. Also, unlike other Java platforms, on TINI there is usually no system administrator to perform configuration and maintenance. This means that the application is responsible for configuring as well as controlling the entire system. For these reasons an application that controls an embedded system must have complete access to even low-level functionality provided by the OS.

1.4.1   API Overview

The API portion of the runtime environment combines classes from several packages defined in Sun's Java Developer's Kit (JDK) version 1.1.8 with TINI specific classes that expose system capabilities that have no analog on other larger Java platforms. The TINI-specific classes are all defined as subpackages underneath the root package com.dalsemi. The classes that are included in the runtime environment are known as the built-in portion of the API. There are also other classes defined in TINI's API that can be included in an application during the build process. The application build process is described in detail in the next chapter.

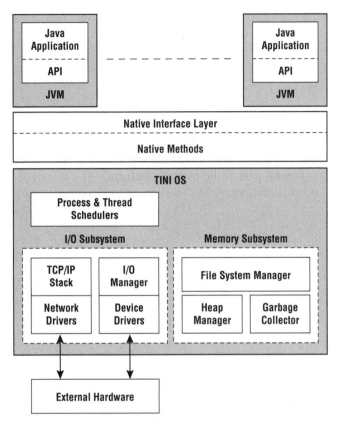

Figure 1.5   The TINI runtime environment

The Core Java Packages.   The API includes implementations for most of the classes in the following core Java packages.

- `java.lang`
- `java.io`
- `java.net`
- `java.util`

The differences between the JDK1.1.8 API specification and TINI implementation of the classes in these packages is described in a text file named "API Diffs.txt." This file is included in TINI's SDK documentation. As the platform evolves, it is our hope that this file will approach zero length. However, it is unlikely that functionality that is seldom useful in small embedded applications, such as the methods defined in `java.lang.Math` that perform trigonometric calculations, will be supported on TINI in the foreseeable future. Currently, the most notable omissions from the packages in the preceding list are the classes that support reflection and object serialization. Both reflection and object serialization will be supported in a future version of the runtime environment.

The com.dalsemi Packages

- com.dalsemi.system. Classes in this package provide access to several forms of integrated I/O including the 2-wire synchronous serial port, the microcontroller's data bus, and individual port pins. It also contains classes for configuring system resources such as the clock, watchdog timer, and external interrupt (see Chapter 10).
- com.dalsemi.tininet. This package contains a class named TININet that provides static methods for querying and setting several system-wide network parameters, such as the IP address and subnet mask. Subpackages of com.dalsemi.tininet provide support for networking protocols such as DHCP (Dynamic Host Configuration Protocol), ICMP (Internet Control Message Protocol), and DNS (Domain Name System). The com.dalsemi.tininet package and its subpackages are described in Chapter 5 and Chapter 6.
- com.dalsemi.shell. Classes in this package and its subpackages implement infrastructure for command shell applications. Classes in the subpackages of com.dalsemi.shell implement Telnet and FTP (File Transport Protocol) servers. These servers can also be used by applications other than command shells to provide access to Telnet and FTP client applications.
- com.dalsemi.comm. This package contains fairly low-level classes for accessing the CAN controllers. It also contains several classes for configuring and communicating with the system's serial ports. However, these classes are seldom used by applications. Serial port access is provided by an implementation of Sun's Java Communications API, which is defined in the javax.comm package. Serial communication using the Java Communications API is presented in Chapter 3.
- com.dalsemi.onewire. This is the root of the package hierarchy for the 1-Wire API. Unlike the packages listed above, the 1-Wire API is also supported on Java platforms other than TINI. The package com.dalsemi.onewire.container provides classes, known as containers, that comprehend the behavior of specific 1-Wire chips. To avoid consuming precious space in the flash memory, device specific container classes are not included in the built-in API. Container classes must therefore be included as a part of the application. The 1-Wire API is discussed in Chapter 4.

All of the public classes, built-in or otherwise, in the com.dalsemi package hierarchy are listed in almanac form in the appendix.

1.4.2 The Java Virtual Machine

The memory footprint of TINI's Java Virtual Machine (JVM) is less than 40 kilo-bytes. Despite its small size, it supports much of the functionality provided by full JVM implementations, including the following.

- Full support for threads
- Support for all primitive types
- Strings

However, there are also important omissions such as these.

- Dynamic class loading
- Object finalization[5]

Stating that the JVM doesn't support the dynamic loading of class files may leave the impression the methods Class.forName and Class.newInstance are not supported. In fact, both are implemented along with several other methods defined in class Class. Many of the classes in the API rely on this capability for several tasks, including creating character-to-byte converters and loading 1-Wire chip containers. However, if a thread of execution invokes forName and passes it a String specifying a class that does not exist in either the built-in API or the currently executing application, forName will throw a ClassNotFoundException rather than loading the specified class into the current application's binary image.

Class loading is effectively split into two phases. The first is performed by a convertor utility (TINIConvertor which is described in the next chapter) on a host development machine. The convertor performs complete constant pool[6] resolution of all of the classes used by an application. Application classes may reference methods and fields in other classes in the application or in the built-in API. The output of this conversion process is a binary image that can be directly executed by TINI's JVM. Any unresolvable constant pool entry results in the convertor aborting before generating an executable image. The second phase of the class loading process, running the class initializer methods, takes place on TINI. When a new Java application is launched, all of the class initializer methods are run for the classes in the API, followed by all of the application's class initializer methods. The net effect of this split class loading model is that an application, by default, has loaded all of the classes defined in the built-in API as well as application specific classes. This

---

5. An object's finalize method can be explicitly invoked by a Java thread of execution but is not automatically run before it is reclaimed by the garbage collector.
6. Every class file contains an area known as the constant pool that contains symbolic information required by the class during runtime execution, such as references to fields, methods, and classes.

doesn't increase the footprint of the application's binary image because converted images of the built-in API classes are stored separately in the flash memory as part of the runtime environment.

Besides the preceding functional omissions, there are also hard limits on certain resources, such as a maximum of 16 actively executing threads. These limits are documented in a file named "Limitations.txt" distributed with TINI's SDK documentation. As the platform evolves, the majority of these limits will disappear.

1.4.3   Native Methods

The native layer, shown in Figure 1.5, represents the collection of native methods that support the API by exposing the infrastructure provided by TINI OS. This includes access to the network protocol stack's socket layer as well as non-networking device drivers. It also includes methods for configuring and accessing system resources such as the watchdog timer and real-time clock.

Between the actual native method implementations and interpreted Java code is a very thin layer known as the native method interface. The native method interface is a boundary that must be crossed to switch execution contexts between code being executed by the JVM and a native method. TINI's native method interface (TNI) provides a very lightweight mechanism to cross this boundary. Its analog on most other Java platforms is the Java Native Interface (JNI). TNI is much lighter weight, and therefore less flexible, than JNI. Because the majority of TINI applications can be written entirely in Java, the details of TINI's native interface are unimportant to most developers. The only thing that matters is that the context switching overhead incurred when invoking the runtime environment's native methods is as low as possible.

Applications that require custom native methods can provide a native library that can be loaded into the system at runtime using the `loadLibrary`[7] method defined in the class `java.lang.Runtime`

```
public static void loadLibrary(String libname)
```

where the `libname` parameter specifies the file name of the native library. The details of writing native libraries are beyond the scope of this text. A pair of documents named "Native_Methods.txt" and "Native_API.txt" are included in the TINI SDK distribution, and they describe the process of writing and building native libraries.

---

7. The class `java.lang.System` also defines a method named `loadLibrary` that performs the identical task.

1.4.4 TINI OS

TINI's operating system is the lowest layer of the runtime environment. It is responsible for managing all system resources including access to the memory, scheduling multiple processes and threads of execution, and interacting with both internal and external hardware components. Though the operating system is a complex body of code that performs many independent tasks, it is reasonably well represented as being the sum of the following three major components.

- Process and thread schedulers
- Memory management subsystem
- I/O management subsystem

The following sections describe each of these components in some detail.

The Schedulers.   The operating system contains both process and thread scheduler modules that drive application-level (as opposed to operating system) code execution. The schedulers are launched by one of the microcontroller's timers that generates a high-priority interrupt every millisecond. The timer's interrupt service routine (ISR) either performs or initiates the following tasks.

- Update a millisecond system uptime count[8]
- Launch the thread schedulers every 2 milliseconds
- Run device driver modules every 4 milliseconds
- Launch the process scheduler every 8 milliseconds

Processes are scheduled in a simple round-robin fashion. Each process is given an 8-millisecond time slice. After the time slice expires, the process is sent to the end of an active process queue to wait its turn for another time slice. Even if multiple processes exist in the system, a single process can utilize nearly all of the CPU if it is the only process actively competing for execution time. Each process has its own independently operating thread scheduler. At the native level threads are cooperative, each thread voluntarily relinquishes control of the CPU. From a Java application's perspective, however, threads appear to be preemptive because the JVM ensures that each thread relinquishes the CPU after its 2-millisecond time slice has expired. Threads are also scheduled in a round-robin fashion.

Scheduling multiple threads is a lighter-weight operation than scheduling multiple processes. Because process scheduling is expensive compared to thread scheduling, most applications perform multiple independent execution tasks by

---

8. This count is accessible to applications using the `uptimeMillis` method defined in class `com.dalsemi.system.TINIOS`.

creating multiple threads to perform each task rather than spawning additional heavyweight processes. Synchronization is also easier to implement and more efficient with multiple threads than with multiple processes because there are no formal interprocess communication (IPC) mechanisms such as semaphores, shared memory or named pipes. Multiple processes can use sockets bound to the network stack's loopback interface or the file system using a crude mechanism such as a lock file. The network interfaces, including the loopback interface, are covered in Chapter 5. Both of these methods are slow compared to the built-in Java synchronization primitives for threads provided by the JVM.

However, it is useful to be able to have multiple Java processes during the application development phase. In this case, a command shell application runs as a separate Java process, allowing the developer to easily load and execute an application. Also, on TINI, the garbage collector runs as a separate process.

The Memory Management Subsystem.   The memory management system performs the following three tasks.

1. Allocates memory from the heap for both Java and system processes
2. Automatically collects garbage generated by Java processes
3. Manages the file system

As shown in Figure 1.4, the data segment contains all fast read/write memory used by the runtime environment. The portion of memory from the system area to the end of the data segment is called the heap. The heap represents the bulk of data memory available to the system. Access to the heap is controlled by a central set of memory allocation routines. The basic operation these routines perform is very similar to a C malloc operation. One exception is that most allocation operations clear all of the bytes of an allocated memory block to 0 before returning the block to the caller. Most blocks of memory are allocated from the heap on behalf of a new operation executed by the JVM or by file system operations.

Memory blocks are seldom freed explicitly. This is true of most of the memory consumed by system tasks and of all of the memory consumed by the JVM on behalf of a Java application. Memory is freed by a garbage collector that is run as a separate system process. The garbage collector (gc) process is created when the system boots. It is the only non-Java process that is ever created. Under normal memory use conditions, the gc process spends the majority of time in an inactive state. When the gc—or any other process for that matter—is inactive, it consumes no processing time. It is launched (that is, transitioned to an active state) in one of these three ways.

- An application explicitly invokes the gc method defined in the class java.lang.System.

- A new operation reduces the amount of available memory below a low-memory threshold of 64 kilobytes.
- A Java process terminates.

When the garbage collector runs, it does not clean up all of the garbage in the entire heap. It cleans up only the garbage created by the process that launched it. When a process terminates, all memory consumed by the process, including that held by objects and internal JVM structures, is freed.

All files are created, deleted, read, and written by Java applications, using classes in the java.io package such as File and FileOutputStream. All memory occupied by the file system, including file data and directories, is allocated from the same heap used for the storage of Java objects. When the file system manager allocates memory, it "tags" the memory to indicate that it is a part of the file system. This prevents memory held by file system structures from being reclaimed by the garbage collector. Memory used by the file system manager is explicitly freed during file deletion operations.

The fact that file system data structures are allocated from the same heap as Java objects may seem odd at first, but there is no local hard disk associated with TINI. Using the heap, which is contained within fast static RAM, has the advantage that file write operations are as fast as file read operations. With most other rewritable memory technologies, writes would be much slower than reads. The downside to this approach is that TINI hardware implementations that do not provide the static RAM nonvolatizing circuitry, shown in Figure 1.3, lose file system data when power is removed from the system. File system data will remain intact even in the absence of main system power in systems that nonvolatize the static RAM. The other obvious disadvantage is that as the file system grows, it consumes more memory from the heap, leaving less memory available for Java object creation.

The file system can contain arbitrary data files as well as executable binary images. All executable files are assumed to be binary images of Java applications that can be executed directly by the JVM. Large files are fragmented into smaller 512-byte blocks and therefore occupy a noncontiguous range of memory. Before an executable file can be interpreted by the JVM, it must be contiguous. Therefore, the first time an executable file is run, the file system manager defragments the file in order to generate a contiguous binary image. The memory consumed by the original file fragments is freed. From this point forward the file can be executed without the overhead of defragmentation. In the next chapter we'll take a much higher-level look at the file system.

The I/O Subsystem. The I/O subsystem is divided into two major components: network and non-network I/O. Referring to CAN and 1-Wire as non-networking I/O can be somewhat confusing because both are in fact networking technologies. However for the sake of this discussion, network I/O refers strictly to "big world" TCP/IP (Transmission Control Protocol/Internet Protocol) networking.

Both the TCP/IP stack and the I/O manager are implemented as independent lightweight kernel processes.[9] These processes are driven by a 4-millisecond system timer tick. The I/O manager controls all non-networking device drivers. I/O requests generated from application code all pass through the I/O manager to the appropriate driver and back. Certain I/O requests go directly to attached hardware devices. For example, there are no built-in drivers to communicate with arbitrary devices attached to the parallel expansion bus. In this case, the Java application is responsible for managing all of the low-level details of communicating with the device.

The TCP/IP network protocol stack is one of the largest blocks of native code in the runtime environment. It provides much of the same networking capability found on larger platforms and is sufficiently rich in functionality to support a full implementation of the java.net package. The protocol stack supports multiple network interfaces, including Ethernet, for high-speed local area networking and PPP (PPP—Point-to-Point Protocol) over a serial link for remote dial-up networking using an analog modem. The Ethernet interface is managed by a separate device driver that performs all communication with the Ethernet controller. PPP is a little different in that it actually relies on a lower-level serial port driver to deliver network messages to the physical communications port.

1.4.5   Bootstrapping the System

To understand the sequence of events that occurs when the system boots, we'll first need to take an expanded look at the "code area" section of the entire memory map shown in Figure 1.4. The code area is broken into these three distinct pieces, shown in Figure 1.6.

- Bootstrap loader
- Runtime environment
- Primary Java application

The combination of the bootstrap loader and runtime environment consumes the first 468 kilobytes in the code area. The primary application always begins at the fixed address of 0x70000. Because the minimum amount of flash memory required by TINI is 512 kilobytes, a minimum of 64 kilobytes[10] is reserved for storage of the primary application. Hardware implementations that provide the

---

9. Kernel processes should not be confused with application-level processes.
10. The exact minimum is a little smaller (65280 bytes) because 256 bytes are reserved for persistent storage of static network parameters. (See Section 5.2.1 for details.)

full 1024 kilobytes of flash memory can have a primary application up to 576 kilobytes in length.

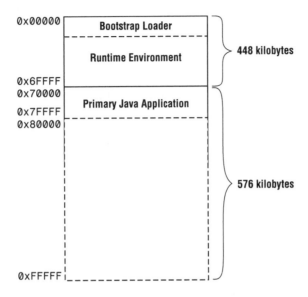

Figure 1.6 Code area—expanded

At a high level, the boot sequence can be described in very simple terms. The bootstrap loader is the first code executed by the microcontroller. Under normal startup conditions, the boot loader quickly transfers control to the runtime environment. After some system initialization routines have been executed, the runtime environment launches the primary Java application. Next we'll take a more detailed look into the boot sequence to better understand this important phase of system operation.

1.4.6   Step 1: Execute the Bootstrap Loader

The bootstrap loader is a very small autonomous program (consuming about 4 kilobytes of code space) that controls the loading of the runtime environment and primary Java application into the flash ROM. The behavior of the bootstrap loader depends on the source of the reset that preceded the microcontroller's execution of the first machine instruction. There are two classes of reset with which the bootstrap loader is concerned: a power-on reset and an external reset. As the name suggests, a power-on reset (POR) occurs as soon as power is applied to the system and reaches an acceptable minimum level. An external reset is generated by an external source by driving the microcontroller's reset pin to its active state. This provides an out-of-band reset that can be generated without cycling power.

After a POR, the boot loader immediately transfers control to the runtime environment's initialization code, and the "normal" boot process continues. In the event of an external reset, the bootstrap loader waits to receive a specific data pattern[11] on the microcontroller's default serial port (also known as "serial0"). It uses the first character of the pattern to determine the serial data rate. If the correct sequence is received, the loader enters a small command shell and awaits further instructions over the serial port. Once in the loader shell, the attached serial device, typically a PC or workstation, can reload any or all of the contents of the flash memory. The bootstrap loader will only wait for the data sequence for three seconds before continuing normal system startup. The next chapter will discuss the specifics of interacting with the bootstrap loader for the purposes of loading the runtime environment.

1.4.7   Step 2: Initialize the Runtime Environment

After the bootstrap loader transfers control to the runtime environment, a set of initialization routines is executed. The following tasks are performed during the initialization phase.

- Heap integrity check
- File system integrity check
- Device driver initialization
- Create initial processes

Both the heap and file system managers maintain static system buffers that are used to back out of any incomplete operations. This is intended to prevent either the loss or corruption of data due to an unexpected power interruption. During the initialization phase both the heap and file system are checked for any inconsistencies. Any incomplete transactions are "rolled back." If for any reason the heap is structurally damaged, it is reset to allow the system to boot in a consistent state. The integrity checks are skipped for systems that do not battery back the memory (SRAM) that contains the heap. In this case the heap is unconditionally reset when the system boots.

If the heap check passes, the sweeper (the second phase of the mark-and-sweep garbage collector) is executed to look for any garbage left by applications that were terminated abruptly. Abrupt termination usually occurs due to loss of power. When an application terminates normally, all memory it was using is immediately reclaimed. Any memory that is not part of the file system or otherwise marked as

---

11. The current version of the bootstrap loader waits for a carriage return (0x0d) character.

persistent is returned to the free memory portion of the heap. Determining what actions were taken by the heap or file system manager during the boot process is covered further in Section 11.6, which presents "application hardening" tips.

After the integrity checks, the I/O manager runs the initialization routines for the serial port and Ethernet drivers as well as other operating system modules. Drivers for other I/O resources such as CAN and 1-Wire are initialized as needed by the system.

In the last phase of initialization these two processes are created.

- The garbage collector (gc)
- The primary Java application

The gc process is created first and is alive as long as the system is running. However, it spends most of its time in a suspended state, consuming virtually none of the CPU's resources. When it is first created, it has no work to do and therefore immediately suspends itself. It remains in a suspended state until the memory manager wakes it up because of either a low memory condition or a garbage collection that has been requested by a Java application. Finally, a process is created to execute the primary Java application. After both processes have been created, the runtime environment's initialization phase is complete and the task scheduler begins executing the primary application.

1.4.8   Step 3: Start the Primary Java Application

The primary Java application is in a sense analogous to the primordial thread of any Java application. The primordial thread is automatically created by the system, and all other threads are created as a direct result of actions taken by the application. The primary application is always the first Java process launched by the runtime environment and is, in fact, the only application launched automatically by the runtime environment. Without further direction from the primary application no other system processes, Java or native, are created by the system.

As with all Java processes, TINI's JVM first executes the class initializer methods in the API classes, followed by the applications class initializer methods. After all class initialization is complete, the primordial thread is launched and execution continues from the application's main method. The amount of time from the moment that power is applied to execution of the main method is around three seconds. This can of course vary depending on the amount of code that must be executed in the application's class initializer methods. The bulk of the startup time is spent executing the API class initializer methods. The exact behavior of the primary application, from this point forward, is determined by the developer based on the requirements of the overall embedded system. Typically the primary application assumes control of the entire system and is responsible for any configuration and hardware device initialization that may be required.

The primary application can launch other Java processes, but most applications accomplish multiple execution tasks simply by creating additional threads rather than spawning new processes. Thread swapping is much lighter weight than process swapping, leading to smaller system delays due to context-switching overhead. One class of application in which it makes sense to launch independent processes is a command shell. For development purposes a command shell program can be very useful as the primary application. The shell provides a convenient way to configure the system parameters such as network settings and run and test applications. After the application has been debugged and hardened for production deployment, it can replace the shell as the primary Java application and assume control of the entire embedded system. A small command shell, known as "slush," is provided in the TINI software developer's kit and is described further in the following chapter.

1.5 THE FUTURE

This chapter described the TINI platform as it exists today. Both the hardware (chip-set) and software (runtime environment) components of the platform will continue to evolve over time. On the software front the main focus will be the addition of more support for the Java runtime environment with the addition of features such as object serialization and reflection. At the operating system level, strict priority-based schedulers will be added for both process and thread scheduling to offer better support for real-time applications. The migration path for the chip-set is very clear: faster microcontroller cores for enhanced system performance and higher levels of integration to reduce the number of chips in the chip-set. The next generation controller, already in development, will widen TINI's address space and integrate the Ethernet controller onto the same core as the microcontroller. Other microcontroller enhancements will also provide chip level support aimed at enhancing the performance of the JVM and the runtime environment as a whole. Regardless of how the platform evolves, care will be taken to ensure that TINI's minimum resource requirements remain low even as its capabilities continue to grow.

CHAPTER 2 # Getting Started

The chapters that follow contain many examples that run directly on TINI and illustrate the use of the various application programming interfaces. These examples also demonstrate programming practices and concepts used in developing Java code targeted for small footprint, embedded-network computing applications. This chapter provides a description of both the hardware and software environment needed to develop and execute TINI applications written in Java, including the examples presented in this text. Readers already familiar with TINI technology can skip this chapter.

2.1 HARDWARE REQUIREMENTS

This section describes the core hardware configuration[1] used to develop and test the example programs listed in this book. Other configurations are certainly possible and can be assembled in piecemeal fashion by readers already in possession of, or familiar with, TINI.

---

1. The hardware configuration used to develop and test the examples in this book is available from Dallas Semiconductor (see *http://www.ibutton.com/TINI/ getting_started.html* for details).

2.1.1   The TINI Board Model 390

The TINI board model 390 (TBM390), which was described in Section 1.3.3, is a complete TINI hardware reference design that is embodied in a full commercial product. The TBM390 is currently available with either 512 kilobytes or 1 megabyte of nonvolatile, static RAM. It is available as a 72-pin SIMM module and is shown in Figure 2.1. All examples in this book are executed and tested using a TBM390 with 512 kilobytes of SRAM. Unless it's important, we'll just say TINI, avoiding further qualifiers, when referring to TINI hardware.

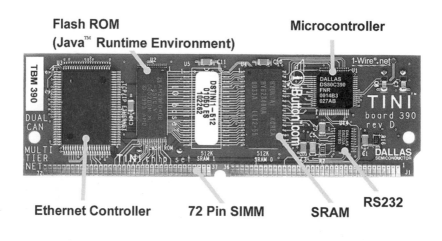

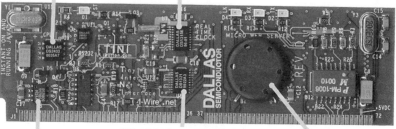

Figure 2.1   TBM390 (top and bottom views)

2.1.2 The E10 Socket

For application development and prototyping, a TINI board, as shown in Figure 2.1, isn't terribly useful without the ability to connect necessities such as serial, Ethernet, and power. A socket board's main function is to provide the physical connectors to interface the TBM390 with other equipment such as an Ethernet network, a serial device, or a 1-Wire network.

The E10 socket board is aimed at aiding the application development process. It provides the following physical connectors.

- *72-pin SIMM connector.* The SIMM connector accepts the TINI board shown in Figure 2.1.
- *9-pin female DB9 connector.* This connector provides a limited DCE (Data Communications Equipment) type serial port that provides connection to a standard PC DTE (Data Terminal Equipment) serial port using a straight-through serial cable. This port is typically only used for loading the run-time environment and bootstrap application (Section 2.3). Hardware hand-shake lines, such as RTS (Request To Send) and CTS (Clear To Send), are not supported by the DCE port.
- *9-pin male DB9 connector.* This connector provides a DTE serial port for straight-through connection to DCE devices such as analog modems. Most TINI applications that control serial devices use the DTE port. In this case TINI is the DTE device, replacing the PC or workstation. The DTE serial port supports all hardware handshake lines except DSR (Data Set Ready) and RI (Ring Indicate).
- *RJ45.* The RJ45 connector accepts a standard 10Base-T Ethernet cable providing connectivity to an Ethernet network. Use a straight-through cable for connecting TINI to the network, using a hub or a crossover cable for connecting TINI directly to a PC or workstation.
- *RJ11.* The RJ11 connector provides access to the 1-Wire network using standard telephone cable. 1-Wire networking is discussed in Chapter 4.
- *Power jack.* The E10 accepts a regulated +5V DC power supply.

The E10 also provides IC (Integrated Circuit) and discreet component footprints to support additional I/O options such as parallel, CAN and additional serial ports.

The "E" in E10 stands for Eurocard and suggests that the size of the socket board itself is identical to one of the standard Eurocard sizes, allowing it to be placed inside a Eurocard enclosure. The E10 socket board is 160mm × 120mm. Figure 2.2 shows the E10 socket with a TINI board inserted and labels the connectors just described.

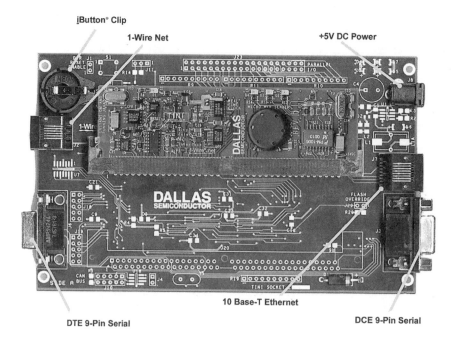

iButton® Clip

1-Wire Net

+5V DC Power

1-Wire

10 Base-T Ethernet

DTE 9-Pin Serial

DCE 9-Pin Serial

Figure 2.2 The E10 socket with TINI board

2.2 DEVELOPMENT PLATFORM REQUIREMENTS

We use the term "development platform" to refer to the computer used for creating, building, and loading TINI applications. This is the machine that runs the JDK or equivalent Java development and runtime environment and is connected to TINI using Ethernet and/or a serial cable. Typically we'll just refer to the host development machine as "the host."

Since all of the required tools have been written in Java, TINI applications can be developed on any of the following operating systems.

- Any Win32 OS (Windows 95, 98, NT, 2000)
- Linux
- Solaris

To load TINI's runtime environment (see Section 2.3) the host must also have an RS232 serial port. This requirement is met by nearly every PC and workstation.

Besides one of the operating systems mentioned above and a serial port, the host machine must also have the following software correctly installed.

- Java Development Environment
- Java Communications API
- TINI Software Development Kit

These software components are described briefly in the following sections.

2.2.1 A Java Development Environment

All examples in this text were compiled using javac from Sun's JDK, standard edition 1.2.2.[2] Sun's JDK is free and available for most platforms that support Java development of any sort. However, you can certainly use your favorite Java IDE such as JBuilder or Visual Cafe to edit and compile your TINI applications. In fact there are OpenSource extensions to JBuilder that allow for a purely graphical development environment for TINI.

2.2.2 The Java Communications API

The Java Communications API (comm API) is also available from Sun Microsystems and provides the infrastructure required to communicate with RS232 serial ports in a platform-independent fashion. This API is used by the serial communications utility, provided in the TINI SDK, that manages the process of loading the TINI runtime environment. At the time of this writing, comm API drivers supplied by Sun supported only the Win32 and Solaris platforms. However, the OpenSource project RXTX provides driver support for Linux. The installation process for the comm API for Win32 and Solaris is described in the comm API's distribution Readme.html and is straightforward. There is extra work, such as compiling the driver source, involved for those installing the comm API on Linux. Detailed instructions are provided at the RXTX Web site.[3]

2.2.3 The TINI SDK

The latest release of the TINI software distribution can be freely downloaded from Dallas Semiconductor's Web site.[4] At the time of this writing, the current release of the software is 1.02. The SDK is distributed as a single compressed tar file

---

2. Any version of the JDK starting from 1.1.8 will suffice.
3. More information on RXTX including all source is available from *http://www.rxtx.org/*.
4. The latest version of the TINI SDK can be downloaded from *http://www.ibutton.com/TINI/software/index.html*.

(.tgz).[5] After downloading the distribution and extracting its contents, the SDK is installed. There is no setup.exe to run that installs DLLs or modifies the registry, and there is no need to reboot your system. These are some of the important files included in the SDK. It is important to understand the contents of these files because we will use them to build the examples later in this chapter.

- **README.txt**. The README.txt file is located in the root of the SDK hierarchy. Start by completely reading this document. It contains detailed instructions on how to install the TINI runtime environment, boot the TINI system, and initialize its network settings. It also contains references to other documents in the SDK that further describe the process of creating a full development environment.
- **tini.jar**. This jar file is located in the bin directory and includes two important utility programs: JavaKit and TINIConvertor. The JavaKit utility manages the firmware-loading process and performs other system maintenance tasks. It can also be used to run slush (see Section 2.4) user sessions over a serial connection. The TINIConvertor utility takes the class files in your application as input and generates a binary image suitable for execution on TINI.
- **tiniclasses.jar**. The tiniclasses.jar file is located in the bin directory and contains all of the class files in TINI's API. In this sense it is similar to the rt.jar file distributed with Sun's JRE and JDK 1.2 and higher. This file must always be included as the first file in the classpath when compiling applications for TINI.
- **tini.db**. The tini.db file is an ASCII file that contains information about the API class files. This file is used by TINIConvertor along with the class files in your application to produce a binary image suitable for interpretation by TINI's JVM.
- **tini.tbin**. The .tbin extension is short for "TINI binary" and is the default extension used for binary images that are targeted for execution from the flash ROM. The tini.tbin file is located in the bin directory and contains the binary image of TINI's runtime environment. It is a combination of the native operating system and the API. This file must be loaded before any Java applications can be executed.
- **slush.tbin**. The slush.tbin file is located in the bin directory and contains the binary image of the user shell known as slush. Section 2.4 provides a description and a quick tour of slush.

---

5. The commonly used Win32-based winzip utility will handle gzipped tar files correctly.

2.3 LOADING THE TINI RUNTIME ENVIRONMENT

At this point, it is assumed that you have successfully installed your favorite Java development environment, the Java Communications API, and the TINI SDK on the host machine. Installing the runtime environment on your TINI board consists of these two steps.

1. Loading `tini.tbin` and `slush.tbin`
2. Initializing the heap

Both steps require the use of the `JavaKit` utility. `JavaKit` runs on the host and communicates with TINI's bootstrap loader (Section 1.4.5) over an RS232 serial port using the comm API. `JavaKit` is a Swing-based GUI utility, so if you're using a version of the JDK released prior to 1.2, make sure that you have the `swing.jar` file somewhere in your classpath. Before starting `JavaKit`, make sure that you've connected TINI and the host machine using a straight-through (not a null-modem) serial cable. Start `JavaKit` with a command similar to this one.

```
c:\jdk1.2.2\bin\javaw -classpath c:\tini1.02\bin\tini.jar JavaKit
```

Once you've successfully launched `JavaKit`, you should see a window similar to the one shown in Figure 2.3.

Using the "Port Name" drop down selection box, choose the serial port to which TINI is attached and click the "Open Port" button. If `JavaKit` is able to open the selected serial port, the name of "Open Port" button will change to "Close Port." If the open operation fails, `JavaKit` will display an error message indicating the failure. If an attempt to open a serial port fails, it is usually because another application currently owns the port. In this case, close the application that owns the serial port and try the "Open Port" button again. Next, click the "Reset" button. This should result in TINI's loader generating a prompt similar to this.

```
TINI loader 05-15-00 17:45
Copyright (C) 2000 Dallas Semiconductor. All rights reserved.
>
```

Now that we have the loader's attention, we can load the runtime binaries. Select "Load File" from the File menu. Use the directory drop down box to select the bin directory in the SDK hierarchy. Select the files named `tini.tbin` and `slush.tbin` and click the "Open" button. You should see the following text displayed in the `JavaKit` window.

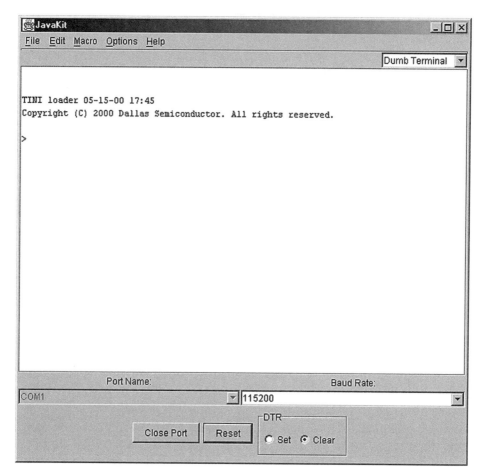

Figure 2.3   JavaKit (Loader utility)

```
Loading file: C:\tini1.02\bin\slush.tbin.
Please wait... (ESC to abort.)
Load complete.

Loading file: C:\tini1.02\bin\tini.tbin.
Please wait... (ESC to abort.)
Load complete.
```

These files are rather large and at JavaKit's default serial data rate of 115,200 bps, loading tini.tbin and slush.tbin takes a couple of minutes.

Now we've loaded the binary images that comprise TINI's runtime. But before the system is booted for the first time, the heap must be initialized. At the boot loader prompt, type "BANK 18" and hit Enter. This selects the lowest 64K portion of TINI's heap. See Section 1.3.1 for details of the memory map. Next type "FILL 0" and hit Enter.

```
>BANK 18
>FILL 0
```

This rather cryptic two-step sequence fills the low 64K of heap with 0s, forcing the OS to initialize the heap, file system, and all other persistent settings.

Now we're ready to boot the system for the first time. To exit the serial loader and boot the TINI runtime, type "EXIT" at the prompt. These are the first few lines of text generated by the OS early in the boot process.

```
----> TINI Boot <----
TINI OS 1.02
API Version 8009
Copyright (C) 1999 - 2001 Dallas Semiconductor Corporation
```

The system boot flow is described in detail in Section 1.4.5. After a couple of seconds the system will have completely booted, and the following prompt is displayed by slush.

```
Hit any key to login.
```

After pressing a key, slush prompts the user for a login name.

```
Welcome to slush.  (Version 1.02)
TINI login:
```

The next section provides a brief introduction to slush that will cover, among other things, the login process.

2.4 SLUSH: A QUICK PRIMER

This section provides a brief overview of slush and a look at just enough of the commands and features we need to load and run the example applications at the end of this chapter and later chapters. A more complete description of slush is provided in the Slush.txt file included in the SDK.

2.4.1 Slush Defined

Slush is a small command shell intended to provide a UNIX-like interface to TINI's runtime environment by providing Serial (TTY), Telnet, and FTP servers. Slush is itself a Java application that is interpreted by TINI's JVM. Slush is less than a full operating system but more than a simple shell. It provides a way to view and manipulate the file system, run other Java applications, and control system functions such as the watchdog timer and network configuration.

Slush is designed to be a multi-threaded, multi-user system allowing simultaneous user sessions. It is typically used in the development phase. It provides conveniences such as network accessibility using the ubiquitous networking client application Telnet for user interaction and FTP for transferring applications and data files to and from the file system. After an application has been developed and debugged, it is typically built and targeted for installation in the flash ROM, replacing slush. Transitioning an application from the development phase to production deployment is discussed in Chapter 11.

2.4.2 Starting a New Session

Slush uses a user name and password to authenticate a login request and start a new user session. When slush is booted for the first time (as in the previous section), it creates two new default accounts: a root account with "super user" or administration privileges and a guest account with more limited access to system resources. Additional users can be added or removed by a user with administrative privileges. The user names and password for the default accounts are shown in Table 2.1.

Table 2.1 Default user accounts

Account Name	User Name	Initial Password
root	root	tini
guest	guest	guest

When we left the previous section we had booted slush for the first time and left it at the login prompt. It is important to note that both slush and TINI's file system are case sensitive. All characters in the user name and password for both default accounts are lower case. Log on to the system to establish a user session with slush. Use the root account by typing "root<CR>" at the login prompt and "tini<CR>" at the password prompt.

```
TINI login: root
TINI password:
```

The password characters typed at the password prompt are not echoed by the system. After successfully logging on to the system, slush returns a prompt comprised of the host name, TINI in this case, and the login session's current working directory in the file system. Immediately after logging on to the system, the current working directory is the root directory of the file system.

```
TINI />
```

2.4.3 Exploring the File System

Using slush, we can explore the file system in its initial state, just after the first slush boot. A detailed listing of the files in a directory can be displayed using the ls command with the "-1" option.

```
TINI /> ls -1
total 2
drwxr-x     1 root     admin         1 Jan 27 15:13 .
drwxr-x     1 root     admin         3 Jan 27 15:14 etc

TINI>
```

The first line after the prompt displays the total number of files and directories contained within the current directory. In the preceding sample listing, the second file is a directory named "etc." This directory is created automatically by slush the first time it boots and contains several system files. Changing to the "etc" directory using the cd (change directory) command and displaying its contents using "ls -1" produces the following listing.

```
TINI /> cd etc

TINI /etc> ls -1
total 5
drwxr-x     1 root     admin         3 Jan 27 15:14 .
drwxr-x     1 root     admin         1 Jan 27 15:13 ..
-rwxr--     1 root     admin        28 Jan 27 15:14 .tininet
-rwx---     1 root     admin       225 Jan 27 15:14 .startup
-rwxr--     1 root     admin       101 Jan 27 15:14 passwd

TINI /etc>
```

This detailed listing displays, from left to right, the following information about each file or directory contained within the current working directory.

- Permissions
- Number of links
- Owner
- Group
- File count/size
- Last modification date
- Name

Let's look at the listing for the .startup file in detail. The permissions for the .startup file, from left to right, indicate that it is not a directory(-). The owner (root in this case) has read (r), write (w), and execute (x) privileges, while others have no read, write, or execute privileges. The file system does not support different groups, but this entry is present for UNIX-listing compatibility when using the FTP server. The link count is also purely for compatibility, since the file system doesn't support links.

All three of the files in the "etc" directory are created by slush during the initial boot sequence. The .tininet file stores the host and domain names. By default the host name is "TINI." The passwd file stores the user name along with the SHA1 (Secure Hash Algorithm) hash of the password for every account on the system. The most interesting of the autogenerated files is .startup. This file is parsed and interpreted by slush on every reboot. It allows a user with administrative privilege to set environment variables and automatically launch applications on system boot. We can view the contents of .startup, or any other ASCII text file, using the cat command.

```
TINI /etc> cat .startup
########
#Autogen'd slush startup file
setenv FTPServer enable
setenv TelnetServer enable
setenv SerialServer enable
##
#Add user calls to setenv here:
##
initializeNetwork
########
#Add other user additions here:
```

Each line of the file is either a command to be interpreted by slush or a comment that begins with the "#" character. The three lines that begin with "setenv" enable the FTP, Telnet, and serial servers, respectively. So, for example, if an application needed to use the same serial port that slush uses for the serial server, a user with administrative privilege could comment out the "setenv" line that enabled the serial server. The next time the system is booted, slush will only start the FTP and Telnet servers. This allows another application to claim exclusive ownership of the serial port.

Applications can be launched on system boot by adding the appropriate commands to the .startup. For example, adding this command

```
java /bin/MyApp.tini > /log/debug.out
```

causes slush to run MyApp.tini from the bin directory and redirect all output from java.lang.System.out and java.lang.System.err to a log file named debug.out. All applications launched from the .startup file are forced to run in the background.

This concludes our mini-tour of our new file system. Type "cd /" at the command prompt to return to the root directory.

```
TINI /etc> cd /
TINI />
```

2.4.4 Getting Help

The help command provides a hands-on approach to exploring slush as well as some insight into the capabilities of TINI's runtime environment. Type help at the prompt at any time to obtain a complete list of all commands supported by slush.

```
TINI /> help
Available Commands:

    append        arp           cat           cd
    chmod         chown         clear         copy
    cp            date          del           df
    dir           downserver    echo          ftp
    gc            genlog        help          history
    hostname      ipconfig      java          kill
    ls            md            mkdir         move
    mv            netstat       nslookup      passwd
    ping          ps            pwd           rd
    reboot        rm            rmdir         sendmail
    setenv        source        startserver   stats
    stopserver    su            touch         useradd
    userdel       wall          wd            who
    whoami
```

A command's description and usage is obtained by typing help followed by the name of the command at the prompt. Typing "help java" at the prompt displays the usage message for the java command.

```
TINI /> help java
java FILE [&]

Executes the given Java application.
'&' indicates a background process.
```

The java command is used to launch new Java processes. The usage message specifies the required and optional parameters. In this case, the java command requires the name of the application binary file to be executed and optionally allows the user to launch the application as a background process using the & parameter. We'll use the java command in Section 2.6 to run the example programs.

At this point we can start a user session, navigate the file system, and get help with unfamiliar commands. We will continue interacting with our "slush user session" in the next couple of sections to configure the network as well as load and run some small example applications. The sections that follow describe new slush commands and functionality as they are encountered.

2.5 CONFIGURING THE NETWORK

Network configuration information can be set by using the slush command ipconfig. The ipconfig command provides several options that allow for complete control of all important network parameters. Executing ipconfig with no parameters displays the current network settings.

```
TINI /> ipconfig
Hostname          : TINI.
Current IP        :
Default Gateway   :
Subnet Mask       :
Ethernet Address  : 00:60:35:00:10:bb
Primary DNS       :
Secondary DNS     :
DNS Timeout       : 0 (ms)
DHCP Server       :
DHCP Enabled      : false
Mailhost          :
Restore From Flash: Not Committed
```

Since we have just installed the runtime and cleared the heap, nothing but the Ethernet address and default host name, TINI, have been configured. The Ethernet address is an IEEE registered MAC id to avoid any possible collision on an Ethernet network. It is read from the read-only memory of a 1-Wire chip on the TINI board and is not user configurable. This implies that it is always available and always the same, allowing it to serve as a general purpose unique identification for the TINI board as well as the Ethernet address.

Use the help command to obtain the list of options supported by ipconfig.

```
TINI /> help ipconfig
ipconfig [options]

Configure or display the network settings.
  [-a xx.xx.xx.xx]    Set IP address.  Must be used with the -m option.
  [-n domainname]     Set domain name
  [-m xx.xx.xx.xx]    Set subnet mask.  Must be used with -a option.
  [-g xx.xx.xx.xx]    Set gateway address
  [-p xx.xx.xx.xx]    Set primary DNS address
  [-s xx.xx.xx.xx]    Set secondary DNS address
  [-t dnstimeout ]    Set DNS timeout (set to 0 for backoff/retry)
  [-d]                Use DHCP to lease an IP address
  [-r]                Release currently held DHCP IP address
```

```
[-x]                    Show all Interface data
[-h xx.xx.xx.xx]        Set mailhost
[-C]                    Commit current network configuration to flash
[-D]                    Disable restoration of configuration from flash
[-f]                    Don't prompt for confirmation
```

As you can see from the preceding usage message, ipconfig provides fine-grain configuration and control of network settings and parameters. We won't cover all of them here, just enough to get TINI up and running on the network. If there is a DHCP (Dynamic Host Configuration Protocol) server available on your network, you can use the -d option to dynamically obtain an IP address and subnet mask as well as several other network parameters, depending on the configuration of the DHCP server. Usually, if TINI is to be used as a server, you'll want to use a static IP address, making it easy for network clients to access the service(s) TINI is providing. For static network configuration we need to set the IP address and subnet mask at a minimum. The following command sets the IP address and subnet mask.

```
TINI /> ipconfig -a 192.168.0.15 -m 255.255.255.0
Warning:  This will disconnect any connected network users
and reset all network servers.
OK to proceed? (Y/N): y

[ Sun Jan 28 14:52:46 GMT 2001 ]  Message from System: Telnet server
    started.
[ Sun Jan 28 14:52:46 GMT 2001 ]  Message from System: FTP server started.
```

You will of course substitute the IP address and subnet mask used here with values provided by your network administrator. We can test our new settings by "pinging" the TINI board from the host machine, using the ping command. Also, we can see from this command that slush automatically starts Telnet and FTP servers after setting the network information. At this point you should be able to establish a Telnet session with TINI, using the host's Telnet client. Win32, Solaris, and Linux all provide command line Telnet client programs. There are also graphical Telnet clients available for most platforms that should work fine with TINI.

```
C:\>telnet 192.168.0.15
Connecting To 192.168.0.15...
Welcome to slush.  (Version 1.02)

TINI login: root
TINI password:
TINI />
```

Once connected, slush prompts the user for a user name and password. Use the same name and password (root, tini) that we used to log in to the serial session from JavaKit in the previous section. We can kill the Telnet session by using the exit command.

Now TINI is on the network and ready for action. However, with only the IP address and subnet mask set, network messages intended for machines on different physical networks can't reach their destination. To extend TINI's reach beyond its physical network, we will need to set at least one more network parameter: the IP address of the default gateway (or router). The default gateway address is set using the -g option. The other network parameter we would like to set now is the IP address of the DNS (Domain Name System) server using the -p option. This allows us to use host names rather than raw IP addresses when communicating with other hosts. Running the following command from our serial session adds the default gateway and primary DNS server's IP addresses to the current network configuration.

```
TINI /> ipconfig -g 192.168.0.1 -p 192.168.0.2
Warning:  This will disconnect any connected network users
and reset all network servers.

OK to proceed? (Y/N): y

[ Sun Jan 28 15:02:53 GMT 2001 ]  Message from System: FTP server stopped.
[ Sun Jan 28 15:03:00 GMT 2001 ]  Message from System: Telnet server
   stopped.
[ Sun Jan 28 15:03:00 GMT 2001 ]  Message from System: Telnet server
   started.
[ Sun Jan 28 15:03:01 GMT 2001 ]  Message from System: FTP server started.
```

Note that if the FTP and Telnet servers are running, slush stops them before changing the requested network settings. After aborting any active FTP or Telnet sessions, the new network parameters are set and the servers are restarted. We can test both of the new settings by pinging a host machine on another network, using that host's name as opposed to its IP address.

```
TINI /> ping www.ibutton.com
Got a reply from node www.ibutton.com/198.3.123.121
Sent 1 request(s), got 1 reply(s)
```

At this point we'll want to log out of the serial session and close JavaKit. Now we can interact with TINI and run our examples over the network using the host's Telnet and FTP clients. From this point forward in the book nearly all examples will be run from a Telnet client. Start a new Telnet session and run ipconfig with no parameters.

```
Welcome to slush.  (Version 1.02)

TINI /> ipconfig
Hostname          : TINI.
Current IP        : 192.168.0.15
Default Gateway   : 192.168.0.1
Subnet Mask       : 255.255.255.0
```

```
Ethernet Address  : 00:60:35:00:10:bb
Primary DNS       : 192.168.0.2
Secondary DNS     :
DNS Timeout       : 0 (ms)
DHCP Server       :
DHCP Enabled      : false
Mailhost          :
Restore From Flash: Not Committed
```

Allow this session to remain active because it will be used to run the examples in the following section.

2.6   SOME SIMPLE EXAMPLES

At this point we've loaded the runtime environment and configured TINI for network operation, and now we can interact with the runtime environment, using slush. Now we'll create three very small applications from scratch and detail the process of building, loading, and running the examples. We'll use slush via a Telnet session to run the applications, display any output, interact with the file system, and control processes.

2.6.1   HelloWorld

Naturally, we simply must begin with the canonical `HelloWorld` program. While it won't exactly enhance our skills as Java coders, it does provide a nice vehicle for describing the application development process in a step-by-step fashion. Typically, to develop and test your application requires these five steps.

1. Create the source file.
2. Compile the source file.
3. Convert the class file.
4. Load the converted image.
5. Run the converted image.

The remainder of this section will detail all five steps. We'll recycle this experience for the remaining examples, allowing us to focus on other details. For the sake of becoming familiar with the development process, we'll perform all of these steps manually. Since this quickly becomes tedious for real-world application development, the process of building and loading applications should be automated using a reasonable combination of make files and shell scripts (batch file in Windows lingo).

Step 1: Create the source file.   Create and save a file named `HelloWorld.java` containing the source code in Listing 2.1.

Listing 2.1   HelloWorld

```
class HelloWorld {
    public static void main(String[] args) {
        System.out.println("Hello World");
    }
}
```

Step 2: Compile the source file.   Compile `HelloWorld.java` to a class file, using your favorite Java compiler. If you're using Sun's JDK and the JDK's bin directory is in your path, change to the directory that contains the file we just created and execute the following command.

```
javac HelloWorld.java
```

If the compile completes successfully, you should have a new file named `HelloWorld.class` in the current working directory.

Step 3: Convert the class file.   The utility program `TINIConvertor` performs a conversion on input, specifically one or more Java class files, and outputs a binary image suitable for execution on TINI. `TINIConvertor`'s function is described in Section 1.4.2. However, it is worth mentioning that `TINIConvertor` is performing a portion of the class loading process. The binary file produced by `TINIConvertor` is typically about 25 to 35 percent of the size of the sum of the original class files. `TINIConvertor` does not generate code native to TINI's microcontroller; rather, it generates a binary file containing Java bytecodes that are interpreted by TINI's JVM.

TINIConvertor is a Java application that lives in the tini.jar file and is run from a command shell on the host. It is controlled by a series of command line parameters that specify the converter's input and output. A list of all required and extended parameters can be obtained by running `TINIConvertor` with no parameters.

To convert `HelloWorld.class` to a binary image that we can execute on TINI, run `TINIConvertor` supplying the three mandatory command line parameters: input file or directory (`-f`), API database (`-d`), and output file (`-o`).

```
java -classpath c:\tini1.02\bin\tini.jar TINIConvertor -f HelloWorld.class
        -d c:\tini\tini1.02\bin\tini.db -o HelloWorld.tini
```

In this example, our application consists of only one class file, `HelloWorld.class`, so we can specify the class file's name with the `-f` parameter. In general, our applications will consist of several classes in one or more packages. In this case, supply the directory name of the root of the package structure hierarchy. This causes `TINIConvertor` to include all class files in and below the specified directory when creating the application binary.

The other input required by `TINIConvertor` is the name of the API database distributed in the SDK. This file is named `tini.db` and must be supplied with the `-d` parameter. This file is used by the convertor to resolve information between your application and the API. The `tini.db` file is specific to a version of the SDK, so if you have multiple versions of the SDK installed on the host, be sure to use the correct `tini.db` file.

`TINIConvertor` produces an output file with the name provided with the `-o` parameter. Other than being a legal name, as determined by the file system, there are no specific rules that restrict the name of the final application binary. By convention, the name of the class that contains the `main` method is used for the file name with an extension of ".tini." The extension is used to indicate that this file is a TINI executable. Following this convention produces a binary output file named `HelloWorld.tini`.

Step 4: Load the converted image.   Use the FTP client provided with your operating system to connect to TINI and transfer the binary image, generated in the previous step, to the TINI file system.

```
C:\tini1.02\HelloWorld>ftp 192.168.0.15
Connected to 192.168.0.15.
220 Welcome to slush.  (Version 1.02)  Ready for user login.
User (192.168.0.15:(none)): root
331 root login allowed. Password required.
Password:
230 User root logged in.
ftp>
```

After successfully establishing a connection and logging in to slush we can transfer `HelloWorld.tini` to TINI's file system. First type "bin" at the FTP prompt to ensure that our binary image is not altered during the actual file transfer.

```
ftp> bin
200 Type set to Binary
```

Transfer `HelloWorld.tini`, using this put command.

```
ftp> put HelloWorld.tini
200 PORT Command successful.
150 BINARY connection open, putting HelloWorld.tini
226 Closing data connection.
ftp: 171 bytes sent in 0.00Seconds 171000.00Kbytes/sec.
```

Finally, close the FTP session by typing bye or `quit` at the prompt.

```
ftp> bye
221 Goodbye.
```

We can check that our file transfer completed successfully by using the `ls` command at the slush prompt in our Telnet session.

```
TINI /> ls -l
total 3
drwxr-x      1 root      admin           2 Jan 28 14:45 .
-rwxr--      1 root      admin         171 Jan 28 15:46 HelloWorld.tini
drwxr-x      1 root      admin           3 Jan 28 14:45 etc
```

The file `HelloWorld.tini` now appears in the root directory of the file system and has the same size that was listed during the FTP transfer.

Note that all operating systems that are capable of hosting TINI application development have an FTP client that works nearly identically to the preceding session. There also exist several graphical FTP clients for various platforms. These are useful for developers that prefer not to work from a command shell. For some developers, a command line FTP client is preferable because it allows for easy automation of the file transfer process. For example, using the Windows FTP client, we can create a file with the following contents.

```
root
tini
bin
put HelloWorld.tini
bye
```

If we call this file `load.cmd`, we can use the following command to transfer `HelloWorld.tini` without any interaction with the FTP client command prompt.

```
C:\TINI\tini1.02\myapps\HelloWorld>ftp -s:load.cmd 192.168.0.15
```

Using the `-s` option causes the FTP client to read the specified file and execute each line as if it were typed in manually in response to a prompt.

Step 5: Run the converted image.   Now we're ready to run the application using the `java` command at the slush prompt.

```
TINI /> java HelloWorld.tini
Hello World
TINI />
```

`HelloWorld.tini` executes and produces the output we expect. After the program terminates, control of the user session returns to the command prompt.

2.6.2   Blinky, Your First TINI I/O

Now that we know how to build, load, and execute a Java application, let's try an example that performs the most basic form of I/O by controlling a single microcontroller port pin. There is a status LED (Light Emitting Diode) on the TINI board that is connected to p3.5 (port 3, bit 5) of the microcontroller. This pin is also shared with the internal 1-Wire network (see Table 9.1) but since we're not doing any 1-Wire at the moment, we're free to play with it.

The relevant portion of the TBM390 schematic is shown in Figure 2.4. The anode side of the LED is connected to V_{cc} (the power supply voltage). A 680-ohm current limiting resistor separates the LED's cathode and the source of transistor Q2. In this circuit, Q2 is just used as a saturation switch to ground. So we can think of it as either being off (nonconducting) or on (conducting). The port pin drives the gate of Q2. Setting the pin high (a logic 1) forces Q2 into a conducting state, causing current to flow through the LED and turning it on. Setting the pin low (a logic 0), forces Q2 to a nonconducting state, stopping the flow of current through the diode, thereby turning it off.

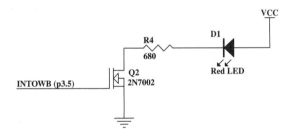

Figure 2.4   TINI's status LED

The Blinky program, shown in Listing 2.2, uses the class BitPort from the com.dalsemi.system package to access p3.5. Once we have an instance of BitPort, we can invoke the methods set and clear, to turn the LED on and off, respectively.

```
public void set()
public void clear()
```

Listing 2.2   Blinky

```java
import com.dalsemi.system.BitPort;

class Blinky {
    public static void main(String[] args) {
        BitPort bp = new BitPort(BitPort.Port3Bit5);
        for (;;) {
            // Turn on LED
            bp.clear();
            // Leave it on for 1/4 second
            try {
```

```
            Thread.sleep(250);
        } catch (InterruptedException ie) {}

        // Turn off LED
        bp.set();
        // Leave it off for 1/4 second
        try {
            Thread.sleep(250);
        } catch (InterruptedException ie) {}
    }
  }
}
```

Compile, convert, and load Blinky following the steps we used for the HelloWorld example. However, we will make one small change to the way in which we run this program. Blinky runs forever just brainlessly blinking the status LED at 2 Hz. If we run it in the same fashion that we ran HelloWorld, as a foreground process, we would never get our command prompt back in the Telnet session.[6] We would either have to start a new Telnet session just to halt Blinky by using the kill command or removing power, forcing the system to reboot. Instead, just execute Blinky in the background.

```
TINI /> java Blinky.tini &
TINI />
```

Now if you take a look at your TINI board, you should see the status LED (D1) blinking about twice per second. It will continue to blink until you kill the process. To kill a process from slush, you use the kill command specifying the process id on the command line. To learn the process id, use the ps command.

```
TINI /> ps
3 processes
1: Java GC (Owner root)
2: init (Owner root)
4: Blinky.tini (Owner root)
```

The ps command shows us the total number of processes and lists each process id followed by its name. Now let's kill Blinky, since the thrill of a blinking light is probably starting to wane.

```
TINI /> kill 4
TINI /> ps
2 processes
1: Java GC (Owner root)
2: init (Owner root)
```

---

6. Slush does not support the use of <ctrl>C to terminate foreground processes.

After killing process 4 and examining the process list, we see that the process count has gone from three to two, and only the background garbage collector and command shell (Notice that the first Java process started during the bootup phase. Slush in this case is always named "init.") are running. Even if you kill and immediately restart the same process, it will not get the same process id. Process ids are always incrementing and are not recycled. So, if you were to run Blinky again and do a ps, the process id would be 5. The process id is an unsigned 16-bit value and therefore rolls to the lowest available value after 65535.

2.6.3 HelloWeb, a Trivial Web Server

Finally, we'll upgrade the HelloWorld example, taking it to the World Wide Web. The HelloWeb program, shown in Listing 2.3, is a very small Web server. The "built-in" HTTPServer class, provided in the com.dalsemi.tininet.http package, does the bulk of the work. HelloWeb creates an instance of HTTPServer that listens for client HTTP requests on server port 80. It also logs all requests to a file named web.log in the "/log" directory. The main loop simply spins forever, invoking the serviceRequests method on the HTTPServer instance.

Listing 2.3   HelloWeb

```
import com.dalsemi.tininet.http.HTTPServer;
import com.dalsemi.tininet.http.HTTPServerException;

class HelloWeb {
    public static void main(String[] args) {
        // Constuct an instance of HTTPServer that listens for
        // requests port 80
        HTTPServer httpd = new HTTPServer(80);
        httpd.setHTTPRoot("/html");
        httpd.setIndexPage("index.html");
        // Specify a name for the log file and turn on logging
        httpd.setLogFilename("/log/web.log");
        httpd.setLogging(true);

        // Spin around forever servicing inbound requests
        for (;;) {
            try {
                // Wait for a new request
                httpd.serviceRequests();
            } catch (HTTPServerException e) {
                System.out.println(e.getMessage());
            }
        }
    }
}
```

Compile, convert, and load HelloWeb, following the steps used in the HelloWorld example. Like Blinky, HelloWeb runs forever and should therefore be executed as a background process. But there's a little more work to do before we can run HelloWeb. Unlike the first two examples, HelloWeb requires some application data in the form of an ASCII file, namely index.html. On the host, create and save a file named index.html with the following contents.

```
<html>
<head><title>Hello Web!</title></head>
<body>
<h1>Hello from TINI!</h1>
</body>
</html>
```

Now let's return to our slush Telnet session to make directories for our Web root and log file.

```
TINI /> mkdir html
TINI /> mkdir log
TINI /> ls -l
total 7
drwxr-x    1 root      admin         6 Jan 28 14:45 .
drwxr--    1 root      admin         0 Jan 28 18:06 log
drwxr--    1 root      admin         1 Jan 28 18:06 html
-rwxr--    1 root      admin       297 Jan 28 18:05 HelloWeb.tini
-rwxr--    1 root      admin       220 Jan 28 17:58 Blinky.tini
-rwxr--    1 root      admin       171 Jan 28 15:46 HelloWorld.tini
drwxr-x    1 root      admin         3 Jan 28 14:45 etc
```

Use FTP again to "put" index.html into the "/html" directory we just created. To make sure we transferred the file successfully, we can, from the slush prompt, change to the "/html" directory and display the contents of index.html, using the cat command.

```
TINI /> cd html
TINI /html> cat index.html
<html>
<head>
<title>Hello Web!</title>
</head>
<body>
<h1>Hello from TINI!</h1>
</body>
</html>
```

Now that we have the Web server application binary (HelloWeb.tini) and the HTML file that it will serve in the Web root, we can return to the root directory and start the program as a background process.

```
TINI /html> cd ..
TINI /> java HelloWeb.tini &
TINI />
```

Typing the ps command at the slush prompt shows that our server is indeed up and ready to receive and process client HTTP requests.

```
TINI /> ps
3 processes
1: Java GC (Owner root)
2: init (Owner root)
5: HelloWeb.tini (Owner root)
```

Now we can test our simple server, using any browser and typing TINI's IP address or DNS name in the URL line. Figure 2.5 shows the results of browsing the elaborate Web site served by HelloWeb, using the Netscape browser.

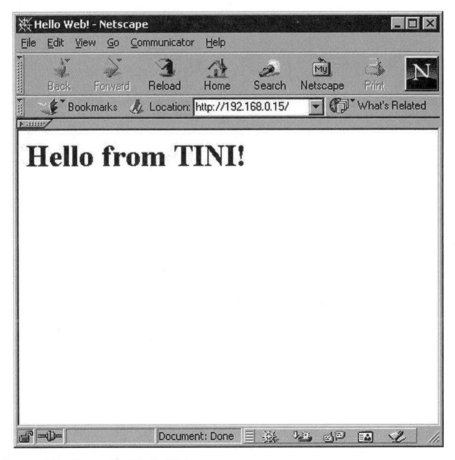

Figure 2.5   Browsing HelloWeb

Recall that when we created the instance of HTTPServer, we specified that it generate a log file. Let's take a look at its contents, using the cat command from the slush prompt.

```
TINI /> cd log
TINI /log> cat web.log
192.168.0.3, GET, index.html
TINI /log>
```

The log file shows us that the server has processed 1 "GET" request for the file index.html from a client with the IP address 192.168.0.3. You can hit the reload (or refresh if you're using Internet Explorer) button on your browser several times and watch the log file grow by one entry for each new request. If this were a real application serving real Web pages, we probably wouldn't enable logging, since we're working with a relatively small memory footprint. If logging were used by a real application, the log file would eventually grow too large to fit in TINI's memory.

2.7   DEBUGGING TIPS

Trivial applications like those in the previous section require little in the way of debugging. So the development cycle of building the application on the host and loading and running it on TINI isn't really much of a burden. Real-world applications are of course much more complicated and involve a fair amount of debugging. This is one of the more difficult areas of TINI application development.

As a general rule, do all of the debugging you possibly can on your development host. On a host machine the use of a full-featured IDE that provides a runtime environment with integrated source-level debugging can further aid in the development and debugging cycle.

There are broad classes of applications that can be developed for the TINI platform that will also run on larger, more traditional Java platforms. These classes include applications that use the following mechanisms for monitoring and controlling external devices and communicating with other networked machines.

- Serial communication
- TCP/IP networking
- 1-Wire networking

If your application uses only the standard Java packages supported by TINI (see Section 1.4.1) and extensions available on most Java platforms—namely, the Java Communications API (Section 3.2) and the 1-Wire API (Chapter 4)—then all debugging can be accomplished using just your host's development environment.

Since TINI's main purpose is interacting with physical devices, it also provides I/O capabilities above and beyond those supported by any other Java platform. Once you're writing applications that make use of the APIs that expose these expanded I/O capabilities, your applications will only run on TINI and therefore must be debugged on TINI. Here are some examples of TINI's expanded I/O capabilities.

- Parallel I/O
- Port pin I/O
- Controller Area Network (CAN)

If your application makes use of APIs that support any of the above, you lose source level debugging capabilities and are relegated to using exceptions with informative detail messages and old-fashioned console (`System.out.println`) debug output.

Also, there's a pretty good chance that if you're using expanded I/O capabilities, TINI is connected to specialized hardware. This often brings traditional hardware diagnostic and debug equipment into the picture—anywhere from expensive DSOs (Digital Storage Oscilloscopes) and logic analyzers to very inexpensive tools like logic probes and DMMs (Digital Multi-Meters). This isn't always a simple and user friendly environment for debugging. It proves to be very challenging at times, but such is life in the murky world where hardware meets software.

CHAPTER 3

Serial Communication

The sheer number of devices that use a serial port as a means for communicating with other electronic devices is staggering: everything from very well-known examples like personal computers and modems to manufacturing and industrial automation equipment. In fact, for many, a serial port provides the sole mechanism of communicating with the outside world. Such devices have no direct means of participating in a larger computer network. For this reason bridging the communications gap between serial-only devices to networked hosts is one of the most popular applications of TINI technology.

This chapter will cover both the hardware and software aspects of developing serial applications on TINI. It focuses on application programming, providing reasonably detailed coverage of the serial portion of the Java Communications API. The chapter concludes with a sample implementation of a general purpose serial to Ethernet network bridge.

3.1 INTRODUCTION AND TERMINOLOGY

The asynchronous serial communication discussed in this chapter is based on a standard that dates back to the earliest days of recorded history. Well, it's not actually that old, but the RS-232-C standard was published way back in 1969, specifically. Most modern serial ports do not support all of the signals defined in the standard. The signals that are implemented are used in a fashion that is fairly close to that defined in the standard.

It's difficult, if not impossible, to discuss asynchronous serial communication based on the RS-232-C standard without delving into fairly tricky terminology that brings with it a significant amount of historical baggage. Over the years, terms commonly used in the industry have diverged somewhat from those defined in the standard.[1] The following text will define a few necessary terms, attempting to stay reasonably close to the RS-232-C standard. It will also describe the hardware and software test environment used to test the examples in this section.

The low-level details of asynchronous serial communication, such as managing tight timing tolerances on receive data sampling, are typically handled by a dedicated piece of hardware known as a UART (Universal Asynchronous Receiver Transmitter). This is often a dedicated piece of silicon that is either integrated into a microcontroller or provided externally as a special purpose external UART chip. TINI's serial driver provides support for both of the internal UARTs as well as optional support for an external dual-UART chip. This allows TINI to communicate with up to four separate serial devices.

The standard specifies that the receiver shall acknowledge voltage levels of +3V to +25V for a "SPACE" (a binary zero) bit and –3V to –25V for a "MARK" (a binary one) bit. This is shown in Figure 3.1. The "no man's land" between –3V and +3V is the switching region. All of the UARTs supported by TINI transmit and receive the much more common (and modern) TTL (Transistor Transistor Logic) voltage levels of 0V and +5V. Special purpose chips commonly known as level translators are used to convert between TTL and RS-232 levels to allow communication with devices that transmit and receive true RS-232 levels. Many small embedded serial devices also use TTL signals obviating the need for level translation. All voltage levels discussed here are measured with respect to signal ground (a.k.a., common, see Table 3.1).

The serial ports that we're concerned with in this chapter come in the following two configurations.

- DCE (Data Communications Equipment)
- DTE (Data Terminal Equipment)

The RS-232-C standard refers to the two endpoints of a communications channel as being data terminal equipment (DTE) and data communications equipment (DCE). A common example of data communications equipment is a modem and a common example of data terminal equipment is a PC or workstation.

---

1. For example, the DCE acronym is now almost exclusively used to refer to data communications equipment, as opposed to the original definition of data circuit-terminating equipment.

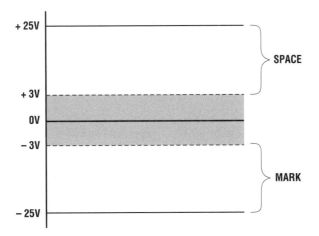

Figure 3.1   RS-232 voltage levels

In general, systems that employ TINI technology can expose either DTE or DCE serial ports. However, in the interest of constructing a concrete test environment, we'll need to refer to specific hardware implementations. For our purposes the most commonly available and generic configuration, which includes a TBM390 and an E10 socket, is used.

For most serial applications, TINI controls or acts as a network bridge for DCE serial devices and is therefore more likely to be used as data terminal equipment. For this reason the E10 socket provides a DTE serial port that supports most of the hardware handshake (flow control) lines. As we'll see in the next section, this serial port is identified by the system as serial0. It is often called the "default serial port" because the UART is integrated within the microcontroller.

The pinout, along with signal names and descriptions for a DB-9 DTE serial port connector, is shown in Table 3.1.

Table 3.1   DB-9 DTE serial connector pinout

Pin #	Signal Name	DTE Sense	Description
1	CD (Carrier Detect)	INPUT	Asserted by DCE when it has received a data carrier signal
2	RD (Receive Data)	INPUT	Data receive from DCE
3	TD (Transmit Data)	OUTPUT	Data transmit to DCE
4	DTR (Data Terminal Ready)	OUTPUT	Asserted by DTE when it is ready for communication

continues

Table 3.1   DB-9 DTE serial connector pinout (continued)

Pin #	Signal Name	DTE Sense	Description
5	Common (Signal Ground)	N/A	0 volt reference
6	DSR (Data Set Ready)	INPUT	Asserted by DCE when it has established a communications channel and is ready to transmit
7	RTS (Request To Send)	OUTPUT	Asserted by DTE to request permission to transmit data
8	CTS (Clear To Send)	INPUT	Asserted by DCE to grant permission to DTE to transmit data
9	RI (Ring Indicator)	INPUT	Asserted by DCE when it receives a ringing tone

The BlackBox example application, distributed with the comm API, is very useful for test purposes. In fact, it was used to test all of the examples in this chapter. BlackBox is a GUI application that allows the user to configure port settings such as the baud (or bit) rate, number of data and stop bits, and flow control modes.

The difficulty is that the host machine on which BlackBox executes also has DTE serial ports. So the same straight-through serial cable that connected to TINI's DCE connector to load the firmware is not sufficient by itself to allow TINI and the development host to communicate over a serial link to TINI's DTE connector. If only a straight-through serial cable were used, both computers would transmit data on the same pin (TD), causing an electrical contention. This contention shouldn't cause any damage since RS-232 outputs are current-limited. However, it certainly prevents any communication. The hardware handshake outputs (RTS and DTR) will also collide.

The use of a null modem solves this problem. At a minimum a null modem swaps RD and TD and passes through signal ground. This would allow two machines with DTE serial ports to communicate, assuming none of the hardware handshake lines are required. We'll make use of the handshake lines in a couple of the following examples. For our testing we'll use the common null modem configuration shown in Figure 3.2. This configuration also swaps RTS and CTS, which is used for "hardware" flow control.

The entire hardware test configuration is shown in Figure 3.3. A straight-through cable and null modem are used to connect TINI with the development host machine. Both the TINI and development host have pin-male DB-9 connectors. Both connectors on the null modem are pin-female DB-9.

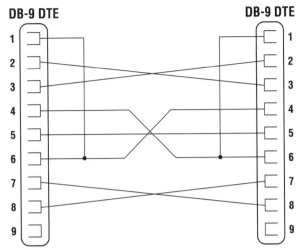

Pin names and descriptions are identical to those shown in Table 3.1.

Figure 3.2   Null modem

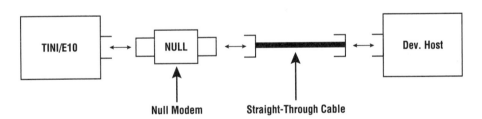

Figure 3.3   Test configuration

The null modem shown in Figure 3.3 is in a brick form factor. Null modems are also available as cables. This would obviate the need for both a null modem and a straight-through cable. Since straight-through cables are more common and typically used with TINI anyway for loading the runtime environment, we have chosen to use a separate null modem brick. If the development host has a DB-25 pin connector, you will need a DB-9 to DB-25 adapter as well. Depending on whether your development host is pin-male or pin-female you may also need a gender changer. With the hardware configuration shown in Figure 3.3 (or equivalent) and BlackBox running on the development host, we're ready to begin writing and testing serial applications.

3.2 THE JAVA COMMUNICATIONS API

The Java Communications API (or comm API for brevity) has been defined by Sun Microsystems as an extension to the Java platform. The API is defined and partially implemented in the `javax.comm` package. The platform specific portion of the comm API implementation exists in the `com.dalsemi.comm` package. For most applications there isn't a compelling reason to use the serial port classes in `com.dalsemi.comm` directly, so this section will focus entirely on the public specification in `javax.comm`. Unless explicitly stated otherwise, all classes described in the next section are defined in the `javax.comm` package.

You may recall that when you installed the comm API on your host development machine, you copied a file named `javax.comm.properties` to the "jre/lib/ext" directory under the root of your JRE or JDK installation. This text file contains a line that specifies a driver to be loaded to manage serial port communication. On TINI the serial port drivers are always installed and available in the runtime environment and therefore the `javax.comm.properties` file is not required or supported.

3.2.1 Acquiring and Configuring Serial Ports

Ultimately we'll be working with `SerialPort` objects. `SerialPort` is a subclass of the abstract class `CommPort`. `CommPort` provides a fairly generic abstraction of a communications port. It provides methods for configuring port settings and acquiring streams for reading data from and writing data to the underlying physical port. `CommPort` objects can't be created directly using the new operator. Rather, they are created by invoking the open method on a `CommPortIdentifier` object.

The `CommPortIdentifier` class manages access to the ports exposed by the platform's physical port drivers. It also provides a mechanism for notifying applications when port ownership status changes. This can be useful when multiple applications need to share a single port. The ability to share ports among multiple processes on TINI is supported, but it isn't typically important and is therefore not covered here. `CommPortIdentifier` objects can be created by invoking one of the following `getPortIdentifier` methods.

```
public static CommPortIdentifier getPortIdentifier(String portName)
    throws NoSuchPortException
public static CommPortIdentifier getPortIdentifier(CommPort port)
    throws NoSuchPortException
```

An enumeration of `CommPortIdentifiers` for all communication[2] ports supported by the system can be obtained by invoking the `getPortIdentifiers` method.

---

2. On TINI this specifically means all serial ports.

```
public static Enumeration getPortIdentifiers()
```

The `PortLister` example, shown in Listing 3.1, gets an enumeration of all `CommPort` objects on the system and displays their names.

Listing 3.1 PortLister

```
import java.util.Enumeration;
import javax.comm.CommPortIdentifier;

class PortLister {
    public static void main(String[] args) {
        Enumeration ports = CommPortIdentifier.getPortIdentifiers();
        while (ports.hasMoreElements()) {
        System.out.println(
            ((CommPortIdentifier)(ports.nextElement())).getName());
        }
    }
}
```

When this application is run on a Win32 machine with the communications API properly installed, it will list both parallel and serial ports. On a system with two serial ports and two parallel ports, it will generate output similar to the following:

```
COM1
COM2
LPT1
LPT2
```

On TINI, however, there are no parallel ports—at least not the IEEE-1284 type parallel ports that are comprehended by the comm API. In fact, there is no implementation for the parallel classes defined by the comm API. TINI does support parallel I/O, but in a far more flexible and powerful fashion by exposing the processor bus to allow for arbitrary I/O expansion. From a programmer's perspective, parallel I/O on TINI-based systems is accomplished using the `com.dalsemi.system.DataPort` class and is covered in Chapter 8.

The output of `PortLister` when executed on TINI shows that four serial ports are supported by the system. They are named `serial0` through `serial3`.

```
TINI /> java PortLister.tini
serial0
serial1
serial2
serial3
```

After we have a `CommPortIdentifier` object, we can invoke open to obtain a `CommPort` object.

```
public synchronized CommPort open(String appname, int timeout)
    throws PortInUseException
```

Ownership of a communications port is mutually exclusive. In other words, multiple processes cannot simultaneously access the underlying physical port. The open method only returns when it has either obtained exclusive access to the port or the input time-out value, specified in milliseconds, has elapsed. If the port is owned by another process and a time-out occurs waiting for the process to relinquish ownership of the port, open throws a PortInUseException. The open method also requires a string representation of the name of the application. This string is used to identify the owner of the port. There is another open method that takes a java.io.FileDescriptor object. Because the runtime environment does not represent physical devices as files, TINI's comm API implementation does not support this version of open. Ownership of the port is relinquished by invoking the close method on the CommPort object.

```
public void close()
```

The CommPort object returned from open must be cast to a SerialPort object before we can begin altering the port settings. The SerialPort class provides public "setter" methods for configuring individual parameters as well as symmetric public "getter" methods for querying the parameters current value. These are a few of the parameters that are typically set before transmitting or receiving data on the underlying physical port.

- Baud rate
- Number of data bits
- Number of stop bits
- Type of parity checking (if any)
- Flow control (if any)

On TINI, the default settings are $115,200^3$ bps, 8 data bits, 1 stop bit, no parity, and no flow control. The supported values for the number of data bits, stop bits, flow control, and parity types are defined as public integer constants in the SerialPort class. The most common set of serial port configuration parameters can be set with a single invocation of the setSerialPortParams method.

```
public void setSerialPortParams(int baudrate, int dataBits,
                                int stopBits, int parity)
    throws UnsupportedCommOperationException
```

All of the settings are supplied as integers. The number of data bits, stop bits, and parity mode are supplied using the SerialPort constants. The baud rate is

---

3. The javax.comm documentation of setSerialPortParams specifies a default of 9600 bps.

simply an integer value equal to the desired speed. In the following code snippet the serial port (represented by the `SerialPort` object sp) is configured for transmitting and receiving data at 115,200 bps with 8 bit serial characters followed by 1 stop bit and no parity checking.

```
try {
    ...
    sp.setSerialPortParams(115200, SerialPort.DATABITS_8,
                        SerialPort.STOPBITS_1, SerialPort.PARITY_NONE);
    ...
} catch (UnsupportedCommOperationException usc) {
    ...
}
```

If any of the parameter values are invalid, `setSerialPortParams` will throw an `UnsupportedCommOperationException`. If this occurs, all four parameters will remain the same as before the `setSerialPortParams` method was invoked.

3.2.2 Flow Control

Another setting that should be configured before beginning serial data transfer is the flow control mode. Flow control is a mechanism that allows a receiver to tell the sender to pause when its internal receive data buffer is close to full. This avoids lost data due to buffer overflow. The following flow control modes are supported by the comm API.

- None
- RTS/CTS (often loosely termed hardware flow control)
- XON/XOFF (often loosely termed software flow control)

If no flow control is specified, both sides of the communication transmit at will, leaving no inherent protection against receive buffer overrun. This may not be a problem, depending on the serial protocol employed by the end points of the data channel. However, if one side of the channel transmits a continuous data stream, the receiver must be dedicated to the task of servicing the receive buffer or risk losing data. This is potentially a problem for multitasking systems, especially those that are not driven by a real-time kernel.

XON/XOFF flow control works as follows. When the receiver's (call it A) internal receive buffer begins to reach capacity, it transmits an XOFF (0x13) character back to the sender (call it B) requesting that it pause its transmission. After the application has unloaded some or all of the data, A transmits an XON (0x11) character notifying B that it is ready to receive more data. XON/XOFF flow control has the advantage of not requiring support for any hardware handshake lines. Its main drawback is that the in-band signalling is somewhat awkward in that an application can inadvertently stop the remote endpoint from transmitting by sending an XOFF character in a binary data stream. Also, it inhibits an application's ability to receive the XON or XOFF control characters because they are absorbed by the serial driver.[4]

If available, RTS/CTS (hardware) flow control is the best way to avoid buffer overflow. In this scheme the endpoint (call it A) wishing to transmit asserts the request to send (RTS) signal. If the other endpoint (call it B) has sufficient room in its buffer and is willing to receive data, it will assert the clear to send (CTS) signal. At this point device A begins transmitting. If B's receive buffer approaches capacity, it de-asserts CTS and A pauses its transmission. Eventually the application will read the available serial data, and B's serial port driver will assert CTS, allowing A to resume data transmission.

The default flow control setting is no flow control. This is appropriate because many devices have no support for hardware or software flow control. However, if the device with which you are communicating supports flow control, this default should be overridden. In fact, some devices may require the use of flow control.

The flow control mode is configured by invoking the `setFlowControlMode` method on a `SerialPort` object. The current flow control mode in use by the driver can be retrieved at any time using the `getFlowControlMode` method.

```
public void setFlowControlMode(int flowcontrol)
    throws UnsupportedCommOperationException
public int getFlowControlMode()
```

The desired flow control setting is passed to `setFlowControlMode` encoded as an integer equal in value to any of the following constants. The value can also be the bitwise-or of one input (_IN) mode constant and the matching output (_OUT) constant.

```
public static final int FLOWCONTROL_NONE
public static final int FLOWCONTROL_RTSCTS_IN
public static final int FLOWCONTROL_RTSCTS_OUT
public static final int FLOWCONTROL_XONXOFF_IN
public static final int FLOWCONTROL_XONXOFF_OUT
```

Flow control can be specified as unidirectional only. For example, the application can require that the remote endpoint specify RTS/CTS flow control without implementing any flow control during its own data transmission. The use of flow control can also be required of both devices protecting each endpoint in the communication from receive buffer overflow. However, input and output flow control modes can't be mixed between RTS/CTS and XON/XOFF flow control. For example, an application can't specify RTS/CTS flow control for outbound data and XON/XOFF flow control for inbound data.

---

4. Applications would have to "escape" XON/XOFF characters.

```
// Illegal setting!
SerialPort.FLOWCONTROL_RTSCTS_IN | SerialPort.FLOWCONTROL_XONXOFF_OUT
```

The following code snippet shows how to correctly select the use of RTS/CTS flow control for both serial data input and output.

```
try {
    sp.setFlowControlMode(SerialPort.FLOWCONTROL_RTSCTS_IN |
                          SerialPort.FLOWCONTROL_RTSCTS_OUT);
} catch (UnsupportedCommOperationException usc) {
    // Can't use hardware flow control with this serial port!
    ...
}
```

If the underlying driver or UART does not support the specified type of flow control or the flow control mode is an invalid combination of the mode constants that are listed above, the `setFlowControlMode` method throws an `UnsupportedCommOperationException`. In this event the actual flow control mode remains the same as it was before `setFlowControlMode` was invoked.

3.2.3 Sending and Receiving Serial Data

An application transmits and receives serial data using the `read` and `write` methods on input and output streams, respectively. `java.io.InputStream` and `java.io.OutputStream` objects are acquired by invoking the `getInputStream` and `getOutputStream` methods on a `SerialPort` object.

```
public InputStream getInputStream() throws IOException
public OutputStream getOutputStream() throws IOException
```

There is exactly one `InputStream` and one `OutputStream` attached to a serial port. Multiple calls to either method will return a reference to the same stream.

The comm API supports the notion of receive time-outs and thresholds. Receive time-outs and thresholds allow the application to control blocking reads on serial port `InputStream` objects. A read time-out can be set by invoking the `enableReceiveTimeout` method on a `SerialPort` object.

```
public void enableReceiveTimeout(int rcvTimeout)
    throws UnsupportedCommOperationException
public void disableReceiveTimeout()
```

The specified time-out value represents the number of milliseconds that any of the `InputStream`'s read methods should block waiting for receive data. If the specified number of milliseconds elapses before the number of bytes requested by the `read` method is received, the `read` method will return immediately with any data that was received. The receive time-out can be disabled at any time, using the `disableReceiveTimeout` method.

A receive threshold value can be set by invoking the method enableReceiveThreshold on a SerialPort object.

```
public void enableReceiveThreshold(int thresh)
    throws UnsupportedCommOperationException
public void disableReceiveThreshold()
```

The thresh parameter passed to enableReceiveThreshold represents a minimum number of bytes that should be returned when reading serial data. Setting a threshold value will cause the serial port InputStream's read methods to block until either thresh bytes have been received or a time-out (if one has been set by enableReceiveTimeout) occurs. The receive threshold can be disabled at any time, using the disableReceiveThreshold method.

Both enableReceiveTimeout and enableReceiveThreshold declare that an UnsupportedCommOperationException will be thrown in the event that the native serial driver doesn't support the requested functionality. This exception should never be thrown on TINI from either of these methods, since all serial port drivers do in fact support receive time-outs and thresholds.

Using receive time-out values and receive threshold settings, an application can read serial data from the serial port's InputStream without polling the InputStream's available method to determine when data is available in the serial driver's receive buffer.

Since the receive buffers are of finite size, they can overflow if not serviced (unloaded) frequently enough by the application. Without the use of any flow control, both sides must ensure that they can service the receive buffer before losing any data. This problem can be avoided to some extent by using a large enough receive buffer to give the application plenty of time to read the data. A receive buffer of a specific size can be requested by invoking the setInputBufferSize method on a SerialPort object.

```
public void setInputBufferSize(int size)
public int getInputBufferSize()
```

The requested buffer size is passed as an integer. On TINI the maximum supported input buffer size is 65535. If an invalid size is specified or another error, such as insufficient memory for the new buffer occurs, the input buffer remains the same size as it was before setInputBufferSize was invoked. No exception is thrown. However, the actual input buffer size can be verified at any time using the getInputBufferSize method. The combination of controlling the input buffer size and using well-chosen receive thresholds and time-out values can allow an otherwise busy application to service the serial port input buffer with little overhead.

An application can manually query the state of all of the hardware flow control lines that are supported by the underlying serial port.

```
public boolean isCD()
public boolean isRI()
public boolean isDSR()
public boolean isCTS()
public boolean isRTS()
public boolean isDTR()
```

These methods return `true` if the signal was asserted at the exact time it was sampled by the native driver and `false` otherwise.

The comm API only allows the DTR and RTS signals to be altered by the applications. This is because DTR and RTS are the only two lines that are outputs in a DTE serial port configuration, and the comm API assumes that it is implemented on data terminal equipment. The state of DTR and RTS can be set using the `setRTS` and `setDTR` methods.

```
public void setDTR(boolean dtr)
public void setRTS(boolean rts)
```

Passing either method a `boolean` value of `true` asserts the signal, while a value of `false` de-asserts the signal. An application using RTS/CTS flow control should not attempt to alter the state of RTS as it's managed by the driver. We'll utilize the comm API's ability to toggle the state of data terminal ready (DTR) to reset an external modem in Section 7.6.2.

On TINI, the internal serial ports (`serial0` and `serial1`) don't support all of the hardware handshake signals. We'll cover the details of TINI's serial port hardware and driver support in Section 3.3

3.2.4   Serial Port Events

The communications API provides a mechanism for asynchronous notification of interesting serial port events such as state changes in the modem control lines and when data is available. On TINI the events are propagated by a daemon thread that listens for state changes in the serial port drivers. The daemon thread is created when the first event listener is registered using the `addEventListener` method in the `SerialPort` class. The argument `listener` passed to method `addEventListener` requires an instance of a class that implements the `SerialPortEventListener` interface.

```
public void addEventListener(SerialPortEventListener listener)
    throws TooManyListenersException
public void removeEventListener()
```

The `removeEventListener` can only be invoked by a listener. Event listeners are automatically removed when the port is closed.

For every serial port event there exists one method with a `notifyOn` prefix. The listener chooses the events for which it wishes to be notified by invoking the appropriate notifyOn* method on a SerialPort object. So, for example, to receive notification when serial data is available, a listener invokes the notifyOnDataAvailable method.

```
public void notifyOnDataAvailable(boolean enable)
```

An enable value of true enables notification for the specified event. Notification can be disabled at any time by invoking the same method with an enable value of false.

The SerialPortEventListener interface defines the serialEvent method that is invoked when an event for which the listener has requested notification occurs.

```
public void serialEvent(SerialPortEvent ev)
```

Listeners invoke the getEventType method on the SerialPortEvent object passed to serialEvent to determine the source of the event.

```
public int getEventType()
```

getEventType returns the type of the event encoded as an integer. There are several serial port events defined as public constants in SerialPortEvent. We'll only cover the types supported by TINI's comm API implementation. Other events, such as FE (Framing Error), are also defined by the comm API but are not supported by TINI's serial drivers.

These are two of the most important events.

- DATA_AVAILABLE
- OUTPUT_BUFFER_EMPTY

These provide notification of the state of the serial driver's transmit and receive buffers. When these events are used properly it allows the application to maximize serial port throughput with a minimum of CPU overhead and without dedicated threads.

An application can periodically poll the available method on the serial port input stream to determine when serial data has been received. However, polling is typically inefficient in terms of CPU usage. Depending on the type of serial device and the other things that the application is doing, it can be difficult to determine the frequency at which to check for inbound data. If the application polls too frequently, then much of the CPU is wasted asking the question "Any data yet (huh, huh, is there, how about now)?" Even if the application can dedicate much of the CPU to polling for receive data, there is no guarantee that other system operations such as garbage collection won't delay polling from time to time. If the serial device doesn't support either RTS/CTS (hardware) or (XON/XOFF) software flow control, infrequent polling can lead to loss of data due to the receive buffer overflowing.

An application can avoid polling either by using the receive time-outs and thresholds discussed in Section 3.2.4 or the DATA_AVAILABLE event. The DATA_AVAILABLE event is generated when data is received by the serial port. When the listener receives notification of this event, it typically reads all data available from the input stream and supplies it to another thread in the application for further processing. The advantage of the DATA_AVAILABLE event is that it doesn't require a blocking invocation of one of the input stream's read methods.

Managing the flow of outbound data is typically less critical and a little easier. The OUTPUT_BUFFER_EMPTY event is generated when the serial driver's transmit buffer is empty. The listener can use this event to move data from an arbitrarily large buffer to the serial port in smaller, more manageable blocks. This event can be used as an alternative to invoking a write method that will block if the serial transmit buffer is full.

Changes in the state of the control lines defined as inputs for DTE serial ports can be detected by registering for any of the following events.

- CD (Carrier Detect)
- CTS (Clear To Send)
- DSR (Data Set Ready)
- RI (Ring Indicate)

The getNewValue method of class SerialPortEvent can be used to determine the sense of the transition.

```
public boolean getNewValue()
```

It returns true if the specified signal is asserted and false otherwise. A common example of how control line change notification is useful is found in managing communications with a serial modem. When the modem has established a connection with another modem, it asserts carrier detect. If the remote modem "hangs up," a SerialPortEvent.CD change event will be generated and getNewValue returns false. The listener can use this information to notify the rest of the application that the modem connection is no longer valid.

The CTSMonitor example, shown in Listing 3.2, listens for changes on the CTS line.

Listing 3.2   CTSMonitor

```
import java.io.IOException;
import java.util.TooManyListenersException;
import javax.comm.*;
import com.dalsemi.system.TINIOS;

class CTSMonitor implements SerialPortEventListener {
```

```
    SerialPort sp;

    CTSMonitor() throws NoSuchPortException, PortInUseException {
        // Specify a timeout value of at least a few seconds before
        // failing on 'open' attempt. This allows another process
        // (probably slush) to relinquish port ownership.
        sp = (SerialPort)
            CommPortIdentifier.getPortIdentifier("serial0").open(
                                            "CTSMonitor", 5000);
        try {
            // Enable the use of hardware handshake lines for serial0
            TINIOS.setRTSCTSFlowControlEnable(0, true);
        } catch (UnsupportedCommOperationException usce) {
            // Won't happen on serial0
        }

        try {
            sp.addEventListener(this);
            sp.notifyOnCTS(true);
        } catch (TooManyListenersException tmle) {}
    }

    public void serialEvent(SerialPortEvent event) {
        switch (event.getEventType()) {
            case SerialPortEvent.CTS:
                System.out.println("CTS change, new value="+
                                event.getNewValue());
                break;
            default:
        }
    }

    public static void main(String[] args) {
        try {
            CTSMonitor cm = new CTSMonitor();
            try {
                Thread.sleep(Long.MAX_VALUE);
            } catch (InterruptedException ie) {}
        } catch (Exception e) {
            System.out.println(e.getMessage());
            e.printStackTrace();
        }
    }
}
```

During construction CTSMonitor creates and opens a SerialPort object that encapsulates serial0. It then adds itself as an event listener and requests notification for CTS change events. After the CTSMonitor object is created, the primordial thread puts itself to sleep for an almost infinite amount of time because the event notifications are generated by a daemon thread. If we were to allow the primordial thread to terminate by falling out of the main method, the event notification daemon would also exit and the application would terminate.

From this point forward the application just waits for notification of a change in the state of the serial port's CTS line. We can test the application using the BlackBox utility and the null modem configuration shown in Figure 3.2. The null modem swaps, among other things, RTS and CTS. So by toggling RTS from the BlackBox utility, we can generate transitions on the CTS pin of the TINI serial port. When the BlackBox utility starts, RTS is asserted (high in this case), and CTS on the TINI serial port should also be asserted. Toggling RTS from the BlackBox will produce an event of type SerialPortEvent.CTS. Invoking getNewValue on the SerialPortEvent object will return false, indicating that CTS has been de-asserted.

In Chapter 7 we'll use the comm API to control an analog phone line modem with a serial interface. It takes advantage of much of the functionality described here including carrier detect (CD) change notification to provide asynchronous notification that the modem has lost the carrier signal (that is, the modem connection has been lost).

3.3 TINI'S SERIAL PORTS

This section covers details that are specific to TINI's serial port hardware and drivers. Limitations and configuration options for each port are described. If your application requires only one serial port, then it can likely use the default serial port (serial0) without worrying about many of the following details. However, if your application targets unusual serial devices or requires the use of multiple serial ports, you should read this section.

As mentioned earlier, the TINI runtime environment supports up to four serial ports. The serial ports are designated serial0 through serial3. The UARTs used by serial0 and serial1 are integrated within TINI's microcontroller. For this reason they are termed "internal" serial ports. The UARTs used by serial2 and serial3 require a dedicated external dual-UART[5] chip. These are referred to as "external" serial ports. Because serial0 and serial1 use internal UARTs, they are more efficient. The internal serial port drivers don't have to do nearly as much work to load or unload data from the UART. However, the internal serial ports are somewhat limited in terms of configuration options. The serial character configurations supported by serial0 and serial1 are the following.

- 8 data bits, 1 stop bit, no parity (default)
- 8 data bits, 1 stop bit, with parity (odd/even only)
- 7 data bits, 2 stop, no parity
- 7 data bits, 1 stop, with parity (odd/even only)

---

5. See the E10 socket schematic for details.

Configurations that use only 5 or 6 data bits or 1.5 stop bits are impossible if using the internal ports. However, this is seldom of practical concern. The options listed allow the internal ports to communicate with most common serial devices. The external serial ports support all configurations that can be achieved using the comm API with the exception of XON/XOFF flow control.

Both internal ports support XON/XOFF flow control. A single set of hardware handshake lines is shared between the internal ports. This implies that only one port at a time can be used with RTS/CTS flow control. By default `serial0` does not own the hardware handshake signals. This default can be changed using the method `setRTSCTSFlowControlEnable` defined in class `com.dalsemi.system.TINIOS`.

```
public static boolean setRTSCTSFlowControlEnable(int portNumber,
                                                 boolean enable)
    throws UnsupportedCommOperationException
```

The port number must specify one of the internal serial ports (0 or 1). If `enable` is `true`, the hardware handshake signals will be dedicated for use as hardware handshake signals for the specified serial port. If `enable` is `false`, the signals are released to be used with the `com.dalsemi.system.BitPort` (see Chapter 9) class as general purpose TTL I/O.

There are a couple of additional points to keep in mind when using `serial1`. First, `serial1` is by default dedicated to the task of communicating with the external 1-Wire line driver. If your TINI hardware implementation does not require (or support) the use of the external 1-Wire adapter, `serial1` can be reclaimed for use with a general purpose serial port. To override `serial1`'s default usage, an application must invoke the `enableSerialPort1` method defined in the `TINIOS` class.[6]

```
public static final void enableSerialPort1()
```

This option persists across system boots. The other thing to keep in mind, with respect to `serial1`, is that it does not support any data rates below 2400 bps. This is seldom of practical concern when communicating with modern serial devices.

The external serial ports must also be enabled using the method `setExternalSerialPortEnable` in class `TINIOS`.

```
public static void setExternalSerialPortEnable(int portNum, boolean enable)
```

---

6. If you're using `serial1` on a TBM390, you will also need to disable the DS2480 1-Wire driver. This is accomplished by grounding the EN2480 signal (pin 26 of the SIMM connector).

The port number must specify one of the external ports (2 or 3). An enable value of `true` enables the use of external serial drivers. The settings established by `setExternalSerialPortEnable` persist across system boots.

The external serial drivers allow flexibility where the external UART hardware is mapped into TINI's memory space. The default base address for the external UART is 0x380020. This method can be overridden using the `setExternalSerialPortAddress` method in TINIOS.

```
public static void setExternalSerialPortAddress(int portNum, int address)
```

The port number must specify one of the external ports (2 or 3). The address refers to the base (or lowest) address consumed in the memory map. The settings established by `setExternalSerialPortAddress` persist across reboots.

There is one final tidbit to keep in mind when developing applications that control serial devices. When TINI boots, it transmits progress messages on `serial0` at the data rate of 115,200 bps. This can cause confusion for certain embedded serial devices because the data is unsolicited and is transmitted at a speed that may be different from the speed for which the device is configured to receive data. Applications can disable boot progress messages using the `setSerialBootMessageState` method in class TINIOS.

```
public static final void setSerialBootMessagesState(boolean on)
```

The serial boot message state is also persistent across system boots. If slush is involved, the line "`setenv SerialServer enable`" should be removed from the `.startup` file. This will prevent slush from chattering over `serial0`.

3.4 A SMALL TERMINAL EXAMPLE

A serial terminal program provides a reasonably small example that ties together much of the functionality provided by the communications API. The `TiniTerm` program presented in this section reads characters from the console (`System.in`) and writes the same characters to a serial port. Data flow in the other direction is supported as well. All characters received on the serial port are written to the console (`System.out`).

`TiniTerm`'s constructor and main method are shown in Listing 3.3. The baud rate must be specified on the command line. The `main` method simply creates and starts a new thread that blocks waiting for console input.

Listing 3.3 TiniTerm

```
...

class TiniTerm extends Thread implements SerialPortEventListener {
```

```java
private SerialPort sp;
private InputStream sin;
private OutputStream sout;

private TiniTerm(String portName, int baudRate)
    throws NoSuchPortException,
           PortrtInUseException,
           UnsupportedCommOperationException,
           IOException {

    try {
        // Create SerialPort object for specified port
        sp = (SerialPort)
            CommPortIdentifier.getPortIdentifier(portName).open(
                                            "TiniTerm", 5000);
        // Configure port for 8 databits, 1 stop bit and no parity
        // checks
         sp.setSerialPortParams(baudRate, SerialPort.DATABITS_8,
                               SerialPort.STOPBITS_1,
                               SerialPort.PARITY_NONE);

        // Get input and output streams for serial data I/O
        sin = sp.getInputStream();
        sout = sp.getOutputStream();
    } catch (NoSuchPortException nsp) {
        System.out.println("Specified serial port ("+portName+
                           ") does not exist");
        throw nsp;
    } catch (PortInUseException piu) {
        System.out.println("Serial port "+portName+
                           " in use by another application");
        throw piu;
    } catch (UnsupportedCommOperationException usc) {
        System.out.println("Unable to configure port:"+portName);
        throw usc;
    } catch (IOException ioe) {
        System.out.println(
            "Unable to acquire I/O streams for port " + portName);
        throw ioe;
    }
}

...

public static void main(String[] args) {
    if (args.length != 1) {
        System.out.println("Usage: java TiniTerm.tini data_rate");
        System.exit(1);
    }

    try {
        TiniTerm term = new TiniTerm("serial0",
                                    Integer.parseInt(args[0]));
        term.start();
```

```
        } catch (Exception e) {
            System.out.println(e.getMessage());
            e.printStackTrace();
        }
    }
}
```

The getCommPortIdentifier method of class CommPortIdentifier is used to obtain a CommPort object representing the port specified by name to the constructor. The CommPort object is immediately cast as a SerialPort object. The resulting serial port object is then initialized to transmit and receive data at the rate specified on the command line. The serial characters will contain 8 data bits and 1 stop bit. All parity checking is disabled. Finally, the constructor invokes the getInputStream and getOutputStream methods on the SerialPort object to acquire streams for receiving data from and transmitting data to the underlying serial port.

For the purpose of illustration, TiniTerm's constructor catches each checked exception that can be thrown during initialization and displays an appropriate error message. The following are exceptions from the preceding catch blocks along with a likely culprit.

- PortInUseException. The port specified is being used by another application.
- NoSuchPortException. This exception won't actually be thrown in this example because it specifies serial0 as a hard-coded value. NoSuchPortException is thrown if an invalid port name, such as "serial5" or "Serial0," is specified.
- UnsupportedCommOperationException. An unsupported baud rate was specified.

Listing 3.4   TiniTerm's run method

```
public void run() {
    // Return from read as soon as any bytes are available
    // (i.e. don't wait for line termination)
    ((SystemInputStream) System.in).setRawMode(true);

    while (true) {
        try {
            byte b = (byte) System.in.read();
            if (b == (byte) '~')
                break;
            // Send the byte out the serial port
            sout.write(b);
        } catch (IOException ioe) {
            ioe.printStackTrace();
        }
    }
}
```

By default on TINI, a `PrintStream`'s read method will block until a line separator has been received. In general this behavior varies from platform to platform. Win32 platforms perform the same buffering as TINI. However, in Linux this behavior depends on how the shell that launches the application is configured. For a terminal application it is nicer to have `read` return as soon as a character is available so that it can immediately be transmitted to the remote terminal and echoed to the console. When an application is launched from slush, it inherits a `System.in` that extends the class `SystemInputStream`. `SystemInputStream` is defined in the `com.dalsemi.shell.server` package. It provides the `setRawMode` method to override the default `readLine` type behavior. In Listing 3.4 on the previous page, the first thing the `run` method does is cast `System.in` to a `SystemInputStream` and set its mode to "raw," using the `setRawMode` method, so that the terminal application behaves as we would expect. If you comment out the statement that invokes `set-RawMode`, `TiniTerm` should run on any Java platform for which an implementation of the communications API exists. However, you may have to hit <ENTER> before the data you type is transmitted to the remote terminal or echoed to the console.

Next, the `run` method enters an infinite loop that blocks waiting for input on `System.in`. It reads a byte at a time and echoes it to the serial port. The only escape from the `run` method is to type the tilde (~) character at the prompt. Typing the tilde character should cause the read thread to terminate, and the application should exit gracefully.

`TiniTerm` implements `SerialPortEventListener`, which means it must provide an implementation for the `serialEvent` (Listing 3.5) method. In this case, we requested notification whenever data is received on the serial port. `serialEvent` invokes the `getEventType` method on the `SerialPortEvent` object. If it is a `DATA_AVAILABLE` event, the serial port `InputStream`'s `available` method is queried to determine how many bytes can be read without blocking. Since we received a `DATA_AVAILABLE` event, the number of bytes available should be at least 1. If the delay between when the first byte of data was received and when we read the data is high enough, it is possible that multiple characters will be in the serial receive buffer. In this example, the bottleneck is the speed at which a human can type characters from a keyboard, so we'd expect to always read just one byte. Regardless, all characters received from the serial port input stream are read from the input stream attached to the serial port and immediately written to the system output stream. Any events other than `DATA_AVAILABLE` are ignored.

Listing 3.5   serialEvent

```
public void serialEvent(SerialPortEvent ev) {
    switch (ev.getEventType()) {
        case SerialPortEvent.DATA_AVAILABLE:
```

```
        try {
            int count = sin.available();
            if (count > 0) {
                byte[] buf = new byte[count];
                count = sin.read(buf, 0, count);
                System.out.write(buf, 0, count);
            }
        } catch (IOException ioe) {
            // Drain it
        }
        break;

    default:
        // Ignoring any unexpected events
        break;
    }
}
```

We can test `TiniTerm` using `BlackBox` and the null modem configuration shown in Figure 3.2. `BlackBox` allows the user to select all necessary parameters to communicate with the terminal program. For our purposes select the following settings.

- Data bits: 8
- Stop bits: 1
- Parity: none
- Data rate: 115,200

Assuming that the data rate selected in `BlackBox` is 115,200 bps, you can start `TiniTerm` in your Telnet session using a command similar to the following.

```
TINI /> java TiniTerm.tini 115200
```

Notice that the application is launched as a foreground process (that is, no "&" at the end of the command). This is important because background processes cannot read from `System.in`. For background processes, `System.in` is fed from a `com.dalsemi.comm.NullInputStream`. This allows the Telnet session itself to continue to process characters typed at the prompt, while other processes run in the background. In this case, we want the application, `TiniTerm`, to process all console input.

If the `BlackBox` settings and serial cable are correct, you should be able to type data at the Telnet prompt and see the characters echoed at both the Telnet prompt and the `BlackBox` receive window. You should also be able to type characters in the `BlackBox` transmit window and see them written to the Telnet prompt.

3.5   A SERIAL ⇔ ETHERNET CONVERTER

Although it may not be obvious, we actually implemented a simple serial to Ethernet converter in the last section. When TiniTerm is run, it takes console input System.in, which was most likely receiving data typed from a Telnet session. The characters typed at the Telnet prompt ultimately wind up as network data traveling over a TCP connection. In this section we'll do a more formal job of making a bridge between a serial device and another host on an Ethernet network. The big difference is that the example presented in this section, SerialToEthernet, is designed for communication with serial devices that transfer potentially large amounts of information with very little delay between characters. This is as opposed to TiniTerm that only needed to perform well enough to keep up with a human typist. The main difference is the need to move large buffers, in the form of byte arrays, in single, relatively few I/O operations. The need for fast, full-duplex I/O over both the serial and network connections will lead to an application with a different structure that configures and uses the serial port in a much different fashion than TiniTerm.

The SerialToEthernet application reads data from an attached serial device and writes it to a network server. Data received from the same network server is transmitted to the serial device. Potentially network and serial data are traveling in both directions simultaneously, as shown in Figure 3.4.

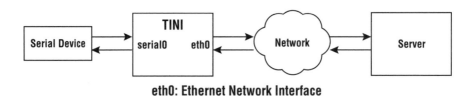

eth0: Ethernet Network Interface

Figure 3.4   Serial to Ethernet bridge data flow

SerialToEthernet's main method extracts the network server name, server port, and serial port data rate from the command line and passes them to the constructor (shown in Listing 3.6). The constructor opens serial0 and configures the port for operation at 8 data bits, 1 stop bit, and no parity. The baud rate is set to the speed passed to the constructor. Since both serial and network I/O are potentially full duplex, the serial port flow control mode is set for RTS/CTS flow control. This will protect the serial receive buffers of both TINI and the attached device from overflow under a potentially heavy load. Next, the constructor acquires an InputStream and an OutputStream for reading from and writing to the serial port.

Listing 3.6   SerialToEthernet

```
...
class SerialToEthernet extends Thread {
    // Use a 1K buffer for serial data receive
    private static final int INPUT_BUF_LEN = 1024;

    // Serial port and associated streams
    private SerialPort sp;
    private InputStream spin;
    private OutputStream spout;

    // Socket and associated streams
    private Socket s;
    private InputStream sin;
    private OutputStream sout;
    ...
    private SerialToEthernet(String server, int port, int speed)
        throws Exception {

        // Create and initialize serial port
        sp = (SerialPort)
            CommPortIdentifier.getPortIdentifier("serial0").open(
                                        "SerialToEthernet", 5000);

        // Enable the use of hardware handshake lines for serial0
        TINIOS.setRTSCTSFlowControlEnable(0, true);

        // 8 data bits, 1 stop bit, no parity
         sp.setSerialPortParams(speed, SerialPort.DATABITS_8,
                                SerialPort.STOPBITS_1,
                                SerialPort.PARITY_NONE);
        // Require RTS/CTS flow control from both serial channel
        // endpoints
        sp.setFlowControlMode(SerialPort.FLOWCONTROL_RTSCTS_IN |
                                SerialPort.FLOWCONTROL_RTSCTS_OUT);

        // Initialize serial port input and output streams
        spin = sp.getInputStream();
        spout = sp.getOutputStream();
        // Set a 100 millisecond receive timeout
        sp.enableReceiveTimeout(100);
        // Set the receive threshold equal to buffer length
        sp.enableReceiveThreshold(INPUT_BUF_LEN);

        // Connect to network server
        s = new Socket(server, port);
        sin = s.getInputStream();
        sout = s.getOutputStream();

        // Create and launch Serial -> Ethernet thread
        (new Thread(new SerialReader(this, INPUT_BUF_LEN))).start();
        // Create and launch Ethernet -> Serial thread
        (new Thread(new SerialWriter(this))).start();
```

```
        // Launch maintenance thread
        super.start();
    }
    ...
}
```

A receive time-out of 100 milliseconds and a receive threshold equal to the length of the serial port receive buffer are set to allow fairly large blocks of data to be read in an efficient fashion from the input stream attached to the serial port. After finishing the serial port configuration, a connection is established with the network server, and input and output streams are obtained for data transfer to and from the server.

Finally the constructor starts three new threads of execution. Their tasks are as follows.

1. *SerialReader.* Reads from the serial port, writes to the socket
2. *SerialWriter.* Reads from the socket, writes to the serial port
3. *SerialToEthernet.* Provides periodic statistical updates

The run method of the maintenance thread is shown in Listing 3.7. It writes the total number of bytes received from the serial port and the total number of bytes received from the network to the console (System.out) and sleeps for about a minute. This process is repeated as long as running is true. The cumulative byte counts are maintained by the SerialReader and SerialWriter threads. Both of the aforementioned threads keep a reference to the maintenance thread. If a java.io.IOException occurs in or the network connection is closed by the remote server, the thread (either SerialReader or SerialWriter) that detected the problem sets the running boolean to false and interrupts the maintenance thread. The maintenance thread then falls out of the while loop and closes the serial port, socket, and all associated streams.

Listing 3.7 run

```
...
private volatile boolean running = true;
private int serialTotal = 0;
private int networkTotal = 0;
...
public void run() {
    while (running) {
        try {
            Thread.sleep(60000);
        } catch (InterruptedException ie) {}
        System.out.println("Bytes received from serial:"+serialTotal);
        System.out.println("Bytes received from network:"+networkTotal);
    }
```

```
    try {
        // Close serial port and associated streams
        ...
        // Close socket and associated streams
        ...
    } catch (IOException e) {}
}
```

`SerialToEthernet` contains two inner classes: `SerialReader` and `SerialWriter`. Each implement the `Runnable` interface so that they can each run as separate threads of execution. This prevents either of the threads from having to block while the other is performing serial or network data transfer. This helps achieve the goal of high-speed, full-duplex I/O.

The inner class `SerialReader`, shown in Listing 3.8, creates a byte array of the specified size that serves as a reusable buffer for serial receive data. The run method enters a loop that reads data available from the serial port's `InputStream` and immediately writes that data to the socket's `OutputStream`.

In `SerialToEthernet`'s constructor, we set a serial port read time-out of 100 milliseconds and a receive threshold equal to the length of the serial receive data buffer length (1024 bytes in this case). The number of bytes read (that is, the value of `count`) from the serial port's `InputStream` will be the minimum of the number of bytes received and the length of the input buffer.

- count = min(serial bytes received, serBuf.length)

At slower speeds the `read` method should not return due to receiving the number of bytes specified by the threshold value. For example, if the baud rate is set at 9600 bps, we'd expect to receive about 1 serial character (or byte[7]) every millisecond[8] assuming that the attached serial device is continuously transmitting. In this case, we would expect the `read` method to return after the 100 millisecond time-out has expired with approximately 100 bytes of receive data copied to the supplied byte array. At the highest supported baud rate of 115,200 bps, we'd receive about 12 serial characters per millisecond (9600 bps * 12 = 115,200 bps). Again, assuming that the attached serial device is transmitting continuously, the number of bytes received in the 100 ms time-out window—approximately 1200—is larger than `serBuf`. In this case, `read` will return after the receive threshold of 1024 bytes

---

7. We're reasonably safe in referring to the received serial characters as bytes because the port is configured for 8 data bits.
8. With 8 data bits, 1 stop bit, and the mandatory start bit result in 10 bits received on the wire for every 8 bits of data. At 9600 bps, 1 bit is received every 104 microseconds. This results in a total time of 1040 microseconds (or 1.04 milliseconds) per byte of serial data.

is reached. We would expect to hit the receive threshold in less than the 100 ms time-out window.

Listing 3.8   SerialReader

```
...
private class SerialReader implements Runnable {
    private byte[] serBuf;
    private Thread maint;

    private SerialReader(Thread maint, int size) {
        serBuf = new byte[size];
        this.maint = maint;
    }

    public void run() {
        while (running) {
            try {
                // Read all available data in serial input buffer
                int count = spin.read(serBuf, 0, serBuf.length);
                if (count > 0) {
                    // Blast serial data to network server
                    sout.write(serBuf, 0, count);
                    serialTotal += count;
                }
            } catch (IOException ioe) {
                // Trouble communicating with server
                System.out.println(ioe.getMessage());
                ioe.printStackTrace();
                running = false;
                maint.interrupt();
                break;
            }
        }
    }
}
```

The inner class SerialWriter is shown in Listing 3.9. SerialWriter's run method enters a loop that reads data available on the socket's InputStream and immediately writes the data to the serial port's OutputStream. It also maintains a single 1024-byte buffer that is (re)used for moving data from the socket to the serial port.

SerialWriter's job is just a bit less complicated than that of SerialReader as it doesn't need to be concerned with receive time-outs and thresholds. A time-out could be set for reads from the socket's InputStream, but in this example, it simply blocks until 1 or more bytes of data are available and returns the minimum of the data available and the buffer length. If the remote server closes the network connection, the socket's InputStream read method returns –1. When this occurs, running is set to false and the maintenance thread is interrupted. This will cause all three threads to eventually fall out of their run methods, and the application will terminate.

Listing 3.9   SerialWriter

```
...
private class SerialWriter implements Runnable {
    private byte[] ethBuf = new byte[1024];
    private Thread maint;

    private SerialWriter(Thread maint) {
        this.maint = maint;
    }

    public void run() {
        int count = 0;
        while (running) {
            try {
                // Read all available data from network server
                count = sin.read(ethBuf, 0, ethBuf.length);
                if (count > 0) {
                    // Write data received from network out serial port
                    spout.write(ethBuf, 0, count);
                    networkTotal += count;
                } else if (count == -1) {
                    running = false;
                    maint.interrupt();
                }
            } catch (IOException ioe) {
                System.out.println(ioe.getMessage());
                ioe.printStackTrace();
                running = false;
                maint.interrupt();
                break;
            }
        }
    }
}
```

For this application we wanted to move relatively large amounts of data between the serial port and the network. If we only moved a byte (or even a few bytes) at a time, the CPU would be consumed, performing relatively heavyweight context switches moving back and forth from Java to the native OS. This would dramatically reduce the overall throughput. For this reason, a large receive threshold and buffer size were chosen for serial input. Moving large buffers prorates the overhead of the expensive context switches mentioned previously. Another way to possibly increase the overall throughput is to provide a large buffer for the driver's receive buffer, using the setInputBufferSize method described in Section 3.2.3. If the driver maintains a large receive buffer, it gives the application more time to service the buffer before the driver must tell the attached serial device to stop transmitting. Ideally, how large to make the receive time-out, threshold, and the driver's serial input buffer should be computed as a function of the serial data rate and an estimate of the CPU load imposed by any other tasks your application may be performing.

In the event that the `SerialReader` thread is unable, due to other system activity, to unload the serial receive data fast enough, the serial driver's receive buffer is protected by the use of RTS/CTS flow control. On the networking side of things we don't need to worry at all about the flow control. It's automatically handled by the fact that we're using a `Socket`. A `Socket` (as opposed to a `DatagramSocket`) encapsulates a TCP connection. TCP provides built-in flow control.

To test `SerialToEthernet`, the `BlackBox` utility was used to simulate the serial device shown in Figure 3.4. When selected, its "auto transmit" mode will continuously transmit data at the specified rate. Its receive window shows the continuous stream of data that is received simultaneously. For testing the network portion of the application, an echo server[9] was used. With this particular test configuration, all bytes originate from the `BlackBox` transmitter and terminate at the `BlackBox` receiver.

---

9. The source for the `EchoServer` application wasn't shown here, but it, along with all of the source to `SerialToEthernet`, is included in the accompanying CD.

CHAPTER 4 # The 1-Wire Net

Many of the gadgets that you might want to interface to TINI such as cameras, vending machines, lab equipment, and so forth are electronic and have the built-in capability to communicate with the outside world. Perhaps they are stand-alone devices with some type of serial or parallel port. These are usually "smart" devices endowed with their own processor that manages the underlying physical port used to communicate with other electronic devices. What about all the other things that lack the ability to communicate with the outside world—for example, an appliance such as a light, dishwasher, or heater? Or maybe you're trying to gather information about something that isn't even a physical device—the environment in a remote-climate-controlled room, for example.

1-Wire chips provide network connectivity to otherwise mute entities. The various families of 1-Wire chips provide functionality ranging from object tagging for the sole purpose of identification to sensing environmental conditions such as temperature and humidity and scale all the way to secure cryptographic processors that run JavaCard and provide an authentic digital identity. Once 1-Wire chips are attached to an object, it becomes capable of joining a 1-Wire network. Once the object is a part of a 1-Wire network, TINI provides the bridge to the Internet, allowing it to be monitored and controlled by something as common and easy to use as a Web browser.

This chapter begins with a brief introduction to 1-Wire networking. The introduction defines the notion of a 1-Wire network and describes the low-level communication protocols. The introduction is intended to present only the core concepts and terminology necessary to describe and illustrate the use of TINI's 1-Wire API. An in-depth treatment of 1-Wire networking is beyond the scope of this book.[1] The rest of the chapter provides a detailed description of the 1-Wire API and examines adapters and containers, the classes that represent them, and how they are used to monitor and control devices on a 1-Wire network. Even though all of the examples presented in this chapter were tested on TINI, it should be mentioned that the 1-Wire API is also supported on several other Java platforms as well.[2]

4.1   1-WIRE NETWORKING FUNDAMENTALS

A 1-Wire network is a collection of one or more uniquely addressable devices that share a single conductor for communication and power. The single conductor is often referred to as a bus. The 1-Wire devices attached to the bus are always slaves. This implies the existence of a master that initiates all communication with the devices.

4.1.1   1-Wire Signalling

The extremely simple hardware configuration of a 1-Wire network is shown in Figure 4.1.

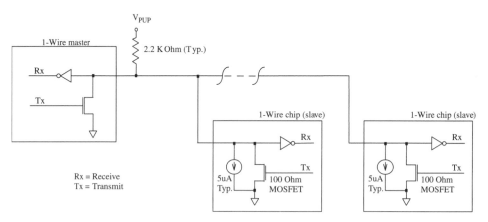

Figure 4.1   1-Wire network hardware configuration

---

1.   A thorough treatment of 1-Wire networking is provided at *http://www.ibutton.com/ ibuttons/standard.pdf.*
2.   Details on platform support for the Java 1-Wire API can be found at *http://www.ibutton.com/software/1wire/1wire_api.html.*

1-Wire devices are open drain driven and can therefore only drive the bus low. The devices rely on either an external pull-up resistor on the master end of the bus or a pull-up resistor integrated into a dedicated master chip to return the bus to a high state. In normal operating conditions the bus is not even driven high by the master. There are, however, circumstances when a properly configured master will actively drive the line high for very brief durations to aid communication over long line lengths.

Most 1-Wire devices can communicate at two different speeds[3]: regular speed and overdrive speed. If not explicitly set into the overdrive speed, devices will communicate at regular speed. Regular speed results in a maximum data rate of 16.3 kilobits per second, while overdrive speed results in a maximum data rate of 144 kilobits per second. The characteristics of the waveforms at the two different speeds are the same except for the duration.

There are four distinct signals (or waveforms) generated by the master on the 1-Wire bus.

1. Reset sequence
2. Write 0
3. Write 1
4. Read data

The reset sequence is used to return all devices on the bus to a known initial state. It consists of a master generated reset pulse followed by a device generated presence pulse. The master transmits a reset pulse by driving the bus low for a minimum 480 μs at regular speed or 48 μs at overdrive speed. The master then releases the bus and goes into receive mode. The bus is pulled to a high state via the pull-up resistor. After detecting the rising edge on the bus, the devices wait 15 to 60 μs at regular speed or 2 to 6 μs at overdrive speed and then transmit the presence pulse by driving the bus low for a time of 60 to 240 μs at regular speed or 8 to 24 μs at overdrive speed. A reset pulse of 480 μs or longer will return any devices communicating at overdrive speed to regular speed.

The read and write data signals are known as time slots. All time slots are initiated by the master driving the bus low for at least 1 μs. The falling edge of the data line synchronizes the slave devices to the master. Each slave device employs a delay circuit that is triggered by this falling edge. During write time slots, the delay circuit determines when the devices will sample the bus. For a read data time slot, if a 0 is to be transmitted, the delay circuit determines how long the devices will hold the data line low overriding the 1 generated by the master. If the data bit is a 1, the device will leave the read data time slot unchanged. An important point to make

---

3. Some of the older 1-Wire devices are only capable of communication at regular speeds. Supported speeds for any device are specified in that device's data sheet.

here is that any device that transmits a 0 in response to a master initiated read time slot will override or hide any 1 transmitted by any other device. Since lows (logical 0s) are actively driven and highs (logical 1s) are soft due to the relatively large pull-up resistor between the bus and power, 0s win any contention. This point is important in understanding the address discovery process described in Section 4.1.3.

Note that the master samples the 1-Wire line whether it is transmitting or receiving. This means that the application receives the data it transmits. This fact can be used by an application as a quick check to ensure that the data it transmitted was not altered by errors such as a momentary short of the 1-Wire line to ground. We'll put this to the test in Listing 4.6. This quick check, however, does not obviate the need to protect 1-Wire data using CRCs (cyclic redundancy checks) as described in Section 4.5.

4.1.2   1-Wire Transactions

A complete communication with a 1-Wire device is called a transaction. A transaction is divided into 3 phases.

1. Initialization
2. Addressing
3. Data exchange

The initialization phase consists of the bus master transmitting a reset pulse. After receiving the reset pulse, all attached devices generate a presence pulse. At this point the master knows that at least one device is attached to the bus. After the initialization phase all devices are in a reset state waiting for the master to transmit one of the address layer commands.

Typically, during the addressing phase, a specific device is targeted by broadcasting its entire 64-bit address. This causes all but the addressed device to "drop off the bus" by transitioning to a high-impedance idle state waiting for the master to begin a new transaction. The device whose address was broadcast is "selected." The 1-Wire addressing commands and the addressing phase is covered in more detail in Section 4.1.3.

After a device has been selected, it is ready to receive device-specific commands that allow access to the services it provides. Different devices have different capabilities. The details of special function commands and associated protocols and data specific to a device family are described in a data sheet associated with the particular device. Most application software doesn't need to worry about these details because the 1-Wire API hides them through an abstraction called a container, described in Section 4.4. However, applications with strict performance requirements may wish to communicate directly with the device.

Table 4.1 details a complete 1-Wire transaction for performing a temperature conversion using a DS18S20 temperature sensor.

Table 4.1   Perform temperature conversion

Master	Data	Comments
Transmit	Reset	Reset all 1-Wire devices
Receive	Presence pulse	All devices announce their presence on the bus
Transmit	Address match (0x55)	Devices wait for an address to be broadcast
Transmit	DS18S20's address	All other devices idle
Transmit	Convert temperature command (0x44)	Send special function command
N/A	None	Master leaves bus high for ~.75s to provide power for conversion

After the DS18S20 has finished with the temperature conversion, a second transaction is required to read the result. This transaction is detailed in Table 4.2. Note that both transactions begin with a reset followed by device selection using the DS18S20's address. This is true of almost all 1-Wire transactions.

Table 4.2   Read temperature conversion results

Master	Data	Comments
Transmit	Reset	Reset all 1-Wire devices
Receive	Presence pulse	All devices announce their presence on the bus
Transmit	Address match (0x55)	Devices wait for an address to be broadcast
Transmit	DS18S20's address	All other devices idle
Transmit	Read scratchpad command (0xbe)	Results of conversion are stored in the scratchpad
Receive	Scratchpad data	Read the temperature data

4.1.3 Addressing 1-Wire Chips

All 1-Wire devices contain a unique 64-bit address. This address consists of three distinct parts, as shown in Figure 4.2.

CRC	Device Id	Family

Figure 4.2 1-Wire address

The family code is used to determine the type (or family) of the 1-Wire device and therefore the services it provides. For example, the family id for the DS2406 Dual Addressable Switch is 0x12.[4] After reading the 1-Wire address and extracting the family id, the application knows it has discovered a switch with two switched I/O channels and 128 bytes of EPROM. The Device id portion of the address can be viewed simply as a large number used to ensure uniqueness. The CRC (Cyclic Redundancy Check) byte is used to ensure the integrity of both the family and device id. The use of CRCs to protect the address as well as other data is covered in detail in Section 4.5.

There are two methods by which 1-Wire devices are addressed.

- Device discovery
- Device selection

When an application that uses a 1-Wire network is started, it doesn't need to know the number, types, or addresses of the attached devices. Device discovery is also referred to as an address search and allows the master to use a process of elimination to discover the addresses of all the devices on the network. Once the host knows a device's address, its type and therefore the services it provides are easily attained by examination of the family id portion of the address. Device selection is also called an address match and is used to select a specific device given its address. After the host application has "discovered" the addresses of all of the devices on the network, it uses the selection process to initiate further 1-Wire transactions targeted at a specific device. Let's consider device discovery and device selection in more detail.

For the following discussion it is helpful to represent a 1-Wire address, A, as an "array of bits." The array has 64 elements labeled A_0 to A_{63}, where A_0 is the 0th element of the array and least significant bit of the address. It is also useful to imagine that both the master and all 1-Wire chips maintain an iteration variable

---

4. A list of all device types and associated family ids can be found online (see *http://www.dalsemi.com/products/autoinfo/families.html*).

(call it i, where $0 \le i \le 63$) that represents the position within the address during the search process.

The process of device (or address) discovery begins with the master transmitting a reset followed by the "search address" command byte (0xf0). The device discovery process continues with the iterative execution of the following three-step sequence: read a bit (R0), read the complement of the bit (R1), write an acknowledgment bit (W). Each iteration of this sequence produces one bit of a device address. The address bits are discovered in little-endian fashion, starting with the least significant bit A_0. This sequence is performed for each bit of the address and terminates after bit A_{63} has been discovered. After one complete pass, the host application knows the complete 64-bit address of one device. The remaining number of devices and their addresses are discovered by additional passes. This implies that a full discovery of every 1-Wire chip on the bus is a process that is linear in time.

Now let's consider the three-step sequence and how it is used to discover the ith bit of a device address (A_i). When the master initiates the $R0_i$ and $R1_i$ time slots, all devices respond with A_i and the bit complement of A_i, respectively. When the master transmits the acknowledgment bit (W_i), each device compares it to A_i. If both W_i and A_i have the same bit value, the device waits for $R0_{i+1}$; otherwise the device transitions to the idle state, where it remains until the master transmits a reset. As this iterative process continues, all but one device "drop off the bus." The address of the single device that remains "on the bus" for all 64 iterations has been discovered. The magic lies with the master's determination of the value of the acknowledgment bit W_i. There are multiple algorithms a master can use in determining W_i and the choice of algorithm determines the order in which device addresses are discovered.[5]

One final important note about the discovery process is that after a pass of the search has completed, the device whose address was just discovered has also been "selected." This implies that the device is ready to accept a "special function" command, the next step in a 1-Wire device transaction.

Device selection is a more straightforward process that begins with the master transmitting a reset followed by the "match address" command byte (0x55). After receiving the match address command, each device on the network initializes its address iterator to 0 and waits for the master to begin transmitting an address. Let's denote the target device's address as T with address bits T_0 to T_{63}. The master then begins transmitting the address T in a bit-serial fashion, starting with T_0. Each device compares T_0 to its A_0 bit. Each device that has an A_0 equal to T_0 increments its own address iterator to 1 and remains in a "listen" state waiting for the master to transmit the next bit, T_1. All other devices transition to the idle state,

---

5. The algorithm used by the Java 1-Wire API is described in the *Book of iButton Standards* (*http://www.ibutton.com/ibuttons/standard.pdf*).

awaiting a reset from the master. This process continues with the master transmitting T_1, T_2, and so on, and completes when the master transmits the most significant bit of the target address, T_{63}. After the entire 64 bits of the address have been transmitted, only the device with that exact address ($A = T$) remains "on the bus." This device has been selected and is now ready to receive a special function command, continuing the 1-Wire transaction.

The addressing modes just described can be bypassed completely by using the "skip address" or broadcast command (0xCC). The broadcast command can be used when there is only one 1-Wire device attached to the bus. This is typically considered bad practice because it precludes adding any more parts to the bus without modifying the software that implements the lowest layer of the 1-Wire communication protocol. The skip address command can also be used when performing a write only operation to many devices of the same family. This command can never be used in an operation that involves reading data from multiple devices. This is due to the fact that the bus is open drain driven and each bit read by the master would be the logical AND of the data transmitted simultaneously by all attached devices. Because the use of "skip address" command is only applicable to very specialized circumstances, it is seldom used. All code examples that follow in this chapter will use the discovery process to attain a device's address. After the address is known to the application, it will use the selection process to begin every communication with that device. This avoids possible collisions with any other devices.

4.1.4   1-Wire Chips and iButtons

Many 1-Wire applications present challenging packaging requirements. Applications such as access control and tagging for inventory management require a physically durable package. iButtons, 1-Wire chips packaged in 16mm diameter stainless steel micro-cans, were created to provide durable, roaming data carriers. While every iButton contains a 1-Wire chip, not all 1-Wire chips are iButtons. Later in this chapter we introduce the notion of containers for 1-Wire devices. Containers exist for every type of 1-Wire device without regard to form-factor or packaging.

4.2   ADAPTERS

The term *port adapter*, or more simply *adapter*, is used to refer to a 1-Wire master. Each 1-Wire network has exactly one master that is responsible for initiating all network communication as well as delivering the power and programming pulses required by certain device families. The term adapter is used because 1-Wire masters typically attach to another physical port—such as a serial, parallel, or USB port—and perform a translation between the host port and the 1-Wire network it controls. At the lowest level adapters receive data from the port and transmit the data in the form of time slots to the devices attached to the 1-Wire bus. Time slots simultaneously received on the 1-Wire bus are returned by the adapter to the host port.

4.2.1 Finding and Creating Adapters

The com.dalsemi.onewire package is the root of the 1-Wire API hierarchy and is purposefully very small and simple in design. This package contains only two classes: OneWireAccessProvider and OneWireException. OneWireAccessProvider provides the static method enumerateAllAdapters, which returns an Enumeration of all adapters registered with the operating system. Adapters are represented by the abstract class DSPortAdapter, defined in the com.dalsemi.onewire.adapter package. The example in Listing 4.1 finds all of the adapters and displays their names.

Listing 4.1   FindAdapters

```
import java.util.Enumeration;
import com.dalsemi.onewire.OneWireAccessProvider;
import com.dalsemi.onewire.adapter.DSPortAdapter;

class FindAdapters {
    public static void main(String[] args) {
        Enumeration e = OneWireAccessProvider.enumerateAllAdapters();
        while (e.hasMoreElements()) {
            System.out.println(
                ((DSPortAdapter) e.nextElement()).getAdapterName());
        }
    }
}
```

Running this application on TINI produces this output.

```
TINIExternalAdapter
TINIInternalAdapter
```

Both TINIExternalAdapter and TINIInternalAdapter are subclasses of DSPortAdapter. If you know exactly the type and name of the adapter your application is using, you can instantiate the adapter directly. For example, the two adapters found in Listing 4.1 using OneWireAccessProvider.enumerateAllAdapters could be created directly as shown in Listing 4.2.

Listing 4.2   CreateAdapters

```
import com.dalsemi.onewire.adapter.TINIInternalAdapter;
import com.dalsemi.onewire.adapter.TINIExternalAdapter;

class CreateAdapters {
    public static void main(String[] args) {
        TINIExternalAdapter external = new TINIExternalAdapter();
```

```
TINIInternalAdapter internal = new TINIInternalAdapter();
System.out.println(external.getAdapterName());
System.out.println(internal.getAdapterName());
   }
}
```

Running this application produces the same result as Listing 4.1.

Often applications know the name of the target adapter and use the direct method shown in Listing 4.2 to create an adapter instance. Once an adapter has been created, there is seldom any reason for an application to create additional adapter instances that reference the same physical port adapter. Adapter objects are typically instantiated during application initialization and remain in use for the lifetime of the application.

If the application simply needs to access one adapter on the system, it can use the OneWireAccessProvider.getDefaultAdapter method. This method returns an instance of the underlying platforms default adapter. Which adapter is the "default adapter" is determined by one of the three following methods (in order of priority).

1. The adapter/port combination specified by the system property specified by the "onewire.adapter.default" and "onewire.port.default" keys
2. The adapter/port combination specified in the "onewire.properties" file[6]
3. A "best guess" default

On TINI the external adapter, represented by TINIExternalAdapter, is the default adapter and the system property specified by the "onewire.adapter.default" key always exists. Therefore, there is seldom the need to create a "onewire.properties" file. Using getDefaultAdapter leads to code that will run on other Java platforms as well as TINI.

4.2.2   The Internal Adapter

The internal adapter is so named because its physical interface is simply one of TINIs microcontroller's port pins and therefore can never be omitted from any hardware implementation. This adapter is used by the operating system during the boot process to read the Ethernet address stored in the EPROM of the on-board 1-Wire chip. The number of attached devices and the line length driven by the internal adapter are limited by the electrical characteristics of the microcontroller port pin used by the adapter. The same port pin is shared by other system functions such as bit-bang serial output for system-level debugging and controlling the status LED. However, assuming TINI is loaded with non-debug firmware

---

6. If this file exists on TINI, it is contained in the "/etc" directory.

and no applications are using the status LED, the internal adapter can be used for controlling very small networks of 1-Wire devices.

4.2.3 The External Adapter

The external adapter uses a serial to 1-Wire converter[7] that is attached to the auxiliary serial port (serial1) of TINI's microcontroller. All TINI hardware designs (including the TBM390) from Dallas Semiconductor include the external adapter chip.

The external adapter is a full-featured port adapter capable of controlling 1-Wire networks that cover a large area and potentially have many attached devices. It is also capable of the power delivery required by many 1-Wire chips to perform special functions such as measuring temperatures and converting analog voltages and currents to digital outputs. Since the external adapter is far more capable, it is the one used for almost all TINI 1-Wire applications. Most of the examples in this chapter will use the external adapter.

4.2.4 Determining an Adapter's Capabilities

The previous section provided a description of the two 1-Wire adapters supported by TINI. This same information is encapsulated in an adapter instance and can therefore be determined programmatically. The methods can* (canOverdrive, canDeliverPower, and so on) defined in DSPortAdapter return the boolean result true if the underlying adapter has that particular ability.

Listing 4.3 AdapterFeatures

```
import com.dalsemi.onewire.adapter.TINIExternalAdapter;
import com.dalsemi.onewire.adapter.TINIInternalAdapter;
import com.dalsemi.onewire.OneWireException;

class AdapterFeatures {
    public static void main(String[] args) {
        try {
            TINIInternalAdapter internal = new TINIInternalAdapter();
            System.out.println("Internal Adapter:");
            System.out.println("   Supports overdrive speeds - " +
                    internal.canOverdrive());
            System.out.println("   Supports flexible timing - " +
                    internal.canFlex());

            TINIExternalAdapter external = new TINIExternalAdapter();
            System.out.println("External Adapter:");
            System.out.println("   Supports overdrive speeds - " +
```

---

7. Specifically, TINI uses the DS2480b (see *http://www.dalsemi.com/datasheets/pdfs/2480b.pdf*) as the 1-Wire line driver.

```
                            external.canOverdrive());
                System.out.println("  Supports flexible timing - " +
                            external.canFlex());
        } catch (OneWireException owe) {
                System.out.println(owe.getMessage());
        }
    }
}
```

The `AdapterFeatures` program, shown above in Listing 4.3, creates instances of `TINIInternalAdapter` and `TINIExternalAdapter` and queries both for their capabilities. Running `AdapterFeatures` produces the following output.

```
Internal Adapter:
    Supports overdrive speeds - true
    Supports flexible timing - false
External Adapter:
    Supports overdrive speeds - true
    Supports flexible timing - true
```

We see here that both adapters are capable of communications at overdrive speeds, but only the external adapter is able to support the flexible timing mode used to communicate with 1-Wire chips over long line lengths.

4.2.5   Searching for 1-Wire Devices

One of the major roles served by an adapter is managing the address discovery (or search) process by which the address of every device attached to the network is discovered. The super class of all adapters, `DSPortAdapter`, contains several methods used to configure and execute the discovery process. The method `getAllOneWireDevices` returns an `Enumeration` of `OneWireContainer` objects (containers are described in Section 4.4). Listing 4.4 uses the `getAllOneWireDevices` method to obtain a "census" of all chips on the 1-Wire network controlled by TINI's default (external) adapter.

Listing 4.4   Census

```
import java.util.Enumeration;
import com.dalsemi.onewire.OneWireAccessProvider;
import com.dalsemi.onewire.container.OneWireContainer;
import com.dalsemi.onewire.adapter.DSPortAdapter;
import com.dalsemi.onewire.OneWireException;

class Census {
    public static void main(String[] args) {
        try {
            DSPortAdapter adapter =
                OneWireAccessProvider.getDefaultAdapter();
```

```
            adapter.targetAllFamilies();
            System.out.println("1-Wire net addresses:");
            Enumeration e = adapter.getAllDeviceContainers();
            while (e.hasMoreElements()) {
                System.out.println(
                    ((OneWireContainer)
                        e.nextElement()).getAddressAsString());
            }
        } catch (OneWireException owe) {
            owe.printStackTrace();
        }
    }
}
```

When executed, Census displays a string representation of every 1-Wire address attached to the network by invoking the getAddressAsString method on each OneWireContainer object.

```
1-Wire net addresses:
F300000018A4BC12
8F00000018A37A12
AD00000018A51612
D600000018A37912
3D34C00000609F21
```

There are a total of five 1-Wire devices in this example configuration.[8] Four of them have the family id of 0x12. These devices are all DS2406-addressable switches. The device with family id 0x21 is DS1921 Thermocron iButton.[9] Thermocrons log temperature over time for the purposes of generating time versus temperature histograms. We'll be using this same network configuration for the next few examples. The important property of this configuration is that we have devices from different 1-Wire families on the same network.

Since our simple network consists of only five chips, it doesn't take long to search the entire network. So, for example, if we're interested only in Thermocrons, it wouldn't be unthinkable to just get an Enumeration of all available devices and slug through the Enumeration looking for Thermocrons. However, if the network contained tens or even hundreds of devices, this approach would be far too cumbersome. For this reason, DSPortAdapter defines several methods that allow the targeting or exclusion of certain families. These methods greatly improve the efficiency with which an application can identify devices of interest.

---

8. The specific test configuration used here is the Systronix 8x1-Wire Digital I/O board with the Thermocron inserted into the iButton clip. See *http://www.systronix.com/ expansion/8x1wire/81w.htm* for details on the 8x1-Wire Digital I/O board.

9. More detailed information on the Thermocron iButton can be found at *http:// www.dalsemi.com/datasheets/pdfs/1921.pdf.*

```
public void targetFamily(int familyID);
public void targetFamily(byte[] familyID);
public void excludeFamily(int familyID);
public void excludeFamily(byte[] familyID);
```

The `targetFamily` methods allow an application to specify exactly which device families it is interested in. The searches that follow will return only devices in the specified families. So, for example, if a program is only interested in discovering the switches currently attached to the network, it would invoke `targetFamily` specifying a value of 0x12 for the `familyID` parameter.

Using the `targetFamily` method, we can create a smarter version of Census that finds only devices of a specified family. Listing 4.5 takes the family id provided on the command line and passes that value to `targetFamily`.

Listing 4.5   FamilyCensus

```
import java.util.Enumeration;
import com.dalsemi.onewire.OneWireAccessProvider;
import com.dalsemi.onewire.container.OneWireContainer;
import com.dalsemi.onewire.adapter.DSPortAdapter;
import com.dalsemi.onewire.OneWireException;

class FamilyCensus {
    public static void main(String[] args) {
        if (args.length != 1) {
            System.out.println(
                "Usage: java FamilyCensus.tini family_id");
            System.exit(1);
        }
        try {
            DSPortAdapter adapter =
                OneWireAccessProvider.getDefaultAdapter();
            // Family id assumed to be input in hex
            adapter.targetFamily(Integer.parseInt(args[0], 16));
            Enumeration e = adapter.getAllDeviceContainers();
            while (e.hasMoreElements()) {
                System.out.println(((OneWireContainer)
                    e.nextElement()).getAddressAsString());
            }
        } catch (OneWireException owe) {
            owe.printStackTrace();
        }
    }
}
```

Running `FamilyCensus` and providing the addressable switches family ID of 0x12 on the command line produces a list of only switch addresses.

```
1-Wire net addresses:
F300000018A4BC12
8F00000018A37A12
```

```
AD00000018A51612
D600000018A37912
```

Running `FamilyCensus` again specifying a family id of 0x21 displays the address of the only Thermocron on the network, ignoring all of the switches.

```
1-Wire net addresses:
3D34C00000609F21
```

The `excludeFamily` methods exclude the specified families from the search process and return only devices that are members of non-excluded families. This is particularly useful for large networks that use 1-Wire digital switches to either isolate or include different network segments. Often when searching for devices on such a network, it is useful to exclude the switches to expedite the search process. The adapter object maintains a list of all excluded family ids. This list can be cleared at any time by invoking the `targetAllFamilies` method.

Certain families are capable of responding to a special type of search called an "alarm search." The alarm search allows parts in need of special attention to be discovered quickly even in a large network of 1-Wire devices. For example, the DS18S20 temperature sensor allows for the setting of high and low thresholds. If the temperature drops below the low temperature threshold or rises above the high temperature threshold, the device will enter an alarm state. Once in an alarm state, a device will respond to alarm-only searches as well as general searches. An alarm search uses a 1-Wire addressing command distinct from the general search, which causes all 1-Wire devices that either don't generate alarms or are not in an alarm state to immediately drop off the bus. The `setSearchOnlyAlarmingDevices` method sets the adapter's internal search state to perform searches that discover only devices in an alarm state.

```
public abstract void setSearchOnlyAlarmingDevices()
public abstract void setSearchAllDevices()
```

This state can be cleared by invoking `setSearchAllDevices`. This causes the adapter to issue searches using the global search command rather than the alarm search.

4.2.6 Adapter Ownership

This section deals with the rather difficult issue of multiple threads or even processes accessing the same adapter. We use the term adapter in a generic sense, applying it to either an instance of a subclass of `DSPortAdapter` or to a physical adapter such as TINI's external adapter. However, to treat the subject of mutual exclusion effectively, we will need to draw a clear distinction between an adapter object and the underlying physical adapter. In the rest of this section we'll use the term *port adapter* to refer to the underlying physical 1-Wire bus master and the term *adapter instance* (or *object*) when referring to an instance of a subclass of DSPortAdapter.

Creating an adapter object provides a means for interacting with the underlying port adapter, but it does not guarantee exclusive access to that port adapter or the 1-Wire network it controls. DSPortAdapter defines the abstract methods beginExclusive and endExclusive, requiring subclasses to override these methods and provide a mechanism for mutual exclusion.

```
public abstract boolean beginExclusive(boolean block)
    throws OneWireException
public abstract void endExclusive()
```

The beginExclusive method is invoked on an adapter object to obtain a lock on the underlying physical adapter. Once the lock is owned by a particular adapter, no other adapter instance can invoke methods that result in communication with either the port adapter directly or the 1-Wire network it controls. Any attempt to do so results in a OneWireException being thrown. The lock applies to other processes as well as other threads within the same process. The lock can be freed by either of two mechanisms. Typically, the adapter instance that owns the lock will invoke endExclusive, voluntarily releasing the lock. Also, the lock will automatically be freed in the event that the owning process terminates without invoking endExclusive.

The boolean value passed to beginExclusive specifies whether the caller wishes to wait until the lock is free or return immediately regardless of the lock's state. If block is false, beginExclusive will immediately return true in the event that the lock was successfully acquired and false otherwise. If block is true, beginExclusive will attempt to acquire the lock; if it is already owned by another adapter instance, beginExclusive blocks indefinitely until the lock has been freed and it can claim ownership. When block is true and beginExclusive returns normally (that is, non-abruptly), it will always return true.

4.3   DIRECT 1-WIRE COMMUNICATION

Typically, once an application has used the adapter's search capability to obtain containers for the devices in which it is interested, all further communication with the device goes through the container, not the adapter. However, while containers provide a very useful abstraction from the low-level device details, there are times when it is better to avoid the overhead of containers and communicate directly with the devices. Several methods in the DSPortAdapter class provide the support necessary to communicate with any 1-Wire chip. The following methods provide the minimum set of primitives that allow any possible communication with any 1-Wire chip.

```
public int reset() throws OneWireIOException, OneWireException
public abstract boolean getBit()
    throws OneWireIOException, OneWireException
public void putBit(boolean bitValue)
    throws OneWireIOException, OneWireException
```

A reset is required to begin any new communication. Invoking reset[10] puts all devices on the 1-Wire net in a known (RESET) state. After the reset signal has been transmitted, all devices are waiting to receive one of the addressing commands. Since there is only one data carrier, communication is done in a bit-serial fashion. So theoretically, the rest of the communication can be accomplished just using getBit for reads and putBit for writes. In practice almost all device commands and data are structured on byte-boundaries. So the methods

```
public void putByte(int byteValue)
    throws OneWireIOException, OneWireException
public int getByte() throws OneWireIOException, OneWireException
```

provide an efficient way to move individual bytes to the bus. The getBit and put-Bit methods are necessary for communication with a few 1-Wire devices. For example, every operation that runs the processor in the Java Powered iButton begins with a release sequence that terminates with a single bit acknowledgment.

Both of the methods that write to the bus, putBit and putByte, throw OneWireIOException if the value written (or transmitted) is not identical to the value read (or received). Consider the example in Listing 4.6.

Listing 4.6   ByteBlast

```
import com.dalsemi.onewire.OneWireAccessProvider;
import com.dalsemi.onewire.OneWireException;
import com.dalsemi.onewire.adapter.DSPortAdapter;
import com.dalsemi.onewire.adapter.OneWireIOException;

class ByteBlast {
    public static void main(String[] args) {
        DSPortAdapter adapter = null;
        try {
            adapter = OneWireAccessProvider.getDefaultAdapter();
            adapter.beginExclusive(true);

            adapter.reset();
            while (true) {
                adapter.putByte(0xFF);
            }
        } catch (OneWireIOException ioe) {
```

---

10. This assumes the adapter is configured for "regular" bus speeds. A reset issued at "overdrive" speed will reset only the devices currently operating at overdrive speed.

```
            System.out.println("1-Wire I/O problem:"+ioe.getMessage());
        } catch (OneWireException owe) {
            System.out.println(owe.getMessage());
        } finally {
            adapter.endExclusive();
        }
    }
}
```

The first thing `ByteBlast` does is transmit a reset to the bus to put all devices into a high-impedance listen-only state. Then it repeatedly writes the value 0xff[11] to the bus, producing a continuous stream of write-1 time slots. All devices should be in a high-impedance state and therefore should not alter the state of the bus. This implies that all data written should simply be echoed and the identical value will be read. To terminate this application we can short the bus to ground, and the logic 1s we were writing to the bus are read back as logic 0s. This causes `putByte` to throw an instance of `OneWireIOException`, which is caught, and the following output is displayed.

```
1-Wire I/O problem:Error during putByte()
```

In practice, `OneWireIOException` should be caught and the operation retried. Transient problems can occur when roaming 1-Wire devices (typically iButtons) attach to or detach from the network, causing a momentary short between the 1-Wire bus and ground. This should not be sufficient to terminate a well-written application. Retry logic must be intelligent enough to determine when a problem is persistent and fatal.

Whenever possible an application should use block reads and writes when accessing sequential memory addresses, as opposed to the less efficient approach of invoking `getByte` or `putByte` in a loop. For example, a memory chip can be read by selecting it, and transmitting a read memory command, followed by a starting memory address. After this, all of the chip's memory can be read using a single invocation of a "block" read method. The following methods provide a very efficient way to send and receive arbitrarily large blocks from 1-Wire devices.

```
public byte[] getBlock(int len) throws OneWireIOException, OneWireException
public void getBlock(byte[] arr, int len)
    throws OneWireIOException, OneWireException
public void getBlock(byte[] arr, int off, int len)
    throws OneWireIOException, OneWireException
```

Writes can also be done in a block fashion using this `dataBlock` method.

---

11. The value 0xff was chosen because it is not a valid address command and all devices will simply ignore it.

```
public abstract void dataBlock(byte[] arr, int off, int len)
    throws OneWireIOException, iButtonException
```

A single invocation of dataBlock can be used for reading and writing multiple bytes. The block transfer methods are put to use in Listing 4.8.

The discovery process can also be controlled directly using the methods findFirstDevice and findNextDevice.

```
public abstract boolean findFirstDevice()
    throws OneWireIOException, OneWireException
public abstract boolean findNextDevice()
    throws OneWireIOException, OneWireException
```

Since different adapters provide different interfaces to control the search process, findFirstDevice and findNextDevice are abstract, forcing the subclasses that encapsulate real adapters to implement the search algorithm. Both methods throw OneWireIOException if any communication error occurs during the search process. To discover the addresses of all devices attached to the network, an application invokes findFirstDevice and then invokes findNextDevice repeatedly until findNextDevice returns false. Listing 4.7 discovers and displays all of the devices attached to the default adapter.

Listing 4.7   FastCensus

```
import com.dalsemi.onewire.OneWireAccessProvider;
import com.dalsemi.onewire.OneWireException;
import com.dalsemi.onewire.adapter.DSPortAdapter;

class FastCensus {
    public static void main(String[] args) {
        DSPortAdapter adapter = null;
        try {
            adapter = OneWireAccessProvider.getDefaultAdapter();
            adapter.beginExclusive(true);
            adapter.setSpeed(adapter.SPEED_REGULAR);
            if (adapter.findFirstDevice()) {
                System.out.println(adapter.getAddressAsString());
                while (adapter.findNextDevice()) {
                    System.out.println(adapter.getAddressAsString());
                }
            }
        } catch (OneWireException owe) {
            System.out.println(owe.getMessage());
        } finally {
            adapter.endExclusive();
        }
    }
}
```

FastCensus produces the same output as Listing 4.4 but without the overhead of creating an Enumeration of OneWireContainer objects. It is important to realize that invoking findFirstDevice does not typically return the address of the 1-Wire device that is physically nearest the adapter. The ordering of device discovery is logical, not physical.

Now that we know all of the methods required for direct access to the 1-Wire network, we can put it all together in a more comprehensive example. Earlier in this chapter it was mentioned that the Ethernet address is contained in a 1-Wire device on TINI's internal 1-Wire network. The Ethernet address is read when the system boots and is written to program memory as well as the Ethernet controller. The Ethernet address can be displayed at the slush prompt by executing the ipconfig command with no command line parameters. The ipconfig command fetches the Ethernet address directly from system memory, using the getEthernetAddress method in the class com.dalsemi.tininet.TININet.

Another method of accomplishing the same result is to read the Ethernet address directly from the 1-Wire source. The device that maintains the MAC id is called a DS2502. The DS2502 has a family id of 0x89 and contains 128 bytes of EPROM memory. During the manufacturing process, the 48-bit Ethernet address is programmed into the DS2502's memory, starting at address 0x06. The memory is programmed in a fashion that allows this address to be determined programmatically. However, performing this exercise would add little value to the example, so we'll just accept the starting address as a magic number.[12]

Listing 4.8   EthernetAddressReader

```
import com.dalsemi.onewire.adapter.TINIInternalAdapter;
import com.dalsemi.onewire.OneWireException;

class EthernetAddressReader {
    static final int TARGET_FAMILY_ID    = 0x89;
    static final int START_ADDRESS       = 0x6;
    static final int READ_MEMORY_COMMAND = 0xf0;

    public static void main(String[] args) {
        TINIInternalAdapter adapter = new TINIInternalAdapter();
        boolean foundIt = false;

        try {
            adapter.beginExclusive(true);
            if (adapter.findFirstDevice()) {
                // Test LSB (family id) against target
                if ((adapter.getAddressAsLong()&0xff) ==
                    TARGET_FAMILY_ID) {
```

---

12. For those interested, the storage format is governed by the UniqueWare specification that can be viewed online (see *http://www.dalsemi.com/datasheets/pdfs/app99.pdf*).

```
                    foundIt = true;
                }
                while (!foundIt && adapter.findNextDevice()) {
                    if ((adapter.getAddressAsLong() & 0xFF) ==
                        TARGET_FAMILY_ID) {
                        foundIt = true;
                    }
                }
                if (foundIt) {
                    /*
                     * data[0] -> read memory command byte
                     * data[1] -> low byte of starting address
                     * data[2] -> high byte of starting address
                     */
                    byte[] command = new byte[3];
                    command[0] = (byte) READ_MEMORY_COMMAND;
                    command[1] = START_ADDRESS & 0xFF;
                    command[2] = (START_ADDRESS >>> 8) & 0xFF;

                    // Send the command and starting memory address
                    adapter.dataBlock(command, 0, command.length);
                    // Read 48-bit ethernet address
                    byte[] macID = adapter.getBlock(6);
                    for (int i = 5; i >= 0; i--) {
                        System.out.print(
                            Integer.toHexString(macID[i] & 0xff));
                        if (i != 0) {
                            System.out.print(":");
                        }
                    }
                    System.out.println();
                } else {
                    System.out.println("Device not found");
                }
            }
        } catch (OneWireException owe) {
            System.out.println(owe.getMessage());
        } finally {
            adapter.endExclusive();
        }
    }
}
```

EthernetAddressReader (Listing 4.8) begins by searching for a device with the correct family id. Note that we assume there is only one DS2502 attached to TINI's internal 1-Wire network. After the correct part has been addressed, a 3-byte write is performed using the dataBlock method to transmit the read memory command and the starting address. This is immediately followed by reading the 6-byte (48-bit) Ethernet address using getBlock. Finally, the result is formatted in a manner similar to that used by "arp" commands on Unix systems.

0:60:35:0:55:27

This result should be identical to the Ethernet address displayed by slush upon execution of `ipconfig`.

4.4   CONTAINERS

The container classes provide high-level access to the services offered by specific families of devices, shielding the programmer from low-level details of possibly complicated communication protocols. Consider, for example, the DS18S20 temperature sensor device. In Section 4.1.2 we detailed the two 1-Wire transactions required to obtain a temperature. For most development purposes we would probably want something as simple as a method that returns a floating point representation of the current temperature rather than worrying about the details of sending and receiving the set of 1-wire commands and data specified in Tables 4.1 and 4.2.

4.4.1   The Class OneWireContainer

The `OneWireContainer` class, defined in the `com.dalsemi.onewire.container` package, is the superclass of all device specific containers and implements default fuctionality that is shared by all 1-Wire devices, specifically the address. It also provides methods for identifying and describing the devices in a textual form.

All 1-Wire device families are represented by a subclass of `OneWireContainer` and also exist in the `com.dalsemi.onewire.container` package. The name of the container is simply a hexadecimal string representation of the device family id appended to `OneWireContainer`'s fully qualified class name. For example, devices with a family id 0x10 are represented by the container class `OneWireContainer10`. The formation of a container class name is done in this fashion to allow instances of device specific container classes to be created as they are discovered on the 1-Wire network. This is discussed in more detail in the next section.

An instance of `OneWireContainer` (or a subclass) maintains a reference to its parent adapter that is used for all communication with the device. `OneWireContainer` methods use the techniques described in Section 4.3 for sending and receiving commands and data to and from the underlying device.

4.4.2   Creating Container Instances

`OneWireContainer` objects are created by invoking any of the following methods on an instance of a subclass of `DSPortAdapter`.

```
public OneWireContainer getFirstDeviceContainer()
    throws OneWireIOException, OneWireException
public OneWireContainer getNextDeviceContainer()
```

```
        throws OneWireIOException, OneWireException
    public Enumeration getAllDeviceContainers()
        throws OneWireIOException, OneWireException
```

The DSPortAdapter methods that create container objects use forName and newInstance of class Class. The string passed to forName to get the Class object is created by appending an uppercase, hexadecimal String representation of the device's family id to the String representation of the fully qualified name of One-WireContainer: com.dalsemi.onewire.container.OneWireContainer.

The Census example in Listing 4.4 used the methods findFirstDevice and findNextDevice to display all devices on the network. We can use the methods getFirstDeviceContainer and getNextDeviceContainer to find the same devices in the same order, but instead of just returning a boolean result, getFirstDeviceContainer and getNextDeviceContainer return OneWireContainer objects representing the devices found during the discovery process. Listing 4.9 is essentially the same as Listing 4.7 except it uses getFirstDevice and getNextDevice to obtain device containers. Once we have containers, we can print out more information specific to the chips discovered during the search, as opposed to just each chip's address.

Listing 4.9   FindContainers

```java
import com.dalsemi.onewire.OneWireAccessProvider;
import com.dalsemi.onewire.OneWireException;
import com.dalsemi.onewire.container.OneWireContainer;
import com.dalsemi.onewire.adapter.DSPortAdapter;

class FindContainers {
    public static void main(String[] args) {
        DSPortAdapter adapter = null;
        try {
            adapter = OneWireAccessProvider.getDefaultAdapter();
            adapter.beginExclusive(true);
            adapter.setSpeed(adapter.SPEED_REGULAR);
            OneWireContainer owc = null;
            if ((owc = adapter.getFirstDeviceContainer()) != null) {
                System.out.println(owc.getName()+","+
                                   owc.getAlternateNames() +
                                   " at address "+
                                   owc.getAddressAsString());

                while ((owc=adapter.getNextDeviceContainer()) != null) {
                    System.out.println(owc.getName()+","+
                                       owc.getAlternateNames() +
                                       " at address "+
                                       owc.getAddressAsString());
                }
            }
        } catch (OneWireException owe) {
            System.out.println(owe.getMessage());
```

```
    } finally {
        adapter.endExclusive();
    }
}
}
```

Running `FindContainers` on the same 1-Wire network as Listing 4.7 outputs each chip's address as well as a short description and formal part name.

```
DS2406,Dual Addressable Switch at address F300000018A4BC12
DS2406,Dual Addressable Switch at address 8F00000018A37A12
DS2406,Dual Addressable Switch at address AD00000018A51612
DS2406,Dual Addressable Switch at address D600000018A37912
DS1921,Thermochron at address 3D34C00000609F21
```

Note that on TINI, device specific container classes are not available by default as part of the API. They must be included with the application during the conversion process (see Section 1.4.2). In Listing 4.9, `OneWireContainer12` and `OneWireContainer21` were both included during the conversion process for `FindContainers`. On large systems with no practical memory constraints, it is reasonable to assume that all device specific containers will be available.

Finally, `OneWireContainer` objects can also be created directly in the event that the application somehow knows a device's address without going through the discovery process. In this case the application can create a `OneWireContainer` object using the container's default constructor and invoking one of the `setupContainer` methods on the newly created container. All `setupContainer` methods require an adapter to be used for device communication and the device's address.

```
public void setupContainer(DSPortAdapter sourceAdapter, byte[] newAddress)
public void setupContainer(DSPortAdapter sourceAdapter, long newAddress)
public void setupContainer(DSPortAdapter sourceAdapter, String newAddress)
```

4.4.3   Example: 1-Wire Humidity Sensor

At the time of this writing there were over 20 containers, one for each device family. Now we'll take a closer look at the container for one of the more interesting 1-Wire device families, the DS2438 A/D (Analog to Digital) converter. The DS2438 includes an A/D converter, a temperature sensor, an elapsed time meter, and 40 bytes of nonvolatile memory. The practical uses for a device that can measure analog voltages and currents as well as sense temperature are nearly unlimited. For example, the DS2438 can be used to create sensors that monitor various environmental conditions including temperature, solar radiance, humidity, and barometric pressure.

We would expect a container designed to encapsulate the DS2438's behavior to provide simple methods for accessing the memory, reading the current temperature, and returning the voltage read on its A/D pin. For our purposes we'll need to be able to read the temperature and the input voltage on the V_{ad} pin as well as the supply voltage (V_{dd}). OneWireContainer26 (the DS2438 has a family id of 0x26) provides the following methods to serve these purposes[13].

```
public void doADConvert(int channel, byte[] state)
    throws OneWireIOException, OneWireException
public double getADVoltage(int channel, byte[] state)
    throws OneWireIOException, OneWireException
public void doTemperatureConvert(byte[] state)
    throws OneWireIOException, OneWireException
public double getTemperature(byte[] state)
```

Both the voltage and temperature measurements are split into two phases: performing a conversion and reading the result. So, for example, to read an analog voltage from the DS2438, an application invokes doADConvert, followed by getADVoltage. The channel parameter of the doADConvert method allows the caller to specify which analog voltage is desired. In Example 4.1 we'll need to read both V_{ad} and V_{dd}.

This example uses a DS2438 and its associated container to create a 1-Wire humidity sensor. The circuit diagram for the humidity sensor is shown in Figure 4.3. This circuit uses a core humidity sensor from Honeywell that outputs an analog voltage that can be used in conjunction with the supply voltage and temperature to calculate the relative humidity using Equation 1 and Equation 2. The DS2438 (U1) provides a 1-Wire communication interface for the composite sensor as well as the analog-to-digital conversion and the temperature measurement. The schottky diode, D2, is used to protect the circuit from negative voltages greater than about 400 millivolts in magnitude. D1 and C1 are used to build a parasite power supply that "steals" energy from the bus during high periods. Finally, R1 and C1 serve as a low-pass filter.

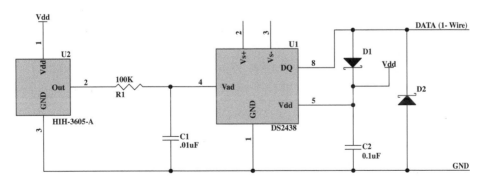

Figure 4.3 1-Wire humidity sensor

---

13. This part actually contains much more functionality and therefore many more methods than needed for our example.

The output of the humidity sensor is an analog voltage proportional to the supply voltage. From the HIH-3605 data sheet, the relative humidity at 25°C can be computed with respect to the supply voltage (V_{dd}) using Equation 1.

$$RH_{sensor} = (V_{out}/V_{dd} - 0.16) / 0.0062 \qquad \textbf{(EQ 1)}$$

Of course, what we're really interested in is the true relative humidity without any dependence on the supply voltage or a fixed temperature. Equation 2 provides the means to compute the true relative humidity.

$$RH_{true} = RH_{sensor} / (1.0546 - 0.00216*T) \qquad \textbf{(EQ 2)}$$

Where T is measured in degrees celsius (°C). From these equations we can see that we need three measurements to compute a value for RH_{true}: V_{out}, V_{dd}, and T. Fortunately, the A-to-D converter can measure both V_{ad} and V_{dd}. Now we're armed with all of the information we need to write a small program to read the relative humidity using `OneWireContainer26`.

Listing 4.10 HumiditySensor

```java
import com.dalsemi.onewire.OneWireAccessProvider;
import com.dalsemi.onewire.adapter.DSPortAdapter;
import com.dalsemi.onewire.OneWireException;
import com.dalsemi.onewire.container.OneWireContainer;
import com.dalsemi.onewire.container.OneWireContainer26;

public class HumiditySensor {
    DSPortAdapter adapter;
    OneWireContainer26 owc;
    byte[] state;

    HumiditySensor(DSPortAdapter adapter) throws OneWireException {
        this.adapter = adapter;
        // Only find DS2438 family devices
        adapter.targetFamily(0x26);
        adapter.setSpeed(adapter.SPEED_REGULAR);
        owc = (OneWireContainer26) adapter.getFirstDeviceContainer();
        if (owc == null) {
            throw new OneWireException("No DS2438 A to D chip found");
        }
        state = owc.readDevice();
    }

    public double getTemperature() throws OneWireException {
        owc.doTemperatureConvert(state);
        state = owc.readDevice();

        return owc.getTemperature(state);
    }

    public double getSensorRH() throws OneWireException {
```

```
        // Read Vad
        owc.doADConvert(OneWireContainer26.CHANNEL_VAD, state);
        double Vad = owc.getADVoltage(OneWireContainer26.CHANNEL_VAD,
                                        state);
        // Read Vdd
        owc.doADConvert(OneWireContainer26.CHANNEL_VDD, state);
        double Vdd = owc.getADVoltage(OneWireContainer26.CHANNEL_VDD,
                                        state);

        return (Vad/Vdd-0.16)/0.0062;
    }

    public double getTrueRH() throws OneWireException {
        return getSensorRH()/(1.0546-0.00216*getTemperature());
    }

    void displayData() {
        try {
            adapter.beginExclusive(true);
            System.out.println("Temperature = "+getTemperature()+" C");
            System.out.println("RHsensor = "+getSensorRH()+"%");
            System.out.println("RHtrue = "+getTrueRH()+"%");
        } catch (OneWireException owe) {
            System.out.println(owe.getMessage());
        } finally {
            adapter.endExclusive();
        }
    }

    public static void main(String[] args) {
        try {
            HumiditySensor humidity =
                new HumiditySensor(
                    OneWireAccessProvider.getDefaultAdapter());
            humidity.displayData();
        } catch (OneWireException owe) {
            System.out.println(owe.getMessage());
        }
    }
}
```

HumiditySensor finds the appropriate container during construction by invoking targetFamily on the adapter object to specify that the search should ignore all devices that are not in the DS2438 family. We then know that when we invoke getFirstDeviceContianer on the adapter, it will return either an instance of OneWireContainer26 or null if no devices with family id 0x26 are discovered on the 1-Wire network. The getSensorRH method uses the container to read both the supply voltage (V_{out}) and the voltage output of the core humidity sensor (V_{ad}) and then uses Equation 1 to compute RH_{sensor}. The getTrueRH method invokes getSensorRH to obtain RH_{sensor} and getTemperature to obtain a current temperature reading. It then uses those two results as input to Equation 2 to compute the true relative humidity (RH_{true}).

Running `HumiditySensor` on the TINI in my home office in the beautiful wilds of Coppell, Texas, produces the following rather unspectacular output.

```
Temperature = 26.875C
RHsensor = 45.766129032258057%
RHtrue = 45.915238770164166%
```

In this case, the relative humidity as measured by the core analog humidity sensor is not far from the true relative humidity computed taking supply voltage and temperature into account. This makes sense because the temperature was close to the nominal 25°C used by the core sensor. As the temperature drifts farther from 25°C in either direction, we would expect wider divergence of RH_{sensor} from RH_{true}.

4.5 ENSURING DATA INTEGRITY USING CRCS

The `com.dalsemi.onewire.utils` package contains two utility classes used exclusively for the computation and verification of Cyclic Redundancy Checks (CRCs). A CRC is a mathematical tool used to verify the integrity of data transferred over an unreliable communication link.

It is common in 1-Wire networks to have devices that are both "hardwired" (permanently attached) and roaming. Roaming devices can cause transient short circuits on the 1-Wire bus that corrupt normal communications. CRCs are employed to detect corruption in the transfer of data over the 1-Wire bus. When errors are detected, the typical remedy is to retry the communication. Once the condition that caused the error is gone, the operation should complete successfully.

Methods for the computation and verification of the two CRCs that are used in the data transfer layers of the 1-Wire protocol, CRC-16[14] and CRC-8[15] are provided by the classes `CRC16` and `CRC8`, respectively. Both classes provide static utility methods only and therefore have private constructors to explicitly disallow their instantiation. The following method descriptions are from the `CRC8` class, but everything following applies to the `CRC16` class as well. The following method is the most flexible of the CRC generators.

```
public static int compute(byte[] data, int off, int len, int seed);
```

This method returns a CRC value computed over the range of bytes specified by [off, off+len), using the specified seed. All of the other methods in the `CRC8`

---

14. The CRC-16 is described mathematically by the polynomial $X^{16} + X^{15} + X^2 + 1$.
15. The 1-Wire CRC is an 8-bit CRC described mathematically by $X^8 + X^5 + X^4 + 1$.

class simply provide some convenient subset of this functionality. For example, the method

```
public static int compute(byte[] data);
```

computes the CRC over the entire byte[] using the default initial seed of 0. The example in Listing 4.11 computes the CRC8 of the data input using hexadecimal notation on the command line.

Listing 4.11   CRCCalculator

```
import com.dalsemi.onewire.utils.CRC8;

class CRCCalculator {
    public static void main(String[] args) {
        byte[] data = new byte[args.length];
        for (int i = 0; i < data.length; i++)
            data[i] = (byte) Integer.parseInt(args[i], 16);
        System.out.println("crc=" +
                        Integer.toHexString(CRC8.compute(data)));
    }
}
```

Running `CRCCalculator` using the least significant 56 bits of the 1-Wire address of the Thermocron on our example network

```
TINI /> java CRCCalculator.tini 21 9F 60 00 00 C0 34
```

produces the output

```
crc=3d
```

This implies that the last byte of the 1-Wire address (the CRC) is 0x3d. Indeed, this agrees with the output from Listing 4.4. If we run the example again with the CRC byte included

```
TINI /> java CRCCalculator.tini 21 9F 60 00 00 C0 34 3D
```

it produces the output

```
crc=0
```

The preceding two example outputs suggest the two different approaches that an application may use to check a CRC value that it computes against the CRC value read from the device. It can either compute the CRC of all of the data up to the CRC byte(s) and then check that the resulting value is identical to the CRC returned by the device, or it can compute the CRC of all of the data including the CRC byte(s) returned by the device and check the computed CRC for a value of 0.[16]

All methods that perform address searches in the API automatically check the address CRC before returning an address to the caller. When a CRC check fails, the search result is discarded. Several 1-Wire devices automatically generate CRCs on various fields as they are being queried or updated. In these cases the container implementation for that family is responsible for checking the CRC before successfully returning to the caller. If the CRC fails, a OneWireIOException is thrown to indicate that the operation failed. Applications that use 1-Wire memory devices for data storage and retrieval should be sure to protect their data using the 16-bit CRC (CRC-16).

---

16. Note that the CRC-16 value is often stored bit-wise inverted (ones complement). Computing the CRC-16 including the inverted CRC16 value results in a final value of 0xB001 (as opposed to 0).

CHAPTER 5 TCP/IP Networking

TINI's main objective is to provide a powerful platform for developing small embedded applications that connect non-networked devices to the network. TINI's broad networking is its most compelling feature, and Java's suitability for writing networked applications is one of the primary reasons TINI provides a Java runtime environment. Java supports basic network access using classes in the java.net package. Since TINI provides a full implementation of the java.net package, many network applications written in Java will run on TINI without modification. However, there are differences between developing a network application for a PC or workstation and a dedicated network application for TINI. These differences come from the fundamental nature of programming for embedded networking devices. For example, configuring the network parameters on general purpose computers or workstations is not handled programmatically as a part of your application. However, in the embedded world, if your application assumes control of the entire system, then it must be capable of configuring the network as well as using it.

This chapter assumes a strong familiarity with writing networked applications in Java. It is not intended to be a general treatment of TCP/IP networking or writing network applications in Java. There are many excellent books that cover both of these subjects in detail. Rather, this chapter focuses primarily on programming for TINI's networking environment.

5.1 TINI NETWORKING ENVIRONMENT AND API OVERVIEW

A diagram of the networking environment is shown in Figure 5.1. The figure displays the following six application layer protocols that are supported in the API.

- HTTP (Hypertext Transfer Protocol)
- DNS (Domain Name System)
- DHCP (Dynamic Host Configuration Protocol)
- Telnet
- FTP (File Transfer Protocol)
- Ping (ICMP echo request/reply)

All of the application layer protocols except Ping are implemented using the socket classes in the `java.net` package as the network transport mechanism. Ping isn't really a protocol. It's an application wrapper over a subset of ICMP (Internet Control Message Protocol). The Ping class, covered in Section 5.5, directly invokes native methods that are exposed in the network stack's ICMP module.

Support for most of the application layer protocols is provided by the sub-packages of `com.dalsemi.tininet`.

- com.dalsemi.tininet.http
- com.dalsemi.tininet.icmp
- com.dalsemi.tininet.dhcp
- com.dalsemi.tininet.dns

We'll cover TINI's API for these protocols in detail in the next few sections. The FTP and Telnet protocols are implemented in the `com.dalsemi.shell.server.ftp` and `com.dalsemi.shell.server.telnet` packages, respectively. Both FTP and Telnet are implemented as servers and are typically only used by system shells such as slush. Support for using FTP as a client is of course available using the URL classes in the `java.net` package.

The protocols in Figure 5.1 are those for which the TINI networking API provides special support. Other networking protocols can and have been written in Java and can run on TINI with little or no change to the code. Examples include both servers and clients for network time and SNMP (Simple Network Management Protocol). Also, there is no reason that the protocol support provided in the networking API cannot be extended or possibly even replaced by third-party implementations.

Parameters specific to the various network interfaces can be queried or configured using the `TININet` class in the `com.dalsemi.tininet` package. `TININet` also provides methods for setting global networking parameters such as the host and domain name. Network configuration is covered in Section 5.2.

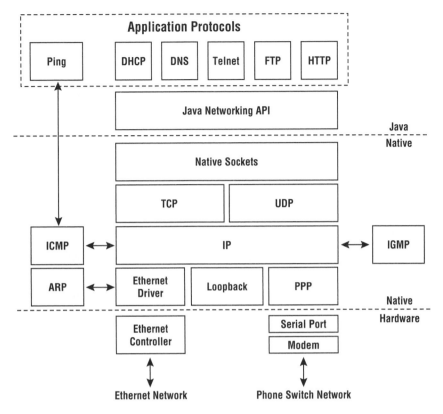

Figure 5.1   Network protocol stack

5.1.1   The Network Interfaces

From Figure 5.1 we can see that TINI supports three distinct network interface types.

- Ethernet
- PPP over a serial link
- Loopback

There are a maximum of four network interfaces supported by the network stack. For the sake of viewing the configuration of individual interfaces, assume they are numbered starting with 0. Interface 0 is always the Ethernet interface (eth0). Interface 1 is always the loopback (lo) interface, and interfaces 2 and 3 are available for use by up to two simultaneous PPP (Point-to-Point Protocol) connections.

You can query the state of all network interfaces using the slush command "ipconfig -x."

```
Interface 0 is active.
Name          : eth0 (default)
Type          : Ethernet
IP Address    : 192.168.0.15
Subnet Mask   : 255.255.255.0
Gateway       : 192.168.0.1

Interface 1 is active.
Name          : lo
Type          : Local Loopback
IP Address    : 127.0.0.1
Subnet Mask   : 255.0.0.0
Gateway       : 0.0.0.0

Interface 2 is not active.

Interface 3 is not active.
```

This sample output shows a fairly typical network configuration. In this case the Ethernet interface (eth0) has been configured and is the default interface. This means that an IP datagram that isn't specifically destined for any host on the networks serviced by the other interfaces will be sent to the default (Ethernet in this case) driver for transmission onto the physical link. Interfaces 2 and 3 as shown above are not in use because there were no PPP connections on the system at the time the ipconfig command was executed.

Network interfaces can be added or removed programmatically using TININet's addInterfaceEntry and removeInterfaceEntry methods. This operation is usually handled indirectly through the PPP class using wrapper methods that provide the details to the TININet methods. Neither the Ethernet nor loopback interface can be removed from the system. Both are created as unconfigured network interfaces by the system during the initial boot.

5.1.2   Ethernet

Ethernet is by far the most popular networking technology used today in constructing Local Area Networks (LANs). Ethernet networking is currently supported on TINI using a separate Ethernet controller to send and receive network messages. All Ethernet nodes have a 48-bit address, usually called the Ethernet address or MAC id. To ensure that networking hardware is built with a unique address, the number pool is managed by the Institute of Electrical and Electronics Engineers[1] (IEEE). Organizations register for an Organizationally Unique Identifier (OUI). The OUI is the most significant 24 bits of the MAC id and is 00:60:35 for TINI. The Ethernet address is stored in the EPROM of a 1-Wire chip on the

---

1. A list, searchable by organization name, of OUIs is online at *http://standards.ieee.org/regauth/oui/index.html*

internal 1-Wire net and is present in every TINI hardware implementation. It can be queried but not altered programmatically. The following `getEthernetAddress` methods are defined in `TININet` and return the ethernet address as either a byte array or `String`.

```
public static void getEthernetAddress(byte[] address)
public static String getEthernetAddress()
```

The Ethernet address can also be used by applications as a unique identifier for the TINI hardware on which it is running. The first method listed above fills in the supplied byte array with the Ethernet address where the most significant byte is stored in the 0th array element. Since the Ethernet address is 48 bits long, the array must be of length 6 or greater. The second method returns a `String` representation of the Ethernet address in a format similar to that output by a UNIX style arp command. In Section 4.3 we read the Ethernet address directly from its storage in the on-board 1-Wire chip. That was for the sake of learning how to communicate directly with 1-Wire chips. But it was definitely the hard way to discover the MAC id. The `SimpleEthernetAddressReader` program, shown in Listing 5.1, produces the same result in a trivial fashion.

Listing 5.1   SimpleEthernetAddressReader

```
import com.dalsemi.tininet.TININet;

class SimpleEthernetAddressReader {
    public static void main(String[] args) {
        System.out.println(TININet.getEthernetAddress());
    }
}
```

Notice that the following sample output is identical to that of the `EthernetAddressReader` example in Listing 4.8.

```
TINI /> java SimpleEthernetAddressReader.tini
0:60:35:0:55:27
```

The Ethernet interface is typically configured as the default interface. It provides the most efficient means to transfer data to other networked hosts. On current TINI hardware implementations, the highest sustainable data rate over a TCP connection is about 1Mbps or 10 percent of the bandwidth of a 10Mbps Ethernet network.

5.1.3 PPP

Just like the Ethernet driver, the Point-to-Point Protocol (PPP) module provides a packet-oriented interface to the IP layer. PPP is actually a very broad and flexible protocol that allows for the transmission of various types of network packets over various types of physical links such as serial, parallel, and even Ethernet. However, on TINI, PPP is used strictly as a mechanism to transmit IP datagrams over a serial link. PPP uses one of the serial port drivers for all data transmission. Usually a modem is attached to the serial port to support dial-up networking applications.

If you're using Ethernet (eth0) or Loopback (lo) interfaces only, you won't need to add or remove network interfaces. Only PPP interfaces can be dynamically added to or removed from the system. By convention PPP interfaces are named by appending the serial port number to the lowercase string "ppp." Any of the four serial ports can be used by the native stack's PPP implementation to provide the physical data link. The network stack can support two simultaneous PPP sessions over two independent serial ports.

For applications that support dial-up networking, the classes in the `com.dalsemi.tininet.ppp` provide an API for establishing and controlling PPP connections. The PPP API is discussed in Chapter 6.

5.1.4   Loopback

The loopback interface (lo) allows a server and (potentially multiple) clients to communicate on the same host from possibly different processes. The class A network id 127 is reserved for use by the loopback interface. Since it is a class A network, it uses the subnet mask 255.0.0.0 so that all of the IP addresses between 127.0.0.1 and 127.255.255.254[2] are valid IP addresses and use the loopback interface. No IP traffic destined to a 127 address is transmitted to any physical network interface. TINI follows the convention of binding the name "localhost" with the IP address 127.0.0.1. If you use the slush "ping" command to ping localhost, you will see the following output.

```
TINI /> ping localhost
Got a reply from node localhost/127.0.0.1
Sent 1 request(s), got 1 reply(s)
```

You should be able to execute this command regardless of whether you've previously configured any of the other network interfaces, since loopback is automatically configured during the boot process and therefore always exists. One minor note here is that unlike "pinging" hosts on other network interfaces, pinging localhost should never fail to get a reply. This is because the IP datagram carrying the ping (ICMP echo request) data is never transmitted "on the wire" removing the possibility of a lost IP datagram.

---

2.   127.0.0.0 is the network address and 127.255.255.255 is the broadcast address for the 127 network.

The loopback interface is generally used by the network stack implementors for testing purposes, but it can also be used by multiple applications running on the same host as a mechanism for IPC (Inter-Process Communication).

5.2 SETTING NETWORK PARAMETERS

On non-embedded hosts, networking applications don't need to worry about configuring basic network parameters such as the IP address and subnet mask. This task is performed by a network administrator using the network utility program provided with the operating system. During application development this is also true for TINI. The network settings are established using the slush `ipconfig` command. Ultimately, however, if your application is going to control the entire system, it will replace slush as the Java application that is launched automatically when the system boots. In this case, your application must be able to query and configure network parameters.

The TININet class in the `com.dalsemi.tininet` package provides static methods for storing and retrieving all of the configuration information used by the different network interfaces, TCP/IP stack, and "built-in" application protocols. The following are networking parameters configurable using TININet, with brief descriptions.

- *IP address.* A 32-bit integer that encodes the host's network identification as well as the identification of the host on that network. Every host on an internet has a unique IP address. Each network interface has its own IP address.
- *Subnet mask.* A 32-bit integer used by the TCP/IP protocol stack as a bit mask to separate the network and host portions of the IP address.
- *Gateway (router) IP address.* The IP address of the default router. A router is (usually) a dedicated machine connected to at least two networks that forwards IP datagrams between the various networks.
- *Primary DNS address.* The IP address of the preferred DNS (Domain Name System) server. A DNS server resolves IP addresses to human readable host names, and vice-versa.
- *Secondary DNS address.* The IP address of an alternate DNS server. If a request to the primary DNS server is unanswered, the DNS client implementation will send the request to the secondary DNS server.
- *DNS time-out value.* The amount of time (in milliseconds) that the DNS client will wait for a response from a DNS server before timing out and possibly retransmitting the request.
- *Domain name.* A string representing the domain name (for example, "dalsemi.com").

- *DHCP server IP address.* The IP address of the DHCP (Dynamic Host Configuration Protocol) server. DHCP is discussed in detail in Section 5.2.2.
- *Host name.* A string representing the local host's (not localhost) name. The host's name is not necessarily the same as its DNS name.
- *Mailhost.* The IP address of the machine running an SMTP (Simple Mail Transfer Protocol) server. This must be set to use the mailto protocol supported by the Java URL classes.
- *HTTP proxy server.* The IP address of a machine that forwards HTTP requests on your behalf. For example, if your TINI is behind a firewall, use of a proxy server may be required to satisfy HTTP requests of hosts outside of the local network.
- *HTTP proxy port.* A 16-bit integer that specifies the port number on which the HTTP proxy server expects to receive HTTP requests.

TININet provides both set (and the symmetric get) methods for each of these parameters.

```
public static boolean setIPAddress(byte[] localIP)
public static boolean setIPAddress(String localIP)
```

The first method requires a byte array of length 4 with the IP address stored using big-endian byte ordering (also known as network byte ordering), such that the most significant byte of the address is stored in array element 0 and the least significant byte is stored in element 3. This byte ordering applies for all of the TININet setters that require a byte array to specify any IP address or subnet mask. The second setIPAddress method here takes a String with an IP address specified in dotted-decimal notation—for example, "192.168.1.1." These methods do not require specification of the target network interface and therefore apply to the default interface. All parameters that are specific to an interface, such as the interface IP address and subnet mask, have an additional setter method that allows the application to specify the interface to which the new settings apply.

```
public static boolean setIPAddress(String interfaceName, byte[] localIP)
```

The interfaceName parameter is a case-sensitive String equal to the target interface—"eth0," for example. All of the preceding methods return true if the address has been successfully set on the targeted interface.

Note that while there are a lot of network parameters listed, it is not necessary to configure each of them. In fact, it is possible to get up and running on an Ethernet network by setting just the IP address and subnet mask. However, if you want to be able to communicate with hosts on other networks, the default gateway IP address must also be configured. Also, if you want to be able to use real names as well as just IP addresses when creating instances of java.net.InetAddress, you'll have to set at least the IP address of the primary DNS server. It boils down to a question of how much networking capability is required by your application(s). We'll cover additional TININet methods used for network configuration as the need arises.

5.2.1   Committing Static Network Parameters

The network parameters are stored in a special system area just beneath the garbage collected heap. By default, they persist across system reboots. However, an application can force the entire RAM, including the system area, to be cleared during the boot process. This provides a known, reliable state to allow the system to boot, but it also wipes out all network configuration information. This is not an issue for applications that use DHCP (described in the next section) to obtain their network parameters, but it is fatal for systems that rely on statically configured network information. The TININet class provides a commit/restore mechanism that allows network parameters to be stored in flash ROM as well the RAM system area. Use of the commit/restore capability assures that an application can always boot up with network access.

The commitNetworkState method that follows copies the configuration information for all network interfaces into a reserved space in flash memory. On boot any change that is detected in the network parameters causes the configuration information to be restored to its exact state at the time the commit operation was executed.

```
public static void commitNetworkState() throws CommitException
```

Before invoking commitNetworkState, an application should set a minimum of the IP address and subnet mask for the default (typically eth0) interface. An application can determine whether a commit operation has been performed using the getNetworkCommitState method.

```
public static int getNetworkCommitState()
```

It returns one of the following integer constants, also defined in TININet.

```
public static final int UNCOMMITED
public static final int COMMITTED
public static final int RESTORE_DISABLED
```

If commitNetworkState has never been invoked, getNetworkCommitState returns UNCOMMITED. In this case, the commit/restore functionality is not used on system reboot, and all network parameters are left unchanged. This is the only state in which a call to commitNetworkState is guaranteed to succeed. If the persistent memory technology used is the Flash ROM, the network parameters may be committed only once without reloading the flashed application. In the future, external memory devices may be used to provide alternate storage in support of multiple commit operations. If an attempt to commit network parameters is made and the underlying persistent storage can be written only once, commitNetworkState will throw a CommitException.

An application can override the system's network restore operation using the disableNetworkRestore method.

```
public static void disableNetworkRestore()
```

This allows the application to make changes to the network parameters without the operating system overriding them on every reboot.

Finally, an application can determine whether a restore operation was required during the last system boot using the getBootState method in the TINIOS class.

```
public static native int getBootState()
```

The value that getBootState returns is an integer that encodes information about the state of the system during the boot process. The boot state value is the bitwise-or of several possible bit masks. To extract the network restore bit, the returned value from getBootState is bitwise anded with the NETWORK_CONFIGURATION_RESTORED mask defined in TINIOS. If the result is non-zero, then the network parameters were copied from the ROM to the RAM system area during the system boot. This can serve as a warning that persistent data in the heap may have been damaged, forcing the restore operation.

The network commit/restore capability can be tested using slush without writing a line of code or running any other applications. First execute the ipconfig command with no command line parameters. The last line displayed shows whether the network parameters have already been committed.

```
TINI /> ipconfig
...
Restore From Flash: Not Committed
```

Next, use the ipconfig command to configure your static network settings. After verifying that the settings are correct, you can run ipconfig again, but this time supply the -C option. You should see the following output.

```
TINI /> ipconfig -C
Network configuration committed to flash memory
```

If you were to run this exact command a second time, ipconfig would display an error message due to a CommitException. Finally, use the "reboot -a" command to reboot and force both the heap and system area to be cleared. When the system boots, slush uses getBootState to determine whether the network parameters were restored. Immediately after logging on you should see output similar to the following.

```
[ Thu Feb 01 21:00:05 GMT 2001 ]  Message from System: Network recovery
routines have run.
```

Executing `ipconfig` one final time, you can verify that the network settings are identical to those committed prior to the heap clearing reboot.

5.2.2 Dynamic IP Configuration Using DHCP

The previous section dealt with directly setting static network configuration parameters using the TININet class. It is possible, under certain circumstances, to write your application so that it can dynamically obtain required network parameters using the Dynamic Host Configuration Protocol[3] (DHCP). A DHCP client can obtain several network parameters without knowing anything other than its own Ethernet address in advance. DHCP is an extension of the BOOTP protocol that was designed to allow a diskless workstation to boot, determine its network configuration information, and download a binary image of its operating system. One of the big improvements with DHCP is that IP addresses are assigned dynamically from a predetermined pool of available addresses.

When a client boots, it issues a DHCPDISCOVER message, looking for a DHCP server. The discover message is a broadcast message that means that every host on the same physical network as the client receives the message. It contains information describing the network parameters requested by the client. If a DHCP server is available and it receives the message and chooses to respond to the discover message, the server will respond with a DHCPOFFER message. The offer contains a set of network parameters the server is willing to let the client use. The client inspects the contents of the offer and, if acceptable, transmits a DHCPRE-QUEST message to the server. After receiving the request, the server transmits a final acknowledgment to the client.

It is possible that multiple DHCP servers can respond to the clients discover message. In this case, the client chooses the offer it likes and issues a request to only that offer. DHCP servers that made the offers that weren't selected by the client are notified of this rejection because the request message is also broadcast. In the case of TINI's DHCP client implementation, the offer that it chooses is the first offer that contains at least an IP address and subnet mask.

At this point the client has successfully "leased" the IP address from the server. With no further involvement from the client, however, the lease will expire and the server will allow the IP address to be vended to another client at a later time. This prevents IP addresses from being permanently consumed by clients that

---

3.   The current version of DHCP is defined in RFC 2131.

have "gone offline" for whatever reason. The amount of time for which the lease is valid is determined during the negotiation phase. To maintain its lease, the client periodically sends DHCPREQUEST messages with the same content as the initial request message.

The description above assumed everything went perfectly; there was at least 1 DHCP server running on the network, and all messages transmitted were received by their intended recipient. But DHCP requests and responses travel within UDP messages, and since UDP provides an unreliable datagram delivery service, any of the messages previously mentioned may fail to reach the intended recipient. The details about how messages are retried and how this affects the DHCP client state machine are all handled internally by the DHCP client. TINI's client does, however, notify the application of important changes in state, including repeated failures when attempting to lease network configuration parameters.

If you're running slush, you can use DHCP to configure your network settings by using the ipconfig command with the -d option. An IP lease can be relinquished nicely (without the lease expiring) at any time using "ipconfig -r." For normal development purposes, your application can remain blissfully unaware of whether the network settings were obtained statically or dynamically. However, if your application is to acquire the network settings using DHCP, it will need to start the DHCP client and process a few different types of events to ensure that the networking portion of the application can execute properly. The rest of this section describes how to interact with TINI's DHCP client from within an application.

The DHCP client is implemented by the following two classes in the com.dalsemi.tininet.dhcp package.

- DHCPClient
- DHCPListener

DHCPClient runs as a separate thread of execution that acquires and maintains a lease on an IP address. It spends the vast majority of the time sleeping, waking only to renew the leased IP address. The sleep time is typically hours or even days. So once DHCPClient has leased the IP address, it imposes very little overhead on the overall system.

Both DHCPClient constructors require an instance of a class that implements the DHCPListener interface. The listener is notified of important changes in the DHCP client's internal state machine.

```
public DHCPClient(DHCPListener listener) throws IllegalStateException
public DHCPClient(DHCPListener listener, byte[] serverIP, byte[] localIP)
    throws IllegalStateException
```

The first constructor is used to obtain a new lease on a new IP address. The second constructor requires the IP address obtained during a previous execution of the DHCP client. This is typically the IP address acquired before the last time the system was rebooted. The serverIP array contains the IP address of the server from which the client (or local) IP address was leased. Both byte arrays require the most significant byte of the IP address to be stored in big-endian fashion with the most significant byte of the address in array element 0 and so on. If this constructor is used, the client will attempt to renew a lease on the specified IP address rather than obtain a new lease on a (possibly) different IP address. If the previously leased IP address is available, the renew operation will likely succeed. If, however, while the client was not executing—and therefore not maintaining—the lease, the server issued the address to a different host, it will reject the client's attempt to renew the lease. This does not have to be fatal. The client can be stopped, and a new DHCPClient object can be created using the first constructor listed to obtain a new lease.

DHCPClient does not begin negotiating for an IP address until the start method, inherited from Thread, is invoked. After the client thread is started, it immediately sends a broadcast discover message in the form of a DatagramPacket. The datagram requests the following parameters from any DHCP server listening on the network.

- An IP address
- The subnet mask
- The default gateway (router) IP address
- Primary and secondary DNS server IP addresses
- The mailhost IP address

Even if a server replies with an offer, there is no guarantee that all of the requested parameters will be specified in the offer datagram. For example, the network on which the DHCP server is running may not have an SMTP server (mailhost) or a secondary DNS server. At a minimum, the client requires an IP address and subnet mask. However, if the application is going to create InetAddress objects using DNS names (Section 5.3), it will need an IP address of the primary DNS server as well. All network parameters that are received from the server are automatically set by the client after it receives acknowledgment of its request from the server. An application can check the network settings using the methods provided in the TININet class to ensure any additional parameters that it requires have been set before initiating network activity.

The DHCPClient thread continues to execute until its stopDHCPThread method is invoked.

```
public void stopDHCPThread()
```

If stopDHCPThread is invoked during a time when the client has successfully leased an IP address, the lease is relinquished by transmitting a DHCPRELEASE message to the server. The only other way the client thread halts is if a fatal error occurs in one of the DatagramSockets used in communicating with the server.

The DHCPListener interface can be implemented by any class that wants to be notified of important DHCP events. The interface defines the following methods for event notification.

```
public void ipLeased()
public void ipRenewed()
public void ipLost()
public void ipError(String error)
```

The ipLeased method is invoked after DHCPClient (or simply the client from this point forward) has successfully negotiated the lease of an IP address with a DHCP server. At this point, it is safe for the application to begin network communication. The ipRenewed method is invoked every time the client thread wakes up and successfully renews the lease. This is for informational and debug purposes only. The listener is not required to perform any action in ipLeased. The ipLost method is invoked when the client fails to renew its lease. At this point the application should close all open sockets and cease all network communication. The ipError method is invoked when a serious error occurs, such as failure to receive any response from a DHCP server. Note that ipError is not invoked every time there is a minor error in communicating with the server. Only after repeated attempts to communicate with the server will DHCPClient invoke the listener's ipError method.

5.3   DNS

The Domain Name System (DNS) is the globally distributed database that provides mappings between humanly readable names and IP addresses. To determine a remote host's IP address given its name, an application uses a DNS client running on the local machine to contact a DNS server, typically running on another host. If the server doesn't have an entry for the specified host, it will ask another DNS server and so on until the name is resolved to an address or it is determined that no entry for that host exists.

On TINI the DNS client (also known as a "resolver") is used primarily to support the InetAddress class in the java.net package. The client is used for both forward lookups—mapping a name to an IP address—and reverse lookups—mapping an IP address to a name. InetAddress objects are used explicitly during construction of Socket and DatagramSocket objects and implicitly when using the URL classes. On most Java platforms lookups are performed by a native DNS client. TINI's runtime environment, however, implements its DNS client in Java. The client may be configured by a Java application.

To be able to use DNS names in creating `InetAddress` objects, the IP address of the primary DNS server must be configured. The IP addresses of both the primary and secondary DNS servers can be set programatically using the following methods. The server string is specified using dotted-decimal notation.

```
public static boolean setPrimaryDNS(String primaryDNS)
public static boolean setSecondaryDNS(String secondaryDNS)
```

It is also useful, but not required, to set the domain name using the `setDomainName` method.

```
public static boolean setDomainname(String domain)
```

If the domain name has been configured and host names are passed to the `getByName` method without specifying the domain portion of the DNS name, the local domain name will automatically be appended before querying the server for the remote host's IP address. If you have configured the domain name on your TINI, you can see this in action by using the `ping` command and pinging another host on the local network. Here is some sample output.

```
TINI /> ping win2kpc
Got a reply from node win2kpc.tinitest.net/192.168.0.3
Sent 1 request(s), got 1 reply(s)
```

The domain name in this example is dalsemi.com. In this case "`ping wally`" produces the same result as "`ping wally.dalsemi.com.`" For application development purposes, all three DNS-related parameters: primary server, secondary server, and domain name can be set from the slush prompt using the `ipconfig` command.

Performing DNS lookups can be a time-consuming process, depending on reachability of the server and how much work it has to do interacting with other DNS servers to complete the lookup. When the `getByName` method of `InetAddress` is used for the first time on a specified host, it can block for several seconds, waiting for a response from the DNS server. A cache of successfully resolved DNS entries is maintained in a private `java.util.Hashtable` to avoid unnecessary DNS requests and delay in creating `InetAddress` objects for which DNS bindings already exist.

DNS requests can travel over either a TCP connection (`Socket`) or within UDP messages (`DatagramSocket`). TINI's DNS client implementation uses UDP with a time-out and retry scheme. The retry scheme deals with the fact that UDP is an unreliable datagram delivery service. This problem can be exacerbated by the fact that some network links come up slowly after periods of inactivity, so the first couple of attempts to resolve a name might fail due to a time-out waiting for a

reply. The initial time-out value used by the client can be set explicitly using the
`setDNSTimeout` method.

```
public static boolean setDNSTimeout(int dnsTimeout)
```

The `dnsTimeout` value is specified in milliseconds, but values of at least 1
second (1000 milliseconds) or greater should be specified. If a non-zero time-out
value is specified, the DNS client will send the request and wait for up to
`dnsTimeout` milliseconds for a response from the server. If no response is
received, it will not retry the request. If the time-out value is set to zero, a fallback
and retry procedure will take effect. The DNS client will retry after a 2-second
period and double the time-out value until it reaches 16 seconds. This produces a
maximum four retries before the DNS client finally gives up. If during the
creation of a new instance of `InetAddress` a forward lookup fails, either due to a
time-out or another DNS server error, an `UnknownHostException` is thrown. If,
however, an error occurs trying to perform a reverse lookup, no exception is
thrown, since the IP address is all that is required to communicate with the remote
host.

The class `DNSClient` in the `com.dalsemi.tininet.dns` package implements
TINI's DNS client. It exposes public methods for performing both forward and
reverse lookups.

```
public String[] getByName(String name)
public String[] getByIP(String ip)
```

The `getByName` method performs a forward lookup, taking a host name as
input. It returns an array of `Strings` encoded in dotted-decimal notation representing all of the IP addresses that map to that name.[4] The `getByIP` method takes as
input a `String` representation of the IP address encoded in dotted-decimal notation. It returns an array of strings representing all of the host names that map to
the input IP address. These methods can be used directly for name resolution
without adding entries to the DNS cache maintained internally by `InetAddress`.
You can interact with the raw (without going through `InetAddress`) DNS client
using the slush command `nslookup`. It takes either an IP address in dotted-decimal
notation or a host name as a command line parameter and performs either a forward or reverse lookup, depending on the input.

It is a simple matter to create our own "nslookup" application using just the
`InetAddress` class. The `DNSTest` application is shown in Listing 5.2. It takes the
same command line input as the `nslookup` command.

---

4. A host name can have multiple IP addresses, and multiple host names can map to the
   same IP address.

Listing 5.2   DNSTest

```
import java.net.InetAddress;
import java.net.UnknownHostException;

class DNSTest {
    public static void main(String[] args) {
        if (args.length != 1) {
            System.out.println("Usage: java DNSTest.tini name");
            System.exit(1);
        }
        try {
            InetAddress[] names = InetAddress.getAllByName(args[0]);
            for (int i = 0; i < names.length; i++) {
                System.out.println(names[i].toString());
            }
        } catch (UnknownHostException uhe) {
            System.out.println("Lookup error:" + uhe.getMessage());
        }
    }
}
```

The getAllByName method is used to generate an array of all DNS entries for the given input. They are displayed using the InetAddress.toString method, which generates a String containing both the host name and IP address. Before this example is run on a TINI, the primary DNS server IP address must be set. The following output shows the IP address of the iButton Web server.

```
TINI /> java DNSTest.tini www.ibutton.com
www.ibutton.com/198.3.123.121
```

If we run DNSTest again but this time supply a bogus host name, getAllByName will be unable to resolve the name to an IP address and will throw an UnknownHostException.

```
TINI /> java DNSTest.tini bogus.aintthere.com
Lookup error:Could not find an entry for bogus.aintthere.com
```

5.4 HTTP

The class HTTPServer in the com.dalsemi.tininet.http package implements a very simple HTTP server. It supports only HTTP GET requests and serves up static information contained within files at or below a specified root directory. It is not intended to be a dedicated Web server application but rather provide HTTP serving capability that an application can launch and forget about. HTTPServer offers reasonable performance, and the overhead it imposes on an application is relatively small. The basic idea is that the server should not detract much from the application's foreground processing requirements.

An HTTPServer object is created using either of the following constructors. If the constructor doesn't specify the port to be used, the TCP port number defaults to 80.

```
public HTTPServer() throws HTTPServerException
public HTTPServer(int httpPort) throws HTTPServerException
```

If the specified port is already in use by another thread or process, the constructor will be unable to create a ServerSocket to listen for connections on the specified port and will throw an HTTPServerException. The HTTP root directory and index page default to "webroot" and "index.html," respectively. To change these defaults, an application can use the setHTTPRoot and setIndexPage methods.

```
public void setHTTPRoot(String httpRoot)
public void setIndexPage(String indexPage)
```

Both of the serviceRequest methods block indefinitely waiting for an inbound connection from a client (for example, a browser).

```
public int serviceRequests() throws HTTPServerException
public int serviceRequests(Object lock) throws HTTPServerException
```

The only difference between the two is that the serviceRequests method that requires the lock parameter will synchronize on the lock before servicing an inbound connection. This method should be used by an application that will be modifying the contents of files, at or below the Web root, from within another thread. Either method will cause the server to create a new thread for each request. The application typically dedicates a single thread that invokes the serviceRequests method in an infinite loop. No other action is required of the application for HTTPServer to continue processing client GET requests.

Because HTTPServer is very small and simple by design, it doesn't meet every application's requirements as a general purpose Web server. However, there exist powerful, full-featured, commercial grade HTTP servers[5] written for TINI that support the Java servlet API.

Applications that need access to information provided by Web servers use the familiar URL classes in the java.net package. There is one additional configuration parameter that can be set by an application using the URL classes: a proxy server. Often corporate networks are protected behind a firewall and the only way HTTP requests can reach the Internet is through a proxy server. A proxy server is simply a machine that receives requests from a client and forwards them to another server. The proxy server has special privileges to communicate with hosts

---

5. One such server (TiniHttpServer), available from Smart Software Consulting, is free and OpenSource. It can be downloaded from *http://www.smartsc.com/tini/TiniHttpServer*.

outside the firewall. The TININet class provides the following methods for configuring the use of a proxy server.

```
public static boolean setProxyServer(String proxyServer)
public static boolean setProxyPort(int proxyPort)
```

The setProxyServer method takes the server name as a String representing either an IP address encoded in dotted-decimal notation or a DNS name. The setProxyPort method takes an integer value specifying the 16-bit port number on which the proxy server receives HTTP requests. Both the server and port are persistent across system reboots. If setProxyServer is invoked with an empty String, it will disable the use of a proxy server. By default, the URL protocol handling classes do not use a proxy.

Listing 5.3 shows a small application that reads the contents of a URL through a proxy server.

Listing 5.3 MiniBrowser

```
import java.net.*;
import java.io.*;
import com.dalsemi.tininet.TININet;

class MiniBrowser {
    public static void main(String[] args) {
        if (args.length != 3) {
            System.out.println(
                    "Usage: MiniBrowser URL proxy_server proxy_port");
            System.exit(1);
        }

        TININet.setProxyServer(args[1]);
        TININet.setProxyPort(Integer.parseInt(args[2]));

        try {
            URL u = new URL(args[0]);
            InputStream in = u.openConnection().getInputStream();
            byte[] content = new byte[512];
            int count = 0;
            do {
                count = in.read(content);
                System.out.write(content, 0, count);
            } while (count != -1);
        } catch (Exception e) {
            System.out.println(e.getMessage());
            e.printStackTrace();
        }
    }
}
```

MiniBrowser requires that the URL, proxy server name (or IP address), and proxy port be specified on the command line. After setting both the proxy server and proxy port, it opens a connection to the specified URL. It then reads the contents of the URL in 512-byte blocks and displays them using System.out. The following is the output from browsing the small HelloWeb application, from Section 2.6.3. In this test configuration one TINI is running the HelloWeb HTTP server application and another TINI (behind a firewall) is running MiniBrowser. The only way for HTTP requests to escape the firewall is through the proxy server named wally on port 576.

```
TINI /> java MiniBrowser.tini http://198.3.123.182/index.html
wally.dalsemi.com 576
<html>
<head>
<title>Hello Web!</title>
</head>
<body>
<h1>Hello from TINI!</h1>
</body>
</html>
```

The output should look familiar as it is identical to the contents of the "index.html" file that we created to be served by HelloWeb.

5.5 ICMP

The Internet Control Message Protocol (ICMP) is the mechanism used by nodes on a TCP/IP network to transfer error and control information. Even though ICMP messages often provide error information regarding IP datagrams, they travel encapsulated within IP datagrams. ICMP is used by routers to transmit error messages and by hosts, like TINI, to determine the reachability of a remote destination.

Unlike DNS, DHCP and the other protocols we've discussed to this point in the chapter, ICMP is not actually an application layer protocol. ICMP is a module that exists in the network stack and is used to send IP control and error messages. However, the ICMP module does provide simple native method hooks to allow Java applications to send ICMP echo requests and read the raw ICMP response. Nearly every host on a TCP/IP network provides an application named "ping" that uses ICMP's echo request/reply mechanism to determine the reachability of other network nodes. When a machine receives an ICMP echo request from a remote host, it responds with an ICMP echo reply message that contains an exact copy of the request packet data.

The pingNode method as follows effectively provides one bit of information: if the remote node was reachable. It can be used to programmatically determine whether just a particular service running on the remote host has died or whether the host machine itself has become unreachable on the network, providing for more precise error reporting.

```
public static boolean pingNode(InetAddress addr)
```

It transmits a single ICMP echo request message to the node specified by addr and waits for a response. The time-out period is about 500 milliseconds. It returns true if a reply is received within the time-out period and false otherwise. Because IP provides an unreliable datagram delivery service, ICMP messages are not guaranteed to reach their destination. So one failure of pingNode does not necessarily mean a node has become unreachable. Multiple successive failures reported by pingNode, however, dictate, with a high probability, that it has indeed gone "off line." A remote host can become unreachable for several reasons, including a failure with the remote host itself or persistent problems with one or more routers between the hosts. The pingNode method used by the slush ping command.

There is another pingNode method that is crude and more difficult to use but provides much more information. It can be used to perform some reasonably sophisticated network analysis.

```
public static long pingNode(InetAddress addr, byte ttl, byte[] response)
```

This version of pingNode requires two additional parameters: the ttl parameter specifying the time to live field in the IP datagram header of the outbound ICMP echo request and a byte array that is filled in with the entire IP datagram received in response to the echo request. The response array should be of length 128 or greater to avoid an ArrayIndexOutOfBounds exception. The method returns the time, measured in milliseconds, between transmitting the ICMP echo request message and receiving a response. The response is typically (but not always, as we'll see later) an ICMP echo reply. If no response is received prior to the time-out period, pingNode returns −1. The round-trip time (RTT) estimate is measured in the native network stack and is therefore reasonably (within a few milliseconds) accurate. Any inaccuracy is on the high side, and therefore the return value of pingNode provides an upper bound on the true round-trip time.

To understand how to make full use of this method, we'll have to dig a little deeper into the format of the IP datagram header as well as the format of certain ICMP messages. We will cover just enough of the details to be able to parse the response array and extract useful information. The remainder of this section is fairly technical and can be skipped by readers not interested in the low-level details of ICMP. Figure 5.2 shows the overall format of an ICMP message encapsulated within an IP datagram.

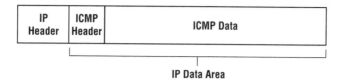

Figure 5.2 ICMP message within an IP datagram

The ICMP header begins immediately following the IP header. The structure of the IP header is shown in Figure 5.3. The exact length of the IP header can be determined by examining its first byte. The IP version number and header length, in 4-byte words, are combined in the first byte. The version number is contained in the most significant nibble (4 bits), and the header word length in the least significant nibble. So a byte value of 0x45 tells us that the IP version is 4 and the header is 5*4 or 20 bytes in length. At the time of this writing, TINI's network stack and the Java platform only support IP version 4. However, due to the rather limited number of IPv4 addresses, both will undoubtedly support IP version 6 in the near future. The length of the entire IP datagram, including headers, is represented by the 16-bit value starting at byte offset 2 in the IP header. This represents the total number of bytes copied into the response array passed to pingNode.

After computing the IP header length, we can extract the TYPE byte from the ICMP header. The format of an ICMP header is shown in Figure 5.4. As the name implies, the TYPE byte specifies the type of ICMP message, providing information as to how the ICMP data should be interpreted. Initially, we'll focus on two types: echo request (8) and echo reply (0). When pingNode is invoked, an ICMP message is transmitted to the remote host with the type byte set to 8. Under normal circumstances we expect to get a reply from the remote host with a type byte of 0.

V/HL—IP version and header length
TL—total length of IP datagram including header
TTL—time to live (hop count)
Scr addr—source IP address
Dest addr—destination IP address
Opt—optional header data (if any)

Figure 5.3 IP datagram header

The code field in the ICMP header specifies additional information about the type. For echo reply and echo response types, there are no code values defined, and this field will always be 0.

The other ICMP type of interest is TIME_EXCEEDED (11) and is generated by a router when the time to live (TTL) field of an IP datagram reaches 0. The TTL field is byte offset 8 in the IP header (see Figure 5.3). The time to live value is often called the hop count and represents the maximum number of routers a datagram can pass through before it expires.[6] Every time a datagram passes through a router, the TTL value is decremented by 1. When a router receives a datagram with a TTL of 1, it (logically speaking) decrements it to 0, discards it, and sends an ICMP time exceeded message to the host that transmitted the original datagram.[7]

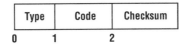

Figure 5.4   ICMP header

By explicitly manipulating the TTL field, we can determine the route a datagram travels when transmitted from the local host to the remote destination. If the TTL field of an outbound ICMP echo request message is set to 1, the message cannot leave the local network. If the message is destined for a host on another network, the message will be sent to a router, and, since the TTL is 1, the router will generate an ICMP TIME_EXCEEDED message. When the local machine receives the TIME_EXCEEDED message, it can extract the router's IP address from the source address field of the IP header. Now we know the address of the first router along with an estimate of how long it took to get a response. This process is repeated with a TTL of 2, yielding the IP address of the second router and so on. Eventually the TTL is set high enough to allow the datagram to be delivered to its final destination. After receiving the final ICMP echo reply, we have the addresses of all routers and estimates for the amount of time required for a datagram to traverse each network segment.

A couple of additional points should be mentioned here. First, you may be unable to ping certain machines on the Internet at all because some hosts don't process ICMP echo requests due to certain types of attacks such as denial of service attacks that attempt to flood a host with ICMP messages, making its response

---

6. Older specifications of the behavior of routers dictated that the TTL should be decremented by 1 for each additional second that a router held on to the datagram. Many routers ignored this requirement and treated the TTL strictly as a hop count. Later versions of the specification relaxed this requirement, making it optional.

7. Under normal circumstances, TIME_EXCEEDED messages will only be seen when there is a "routing loop."

much slower when processing other network messages. Also, the route taken by successive datagrams to the same destination may differ, and the time required to reach a remote host can vary dramatically from datagram to datagram, depending on network congestion. Finally, note that it is not a requirement to use ICMP for the purpose of tracing a route. In fact, older versions of the ICMP specification[8] stated that no ICMP error messages were to be generated in response to another ICMP message. This was to avoid network congestion caused by endless loops of error messages. However, the specification was changed to allow routers to send TIME_EXCEEDED messages in response to echo request messages. The same result can be accomplished using UDP messages. Older implementations of the UNIX traceroute utility used UDP messages with a high, and hopefully bogus, value for the remote port number. The same TTL scheme described previously is used to solicit the ICMP TIME_EXCEEDED messages from the routers, and finally, when the UDP message reaches its ultimate destination, the remote host generates an ICMP PORT_UNREACHABLE message. This is not terribly clean, however, as it assumes that no application on the remote host is listening for UDP messages on the "bogus" port number.

Armed with the information from the previous discussion, we can now parse the response array filled in by the pingNode message. The Pinger example, shown in Listing 5.4, uses pingNode to create a ping type of application that is much more useful than the slush ping command. It requires the remote node, number of ICMP echo requests to be transmitted, and the TTL for the echo requests to be specified on the command line.

Listing 5.4 Pinger

```
import java.net.*;
import com.dalsemi.tininet.icmp.Ping;

class Pinger {
    static final int ICMP_ECHO_REPLY    = 0;
    static final int ICMP_TIME_EXCEEDED = 11;

    public static void main(String[] args) {
        if (args.length != 3) {
            System.out.println(
                        "Usage: java Pinger.tini node count max_hops");
            System.exit(1);
        }
        try {
            InetAddress addr = InetAddress.getByName(args[0]);
            int count = Integer.parseInt(args[1]);
            int ttl = Integer.parseInt(args[2]);
            byte[] response = new byte[256];
```

---

8. ICMP is specified in RFC 792.

```java
        for (int i = 0; i < count; i++) {
            long rtt = Ping.pingNode(addr, (byte) ttl, response);
            if (rtt == -1) {
                System.out.println("No response from host:"+args[0]);
            } else {
                // Compute length of IP header
                int ipHdrLength = (response[0] & 0x0f)<<2;
                int type = response[ipHdrLength];
                switch (type) {
                    case ICMP_ECHO_REPLY:
                        int sequence = ((response[ipHdrLength+6] &
                                        0xFF) << 8) +
                                        (response[ipHdrLength+7] &
                                        0xFF);
                        System.out.println("Reply from:"+
                                        addr.toString()+
                                        " in "+rtt+"ms"+
                                        " ttl="+
                                        (response[8]&0xff)+
                                        " sequence="+sequence);
                        break;
                    case ICMP_TIME_EXCEEDED:
                        // Hack out the source IP address and
                        // convert to a String.
                        StringBuffer sb = new StringBuffer(15);
                        for (int j = 0; j < 4; j++) {
                            sb.append(Integer.toString(
                                        response[12+j] & 0xff));
                            if (j < 3) {
                                sb.append('.');
                            }
                        }
                        System.out.println(
                            "Time exceeded message from:"+
                            InetAddress.getByName(sb.toString())+
                            " in "+rtt+"ms");
                        break;
                    default:
                        System.out.println(
                            "Unexpected ICMP message type: "+type);
                        break;
                }
            }
            try {
                Thread.sleep(1000);
            } catch (InterruptedException ie) { }
        }
    }
    catch (UnknownHostException uhe) {
        uhe.printStackTrace();
    }
  }
}
```

If `pingNode` returns a negative value, then the specified remote node is unreachable. Any nonnegative return value indicates that some type of message was received in response to the outbound ICMP echo request message and the response array contains an IP datagram carrying that response. `Pinger` computes the length of the IP header and uses that value as an offset to extract the ICMP type byte. The only two types processed by `Pinger` are ECHO_REPLY and TIME_EXCEEDED.

If we're just trying to determine the reachability of another network node, we'd typically set the TTL to a large value such as 0xff to give the echo request message the best chance to reach its destination. If the message is an echo reply, `Pinger` displays the round-trip time, the sequence number, and the TTL of the response. The sequence number is a 16-bit value assigned by the native ICMP module immediately following the ICMP header in an echo request or reply. The network stack uses this value along with another 16-bit value known as the identifier to match echo requests with replies. The following is sample output from pinging the remote node "www.awl.com" from a TINI with global Internet access.

```
TINI /> java Pinger.tini www.awl.com 3 255
Reply from:www.awl.com/204.179.152.52 in 65ms ttl=244 sequence=0
Reply from:www.awl.com/204.179.152.52 in 64ms ttl=244 sequence=1
Reply from:www.awl.com/204.179.152.52 in 64ms ttl=244 sequence=2
```

The TTL specified for the outbound echo request messages is 255, so we expect that if the node is reachable at all, it should receive the request and send a reply. In fact all three echo requests generated replies from the remote node, and the round-trip times were all about the same. We're not sure what the initial TTL value was set to by the remote machines network stack, but 255 (0xff) is a pretty good bet, since this is a common value used for echo request and reply messages. If this is the case, then the fact that the datagram's time to live when it reaches the local machine is 244 suggests that it passed through 11 routers on its way from the remote to the local machines.

Now we can play around a bit with the TTL value and begin to trace the route between the local TINI and the remote host. The `Pinger` output for TTL values of 1 and 2 are as follows.

```
TINI /> java Pinger.tini www.awl.com 1 1
Time exceeded message from:gte-ds1-bvi4.fastlane.net/209.197.224.237 in
23ms
TINI /> java Pinger.tini www.awl.com 1 2
Time exceeded message from:dallas.tx.core1.fastlane.net/209.197.224.1 in
23ms
```

So the IP addresses of the first two routers encountered by datagrams traveling between the local host and the destination are 209.197.224.237 and

209.197.224.1, respectively. We can continue this process until we get an echo reply from the final destination node (204.179.152.52). Pinger can easily be modified to automate this process and generate the names and IP addresses of the intermediate routers as well as the time required to pass through each network segment, turning it into a full-blown traceroute type of utility.

CHAPTER 6

Dial-Up Networking Using PPP

In Chapter 5 we touched on PPP (Point-to-Point Protocol) over serial as one of the network interface types supported by TINI's runtime environment. PPP is actually a very general purpose protocol that supports data transfer over many different physical media, including (but not limited to) serial, parallel, and Ethernet. On TINI, however, PPP is currently used strictly as a transport mechanism for IP datagrams over a serial link. In the native network stack, PPP exists below the IP module and above the serial port drivers. To an application developer PPP is exposed through Java classes in the `com.dalsemi.tininet.ppp` package. One of the more compelling aspects of using PPP on TINI is that both endpoints of the connection can be communicating with analog phone line modems. This allows for the development of remote embedded networking applications for deployment in areas where an Ethernet network is not available but the vast phone switch network is.

6.1 THE PPP API CLASSES

The PPP API provides a fairly thin wrapper on the native PPP modules. This allows application developers to choose their own mechanisms for authentication, physical link configuration (that is, control of modem vs. hard serial link) and provides for fine-grained control of error handling. Once a PPP connection has been established, the rest of the networking is business as usual, based on the classes in

139

the java.net package and possibly TINI's networking extensions presented in Chapter 5.

Unless otherwise specified, the methods mentioned in this section are defined in the PPP class. A PPP object is used to control and monitor the state of a PPP connection. An application that creates a PPP object must provide a listener to receive notification of PPP events. A listener is an instance of a class that implements the PPPEventListener interface. Listeners can be added or removed using addEventListener and removeEventListener, respectively.

```
public void addEventListener(PPPEventListener listener)
    throws TooManyListenersException
public void removeEventListener(PPPEventListener listener)
```

PPPEventListener defines the method pppEvent. This method is invoked whenever important state changes occur in the underlying PPP layer and require attention from the listener. The listener is passed a PPPEvent object that encapsulates the event type and any error information. The getEventType method returns the event encoded as an integer.

```
public int getEventType()
```

The types of events and their meanings are discussed in Section 6.2.

Part of the overall process of establishing a PPP connection is the login (or authentication) information. For this purpose TINI's PPP implementation currently only supports the most basic authentication protocol used with PPP, known as Password Authentication Protocol (PAP). PAP passes both the user name and password over the physical data link in clear text. To set login information to be used to authenticate TINI to a remote peer, the setPassword and setUsername methods are used.

```
public void setPassword(String password) throws PPPException
public void setUsername(String userName) throws PPPException
```

To request login information from the remote peer, the setAuthenticate method is invoked with a value of true.

```
public void setAuthenticate(boolean value)
```

This causes PPP to generate an AUTHENTICATION_REQUESTED event when login information is received from the remote peer. This is examined in more detail in the next section. PPP is a peer-to-peer protocol and therefore doesn't have the notion of a client or server. Both sides of the communication are equal and can request authentication information from the other. In a typical configuration only one peer requests authentication information, and in the case that the phone network is being used, this is often the same peer that answers the phone. We'll refer to this node as the authenticating peer. In the next chapter we'll implement a PPP daemon that acts strictly as an authenticating peer. However, the PPP API is sufficiently flexible to allow for the creation of a general purpose PPP daemon.

Before the connection can support IP traffic, the IP addresses of both peers must be established. Both the local and remote peer IP addresses can be set using the following methods.

```
public void setLocalAddress(byte[] address)
public void setRemoteAddress(byte[] address)
```

Both methods require a `byte` array containing the IP address in big-endian byte ordering. If a remote address is specified, it will be vended to the remote peer during address negotiation. If a remote address is specified, the local address must also be specified, and both addresses should be on the same network. If the local address is set and the remote peer attempts to vend a different address, a STOPPED event will be generated and the negotiation of the PPP connection halts. If the local application is connecting to a dial-up server, it is not required to set either the local or remote address. In this case, it is expected that the remote peer will vend the local IP address.

After creating a PPP object, an application will typically set a new value for the asynchronous control character map (ACCM) used by the native PPP implementation.

```
public void setACCM(int newACCM)
```

The `setACCM` method takes an integer that contains a bit map of the characters to be escaped. If a bit in a specified position is 1, the corresponding character is escaped; otherwise, it is transmitted normally. For example, an ACCM value of 0x80000001 would escape only characters 0 and 31. By default, during link negotiation PPP instructs the remote peer to escape all characters between 0 and 0x1f—in other words, the default ACCM of 0xffffffff. Since you'll most often be working with physical links capable of receiving arbitrary binary data, the ACCM should be set to 0. This will allow for more efficient data transfer because it will avoid the unnecessary transmission of escape characters. One important exception to this occurs when the use of software flow control (often referred to as XON/ XOFF flow control) is specified with the underlying serial port. In this case, the software flow control characters XON (17 decimal) and XOFF (19 decimal) must be escaped. This yields an ACCM of 0xa0000. If XON/XOFF flow control is to be used, the `setXonXoffEscape` method must also be invoked.

```
public void setXonXoffEscape(boolean value)
```

When invoked with a value of `true`, the `setXonXoffEscape` method notifies the local PPP interface to escape the XON/XOFF characters.

Another option that an application may want to configure before attempting to establish PPP connections is passive mode. Passive mode can be enabled or disabled using the `setPassive` method.

```
public void setPassive(boolean value)
```

The passive mode option affects the earliest phase in connection establishment: Line Control Protocol (LCP) negotiation. The native LCP module attempts to initiate a connection by sending a configuration request message. It will wait for a certain amount of time for the remote peer to acknowledge receipt of the message. If no acknowledgment is received, LCP will time out and send the configuration request message again. The retry count is finite, however, which means if no remote peer is actually receiving the message, PPP will time out and generate a STOPPED event. Passive mode disables this time-out. LCP will just wait indefinitely for a remote peer to transmit its own configuration request message.

Passive mode should not be enabled when modems are being used to establish the physical data link. In this case, LCP negotiation doesn't begin until the modem connection has been established. The time-out is required to notify the application that the remote peer is not responding. However, in a configuration where a raw serial port is being used in an environment where devices come and go—handheld computers such as a Palm Pilot, for example—the application has no way of knowing when a device will be attached to the serial port. In this case, the use of passive mode frees the application from having to process STOPPED events and restart PPP. When a device eventually attaches to the port, it will transmit a configuration request message, the local LCP module will acknowledge the message, send its own configuration request, and the rest of the connection negotiation will continue in the normal fashion.

After using these methods to configure the PPP session to meet its requirements, the application invokes the open method.

```
public void open()
```

At this point the listener will start receiving PPP events.

6.2   PPP EVENTS

When a PPP object is created, it starts a daemon thread to listen for events in the native PPP module. This thread generates the events that notify PPP event listeners of important changes in the state of a PPP connection. The following events generated by the daemon thread are defined as integer constants in the PPPEvent interface.

- STARTING
- AUTHENTICATION_REQUESTED

- UP
- STOPPED
- CLOSED

6.2.1 STARTING Event

A STARTING event is generated by the application invoking the open method.

```
public void open()
```

The STARTING event provides the application with a chance to bring up the physical communication link. At a minimum this involves initializing the serial port that will be used by all PPP traffic. If a modem is attached to the serial port, the application also initializes the modem and either instructs it to dial a remote modem or waits for the modem to answer an incoming call. After the physical communication link has been established, the application invokes the up method.

```
pubic void up(SerialPort port) throws PPPException
```

The application passes a reference to the serial port that will be used for PPP traffic. At this point, PPP assumes exclusive use of the port. Any other attempt to read from or write to the serial port could disturb the PPP connection and will most likely result in a STOPPED event being generated.

6.2.2 AUTHENTICATION_REQUESTED Event

The AUTHENTICATION_REQUESTED event is generated if the setAuthenticate method is invoked with the parameter value equal to true. This will cause PPP to request authentication information from the remote peer during its negotiation of the connection. This gives the application a chance to verify the login information. The getPeerID and GetPeerPassword methods as follows can be used to retrieve the remote peer's login data.

```
public String getPeerID()
public String getPeerPassword()
```

After the application examines the login information, it invokes this authenticate method.

```
public void authenticate(boolean valid)
```

If the login information is correct, a boolean value of true is passed to authenticate. In this case, PPP continues its negotiation of the connection. If the login information is invalid, the application invokes authenticate, passing a boolean value of false and causing PPP to reject the clients connection request and generate a STOPPED event.

6.2.3 UP Event

If the connection is successfully established, the notifier thread generates an UP event. At this point, the PPP connection is established and is ready for IP network traffic. However, the application must invoke the `addInterface` method before the TCP/IP stack will recognize the new PPP connection as a valid network interface.

```
public void addInterface(String name, boolean default)
```

The name passed to `addInterface` is typically formed by appending the number of the serial port being used for PPP traffic to the lowercase `String` "ppp." So, for example, if serial port 0 is being used, the new PPP interface will be named "ppp0." The name passed to `addInterface` is the same interface name that is viewed when using the "`ipconfig -x`" slush command. If `default` is `true`, the new interface will become the default network interface for the entire system.

6.2.4 STOPPED Event

The STOPPED event is typically generated in response to an error condition. Some of the possible sources of errors include problems negotiating connection options, rejection of authentication information, or the remote peer explicitly closing the connection. The source of the error can be determined by invoking the `getLastError` method on the PPPEvent object passed to the listener.

```
public int getLastError()
```

The PPPEvent class defines the following integer constants used to detect error types.

- NONE—No error condition exists.
- ADDR—One (or both) of the IP addresses could not be negotiated.
- AUTH—The remote peer rejected the local peer's authentication credentials.
- TIME—Link negotiation timed out.
- REJECT—Link options were rejected by the remote peer.

Typically, the listener increments an error (or retry) count. The listener can use a combination of the retry count and the error information to determine the difference between transient and persistent (or fatal) problems. If a persistent problem occurs, the listener may choose to notify the application of the failure rather than trying again to establish a connection. Regardless of the source of the error, the listener invokes the `close` method to allow PPP to shutdown the connection and generate a CLOSED event.

```
public void close()
```

6.2.5 CLOSED Event

After receiving a CLOSED event, the listener frees any resources that were consumed establishing the connection. The removeInterface method is invoked by the listener if an UP event was previously generated, causing a new network interface to be added to the system.

```
public void removeInterface(name)
```

The removeInterface method takes the same String value that was passed to addInterface during UP event processing. After removing the interface, the listener invokes the down method to force PPP to relinquish any claim to the serial port. This makes the serial port available to the rest of the application.

```
public void down()
```

At this point, the listener may choose to invoke open to attempt to establish a new connection.

Handling PPP events and dealing with error recovery can be fairly complicated. The next chapter presents a remote data logging application that uses PPP to allow remote machines to dial in and upload a log file. This example makes extensive use of the PPP API and should help to clarify the concepts presented in this chapter.

CHAPTER 7

Building a Remote Data Logger

7.1   DESCRIPTION

This chapter presents a comprehensive example intended to provide some insight into writing powerful networked applications that take full advantage of big networking capabilities provided by this little computer. TINI will be put to work as a network status reporting device. We'll create a complete example that captures and logs data and implements a TCP/IP network server, making the data available to remote clients. Ultimately, the server will accept connections over both Ethernet and the PSTN (Public Switched Telephone Network)[1] using PPP to manage dial-up connections. Support for dial-up networking is primarily what will make the data logger truly remote. This allows access to any client computer anywhere in the world with Internet access without requiring the presence of an Ethernet network at the data collection site. It assumes nothing more than a serial modem and a connection to the public phone network.

The actual data collected by the application isn't terribly important. The main point is that we can collect information from some sensor or other physical device (or possibly multiple devices) and upload it to any interested client over a TCP/IP network. For this reason we'll try to keep the framework used for data collection relatively general purpose and reusable to allow for collecting data from other

---

1.   Also commonly known as POTS (Plain Old Telephone System).

types of devices. However, to make the finished example reasonably concrete, we'll need some real data to sample. For this purpose we can recycle our effort from the 1-Wire Networking chapter in which we created a humidity and temperature sensing circuit and an accompanying Java class.

The data logging application consists of several classes. The class that contains the main method is in a class named DataLogger. We will also refer to the entire application as "DataLogger," as this is the name of the binary that will be executed on TINI.

The DataLogger example will combine three different concepts from this and two previous chapters.

- TCP/IP networking
- Serial communications
- 1-Wire networking

Since the DataLogger example is rather large, it will be broken down into the following steps.

1. Creating the network server. The TCP/IP server will be implemented in the main class named DataLogger. The server will be implemented in a multithreaded fashion and will handle all inbound connections over an Ethernet network and eventually over the phone network using a modem.
2. Implementing the data collection classes. These classes will be responsible for collecting and managing the data samples as well as writing the results to an output stream to the client.
3. Develop a test client application. After completing these first two steps, we'll have enough functionality to test an intermediate version of the DataLogger application over an Ethernet network only.
4. Adding dial-up networking support. Create a class to manage PPP connections.
5. Managing the serial data link used for PPP communications. We'll develop a set of classes that deal with all of the issues of communicating with both a raw serial port and a modem attached to a serial port.
6. Testing the application. Finally we'll be able to test the entire application with a sample client downloading the data log over both an Ethernet network and the PSTN.

Because the DataLogger example is fairly large, the following sections omit portions of the source code. However, all of the source code for the DataLogger application is provided in the accompanying CD.

7.2 THE DATALOGGER CLASS

We'll start by exploring the main class of the application: `DataLogger`. `DataLogger` implements the network (TCP/IP) server and accepts and manages inbound connections from remote clients. A skeleton of the `DataLogger` class including its constructor is shown in Listing 7.1. The `DataLogger` class extends `Thread` and overrides the `run` method, making it the server's main loop. The primordial thread is allowed to die after successful initialization of the application.

During construction of `DataLogger` an instance of `HumidityLogger` is created specifying the sample count and delay time in seconds between samples. After the logger thread is started, the `DataLogger` thread is not concerned with the operation of the logger or even what kind of data it is collecting. It maintains a reference to the logger object that is used to satisfy log requests for inbound client connections. We'll cover the data collection classes in detail in the next section.

Listing 7.1 DataLogger

```
import java.io.*;
import java.net.*;

class DataLogger extends Thread {
    ...
    static final int SERVER_PORT = 5588;

    HumidityLogger logger;

    DataLogger(int samples, int delay) throws LoggingException {
        // Create and start the logging daemon
        logger = new HumidityLogger(samples, delay);
        logger.start();
    }

    ...
}
```

`DataLogger` requires the number of data readings to be maintained and the delay in seconds between each reading to be specified on the command line. `DataLogger`'s `main` method is shown in Listing 7.2.

Listing 7.2 DataLogger's main method

```
public static void main(String[] args) {
    System.out.println("Starting DataLogger ...");
    if (args.length != 2) {
        System.out.println("Usage: java DataLogger samples delay");
        System.exit(1);
```

```
    }
    int samples = Integer.parseInt(args[0]);
    int delay = Integer.parseInt(args[1]);
    try {
        (new DataLogger(samples, delay)).start();
    } catch (Exception e) {
        System.out.println("Error creating data logger");
        e.printStackTrace();
        // In case any non-daemon threads have been started
        // System.exit(1);
    }
}
```

After extracting the `samples` and `count` values from the command line, the `main` method creates a new `DataLogger` object, which also creates a new thread of execution. After constructing the new instance of `DataLogger`, the `start` method is invoked to kick off the server.

The server spends eternity in the `run` method, processing network connections. `DataLogger`'s `run` method along with the inner class `LogWorker` is shown in Listing 7.3. It starts by creating a `ServerSocket` object to listen for inbound connections from remote clients. The `SERVER_PORT` number used in creating the `ServerSocket` object is simply chosen as a large magic number. Anything that is comfortably above the range of "well-known port"[2] numbers will do. As implemented here, `DataLogger` uses a port number of 5588. The application could easily be modified to use a port number specified on the command line.

Listing 7.3   DataLogger's run method

```
public void run() {
    ServerSocket ss = null;
    try {
        ss = new ServerSocket(SERVER_PORT);
    } catch (Exception e) {
        e.printStackTrace();
        // Abort if we can't create ServerSocket instance
        return;
    }

    while (true) {
        Socket s = null;
        try {
            // Wait for client connections over PPP or Ethernet
            s = ss.accept();
        } catch (IOException ioe) {
            // Shut down the logging daemon
            logger.stopLogging();
            System.out.println("Fatal problem with server socket");
```

---

2.   The well-known ports are listed in RFC 1700.

```
            ioe.printStackTrace();
            // Fall out of run method
            break;
        }

        // Create a new thread to handle this connection
        (new LogWorker(s)).start();
    }
}

private class LogWorker extends Thread {
    private Socket s;

    private LogWorker(Socket s) {
        this.s = s;
    }

    public void run() {
        DataOutputStream dout = null;
        try {
            dout = new DataOutputStream(
                    new BufferedOutputStream(s.getOutputStream()));
            logger.writeLog(dout);
            dout.flush();
        } catch (IOException ioe) {
            System.out.println("I/O error writing log data");
            ioe.printStackTrace();
        } finally {
            try {
                s.close();
                dout.close();
            } catch (IOException e) {}
        }
    }
}
```

After the ServerSocket object is created, the run method enters an infinite loop that accepts and processes inbound client connections. After a new instance of Socket is returned from the ServerSocket object's accept method, a new thread (an instance of LogWorker) is created to manage the connection. The socket's getOutputStream method is invoked to obtain the lowest-level output stream (an instance of SocketOutputStream) for writing data to the underlying connection. This stream is used in constructing an instance of BufferedOutputStream, and the resulting buffered output stream is wrapped in a DataOutputStream.

The idea of using a buffered DataOutputStream for writing the log data is that the data-collecting daemon will write all of the samples it has collected to the output stream in an iterative fashion. If the output stream were not buffered, every write method invoked on the output stream would perform a write to the low-level SocketOutputStream. This forces a write to the native socket layer. Writing the log data in such a fashion could be termed "byte-banging." Byte-banging is very inefficient, since each of these writes is fairly expensive. With the `BufferedOutputStream`, writes to the underlying `SocketOutputStream` occur only when the `BufferedOutputStreams` internal buffer is full or the stream's `flush` method is invoked. The default internal buffer size used in TINI's implementation of all buffered streams is 512 bytes. This allows several log entries to be written to the `DataOutputStream` before the `write` method on the `SocketOutputStream` is invoked to write the contents of the buffer to the native socket layer.

The `DataOutputStream` object is passed to the `writeLog` method of the data collecting daemon. The `writeLog` method is responsible for writing all data points to the output stream. After the `writeLog` method returns, any data remaining in the output stream's internal buffer is flushed and both the stream and underlying socket are closed.

There are two catch blocks in the run method. The first protects the `accept` method. If an `IOException` is thrown from `accept`, the problem is assumed to be fatal. There isn't any good reason for `accept` to throw a runtime exception other than that the port selected is already owned by another thread or process and this problem won't be fixed with retries. In this case, the while loop is exited by the break statement, allowing the `DataLogger` thread to exit. As we'll see in the next few sections, all other threads created in the `DataLogger` process are daemon threads, so when the server thread exits, all of the other threads stop executing and the application terminates. The other catch block protects the writing of the log data to the remote client. In this case, an error could result from the client terminating the connection unexpectedly. While this certainly does prohibit the successful transfer of the log data, it shouldn't cause the application to exit. In this case, we just close down the socket and output stream and wait for a new connection.

In this section we developed the top-level framework necessary to accept network connections and dispatch output requests to the data collector. Next, we'll focus on the details of collecting and managing the data samples.

7.3   COLLECTING THE DATA

The first task is deciding exactly what data we'll be collecting. Since we're using the humidity sensing circuit we developed in Section 4.4.3, we should briefly review its capabilities. The sensor used a 1-Wire chip as a digital front end to the physical humidity sensor. The humidity sensor's only output is an analog voltage. The 1-Wire chip provided analog to digital conversion as well as temperature readings. The `HumiditySensor` class we created to expose the sensor's functionality provides the following public methods.

```
public double getSensorRH() throws OneWireException
public double getTrueRH() throws OneWireException
public double getTemperature() throws OneWireException
```

Of the three readings we can obtain from the above methods, only two are likely to be interesting to a client: the temperature and the true relative humidity. The sensor relative humidity might be interesting for calibration purposes, but we'll ignore it here. We'll also want to put a time stamp on each reading so that clients can build logs and chart environmental change over time.

The next thing we need to decide is how to store the data samples. One obvious approach would be to write the data to a file. Each new entry could be appended to the end of the file. The advantage of using a file is that even if the system loses power, the log data is not lost. When power is restored and the application restarts, it can simply continue logging data samples by appending each sample to the end of the same file. If the system were down long enough to miss one or more samples, any client that downloads the file would be able to detect this by examining the time stamps. The downside to logging the data to a file is that `DataLogger` is running in a memory constrained environment. The file system, Java objects, and all system data structures live in the same memory space. If the log file grows too large, the application will likely terminate with an `OutOfMemoryError` or some other fatal exception. Special tricks would be required to ensure that the file didn't grow beyond a certain size. This is further complicated by the fact that we can't just truncate the file at a certain size by writing the latest sample over the sample at the end of the file. If a sample must be lost, it should be the oldest sample. In this sense, we really want something like a circular buffer. This can still be implemented with the file system using a `RandomAccessFile`, but it is too cumbersome for our example. For our purposes, it will be much simpler and more efficient to store the data in a `Vector`. Of course, if we just continue to add elements to the vector, we'll still run out of memory. But by using a `Vector` we can easily avoid this problem by removing the oldest sample, which will always be at index 0, before adding the new sample after the maximum sample count has been reached.

Note that if we assumed a constant connection to a network, we could structure `DataLogger` so that it just wrote all samples to a socket as they were collected. But we're building this application with the idea that the network isn't always available. This allows the logger to do all of its work without the network. Then when a client is interested in synching up with the logger, it can establish a connection with the server and collect the necessary data. The more "remote" the system is, the more important this ability becomes.

To keep the logging classes reasonably general purpose and reusable, we'll create an abstract class named `LoggingDaemon` to drive the data collection process. Ideally we don't want `LoggingDaemon` to have to be aware of what kind of data is being logged or the details of how it is acquired. To accomplish this isolation, `LoggingDaemon` defines the following abstract methods.

```
protected abstract Object captureSample();
protected abstract void writeLogEntry(Object sample, DataOutputStream dout)
    throws IOException;
```

Subclasses of `LoggingDaemon` implement the `captureSample` method to handle the details of collecting a single data sample. This sample must be encapsulated within an object because it will be stored in a `Vector`. The `writeLogEntry` method is used to write the individual fields contained in the sample object to the supplied instance of `DataOutputStream`.

`LoggingDaemon`'s constructor is shown in Listing 7.4. The constructor requires the maximum number of samples to be held in the `samples` `Vector` along with the delay between consecutive samples. The `maxSamples` field is used to set the initial size of the `Vector`. The `delay` is input to the constructor as a number of seconds. The `delay` is converted to milliseconds so that it can be input directly into `Thread`'s `sleep` method. Finally the `LoggingDaemon` thread is set to a daemon thread. This means that when the last non-daemon thread exits, `LoggingDaemon` will exit, along with any other daemon threads, allowing the process to terminate. We do this because there isn't any point in continuing to log data if there isn't a server running to allow clients to download it.

Listing 7.4   LoggingDaemon's constructor

```java
import java.io.*;
import java.util.*;

public abstract class LoggingDaemon extends Thread {
    private int maxSamples;
    private int delay;
    private Vector samples;

    ...

    public LoggingDaemon(int maxSamples, int delay)
        throws LoggingException {

        this.maxSamples = maxSamples;
        // Convert delay from seconds to milliseconds
        this.delay = delay * 1000;
        samples = new Vector(maxSamples);
        this.setDaemon(true);
    }
    ......

    public void stopLogging() {
        logEm = false;
    }
}
```

`LoggingDaemon`'s run method is shown in Listing 7.5. As long as the `stopLogging` method is not invoked, the `run` method spins in an infinite loop collecting data samples at the specified interval.

Listing 7.5 LoggingDaemon's run method

```
...
public void run() {
    while (logEm) {
        Object smp = captureSample();
        if (smp != null) {
            synchronized (samples) {
                if (samples.size() == maxSamples) {
                    // Remove the oldest entry
                    samples.removeElementAt(0);
                }
                samples.addElement(smp);
            }
        }
        try {
            Thread.sleep(delay);
        } catch (InterruptedException ie) {}
    }
}
```

If the captureSample method returns null, there is no change in samples. The run method simply goes to sleep until it is time to try another sample. This is a rather simplistic mechanism for handling errors that occur during data collection, but it is appropriate for our application. Since every sample carries with it a time stamp, a client can determine that one or more samples were missed by simple analysis of the time stamps.

LoggingDaemon's writeLog method is shown in Listing 7.6. The writeLog method is invoked by the server when a client establishes a connection with the server, requesting a log of the recent data samples. The writeLog method simply enumerates samples, invoking writeLogEntry for every data sample contained within the Vector. The details of extracting and writing the actual field data contained within the sample object are left to the subclass.

Listing 7.6 LoggingDaemon's writeLog method

```
public void writeLog(DataOutputStream dout) throws IOException {
    Vector sc = (Vector) samples.clone();
    dout.writeInt(sc.size());
    for (Enumeration e = sc.elements(); e.hasMoreElements(); ) {
        writeLogEntry(e.nextElement(), dout);
    }
}
```

Since we need to encapsulate the individual data readings within an object, we'll create a class named HumiditySample (shown in Listing 7.7). HumiditySample is just a thin wrapper on the sample data that provides public "get" methods for the individual fields. HumiditySample's constructor takes the readings attained using the `HumiditySensor` class and stores them in the `temperature` and `relHumidity` fields. It also time stamps the readings using the `System.currentTimeMillis` method, which returns the number of milliseconds between the current time and midnight, January 1, 1970. This is much simpler and faster for our purposes than storing the time stamp as a `Date` object. We can put the burden of converting the `timeStamp` value to humanly readable date and time on the client program. In the case that the client is written in Java, this job is trivial. It can simply pass the `timeStamp` value received to the `Date` constructor that takes the long value returned from `currentTimeMillis`. We'll make use of this in the next section, which presents a small sample client application.

Listing 7.7   HumiditySample

```java
public class HumiditySample {
    private double temperature;
    private double relHumidity;
    private long   timeStamp;

    public HumiditySample(double relHumidity, double temperature) {
        this.temperature = temperature;
        this.relHumidity = relHumidity;
        timeStamp = System.currentTimeMillis();
    }

    public long getTimeStamp() {
        return timeStamp;
    }

    public double getRelativeHumidity() {
        return relHumidity;
    }

    public double getTemperature() {
        return temperature;
    }
}
```

Now that we have a simple framework for collecting, maintaining, and outputting a group of samples, we can create the class that performs the actual work of collecting individual samples. The class `HumidityLogger`, shown in Listing 7.8, extends `LoggingDaemon` and provides implementations for the `captureSample` and `writeLogEntry` methods.

Listing 7.8   HumidityLogger

```java
import java.io.IOException;
import java.io.DataOutputStream;
```

```java
import com.dalsemi.onewire.OneWireAccessProvider;
import com.dalsemi.onewire.adapter.DSPortAdapter;
import com.dalsemi.onewire.OneWireException;

public class HumidityLogger extends LoggingDaemon {
    private HumiditySensor sensor;
    private DSPortAdapter adapter;

    public HumidityLogger(int maxSamples, int delay)
        throws LoggingException {

        super(maxSamples, delay);
        try {
            adapter = OneWireAccessProvider.getDefaultAdapter();
            sensor = new HumiditySensor(adapter);
        } catch (OneWireException owe) {
            throw new LoggingException(
                        "Error creating Environmental Sensor:" +
                        owe.getMessage());
        }
    }

    public Object captureSample() {
        try {
            adapter.beginExclusive(true);
            double temp = sensor.getTemperature();
            double humidity = sensor.getTrueRH();
            return new HumiditySample(humidity, temp);
        } catch (OneWireException owe) {
            System.out.println("Error reading sensor");
            owe.printStackTrace();
            // No need to terminate app because of a failed reading
            return null;
        } finally {
            adapter.endExclusive();
        }
    }

    public void writeLogEntry(Object sample, DataOutputStream dout)
        throws IOException {

        dout.writeLong(((HumiditySample)sample).getTimeStamp());
        dout.writeDouble(((HumiditySample)sample).getRelativeHumidity());
        dout.writeDouble(((HumiditySample)sample).getTemperature());
    }
}
```

HumidityLogger creates a new instance of the class HumiditySensor, which is used to perform the humidity and temperature measurements. When the captureSample method is invoked, it simply creates a new HumiditySample object to encapsulate the humidity and temperature values and returns that object to the caller, in this case the run method of LoggingDaemon. It is important that a transient error that could cause a failure while performing an individual measurement not cause the logging thread to terminate. If an exception is thrown while performing the measurements, it is caught, and null is returned.

Since the LoggingDaemon class doesn't know anything about the internal details of the data sample object—HumiditySample, in this case—it invokes writeLogEntry passing it a reference to the sample object and a DataOutputStream used to write the sample object's field information to the underlying socket. The writeLogEntry method extracts the time stamp, humidity, and temperature readings and writes them to the stream using the appropriate methods, writeLong and writeDouble, preserving their primitive types. It is assumed that the client will be using a DataInputStream for easy interpretation of the data.

7.4   A SAMPLE CLIENT

At this point, we have a data logging application capable of capturing data and serving up to any client over an Ethernet network connection. To test the data logger, we'll develop a small client application to connect to the server and download its current log.

The DataLoggerClient class, shown in Listing 7.9, is a simple command line application that can be run on any Java platform. The name of the server, the TINI running the DataLogger application, is extracted from the first argument on the command line. DataLoggerClient then uses the server name to establish a connection to the server. After the connection has been established, the getInputStream method is invoked on the socket instance to get a stream that can be used for uploading the log information from the server. The input stream is buffered, and the result is wrapped in a DataInputStream. Now the client is ready to read the data in the same format in which it is written by the server.

Listing 7.9   DataLoggerClient

```
import java.io.*;
import java.net.*;
import java.util.Date;

class DataLoggerClient {
    static final int PORT = 5588;

    public static void main(String[] args) {
        if (args.length != 1) {
            System.out.println("Usage: java DataLoggerClient server");
            System.exit(1);
        }

        Socket s = null;
```

```
        DataInputStream din = null;
        try {
            s = new Socket(InetAddress.getByName(args[0]), PORT);
            din = new DataInputStream(
                    new BufferedInputStream(s.getInputStream()));
            // Read number of data entries coming our way
            int entries = din.readInt();
            System.out.println("Total readings="+entries);
            for (int i = 0; i < entries; i++) {
                System.out.print("Entry " + i + ":" +
                                new Date(din.readLong()));
                System.out.print(", RH=" + din.readDouble());
                System.out.println(", TEMP=" + din.readDouble());
            }
        } catch (IOException ioe) {
            System.out.println("Error downloading readings:"+
                            ioe.getMessage());
            ioe.printStackTrace();
        } finally {
            try {
                s.close();
                din.close();
            } catch (IOException _) {}
        }
    }
}
```

The first thing the server sends to us is an integer value that tells the client the number of log entries to expect. After the client has read this value, it can loop through all entries, reading each individual sample. The client simply displays each entry as it's being read, but a real client application would probably be logging this information to a database. The individual fields of each entry—timestamp, humidity, and temperature—must be read by the client in the same order they are written by the server. The time stamp is read in as a `long` and passed to a constructor of the `Date` class. The `toString` method of `Date` is then used to display a human readable date and time. The humidity and temperature measurements are simply read as `doubles` and displayed.

Now we have both the client and server programs and are ready to run both applications. The server can be launched on TINI using a command line similar to the following.

```
TINI /> java DataLogger.tini 60 120 &
Starting DataLogger ...
```

A maximum number of 60 samples was specified along with a 120-second delay between each sample. After running the server for several minutes to allow it to acquire a few samples, we can run the client. Here is the sample output for `DataLoggerClient` that is run on a Win2K machine.

```
java DataLoggerClient 192.168.0.15
Total readings=3
Entry 0:Fri Feb 02 14:20:41 CST 2001, RH=27.733103869596295, TEMP=23.53125
Entry 1:Fri Feb 02 14:22:42 CST 2001, RH=28.067076700395877, TEMP=23.4375
Entry 2:Fri Feb 02 14:24:42 CST 2001, RH=27.73123954744912, TEMP=23.28125
```

By examining the time stamp, we can see that each sample was taken just over two minutes apart. If we let the server run more than two hours, it will fill its sample vector, and running the client would result in 60 data samples. If we let the server continue to run for days, weeks, or even months, we would still get 60 samples, but they would always represent readings taken within the last two hours.

In the next section, support will be provided for managing a PPP interface. We can then use the same client we developed in this section to test DataLogger's ability to accept connections over both Ethernet and PPP network interfaces.

7.5 IMPLEMENTING THE PPP DAEMON

Now on to the business of making our "remote data logger" truly remote. We'll accomplish this by adding support for establishing dial-up networking connections to our logger using the PPP network interface and supporting API classes. At this point we're going to bring a second server into the picture, which could become confusing. The top-level network server is what we implemented in the DataLogger class in Section 7.2. It blocks on accept, waiting for a connection over any network interface. It doesn't really care if the connection is established over an Ethernet network or a serial line using PPP. The server we'll implement in this section is a "dial-up" server that allows clients to establish TCP/IP connections to TINI using a PPP interface. For the sake of brevity, we'll just refer to the dial-up server as the "server." However, when both servers are a part of the discussion context, we'll explicitly refer to the "dial-up server."

We'll implement our dial-up server in a class named PPPDaemon. A portion of the PPPDaemon class is shown in Listing 7.10. PPPDaemon implements two interfaces: PPPEventListener to receive PPP event notification and DataLinkListener to receive notification about errors that occur with the physical data link. In this section, we won't get too concerned about the details of the underlying physical link and whether the connection is established over a hard-wired serial link or using modems. Then next section will deal with the low-level data link handling issues.

On construction PPPDaemon requires an instance of a class that implements the PPPDaemonListener interface shown in Listing 7.11. The daemonError interface method is invoked by PPPDaemon to provide asynchronous notification of a PPP or data link error to the listener. The isValidUser method is invoked after the server has received the client's login information. This gives the listener the final say on whether a PPP connection is accepted or rejected.

Listing 7.10 PPPDaemon

```java
import java.io.*;
import com.dalsemi.tininet.ppp.*;

public class PPPDaemon implements PPPEventListener, DataLinkListener {
    private PPP ppp;
    private PPPDataLink dataLink;
    private int maxRetries;
    private PPPDaemonListener listener;

    ...
    public PPPDaemon(PPPDaemonListener listener,
                     String portName, int speed)
        throws PPPException {

        this(listener, portName, speed, 3, true);
    }

    public PPPDaemon(PPPDaemonListener listener, String portName,
                     int speed, int maxRetries, boolean modemLink)
        throws PPPException {

        this.listener   = listener;
        this.maxRetries = maxRetries;
        try {
            if (modemLink) {
                dataLink = new PPPModemLink(portName, speed, this);
            } else {
                dataLink = new PPPSerialLink(portName, speed, this);
            }
        } catch (DataLinkException dle) {
            throw new PPPException("Unable to initialize PPPDaemon:" +
                                   dle.getMessage());
        }

        ppp = new PPP();
        ppp.setLocalAddress(new byte[] {(byte) 192, (byte) 168, 1, 1});
        ppp.setRemoteAddress(new byte[] {(byte) 192, (byte) 168, 1, 2});
        ppp.setAuthenticate(true);
    }

    ...

    public void dataLinkError(String error) {
        System.err.println("Error in data link:"+error);
        ppp.close();
    }
}
```

After initializing the listener and maxRetries fields, PPPDaemon's constructor creates an object to manage the physical data link. It creates either a PPPSerialLink or a PPPModemLink object, depending on the modemLink boolean passed to the constructor. Both of these classes and the PPPDataLink interface they implement will be covered in detail in the next section. For now it's sufficient to know that by using the PPPDataLink object, the daemon can initialize the link and obtain a reference to its underlying serial port. From this point forward the daemon doesn't care if the physical link is over a hard-wired serial connection or a modem.

Next, a new PPP object is created and the IP addresses for both the local interface and the remote peer are set.

Listing 7.11   PPPDaemonListener interface

```
public interface PPPDaemonListener {
    public void daemonError(String error);
    public boolean isValidUser(String name, String password);
}
```

It is easiest to understand the operation of PPPDaemon as a Finite State Machine (FSM). The state diagram for the FSM implemented by the PPPDaemon class is shown in Figure 7.1. The solid lines represent state transitions caused by PPPDaemon invoking methods on its PPP object. The dashed lines represent transition caused by errors detected by the native PPP implementation.

Note that there are actually two finite state machines at work here: the true PPP state machine[3] that is implemented as a part of the network stack beneath the IP module (see Figure 5.1) and the high-level state machine implemented by PPPDaemon, whose state transitions are driven by events generated by the PPP daemon thread and method invocations on a PPP object. The low-level PPP state machine is very complex and has several additional states. For the most part, the arcane details of its implementation are hidden from the application developer by the PPP class. The purpose of the PPPEventListener interface is to provide a mechanism to drive a much simpler, higher-level state machine that gives the application an opportunity to control the physical data link, user authentication, and the handling of error information.

After creating a new PPP object, PPPDaemon is in the INIT state. At this point, there is no PPP traffic traveling across the physical data link. To transition to the STARTING state, the owner of the PPPDaemon object invokes the startDaemon method shown in Listing 7.12. startDaemon adds its own object (this) as a listener for PPP events and invokes the open method on its PPP object.

---

3.   The PPP finite state machine is described in RFC 1661.

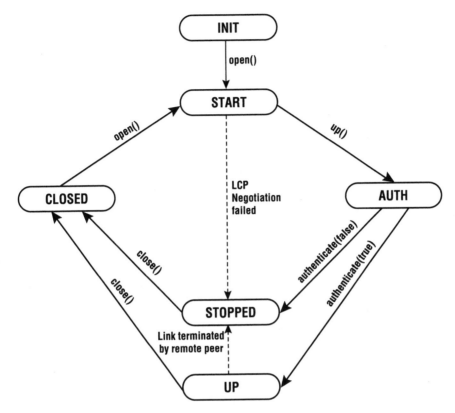

Figure 7.1   PPP daemon FSM

Listing 7.12   StartDaemon

```
public void startDaemon() throws PPPException {
    retryCount = 0;
    try {
        // Add PPP event listener to driver state machine
        ppp.addEventListener(this);
    } catch (java.util.TooManyListenersException le) {
        throw new PPPException("Unable to add event listener");
    }
    ppp.open();
}

public void stopDaemon() {
    // Don't receive any more PPP events
    ppp.removeEventListener(this);
    ppp.close();
}
```

The bulk of the FSM is implemented in the `pppEvent` method shown in Listing 7.13. `pppEvent` is invoked by a daemon thread that is created during construction of the PPP object. It is passed a `PPPEvent` object that is used to determine the event type. The `pppEvent` method switches on the event type to determine the next appropriate action. The event processing usually completes by invoking a method on a PPP object forcing another state transition. The possible events were described in the previous chapter and are listed here for convenience.

- STARTING
- AUTHENTICATION_REQUEST
- UP
- STOPPED
- CLOSED

The `STARTING` state provides the application with a chance to initialize the physical data link. Our sample PPP daemon implementation does so using the `initializeLink` method defined in the `PPPDataLink` (Listing 7.14) interface. If `initializeLink` returns normally, the server invokes the `up` method on its PPP object, passing it a reference to the serial port. All PPP traffic flows over this port. This is really a handoff of serial port ownership. Once the port reference is passed to PPP, it assumes exclusive access to the serial port. If `initializeLink` fails to bring up the link successfully for any reason, it throws a `DataLinkException`, which is caught, and `close` is invoked on the PPP object. This will cause the notifier thread to generate a `CLOSED` event transitioning PPPDaemon to the `CLOSED` state.

At this point, PPP waits for a client to begin LCP (Line Control Protocol) negotiation. Once a client successfully completes the line negotiation, PPP requests login information and the remote peer replies with a user name and password. This generates an `AUTHENTICATION_REQUESTED` event (the AUTH state in Figure 7.1), and `pppEvent` gets the user name and password for the PPP object and passes them to the listener's `isValidUser` method. If the listener likes the login information, PPP completes its negotiation with the client, establishing the IP addresses for both the local and remote peer, and generates an `UP` event. `pppEvent` then invokes `addInterface` on the PPP object, which adds a new network interface to the OS.

Now the communication link is fully established and ready for IP traffic. If the listener didn't like the login information, a `STOPPED` event is generated, and the `retryCount`, which is used to track errors, is incremented. A `STOPPED` event can also be generated by the remote peer breaking the connection. Regardless of how we transitioned to the `STOPPED` state, we'll invoke `close` on the PPP object to generate a `CLOSED` event. This gives both the underlying PPP object and our daemon a chance to perform an orderly shutdown of the connection. If the connection had

been fully established (that is, it had at some point transitioned to the UP state),
then we'll invoke down on the PPP object and remove the network interface that
was added during the UP state processing.

Listing 7.13 pppEvent

```
...
private int retryCount;

public void pppEvent(PPPEvent ev) {
    switch (ev.getEventType()) {
        case PPPEvent.STARTING:
            try {
                // Now we need to bring up the physical link
                dataLink.initializeLink();
                ppp.up((SerialPort) dataLink.getPort());
            } catch (DataLinkException dle) {
                listener.serverError("Data link error:"+
                                        dle.getMessage());
                ppp.close();
            }
            break;

        case PPPEvent.AUTHENTICATION_REQUEST:
            ppp.authenticate(listener.isValidUser(ppp.getPeerID(),
                            ppp.getPeerPassword()));
            break;

        case PPPEvent.UP:
            // Reset error count after successfully bringing
            // up connection
            retryCount = 0;
            ppp.addInterface("ppp0");
            isUp = true;
            break;

        case PPPEvent.STOPPED:
            ppp.close();
            if (++retryCount < maxRetries) {
                ppp.close();
            } else {
                listener.serverError(
                            "Unable to establish PPP connection");
            }
            break;

        case PPPEvent.CLOSED:
            if (isUp) {
                ppp.removeInterface("ppp0");
                ppp.down();
                isUp = false;
            }
            try {
```

```
                    // Sleep before recycling ppp connection
                    Thread.sleep(1000);
                } catch (InterruptedException ie) {}
                ppp.open();
                break;

            default:
                break;
        }
    }
}
```

The state machine as implemented in Listing 7.13 is designed to run continuously, retrying if transient errors occur. Every time a connection is successfully established (the UP state is reached), the error count is reset to 0. Unless a maximum retry count (maxRetries) is reached, the daemon continues to run. Once the error count threshold is reached, the listener is notified that a persistent problem is preventing the daemon from establishing PPP connections. The listener can choose to either stop the daemon entirely by invoking stopDaemon or take some action to fix the problem and recycle the server by stopping and restarting it. The problem may be with the modem or phone line and may require some human intervention.

7.6 MANAGING THE PPP DATA LINK

The PPP daemon we implemented in the previous section maintained a reference to an instance of a class that implemented the PPPDataLink interface. This reference is used by the server to control the data link. Now we'll create the PPPDataLink interface shown in Listing 7.14. Both of the link management classes we will create in this section will implement this interface.

Listing 7.14 PPPDataLink

```
import javax.comm.SerialPort;

public interface PPPDataLink {
    public SerialPort getPort();
    public void initializeLink() throws DataLinkException;
}
```

The initializeLink method is used to perform any specific setup required to use that data link. After the link has been successfully initialized, the PPP daemon invokes getPort to acquire a reference to the link's serial port. This reference is transferred to the native PPP implementation and is used for all PPP communication. Other than during construction and execution of the initializeLink method, the data link classes should not access the serial port.

Because data link errors can occur asynchronously and without the knowledge of the underlying native PPP implementation, an object that owns the data link needs a mechanism for notifying PPPDaemon that an error has occurred. The most common example of a link error is the modem hanging up. This results in loss of carrier detect from the modem. We'll discuss this further in Section 7.6.2. The interface DataLinkListener shown in Listing 7.15 defines the method dataLinkError that will be invoked by the object controlling the data link upon detection of an unrecoverable error.

Listing 7.15   DataLinkListener

```
public interface DataLinkListener {
    public void dataLinkError(String error);
}
```

When the listener's dataLinkError (see Listing 7.16) is invoked, it will typically set some internal state and call the close method on the PPP object. The internal state allows the CLOSED event code to determine why the CLOSED event was generated. In the case of a link error, it will invoke the down method on the PPP object, freeing the serial port and forcing a transition to the START state. This provides a clean way to reset the link and hopefully clear the condition that generated the error.

Listing 7.16   dataLinkError

```
public void dataLinkError(String error) {
    System.err.println("Error in data link:"+error);
    ++linkErrors;
    ppp.close();
}
```

In our example PPP server, we maintain a retry count and put an upper limit on the number of retries that can be caused by a persistent error in either the data link or the underlying PPP object. The retry count is reset to 0 after every successful transition to the UP state.

7.6.1   The Serial Link

All PPP traffic flows over a serial port. The serial port may or may not have a modem attached. Now we'll create a class named PPPSerialLink that provides functionality that is common to both hard-wired serial and modem configurations. PPPSerialLink is shown in Listing 7.17. Notice first that PPPSerialLink implements the PPPDataLink interface providing implementations for the initializeLink and getPort methods. These are the only public methods needed by PPPDaemon to manage the data link.

During construction, `PPPSerialLink` creates a new serial port object and uses that object to configure the physical port. In this example, we set the port for 8 data bits, 1 stop bit, and no parity. This is a very common configuration and shouldn't cause us any problems in communicating with other modems or directly with another serial port. We also select the use of RTS/CTS (Request to Send/Clear to Send) hardware flow control (see Section 3.2.2), assuming that the underlying physical port has support for the necessary hardware flow control lines.[4] Finally, the constructor creates input and output streams for reading from and writing to the serial port, respectively. Note that this class could be made more flexible by adding parameters to the constructor that allowed for the selection of either hardware or software flow control as well as other data transfer settings.

Listing 7.17   PPPSerialLink

```
import javax.comm.*;
import java.io.*;

public class PPPSerialLink implements PPPDataLink {
    protected DataLinkListener listener;
    protected SerialPort sp;
    protected InputStream in;
    protected OutputStream out;

    public PPPSerialLink(String portName, int speed,
                         DataLinkListener listener)
        throws DataLinkException {

        this.listener = listener;
        try {
            // Create and initialize serial port
            sp = (SerialPort)
                CommPortIdentifier.getPortIdentifier(portName).open(
                                                "PPPDataLink", 5000);

            sp.setSerialPortParams(speed, SerialPort.DATABITS_8,
                                   SerialPort.STOPBITS_1,
                                   SerialPort.PARITY_NONE);

            TINIOS.setRTSCTSFlowControlEnable(0, true);
            sp.setFlowControlMode(SerialPort.FLOWCONTROL_RTSCTS_IN |
                                  SerialPort.FLOWCONTROL_RTSCTS_OUT);

            in = sp.getInputStream();
            out = sp.getOutputStream();
        } catch (Exception e) {
```

4. If your TINI hardware does not support the hardware handshake lines on `serial0`, remove the statements that configure flow control or use a serial port that supports RTS/CTS flow control.

```
                throw new DataLinkException("Error configuring serial port"+
                                    e.getMessage());
        }
    }

    public void initializeLink() throws DataLinkException {
    }

    public SerialPort getPort() {
        return sp;
    }
}
```

If the constructor fails to properly acquire ownership or properly initialize the specified serial port for any reason, it throws a DataLinkException. Typical causes of failure would be that the port is already owned by another process or it doesn't support one of the selected options.

A PPPSerialLink object doesn't need to do much after it has initialized the port. The initializeLink method simply returns because the link is always ready for data traffic.[5] In the next section, when we add modem support, we'll have to do a bit of work in initializeLink.

The PPPSerialLink class implements the functionality needed to provide PPP communication over a hard-wired serial link. This type of connectivity is useful as a quick and simple mechanism for testing PPP code written for TINI. No modem is required in this configuration, and it allows for a faster connection because you don't have to wait for normal modem delays such as dialing and answering the phone. In practice, it is probably most useful for direct communication between TINI and a hand-held PDA that supports PPP connections such as the Palm Pilot or Visor.

7.6.2 Controlling the Modem

Most practical uses of PPP on TINI require the use of an external serial modem. Ultimately, if an application similar to DataLogger is deployed in an Ethernet challenged location, its only connection to a TCP/IP network could be using the public phone network. A hardware configuration of TINI plus a serial modem allow applications to either accept or make dial-up network connections with remote clients or servers.

Since all communication with the modem will be over a serial port, we can create the class to manage modem communications as a subclass of PPPSerialLink, defined in the previous section. The class PPPModemLink is shown

---

5. If you're using Windows 2000 or NT for your direct link testing, you will need to modify the initializeLink method to wait for the string "CLIENT" and respond with the string "CLIENTSERVER."

in Listing 7.18. Upon construction PPPModemLink invokes its superclass's constructor to acquire and initialize the serial port. It also creates a ModemCommand object to manage sending commands to and receiving responses from the modem. The ModemCommand class is described later in this section.

Listing 7.18   PPPModemLink

```
import javax.comm.*;
import java.io.*;
import java.util.TooManyListenersException;

public class PPPModemLink extends PPPSerialLink
   implements SerialPortEventListener {
   private ModemCommand mc;

   public PPPModemLink(String portName, int speed,
                       DataLinkListener listener)
      throws DataLinkException {

      super(portName, speed, listener);
      mc = new ModemCommand(sp, in, out);
      try {
         sp.addEventListener(this);
      } catch (TooManyListenersException tmle) {
         throw new DataLinkException(
                     "Unable to register for serial events");
      }
   }
   ...
   public void serialEvent(SerialPortEvent ev) {
      if ((ev.getEventType() == SerialPortEvent.CD) &&
                              !ev.getNewValue()) {

         listener.dataLinkError("Lost carrier detect");
      }
   }
}
```

PPPModemLink implements the SerialPortEventListener interface. In this case we're specifically interested in the SerialPortEvent.CD (Carrier Detect) event because we need to be notified if and when the modem hangs up. When the modem hangs up, the CD signal transitions from high (carrier present) to low (carrier not present). If this happens, the serialEvent method is invoked by the serial port event daemon notification thread. serialEvent checks the event type to see if it is a carrier detect change event. All other events are ignored. If the returned event value is false, this signals that the modem has indeed hung up, and serialEvent invokes the DataLinkListener's (PPPDaemon in this case) dataLinkError method, notifying the listener that the data link is no longer valid.

The PPP daemon then closes the underlying PPP connection and frees any resources that were consumed.

Initializing the modem link involves the following three steps:

1. Reset the modem.
2. Wait for a ring.
3. Answer the phone.

Both the `initializeLink` and `resetModem` methods are shown in Listing 7.19. The modem reset is initiated by dropping the DTR (Data Terminal Ready) line low, delaying for a couple of seconds, and then raising DTR back high. After toggling DTR, `resetModem` sends the string "AT\r" to the modem and waits for a response string of "OK." If the expected response is received, `resetModem` returns normally. If the response is not received within the specified time-out value—six seconds in this case—a `DataLinkException` is thrown by the `sendCommand` method of the `ModemCommand` class. This exception is allowed to propagate up the call stack to notify the method that invoked `initializeLink` of the failure to initialize the modem.

Listing 7.19   initializeLink and resetModem

```
public void initializeLink() throws DataLinkException {
    resetModem();
    mc.receiveMatch("RING", null, 0);
    mc.sendCommand("ATA\r", "CONNECT", 25);
}

private void resetModem() throws DataLinkException {
    // Clear RTS and DTR
    sp.setDTR(false);
    sp.setRTS(false);

    try {
        Thread.sleep(2000);
    } catch (InterruptedException ie) {}

    // Set RTS and DTR
    sp.setDTR(true);
    sp.setRTS(true);

    try {
        Thread.sleep(2000);
    } catch (InterruptedException ie) {}

    // Sync modem to serial port baud rate
    mc.sendCommand("AT\r", "OK", 6);
}
```

Note that depending on the specific modem you're using, you may have to do more or different work in initializeLink. For example, the modems used to test this class all autobaud by default when the "AT\r" string is transmitted immediately after the DTR reset. If your modem initializes to some predefined hardcoded speed after a DTR reset, initializeLink would have to transmit a command at the predefined speed, setting the new desired speed. Other commands may also be required to correctly reset and initialize the modem.

After successfully resetting the modem, initializeLink waits for a ring. When the modem detects a ring on the phone line, it transmits the string "RING." initializeLink blocks indefinitely by specifying a time-out value of 0, waiting for this string. Once it receives the string, it sends the "ATA" command to the modem, instructing it to answer the incoming call. After answering the phone, the modem will respond with the string "CONNECT." We allow a 25-second time-out for the modem to answer the phone and respond because this is a time-consuming process. It should typically complete within 10 or 15 seconds of ring detection. After receiving the "CONNECT" string from the modem, the communication channel is fully established and initializeLink returns normally.

The ModemCommand class, partially shown in Listing 7.20, is a utility class used by PPPModemLink to handle the details of serial communication with the modem. It is passed references to the serial port as well as serial port input and output streams for the actual data transfer. ModemCommand provides these two public methods.

```
public void sendCommand(String command, String response, int timeout)
    throws DataLinkException
public void receiveMatch(String match, String response, int timeout)
    throws DataLinkException
```

The sendCommand method converts command to a byte array and transmits the result over the serial port to the attached modem. After transmitting the command string, sendCommand invokes the waitForResponse method (described below) to wait for the modem to transmit a response equal (ignoring case) to the value supplied in response. If no response is expected from the modem, null can be supplied for the response String. In this case, sendCommand returns immediately after transmitting the command. The receiveMatch command has the opposite sense. It first waits for a transmission from the modem equal (again ignoring case) to the supplied value of match and then transmits a response to the modem. If nothing is to be transmitted to the modem after receipt of the desired match String, null is passed for the response. Both methods throw DataLinkException in the event of a time-out waiting for the desired response.

Listing 7.20 ModemCommand

```java
import javax.comm.*;
import java.io.*;

public class ModemCommand {
    private SerialPort sp;
    private InputStream in;
    private OutputStream out;

    public ModemCommand(SerialPort sp, InputStream in,
                        OutputStream out) {
        this.sp = sp;
        this.in = in;
        this.out = out;
    }

    public void sendCommand(String command, String response,
                            int timeout)
        throws DataLinkException {

        try {
            // Transmit the command
            out.write(command.getBytes());
        } catch (IOException ioe) {
            ioe.printStackTrace();
            throw new DataLinkException(
                            "Error sending command to modem");
        }

        waitForMatch(response, timeout);
    }

    public void receiveMatch(String match, String response, int timeout)
        throws DataLinkException {

        try {
            waitForMatch(match, timeout);
            if ((response != null) && (response.length() > 0)) {
                out.write(response.getBytes());
            }
        } catch (IOException ioe) {
            ioe.printStackTrace();
            throw new DataLinkException(
                            "IO Error receiving a match to:"+match);
        }
    }

    ...
}
```

The waitForMatch method, shown in Listing 7.21, takes a String used for the desired pattern match. The pattern match is performed in a case insensitive manner. It also takes an integer number of seconds used as a time-out value, where a value of 0 seconds is used to specify an infinite time-out. It uses both serial port receive time-outs and thresholds to control the reading of data and manage a timer. The receive time-out is set to 100 milliseconds and the threshold to the number of bytes equal to the length of the match String. The overall time that has elapsed is tracked using System.currentTimeMillis.

Listing 7.21   waitForMatch

```
private void waitForMatch(String match, int timeout)
    throws DataLinkException {
    try {
        sp.enableReceiveTimeout(100);
        sp.enableReceiveThreshold(match.length());

        byte[] mb = new byte[match.length()];
        long timer = 0;
        if (timeout > 0) {
            // Time out when timer > currentTimeMillis
            timer = timeout*1000+System.currentTimeMillis();
        }

        StringBuffer modemSpew = new StringBuffer();
        while ((timer == 0) || (System.currentTimeMillis() < timer)) {
            int count = in.read(mb);
            if (count > 0) {
                modemSpew.append((new String(mb,0,count)).toUpperCase());
                if (modemSpew.toString().indexOf(
                                        match.toUpperCase()) >= 0) {
                    return;
                }
            }
        }

        throw new DataLinkException("Timed out waiting for match:"+
                                match);
    } catch (Exception e) {
        e.printStackTrace();
        throw new DataLinkException("IO Error receiving a match to:"+
                                match);
    }
}
```

The trick here is that the modem might send other unwanted bytes of information in the same stream of data that has the pattern that we're trying to match. To deal with this problem, waitForMatch reads all serial bytes and stores them in a StringBuffer. Each time data is available, the new bytes are appended to the end of the `StringBuffer`. To check for a match, the `StringBuffer` is converted to a `String`, and the `indexOf` method is used to check to see if the desired response is contained anywhere within the resulting `String`. If a match is found, `waitForMatch` returns normally. Otherwise, it performs another blocking read until either the number of bytes equal to the length of the `match` `String` is available or until 100 milliseconds elapses. If no match is found within the specified overall time-out, a `DataLinkException` is thrown. The `DataLinkException` propagates up the call stack eventually notifying the PPP daemon of the modem's failure to respond.

7.7 ADDING THE PPP DAEMON TO DATALOGGER

Now that we have an implementation of a PPP daemon and the supporting data link classes, we can enhance the `DataLogger` class to accept network connections over both PPP and Ethernet interfaces.

Listing 7.22 shows the additions and modifications made to the `DataLogger` class for the purpose of adding PPP daemon support. The first change to notice is that `DataLogger` creates and starts a new instance of `PPPDaemon` on construction. The other change to `DataLogger` is that it now implements the `PPPDaemonListener` (Listing 7.11) interface and therefore provides implementations for the `daemonError` and `isValidUser` methods. The `daemonError` method is invoked when a persistent error is preventing `PPPDaemon` from establishing PPP connections. As implemented below, `daemonError` stops the PPP server. However, `DataLogger` continues to run, allowing connections over the Ethernet network interface only.

Listing 7.22 DataLogger changes

```
class DataLogger extends Thread implements PPPDaemonListener {
    ...
    PPPDaemon pppd;
    private String name;
    private String password;

    DataLogger(int samples, int delay, String name, String password)
        throws PPPException, LoggingException {

        // Set authentication information
        this.name = name;
        this.password = password;
        ...
        // Create a server to manage PPP dial-up requests
        PPPDaemon pppd = new PPPDaemon(this, "serial0", 19200);
        pppd.startDaemon();
    }
```

```java
    public void daemonError(String error) {
        System.err.println("Error in PPP server:"+error);
        pppd.stopDaemon();
    }

    public boolean isValidUser(String name, String password) {
        return (this.name.equals(name) &&
                this.password.equals(password));
    }

    ...

    public static void main(String[] args) {
        System.out.println("Starting DataLogger ...");
        if (args.length != 4) {
            System.out.println(
                "Usage: java DataLogger samples delay username password");
            System.exit(1);
        }
        ...
        try {
            (new DataLogger(samples, delay, args[2], args[3])).start();
        } catch (Exception e) {
            ...
        }
    }
}
```

Since DataLogger is now responsible for validating login requests, we'll add instance fields to store a user name and password. Rather than choose arbitrary hard-coded strings to use for validation of login information, we'll modify the main method to require the user name and password on the command line. We'll also modify the constructor as well to accept login information and store it in the name and password private instance fields. These strings will be used as a direct comparison to the login information passed to the isValidUser method. Note that the login scheme that we're supporting in this example with our simple user name and password match is PAP (Password Authentication Protocol). PAP was chosen because it is the most straightforward to implement. The main goal of this example is to focus on the mechanics of writing multihomed network servers rather than getting bogged down with security details.

7.8 TESTING THE ENTIRE APPLICATION

Now our remote data logging example is multihomed. That is to say that it will accept TCP connections (sockets) from multiple network interfaces—specifically, the PPP and Ethernet interfaces. We tested DataLogger over Ethernet only using the DataLoggerClient developed in Section 7.4. Testing our new PPP functionality is going to take a little more work. However, we can use `DataLoggerClient` without modification for testing both interfaces simultaneously.

The test setup tests the full dial-up networking capabilities provided by `PPPDaemon` using analog modems and a phone line simulator. However, you can also test `DataLogger`'s PPP support using a hard-wired serial connection. The test configuration used here includes the following equipment.

- A TINI board—running the DataLogger server
- A Windows 2000 machine—dial-up networking client
- A Linux machine—Ethernet networking client
- Two analog modems—one attached to the Windows 2000 PC and the other attached to serial port 0 of the TINI
- The humidity sensing circuit detailed in Section 4.4.3

A diagram of a sample test configuration is shown in Figure 7.2. This is one of the smallest test configurations that can be used to test the full networking capabilities of the `DataLogger` application. TINI's network interface IP addresses are 192.168.0.15 and 192.168.1.1 for Ethernet and PPP, respectively.

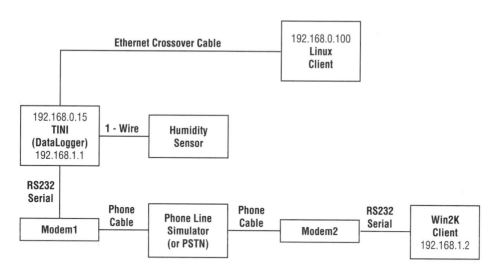

Figure 7.2 Sample test configuration

To keep the necessary equipment to a minimum, the Linux (Ethernet) client connects directly to TINI using an Ethernet crossover cable. The Linux box and TINI could also be connected using straight-through cable with an Ethernet hub. The PPP connection is made using two analog modems on either side of a phone line simulator. If two different phone lines are available, you can of course use the public phone network instead.

If we add a couple of debug statements (see Listing 7.23) to `DataLogger`'s run method, it will display connection information, including both the remote client's IP address and TINI's local interface IP address.

Listing 7.23   Adding debug statements

```
public void run() {
    ...
    while (true) {
        ...
        s = ss.accept();
        ...
        System.out.println("New client:" + s.toString());
        System.out.println("Local interface:" + s.getLocalAddress());
        ...
    }
}
```

Now we can launch `DataLogger`, supplying the sample count, sample rate, and client authentication information as command line parameters.

```
TINI /> java DataLogger.tini 60 120 ducto kid
Starting DataLogger ...
```

To test the PPP interface, you'll need to create a new dial-up network connection. The details on how this is accomplished are platform specific and are not covered here. After you've created the new dial-up connection, you can use it to manually connect to the TINI or optionally use whatever dial-on demand capability is provided on the client OS. Regardless, once you initiate the connection, the following sequence of events occurs.

1. Client modem dials TINI's modem.
2. TINI's modem answers the incoming call.
3. PPP option negotiation begins.
4. Authentication information is transmitted from the remote peer to TINI.
5. IP addresses of TINI and remote peer are established.

At this point, the communication link is ready for network traffic. After successfully establishing the link, executing the "`ipconfig -x`" command at the slush prompt will produce the output shown here. Note that the Ethernet and loopback interfaces are not shown for brevity.

```
...
Interface 2 is active.
```

```
Name          : ppp0
Type          : Point-to-Point Protocol
IP Address    : 192.168.1.1
Subnet Mask   : 255.255.255.0
Gateway       : 0.0.0.0
...
```

A new network interface has been added to the system as a result of the PPPDaemon invoking addInterface on its PPP object after the modem link was established. The local address is set to the value specified during construction of PPPDaemon, and the interface name is the same as supplied by addInterface. The "ppp0" interface will remain in the system until removeInterface is invoked in response to a PPP CLOSED event.

Now that both the Ethernet (eth0) and PPP (ppp0) interfaces are active, we can connect to the server over both using the DataLoggerClient.

Output from launching the Linux (Ethernet) Client

```
java DataLoggerClient 192.168.0.15
Total readings=2
Entry 0:Fri Feb 02 14:31:06 CST 2001, RH=27.738698340362145, TEMP=23.40625
Entry 1:Fri Feb 02 14:33:07 CST 2001, RH=27.402815524359628, TEMP=23.46875
```

Output from launching the Win2K (PPP) Client

```
java DataLoggerClient 192.168.1.1
Total readings=2
Entry 0:Fri Feb 02 14:31:06 CST 2001, RH=27.738698340362145, TEMP=23.40625
Entry 1:Fri Feb 02 14:33:07 CST 2001, RH=27.402815524359628, TEMP=23.46875
```

DataLogger *(TINI) output*

```
New client:Socket[addr=192.168.0.100/192.168.0.100,port=1056,
                   localport=5588]
Local interface:192.168.0.15/192.168.0.15
New client:Socket[addr=192.168.1.2/192.168.1.2,port=1949,localport=5588]
Local interface:192.168.1.1/192.168.1.1
```

From the output above we can see that DataLoggerClient was launched on both the Linux and Win2K client at about the same time and within a few minutes of starting the DataLogger application on TINI. Each client receives the same log data, but each connects to the server using a different IP address. Notice, however, that the local port value displayed in the TINI output is DataLogger's SERVER_PORT number (5588) for both connections. When the Linux box establishes its connection, DataLogger displays the remote client's IP address (192.168.0.100) and the IP address of its own local Ethernet interface (192.168.0.15). When the Win2K client connects the client (192.168.1.2) and server (192.168.1.1) the IP addresses displayed are those selected in

PPPDaemon's constructor during initialization of the PPP object. In the Ethernet case, both IP addresses were statically configured outside of program control. In the PPP case, however, the IP addresses were set programatically by PPPDaemon.

Further improvements to the DataLogger application are certainly possible. For example, we could improve its flexibility by allowing more parameters to be supplied on the command line or perhaps read from a configuration file. Some examples of additional useful parameters are serial port number, serial port data rate, and client and server IP addresses to be used by the PPP network interface. We could also modify PPPDaemon to support multiple PPP interfaces. This requires using multiple serial ports to allow two different clients to establish dial-up connections simultaneously.

CHAPTER 8 Parallel I/O

For our purposes, we'll use the term *Parallel I/O* to refer to communication with devices interfaced to the microcontroller's address and data busses. The parallel data interface can be thought of as a catchall, since it can be used for interfacing with a very broad range of devices from LCDs to external memory devices or even other microcontrollers. TINI hardware implementations, such as the TBM390, communicate with the real-time clock and Ethernet controller over the controller's bus. The parallel I/O bus is very fast and very flexible. However, this flexibility often comes at the cost of additional interface circuitry such as octal buffers, latches, and address decoders.

This, more than any other chapter, requires some comfort with hardware and device driver software concepts. To fully understand this section the reader must, at a minimum, be able to study a simple schematic to determine the address range used to communicate with attached devices. Despite the complexities of the parallel bus interface, the TINI API provides a very simple abstraction, known as a DataPort, to communicate with devices attached to the bus. Given the address range and device speeds, a pure software engineer can focus on code and write Java drivers for attached devices without fully understanding the details of the underlying hardware design.

This chapter begins by describing TINI's parallel bus interface, providing an operational description of the relevant bus signals. A memory map, used to access the microcontroller's entire address space, is presented. This is followed by a description of how a Java application can communicate with devices interfaced to the parallel bus. The chapter concludes with a couple of detailed examples aimed at solidifying both the hardware and software details of communicating with parallel devices on TINI.

8.1   TINI'S PARALLEL BUS

TINI's parallel bus is used, at a minimum, for interfacing with external memory chips for code and data storage. Peripheral devices such as an Ethernet controller and real-time clock are also accessed via the parallel bus. The block diagram shown in Figure 8.1 presents a fairly generic configuration for interfacing external devices to the bus. As their names suggest, the address bus specifies the target address of the read or write operations, while the data bus transfers the binary data to and from the device. The combination of certain control signals and possibly certain address lines can be used in conjunction with decoding logic to act as an enable signal for the peripheral. The purpose of the enable signal is to ensure that only bus operations intended for the device are actually seen by the device. Note that some devices, including many memory chips, can be interfaced directly to the bus without using any decode logic. (See Section 8.3.2 for an example of interfacing a memory device to the parallel bus.)

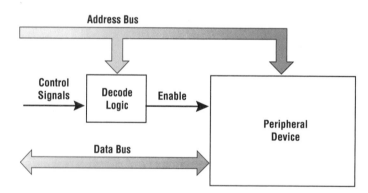

Figure 8.1   Interfacing to the controller bus

An important point to be made here is that Figure 8.1 shows the address and data bus signals connected directly to the external device. This is often appropriate. However, depending on the total number of devices on the parallel bus, either or both the address and data signals may require external buffering to ensure reliable system operation.[1] Buffers are chips that provide isolation from the capaci-

---

1. See *http://www.ibutton.com/TINI/dstini1.pdf* for bus loading specifications for the TBM390.

tive loading of bus interfaced peripherals. Whether or not buffering is required, and how to buffer the bus if it is required, are design specific issues.

The signals that comprise the microcontroller's parallel bus can be grouped into the following categories.

- Data—bidirectional data bus
- Address—unidirectional address bus, driven by the controller
- Control—provides signals for distinguishing between read and write operations as well as device (or chip) selection

All data, address, and control signals are listed, along with brief descriptions, in Table 8.1.[2] The data bus (D0–D7) is an 8-bit bidirectional bus. All data transfer occurs on this bus, including code fetches from flash ROM, data fetches from static RAM, and read and write operations to bus interfaced peripherals. External devices are addressed using the 20-bit address bus (A0–A19) along with one of eight predecoded "chip select" signals. The 20-bit address bus provides a 1-megabyte address range. However, this range is extended by the eight chip select lines that each decode a separate megabyte of address space. The chip selects come in two flavors: chip enables (CEs) and peripheral chip enables (PCEs). There are four CE signals ($\overline{CE0}$–$\overline{CE3}$) and four PCE signals ($\overline{PCE0}$–$\overline{PCE3}$).

Table 8.1   Bus control signals

Signal Designator	Full Signal Name	Description
D0–D7	Data Bus	8-bit wide bidirectional data bus
A0–A19	Address Bus	20-bit wide address bus
$\overline{CE0}$–$\overline{CE3}$	Chip Enables	Chip enable lines are used to select memory or attached peripherals. Code fetches must occur from memory chips enabled by one of these signals.
$\overline{PCE0}$–$\overline{PCE3}$	Peripheral Chip enables	Peripheral chip enable lines are commonly used to enable memories for purposes of data storage only. No native code can be fetched from memory chips enabled by these signals.

continues

---

2. A complete description of all of the microcontroller, including the signals described in this table, can be found in the DS80C390 data sheet at *http://www.dalsemi.com/ datasheets/pdfs/80c390.pdf.*

Table 8.1 Bus control signals (continued)

Signal Designator	Full Signal Name	Description
$\overline{\text{PSEN}}$	Program Store Enable	Strobe line used to control code fetches (reads) from external memory devices enabled by CE lines. It can also be used for data fetches.
$\overline{\text{RD}}$	Read Strobe	Read strobe line used for data fetches from memory and other peripheral devices enabled by PCE lines
$\overline{\text{WR}}$	Write Strobe	Strobe line used for data writes to memory and other peripheral devices
DRST	Device Reset	Pin 3.4 of the microcontroller. This is not a formal signal defined in the parallel bus. On TINI it is used to reset external devices.

The memory map, shown in Figure 8.2, is split into two separate 4-megabyte ranges. The CE space contains all memory chips used as program and data storage for the runtime environment. It also contains a 1-megabyte peripheral area for addressing high-speed devices that support a parallel bus interface. A more detailed memory map of the CE space is contained in Figure 1.4.

The primary difference between the CE and PCE signals is that the PCE signals can only be used for data reads and writes. In other words, the microcontroller cannot fetch *native* code from memory devices that are enabled using the PCE signals. This is why the flash ROM and static RAM used by the runtime environment are accessed using the CE signals.

The CE addresses correspond to true physical addresses in the microcontroller's memory map. The starting address of memory enabled by PCE signals is somewhat arbitrary because it's a virtual address mapping. Real PCE addresses actually overlap CE addresses. This requires the microcontroller to change memory maps when transitioning from accessing devices mapped into CE space to accessing devices mapped into PCE space. Applications accessing devices in PCE space don't need to worry about the details of this address map swapping because they are managed automatically by the parallel I/O driver. However, the system designer should be aware that there is overhead associated with swapping between CE and PCE memory maps. Data transfer rates on block move operations are about three times faster when only CE mapped devices are involved.

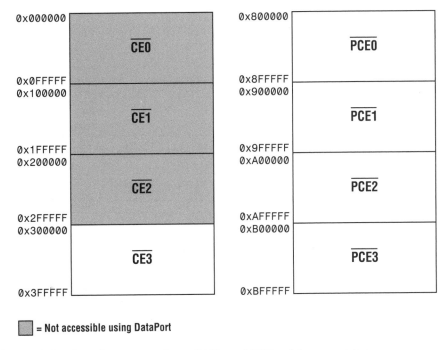

= Not accessible using DataPort

Figure 8.2   DataPort mapping of CE and PCE address ranges

TINI's runtime environment does not reserve any of the PCE space for peripheral devices. This implies that all four PCE signals, and the four megabytes of address space they control, are wide open for system designers. However, many high-speed peripheral devices are mapped into the $\overline{\text{CE3}}$ address space because it can be accessed more efficiently by the microcontroller. If no devices are mapped into PCE space, the four PCE pins can be used as general purpose port pins. The system designer is free to use the peripheral area either for interfacing hardware directly to the microcontroller's parallel bus or as general purpose TTL I/O but not both. The topic of accessing the microcontroller's port pins is covered in Chapter 9.

8.2 THE DATAPORT CLASS

Access to the parallel I/O bus is accomplished using the DataPort class defined in the com.dalsemi.system package. A DataPort object provides a thin, but efficient, encapsulation of the parallel bus. It allows an application to control bus timings and read data from and write data to the bus.

```
public DataPort(int address)
```

The address parameter of DataPort's constructor specifies the initial address for I/O operations. The address must be in either of the following ranges.

- [0x300000–0x3FFFFF]—$\overline{\text{CE3}}$ space
- [0x800000–0xBFFFFF]—$\overline{\text{PCE0}}$–$\overline{\text{PCE3}}$ space

Note that only the last megabyte of CE space, enabled by $\overline{\text{CE3}}$, can be used as a DataPort address. The lower three megabytes, enabled by $\overline{\text{CE0}}$–$\overline{\text{CE2}}$, are reserved for code and data storage and are therefore owned by the operating system. While all addresses in $\overline{\text{CE3}}$ space are legal, two address ranges that should be avoided are those consumed by the Ethernet controller and real-time clock.

- Ethernet controller address range—[0x300000–0x307FFF]
- Real-Time clock—0x310000

A DataPort object can be used to transfer data to and from these devices, though it is not recommended. The operating system[3] assumes that it has exclusive access to these devices and their respective address ranges. However, it is possible that some sophisticated networking applications may benefit from querying certain status registers in the Ethernet controller.

Note that DataPort's constructor does not throw an exception when passed an invalid address. A DataPort object can be initialized with any address and the address can be changed at any time using the setAddress method.

```
public void setAddress(int address)
```

However, any attempt to read from or write to an invalid address will result in an exception being thrown. Parallel bus read and write operations are discussed in the next section.

8.2.1   Data Transfer

For transferring data to and from peripherals interfaced to the parallel bus, the DataPort class provides read and write methods similar to those defined in java.io.InputStream and java.io.OutputStream. After a DataPort object has been properly initialized, the following read and write methods can be used to transfer a single byte of data to or from an attached device.

```
public int read() throws IllegalAddressException
public void write(int value) throws IllegalAddressException
```

---

3. Specifically the Ethernet driver and the clock driver.

The read method returns an integer value between 0 and 255 representing the byte fetched during the bus read operation. The write method writes the least significant eight bits, specified in the value parameter, to the data bus. The value parameter is treated as unsigned and should be between 0 and 255.

When transferring multiple bytes using a DataPort object, the following read and write methods are much more efficient than their single-byte equivalents. In the remainder of the chapter we will refer to the methods below as block read and write methods.

```
public int read(byte[] arr, int off, int len)
    throws IllegalAddressException
public void write(byte[] arr, int off, int len)
    throws IllegalAddressException
```

The read method takes a byte array, an offset into the array and a byte count as parameters. Data is read from the parallel bus and stored in arr starting at the offset specified by the off parameter. A total of len bytes is read from the bus. The read method returns the number of bytes read. If read returns normally (without throwing an IllegalAddressException), the return value will be equal to the number of bytes requested by the len parameter. The write method takes an identical list of parameters but reverses the direction of the data transfer. In this case, bytes are fetched from the array and are written to the parallel bus.

Both the block and single-byte read and write methods will throw an IllegalAddressException if the address specified during construction of the DataPort object (or later using the setAddress method) is not in either of the valid ranges specified previously. The IllegalAddressException class is also defined in the com.dalsemi.system package.

Depending on the speed of the attached device, parallel I/O can be the fastest form of data transfer supported by the TINI platform. With current implementations of TINI hardware, speeds of up to 170 kilobytes per second when accessing devices in PCE space and up to 650 kilobytes per second when accessing devices in CE space are achievable on large block move[4] operations. In contrast, moving data using the single-byte read and write methods results in transfer rates of about 750 bytes per second, a difference of nearly three orders of magnitude!

8.2.2 Memory Access Modes

DataPort provides two addressing modes that can be used with the read and write methods: FIFO (First In First Out) mode and sequential memory mode. In FIFO mode, the address is not altered when performing block read or write operations. So, for example, if a 32-kilobyte block write is performed using a DataPort

---

4. In this context, a "large block move" refers to moving several kilobytes of data, contained within a byte array, to a parallel device with a single method invocation.

object in FIFO mode, all 32,768 writes will occur at the same address. In sequential memory mode, the address is automatically incremented following each bus read or write operation. After a block `read` or `write` method returns, the address is restored to its value prior to the operation.

The addressing mode is only relevant when using the block `read` and `write` methods. The single-byte `read` and `write` methods don't cause the address to be incremented. This implies that performing successive single-byte operations results in behavior that, from an addressing perspective, is identical to FIFO mode. So, if sequential memory mode is desired, the application must increment the address between single-byte reads or writes by using the `setAddress` method. In most cases, an application that must perform parallel I/O in sequential memory mode should be using the more efficient block `read` and `write` methods.

The `setFIFOMode` method is used to change the addressing mode for block read and write operations.

```
public void setFIFOMode(boolean useFIFOAccess)
public boolean getFIFOMode()
```

Invoking `setFIFOMode` with the boolean value of `true` for the `useFIFOAccess` parameter will force successive block reads and writes to use FIFO mode addressing. When a `DataPort` object is initialized, the addressing mode defaults to sequential memory mode. The addressing mode can be changed at any time. The current mode can be queried using `getFIFOMode`. This method returns true if the `DataPort` object is using the FIFO addressing mode and false if it is using sequential memory mode. Examples of parallel I/O using both addressing modes are presented in Section 8.3.

8.2.3 Controlling Bus Timing

To accommodate different logic families and peripherals with varying speeds, the `DataPort` class provides a method for specifying the number of stretch cycles[5] to be used for bus access. Stretch cycles are used to increase data setup and hold times for bus accesses. One stretch cycle adds exactly one machine cycle to the execution time of a bus access instruction. In the case of a TINI hardware implementation executing at a clock rate of 36.864 MHz, one machine cycle requires approximately 110 nanoseconds. This implies that each stretch cycle adds 110 nanoseconds to the total time required for each read or write operation.

The valid ranges of stretch cycles are [0–3] and [7–10].

The low range is fine for most CMOS logic families and medium- to high-speed peripherals. However, there are some slow devices, such as certain LCDs, that may require a large number of stretch cycles. For these devices the high

---

5. Stretch cycles are also commonly referred to as wait states.

range may be appropriate. The number of stretch cycles is specified using the setStretchCycles method.

```
public void setStretchCycles(byte stretch) throws IllegalArgumentException
public int getStretchCycles()
```

Each valid stretch cycle value is represented by a public constant that is defined in the DataPort class. If values outside of either of those ranges are specified, setStretchCycles throws an IllegalArgumentException. The number of stretch cycles being used by the DataPort object can be queried at any time using the getStretchCycles method.

The stretch cycle count can be changed at any time. The change will apply to successive read and write operations. However, in most cases, the stretch cycle count only needs to be specified once. The default stretch cycle count is 0, which assumes that attached peripherals have fast bus access times. Determining the correct number of stretch cycles requires analysis of both the microcontroller's bus timing diagrams[6] as well as the peripheral's timing diagrams.

8.3   PARALLEL I/O EXAMPLES

This section contains a couple of examples to help clarify the somewhat technical nature of managing devices interfaced to the parallel bus. Both the hardware and software portions of each example are presented. A fair amount of time is spent describing the hardware configuration for each example. These descriptions are aimed at software engineers with an only modest hardware background and will therefore be rather obvious to hardware designers.

8.3.1   Additional TTL I/O

Many embedded applications use microcontroller port pins as general purpose digital I/O for monitoring and controlling external hardware. (Controlling microcontroller port pins is the subject of Chapter 9.) However, on TINI, many of the microcontroller's port pins are dedicated to the purpose of addressing a relatively large amount of memory. For many embedded applications this doesn't leave enough general purpose digital I/O. The example presented in this section solves this problem by creating eight additional digital inputs and eight digital outputs, interfaced to the microcontroller's parallel bus using a few commonly available CMOS chips.

The circuitry, shown in Figure 8.3, uses an octal latch (74HC574) to provide eight output lines and an octal buffer (74HC541) for eight input lines. Each input

---

6.   The bus timings are provided in the microcontroller's data sheet, which can be viewed online at *http://www.dalsemi.com/datasheets/pdfs/80c390.pdf.*

is pulled to V_{cc} using a 10-k ohm resistor. Both chips are decoded in the 1-mega-byte space controlled by $\overline{CE3}$. One important requirement for this circuit is that the I/O lines occupy an address range distinct from the Ethernet controller and real-time clock, both of which are mapped within the $\overline{CE3}$ address space in the ranges listed in Section 8.2.

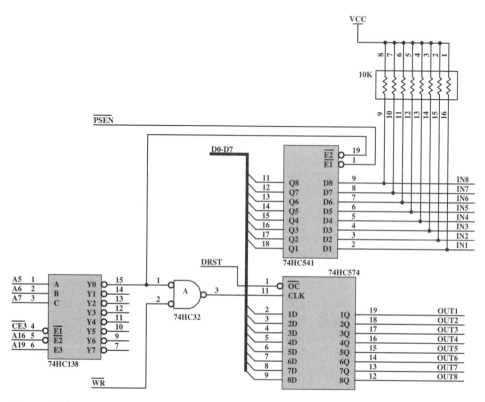

Figure 8.3 Eight I/O lines decoded in CE space

The decoder chip used in this circuit, a 74HC138, provides a one of eight decode. If the decoder's three enable lines ($\overline{E1}$, $\overline{E2}$, and E3) are in their active states (low, low, and high, respectively), the three address lines (A5, A6, and A7) are used to provide eight (2^3) distinct input values. The state of these three address lines causes exactly one of the decoder's eight outputs to be in its active low state, as shown in Table 8.2. Because the least significant five address lines are not used in this circuit for decoding purposes, each output decodes a 32-byte (2^5) range in memory.[7] In this example, we only use one of these outputs (Y0) for selecting the latch and buffer used for output and input, respectively.

Table 8.2 74HC138 truth table

A	B	C	Y0	Y1	Y2	Y3	Y4	Y5	Y6	Y7
0	0	0	0	1	1	1	1	1	1	1
1	0	0	1	0	1	1	1	1	1	1
0	1	0	1	1	0	1	1	1	1	1
1	1	0	1	1	1	0	1	1	1	1
0	0	1	1	1	1	1	0	1	1	1
1	0	1	1	1	1	1	1	0	1	1
0	1	1	1	1	1	1	1	1	0	1
1	1	1	1	1	1	1	1	1	1	0

The signals $\overline{CE3}$, A16, and A19 drive the decoder's enable lines. By studying the chip enable and all of the address lines used by the decoder, we can determine an address that can be used to access the additional I/O lines using a `DataPort` object. `DataPort` operates with 32-bit addresses. For the purposes of this discussion, we'll refer to the address bits as a0 through a31, where a0 is the least significant address bit and a31 is the most significant address bit. Note that we use a lowercase "a" to avoid confusion with the address bus signal names (A0–A19). Because the circuit is decoded in CE space, we know from the memory map shown in Figure 8.2 that the highest possible address is 0x3FFFFF. This means that a22–a31 must all be 0. Bits a20 and a21 are determined by our choice of chip select signals, as shown in Table 8.3.

Table 8.3 Chip enable to high-order address bit mapping

$\overline{CE0}$	$\overline{CE1}$	$\overline{CE2}$	$\overline{CE3}$	a20	a21
0	1	1	1	0	0
1	0	1	1	1	0

continues

---

7. This decode logic is compatible with, but not identical to, the decode used in the E series socket boards. The E series socket board schematics are included in the accompanying CD and can also be found online at *http://www.ibutton.com/TINI/developers/index.html*.

Table 8.3 Chip enable to high-order address bit mapping (continued)

CE0	CE1	CE2	CE3	a20	a21
1	1	0	1	0	1
1	1	1	0	1	1

Because we're using $\overline{\text{CE3}}$, both a20 and a21 are 1. The lower 20 bits of the address (a0 through a19) are determined simply by a 1 to 1 mapping of the 20-address bus signals (A0–A19). The states of the address lines that are not used in the decode are irrelevant, so we'll refer to them as *don't care* bits (or lines). Figure 8.4 shows the combination of the different address fields. The bit positions marked with an X are *don't care* bits.

a31 —> a22	a21	a20	a19	a18	a17	a16	a15 —>a8	a7	a6	a5	a4 —> a0
0000000000	1	1	1	X	X	X	XXXXXXXX	0	0	0	XXXXX

X => don't care

Figure 8.4 Constructing the DataPort address

Note that because a0–a4 are all *don't cares*, all addresses in the range [0x380000–0x3801F] will enable bus access to the I/O circuitry. Also, because there are higher-order *don't care* bits in the address, there are many such 32-byte address ranges. To select a specific address, we'll simply set all of the *don't care* bits to 0, resulting in an address of 0x380000.

While this is not a precise decode, it does ensure that our new I/O circuitry will not conflict with the other devices attached to the microcontroller's bus. Specifically, the decision to require that address line A19 be high and address line A16 be low keeps the new I/O lines out of the way of the Ethernet controller and the real-time clock.

Now that we've covered the somewhat tricky subject of decoding a valid address for transferring data to and from the additional I/O lines, the overall operation of the circuit can be described simply. During a bus write operation to address 0x380000, both $\overline{\text{Y0}}$ and $\overline{\text{WR}}$ will be in their active states, causing the contents of the data bus (D0–D7) to be written to the latch's output lines (1Q–8Q). Likewise, during a bus read operation from address 0x380000, both $\overline{\text{Y0}}$ and $\overline{\text{PSEN}}$ will be in their active states, causing the contents of the buffers's input lines to be transferred onto the data bus.

The circuit can be tested by connecting IN1 to OUT1, IN2 to OUT2, and so on, producing a simple loopback configuration. The ParallelLoopBack test program, shown in Listing 8.1, creates a DataPort object attached to address

0x380000. The `DataPort` object is used to perform byte-wide writes to the latch and byte-wide reads from the buffer.

Listing 8.1   ParallelLoopback

```
import com.dalsemi.system.DataPort;
import com.dalsemi.system.IllegalAddressException;

class ParallelLoopback {
    static final int ADDRESS = 0x380000;

    public static void main(String[] args) {
        DataPort dp = new DataPort(ADDRESS);
        // All reads and writes go to the same address
        dp.setFIFOMode(true);
        // Allow for use of slow logic
        dp.setStretchCycles(DataPort.STRETCH1);
        boolean passed = true;
        try {
            // Cycle through all possible 8-bit values
            for (int val = 0; val < 256; val++) {
                dp.write((byte) val);
                if ((dp.read() & 0xff) != val) {
                    System.out.println("Loopback test failed at:"+val);
                    passed = false;
                    break;
                }
            }
        } catch (IllegalAddressException iae) {
            iae.printStackTrace();
        }
        if (passed) {
            System.out.println("Loopback test passed");
        }
    }
}
```

Because all reads and writes are to the same address, the `DataPort` object is placed into FIFO mode. Also, to allow for the use of slower logic, the stretch cycle count is set to 1. After the `DataPort` object is configured, a test loop is entered in which each possible byte value (0–255) is written to the latch and then immediately read back from the buffer. If all eight output lines of the latch are connected to the eight input lines of the buffer, as previously described, the test should pass. Due to the pull-up resistors on the input lines, any unconnected signals result in the corresponding bit positions being read back as a logic 1. So, for example, if none of the I/O lines are tied together and all of the input lines on the latch are open, each read from address 0x380000 will return a byte of all logic 1s (0xFF).

If for cost or size reasons total chip count is a serious concern, the same functionality can be achieved without the decoder by mapping the I/O circuitry into

PCE space. This obviates the need to avoid any particular address range. The circuit shown in Figure 8.5 provides the same additional digital I/O capability using the same buffer and latch. However, it uses $\overline{PCE1}$ as the chip select signal. The other important difference is that bus reads from the 74HC541 buffer are now enabled using $\overline{RD}$ as opposed to $\overline{PSEN}$. As a rule, $\overline{PSEN}$ controls bus read operations for devices enabled using $\overline{CE}$ signals and $\overline{RD}$ controls bus read operations for devices enabled with PCE signals.

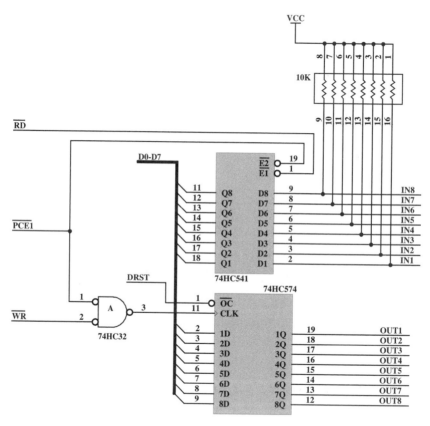

Figure 8.5 Eight I/O lines in PCE space without address decode

Because PCE space ends at 0xC00000, the high-order address bits a31–a24 must all be 0. Also, from the memory map shown in Figure 8.2, the lowest address in PCE space is 0x800000. This implies that a23 must be 1. Setting bit a23 produces the same result as adding an offset of 0x800000. Because there is a hole in the memory map between 0x400000 and 0x800000, a22 must be zero. This range is a no-man's-land because the microcontroller maps several system areas, including the stack, into this address range.

As with all `DataPort` addresses, bits a20 and a21 are determined by the choice of the chip select signal. Table 8.4 shows the values of a20 and a21 for the various PCE signals. Table 8.4 is identical to Table 8.3 with the CE signals replaced by PCE signals.

Table 8.4   Peripheral chip enable to a20 and a21 mapping

$\overline{PCE0}$	$\overline{PCE1}$	$\overline{PCE2}$	$\overline{PCE3}$	a20	a21
0	1	1	1	0	0
1	0	1	1	1	0
1	1	0	1	0	1
1	1	1	0	1	1

Because this circuit uses $\overline{PCE1}$, a20 is 1 and a21 is 0. Finally, we use a 1 to 1 mapping of the address bus lines to determine the values of a19 through a0. In this example, none of the address lines are used to enable the circuit. This makes the low-order 20 bits of the address *don't care* bits.

The address construction for the circuit shown in Figure 8.5 is summarized in Figure 8.6.

```
a31 —>a24  a23   a22   a21   a20         a19 —>a0
00000000    1     0     0     1    XXXXXXXXXXXXXXXXXXXX

X => don't care
```

Figure 8.6   Constructing the DataPort address

Using the convention of choosing the *don't care* bits to be 0 produces an address of 0x900000. So, if we simply change the address used in the `ParallelLoopBack` test application from

```
static final int ADDRESS = 0x380000;
```

to

```
static final int ADDRESS = 0x900000;
```

it will work fine with the circuit shown in Figure 8.5. Note that because no address lines are used to enable the circuit, any address in the 1-megabyte range controlled by $\overline{PCE1}$ (0x900000–0x9FFFFF) can be used.

Finally, it is worth mentioning that even though the two circuits presented in this section produce only eight digital inputs and outputs, more can easily be created in the same fashion by using the other outputs of the decoder to select additional buffers and latches.[8]

8.3.2 Reading and Writing External Memory

Often, embedded applications require nonvolatile storage that is distinct from the garbage collected heap and the file system. It may be used to store critical system data required for bootstrapping the system or some sort of log data. This functional requirement can be met by interfacing a nonvolatile memory device to the parallel bus.

The circuit shown in Figure 8.7 shows the parallel bus interface between the microcontroller and a 32-kilobyte nonvolatile SRAM module.[9] Because the SRAM's density is 32 kilobytes, it uses the 15 low-order address lines.[10] The SRAM is enabled using $\overline{\text{PCE0}}$, which implies that the read strobe ($\overline{\text{RD}}$) is used to control read operations (as opposed to $\overline{\text{PSEN}}$ for CE reads). Because none of the high-order address lines are used in this circuit, the contents of the memory will actually be decoded as many times as its 32-kilobyte "image" can fit in $\overline{\text{PCE0}}$'s 1-megabyte address space. This produces 32 identical images of the 32-kilobyte memory, since 1 megabyte is 2^{20}, 32 kilobytes is 2^{15}, and $2^{20}/2^{15} = 2^5 = 32$. We'll use the lowest address range to access the memory. This results in a DataPort address range from 0x800000 to 0x807FFF.

The MemoryTester application, shown in Listing 8.2, begins by creating a 32-kilobyte array and initializing it with a "checkerboard" test pattern. Next, a DataPort object is created and attached to the base (lowest) address of the SRAM. The stretch cycle count is set to 1 to give the memory plenty of time for bus accesses. Because TINI's bus is operating at a high frequency, memories with access times greater than 55 nanoseconds require at least one stretch cycle for safe I/O. The final step of DataPort initialization is setting the memory access mode to sequential mode by invoking the setFIFOMode method with a boolean value of false. Now the DataPort object is ready to write to and read from the external memory.

---

8. At some point, of course, the data bus will have to be buffered to prevent it from becoming too heavily loaded.
9. An SRAM module includes an SRAM, an SRAM nonvolatizer, and a lithium battery for backup power.
10. $2^{15} = 32768$

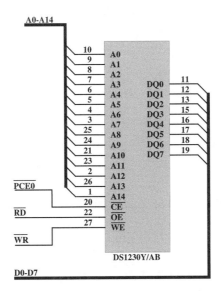

Figure 8.7   32-kilobyte nonvolatile SRAM interfaced to $\overline{\text{PCE0}}$

Listing 8.2   MemoryTester

```java
import com.dalsemi.system.DataPort;
import com.dalsemi.system.IllegalAddressException;
import com.dalsemi.system.ArrayUtils;

class MemoryTester {
    // Assuming a 32 kilobyte SRAM
    static final int MEM_SIZE = 32768;
    // Least significant byte of SRAM
    static final int BASE_ADDRESS = 0x800000;

    public static void main(String[] args) {
        byte[] testPattern = new byte[MEM_SIZE];
        for (int i = 0; i < MEM_SIZE; i += 2) {
            testPattern[i] = 0x55;
            testPattern[i+1] = (byte) 0xaa;
        }
        DataPort dp = new DataPort(BASE_ADDRESS);
        // Need incrementing addresses
        dp.setFIFOMode(false);
        // Allow for communication with slow memories
        dp.setStretchCycles(DataPort.STRETCH1);
        try {
            // Write test pattern to memory
            dp.write(testPattern, 0, testPattern.length);
            // Read back the contents of the memory
```

```
        byte[] ramContents = new byte[MEM_SIZE];
        dp.read(ramContents, 0, ramContents.length);
        // Verify test pattern
        boolean passed = ArrayUtils.arrayComp(testPattern, 0,
                                              ramContents, 0,
                                              MEM_SIZE);
        System.out.print("RAM test results:");
        System.out.println(passed ? "PASS" : "FAIL");
    } catch (IllegalAddressException iae) {
        System.err.println("Invalid address: Memory test aborted");
        iae.printStackTrace();
    }
  }
}
```

The entire test pattern is then written to the memory with just one invocation of the block `write` method. Next, the test pattern is read back into a separate 32-kilobyte array using the block `read` method. The array containing the results of the read operation (`ramContents`) is then compared with the original test pattern data. If the contents of the two arrays are identical, the test is considered successful. Note that the address does not need to be reset to 0x800000 after returning from `write` because `DataPort`'s block `read` and `write` methods automatically restore the address after each operation.

CHAPTER 9 # Just the Bits

Embedded programmers are accustomed to having direct access to microcontroller port pins. This is important for many embedded applications because port pins are often used on an individual basis to provide a single bit of output for driving devices such as LEDs, relays,[1] or stepper motors. Because the port pins we're concerned with are bidirectional, they can also be used to provide a single bit of input for tasks such as reading the state of a switch.

This chapter focuses on the ports and port pins provided by TINI's microcontroller. Specifically, we'll cover their default usage by the native portion of the runtime environment and under what circumstances they can be manipulated directly by a Java application.

9.1 TINI'S PORTS AND PORT PINS

On TINI's microcontroller, all port pins belong to one of six ports. The ports are numbered sequentially starting from 0. A port is a group of eight pins. So, for example, port 3 (or P3) is the collection of the eight port pins [p3.0–p3.7]. Ports 0, 1, 2, and 4 are consumed by the data bus, address bus, and chip enable signals.

---

1. Typically, a port pin drives the gate of a FET (Field Effect Transistor), which drives the actual relay.

This leaves the pins within ports 3 and 5 available as candidates for use as general purpose input and output.

We touched on accessing port pins from Java in Section 2.6.2 with the awe-inspiring "Blinky" application. In this example, we flashed a TINI board's status LED on and off by toggling the state of one of the microcontroller's port pins.[2] There's not much more to it than that. The only real trick is knowing which port pins are available to use with your application, since most port pins serve two, and sometimes three, distinct purposes. Determining which port pins can be used requires a careful study of the "built-in" I/O resources the application is using, such as serial and CAN. Table 9.1 lists all of the port pins that can be controlled directly by a Java application along with their default usage.

Table 9.1   Java accessible port pins

Micro Pin Number/Name	TBM390 Pin Number[a]/Name	Default Use(s)
4 (P3.0)	22 (XRX0)	Receive data for serial0
5 (P3.1)	21 (TX)	Transmit data for serial0
6 (P3.2)	N/A[b]	Ethernet controller interrupt
7 (P3.3)	23 ($\overline{\text{EXTINT}}$)	General purpose external interrupt
10 (P3.4)	18 ($\overline{\text{DRST}}$)	External device reset
11 (P3.5)	17 (INTOW)	Internal 1-Wire net
21 (P5.0)	10 (CTX)	Transmit data for CAN0, clock signal for 2-wire synchronous serial I/O
20 (P5.1)	11 (CRX)	Receive data for CAN0, data transmit and receive for 2-wire synchronous serial I/O
19 (P5.2)	15 (XRX1)	Receive data for CAN1, receive data for serial1
18 (P5.3)	14 (TX1)	Transmit data for CAN1, transmit data for serial1
17 (P5.4)	30 ($\overline{\text{PCE0}}$)	Peripheral chip enable 0
16 (P5.5)	29 ($\overline{\text{PCE1}}$)	Peripheral chip enable 1

continues

2.   The status LED on the TBM390 is controlled by P3.5.

Table 9.1   Java accessible port pins (continued)

Micro Pin Number/Name	TBM390 Pin Number[a]/Name	Default Use(s)
15 (P5.6)	28 ($\overline{\text{PCE2}}$)	Peripheral chip enable 2
14 (P5.7)	27 ($\overline{\text{PCE3}}$)	Peripheral chip enable 3

    a.   These pin numbers are valid for 72-pin TBM390s only.
    b.   This pin is not presented at the TBM390's edge connector.

Consider the four high-order pins of port 5 (p5.4–5.7). Their normal use is for decoding hardware interfaced to the controller's bus. If a system doesn't use any of the PCE signals for logic decoding purposes, then all four of these pins can be used as general purpose port pins.[3] Similarly, if the system isn't using CAN0 or the 2-wire synchronous serial port normally associated with pins p5.0 and p5.1, the Java application can assume direct control of these pins.

9.2   THE BITPORT CLASS

Access to individual port pins is achieved using the `BitPort` class contained in the `com.dalsemi.system` package. The following `BitPort` constructor is used to attach a `BitPort` object to a specific port pin.

```
public BitPort(byte bitname)
```

The port pin is specified by the `bitname` parameter. Valid values for `bitname` are defined as public constants in the `BitPort` class. The constant names are formed by concatenating the "Port" string, followed by the port number to the "Bit" string, followed by the bit's (or pin's) position within the port. So, for example, the following statement creates a new BitPort object attached to the microcontroller's p5.3 port pin.

```
BitPort bp = new BitPort(BitPort.Port5Bit3);
```

The `set` and `clear` methods are used to control the state of the pin.

```
public void set()
public void clear()
```

---

   3.   With the PCE signals it's all or nothing. If a system uses any one of the PCE signals as true "chip enables" then none of the remaining signals can be used as general purpose port pins.

For the `clear` method, the story is simple: When it is invoked, the port pin is actively driven to a low (to a logic 0) voltage level. Likewise, one might naturally expect that when `set` is invoked, the pin is driven to a high[4] (a logic 1) voltage level. This is not necessarily the case. If `set` is invoked following an invocation of `clear`, the pin will be actively driven high for a very brief period of time[5] and then it will transition to a "soft" high[6] through a weak pull-up. This behavior allows the pin to be used as an input because external circuitry can easily overdrive the weak pull-up. So, if the external circuitry is driving a low-impedance low, the actual voltage level of the pin will be low, even following the invocation of `set`. If the external load on the port pin is sufficiently high-impedance, or completely open, then both `set` and `clear` drive true logic levels.

The `read` method returns the value sampled from the port pin. If at the time of sampling the pin was high (logic 1), `read` returns 1. Otherwise, `read` returns 0. The `set` method should be invoked before the first call to `read`. Also, if at any time the port pin is driven low via an invocation of the `clear` method, the `set` method must be invoked to allow external circuitry to override the pin before invoking `read`.

```
public int read()
public int readLatch()
```

The `readLatch` method always returns the state of the last "write" operation, where a write operation is defined as an invocation of either of the `set` or `clear` methods. The `readLatch` method does not perform a true read of a hardware latch; it simply "remembers" the last write operation that was performed by the application. Therefore, it returns a 0 if the previous write operation was a "clear" or 1 if the previous write operation was a "set."

9.3 SYNTHETIC PORT PINS

Some applications require more port pins than are provided by the microcontroller as "built-in" port pins. Depending on your application's I/O requirements, it can be especially difficult to find free (that is, not used by any of the platform's built-in I/O capability) port pins. One solution is to throw hardware at the problem. A small amount of external circuity can be used to synthesize additional port pins. In this section we loosely define the notion of synthetic ports as ports created using

---

4. In this context, high implies a voltage level at or near the controller's supply voltage (V_{cc}), and a low voltage implies a voltage level at or near the ground reference.
5. The pin will be actively driven for two clock cycles (half of one machine cycle). This is about 220 ns on a TINI system running at 36.864 MHz.
6. See the DS803C90 data sheet (*http://www.dalsemi.com/datasheets/pdfs/80c390.pdf*) for details on the electrical characteristics of the port pins for ports 3 and 5.

external I/O circuitry[7] as "external ports." We'll refer to the pins created by these ports as "external pins."

Like internal ports, external ports can contain a maximum of eight pins. However, multiple addresses can be used to decode additional circuitry, producing a practically unlimited number of external port pins. Whether these pins are output-only, input-only, or bidirectional is completely up to the system designer. Because external ports are interfaced to the system using the microcontroller bus, this section assumes that the reader is comfortable with the material presented in Chapter 8.

To access external pins, an application can use a `BitPort` object created using the following constructor.

```
public BitPort(DataPort port)
```

The constructor requires a `DataPort` object attached to the address of the external port. Because TINI's data bus is eight bits wide, a `BitPort` object constructed in this manner can control up to 8 distinct pins. Controlling more than eight pins requires multiple `BitPort` objects, each constructed using a different `DataPort` object associated with a unique address.

Just as with true port pins, `set` and `clear` methods exist for controlling the state of external pins.

```
public void set(int bitpos) throws IllegalAddressException
public void clear(int bitpos) throws IllegalAddressException
```

There are a few differences between these methods and their true port pin analogs. First, the methods used with external pins require the `bitpos` parameter, which specifies the position of a pin within an external port. Because a port can contain a maximum of eight pins, the value of the `bitpos` parameter must be between 0 and 7. Another difference is that the `set` and `clear` methods associated with external pins will throw an `IllegalAddressException` if invoked on a `BitPort` object that was constructed using a `DataPort` object attached to an invalid address. Finally, the I/O characteristics described for `set` and `clear` in Section 9.2 do not necessarily apply to external ports. Rather, the electrical characteristics of external pins depend completely on the circuitry used to implement the external port.

The `readBit` and `readLatch` methods are used to query the state of an external pin. The position of the pin within the external port is specified by the `bitpos` parameter using the same rules just described for the `set` and `clear` methods. The `readBit` method throws an `IllegalAddressException` when invoked on a `BitPort` object that was constructed using a `DataPort` object attached to an invalid address.

```
public int readBit(int bitpos) throws IllegalAddressException
public int readLatch(int bitpos)
```

---

7. Typically octal buffers and latches.

Just as with the `readLatch` method used in conjunction with "built-in" (or true) port pins, this is a "software latch" that simply maintains the state of the last write operation as a convenience. Because `readLatch` is not performing a true bus read operation, it does not throw an `IllegalAddressException`.

9.3.1 Example: Creating Additional Outputs

To make the concepts presented in this section a little more concrete, let's consider a very basic, but useful, example in which eight output-only external pins are created using a minimal amount of circuitry. First, the hardware will be described, and then a small application that controls the hardware will be presented.

The schematic shown in Figure 9.1 shows a simple circuit used to control a bank of eight LEDs. The circuit uses a 74HC574 octal latch (hereafter known as the latch) to control the state of the cathodes of each of the LEDs. When an output is low, the LED that it controls will be "on" (emitting light). So, for example, if output 1Q is low and the remaining outputs (2Q–7Q) are high, D1 will be on and D2 through D8 will all be off. The latch is decoded using $\overline{PCE0}$. This is a very lazy decode in which the goal is to minimize the amount of external logic. In this case, no address lines are used in the decode. This implies that any address in the range [0x800000–0x8FFFFF] can be used to write to the latch. (See the memory map shown in Figure 8.2.) Note that in this example, our eight "external port pins" are output only. Any attempt to read the states of the latch's outputs produces a meaningless result.

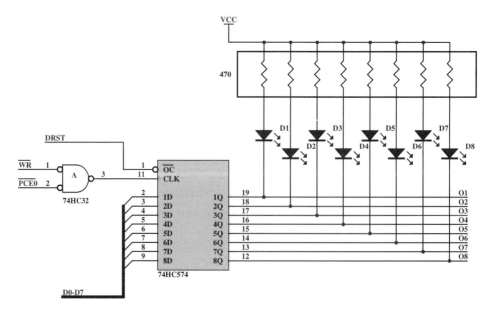

Figure 9.1   8x1 LED test configuration

The `BitTwiddler` example, shown in Listing 9.1, uses a `BitPort` object to individually control each LED in the circuit in Figure 9.1. The application begins by creating a `DataPort` object, attached to address 0x800000, for the purpose of writing to the latch. The `DataPort` object is set to FIFO mode to prevent the address from being incremented on every write. After the `DataPort` object has been correctly initialized, it is handed off to `BitPort`'s constructor to be used for low-level control of the latch.

Listing 9.1   BitTwiddler

```
import com.dalsemi.system.BitPort;
import com.dalsemi.system.DataPort;
import com.dalsemi.system.IllegalAddressException;

class BitTwiddler {
    static final int ADDRESS = 0x800000;

    public static void main(String[] args) {
        // Create and initialize DataPort object
        DataPort dp = new DataPort(ADDRESS);
        dp.setStretchCycles(DataPort.STRETCH2);
        dp.setFIFOMode(true);

        // Create BitPort object to expose 8 independant I/O lines
        BitPort bp = new BitPort(dp);
        try {
            while (true) {
                int pos = 0;
                for (pos = 0; pos < 8; pos++) {
                    bp.set(pos);
                    try {
                        Thread.sleep(100);
                    } catch (InterruptedException ie) {}
                }
                for (pos = 7; pos >= 0; pos--) {
                    bp.clear(pos);
                    try {
                        Thread.sleep(100);
                    } catch (InterruptedException ie) {}
                }
            }
        } catch (IllegalAddressException iae) {
            iae.printStackTrace();
        }
    }
}
```

Next, `BitTwiddler` enters an infinite loop in which all LEDs are repeatedly turned off by driving each latch output high and then turned back on by driving each latch output low. The inner loops invoke the set and clear methods on the

BitPort object to turn the LEDs off and on, respectively. Both loops "touch" every output individually so that only one LED changes state at any given time.

Note that the same exact result can be accomplished using just a DataPort object and by forming appropriate bit masks associated with the write operation. In this case BitPort is simply used as a programming convenience, making it easier to change an individual output of the latch without altering the state of any other outputs.

9.4 THE BytePort CLASS

Besides being able to manipulate individual port pins, embedded programs can also perform single byte-wide read and write operations to and from a port. The BytePort class in the com.dalsemi.system package provides the mechanism to read a byte from or write a byte to a port.

```
public BytePort(byte portname)
```

BytePort's lone constructor requires a byte value specifying the port that is to be the target of any subsequent read or write operations. Note that, unlike BitPort, the BytePort class cannot be used in conjunction with DataPort to access external ports. This is because DataPort already contains methods for byte-wide I/O to external logic.

Legal values for the portname parameter are specified as public constants in the BytePort class. Currently, the only port that can be used to construct a BytePort object is port 5 (P5). You may have noticed in Table 9.1 that, under the correct circumstances, all eight pins that comprise P5 can be used as port pins. The following line of code creates a new BytePort object attached to the microcontroller's port 5.

```
BytePort bp = new BytePort(BytePort.Port5);
```

What's not obvious from the preceding statement are the side effects caused by creating the BytePort object. From Table 9.1 we can see that the pins that comprise port 5 serve several different purposes. The functionality provided by these pins, such as synchronous serial I/O, CAN, and 1-Wire, must all be disabled before all of port 5's pins can be used in a general purpose fashion. Specifically, BytePort's constructor performs the following operations.

- Disables the use of pins 5.0 and 5.1 for use by CAN0 or as a 2-wire synchronous serial interface
- Disables the use of p5.2 and p5.3 for use by CAN1 or serial1; this also disables the external 1-Wire network adapter
- Disables the use of p5.4, p5.5, p5.6, and p5.7 as peripheral chip enables

After taking these steps, the application can safely read from or write to the port. Read and write operations are accomplished using these read and write methods.

```
public int read()
public void write(int value)
```

The read method returns a value between 0 and 255 decimal that represents the state of eight pins of the port at the exact time it was sampled. The value of the 0th position pin (p5.0) is stored in the least significant bit of the return value and so on. So, for example, if the read method is invoked on a BytePort object that is attached to port P5 and read returns a value of 0xc1, then at the time the port was sampled, p5.0, p5.6, and p5.7 were high (logic 1s), and the remaining pins were low (logic 0s).

Notice the lack of read or write methods that take byte arrays as parameters. This is because there is no way for the native code responsible for performing the actual operation to pace the transmission or reception of multiple bytes. This is due to the fact that there are no strobe lines associated with the port for controlling the read and write operations. To write multiple bytes using BytePort, the application must "byte-bang" all data destined for the port.

9.5 PERFORMANCE OF BITPORT AND BYTEPORT

Accesses to either a port or an individual port pin are very fast, single instruction operations in *native* code. The instructions look something like these pseudo-code snippets.

```
mov p5, a // move the 8 bit contents of accumlator to port 5
```

or

```
clr p5.0 //  force bit 5.0 to a logic 0 (low)
```

However, setting the state of a port pin using the set method of BitPort, for example, requires two method invocations. The first is the invocation of the set method itself, and the second is a native method invocation that ultimately sets the desired state of the port pin. Each of these method invocations imposes a non-negligible overhead and requires the execution of hundreds (or even thousands) of native instructions. This brings the overall time required for accessing a port pin from a few hundred nanoseconds to a few hundred microseconds!

This is an instance where the overhead of the Java runtime environment can adversely impact the I/O performance of the system. In many cases, such as serial and network I/O, read and write operations can be performed using large blocks of data. This prorates the overhead of the method invocations and greatly reduces the runtime environment's impact on performance. But in the case of BitPort and BytePort operations, only a single read or write can be accomplished per method invocation(s).

For purposes such as driving status LEDs or relays, this overhead has no practical impact on the overall system performance. Often with such examples the only thing that is important is that the time delay is imperceptible to a human, and a few hundred microseconds easily meets this requirement. However, there are cases where a port pin must be driven at medium to high frequencies. For example, imagine a scenario where a port pin is being used to generate the clock signal for a synchronous serial protocol. For this type of application, a native library may be required to achieve the desired performance levels for reading and writing individual ports or port pins.

CHAPTER 10

Accessing System Resources

In this chapter we'll take a detailed look at the following three very important and distinct system resources.

- The real-time clock—supports the `java.util.Date` class and is often used by embedded applications to provide time-stamping functionality
- The external interrupt—provides asynchronous notification when an interrupt is generated by an attached peripheral device
- The watchdog—adds robustness in the form of system crash detection and recovery

A section is dedicated to each of these topics. Each contains a simple example that demonstrates how to access and control the specific system resource.

10.1 THE REAL-TIME CLOCK

While the real-time clock (RTC) is not a requirement for TINI hardware designs, most implementations provide it. During the development phase when slush is in use, you can set the current date, time, and time zone using the `date` shell command.

For the most part, your interaction with the RTC will be through the `Date` class in the `java.util` package. However, the `Date` class does not provide any method for setting the current date and time in the underlying platform's hardware clock. The Clock class in the com.dalsemi.system package provides the ability to read and write all of the RTC registers, allowing the current date and time to be set programatically. Clock provides *getters* and *setters* for each of the following public fields.

- int year—two-digit year
- int month
- int date—day of the month
- int day—day of the week
- int hour
- int minute
- int second
- int hundredth—the RTC resolution is hundredths of seconds—that is, 0 milliseconds
- boolean is12Hour—12/24-hour mode flag
- boolean pm—true for PM, false otherwise

Each instance field corresponds to a value in one of the real-time clock's hardware registers. Constructing of a new instance of Clock does not force a read of any of the RTC's registers. After construction, all instance fields are set to their default initial values. Invoking the method getRTC on an instance of Clock forces a read of the RTC and copies the raw registers to their respective instance fields. The RTC's register set does not provide any information about the local time zone or the first two digits of the year. Code that uses Clock to set or retrieve the date and time must take both of these facts into account.

The example in Listing 10.1 creates an instance of Clock, invokes getRTC to take a snapshot of the current value of the RTC registers, and displays their values.

Listing 10.1 ReadClockRaw

```
import com.dalsemi.system.Clock;

class ReadClockRaw {
    public static void main(String[] args) {
        Clock rtc = new Clock();
        rtc.getRTC();
        System.out.println("Year: " + rtc.getYear());
        System.out.println("Month: " + rtc.getMonth());
        System.out.println("Day of the month: " + rtc.getDate());
        System.out.println("Day of the week: " + rtc.getDay());
        System.out.println("Hour: " + rtc.getHour());
        System.out.println("Minute: " + rtc.getMinute());
        System.out.println("Second: " + rtc.getSecond());
        System.out.println("Hundredths of seconds: " +
```

```
                              rtc.getHundredth());
          System.out.println("Is pm: " + rtc.getPm());
          if (rtc.get12Hour()) {
              System.out.println("In 12 hour mode");
          } else {
              System.out.println("In 24 hour mode");
          }
      }
  }
}
```

Running `ReadClockRaw` produces output similar to the following.

```
Year: 1
Month: 1
Day of the month: 31
Day of the week: 5
Hour: 22
Minute: 30
Second: 15
Hundredths of seconds: 63
Is pm: true
In 24 hour mode
```

This is the output from the slush `date` command run just two seconds after executing ReadClockRaw.

```
TINI /> date
Thu Jan 31 22:30:17 GMT 2001
Wed Jan 31 16:30:17 CST 2001
```

Note that the first line displayed by the `date` command agrees, within a couple of seconds, with the output from the raw RTC registers. To properly support the platform and location, independent functionality specified in `java.util.Date`, TINI always uses the RTC in 24-hour mode and computes the register values using the GMT (Greenwich Mean Time) zone. If a time zone other than GMT was specified during a previous run of the `date` command, the current date and time are also displayed for the local time zone. The local time zone in this instance is CST (Central Standard Time).

The default (or local) time zone used by the `Date` class can be set and retrieved using the following methods in the class `com.dalsemi.system.TINIOS`.

```
public static String getTimeZone()
public static void setTimeZone(String zone)
    throws IllegalArgumentException
```

The `setTimeZone` method requires a `String` that specifies the time zone. A list of all supported time zones can be acquired using the `getAvailableIDs` method in the class `java.util.TimeZone`.

```
public static String[] getAvailableIDs()
```

All time zone ids are uppercase letters and are three characters in length. You can also view a list of all supported time zones using slush's date command supplying the -t option.

10.1.1 Setting the Current Date and Time

To set the date and time, an application creates a Clock object and sets all of the public fields to their desired values. Invoking the setRTC method commits those values to the real-time clock. This is how the slush date command works. It parses user input from the command line and calculates the correct values for all of the clock registers. If a time zone is specified, it adjusts the input date and time with respect to GMT before setting the Clock instance fields.

There is another method for setting the real-time clock that sets all registers and commits them to the RTC.

```
public synchronized void setTickCount(long millis)
```

The millis parameter required by setTickCount is the difference between the current time and midnight, January 1, 1970 UTC (coordinated universal time). For our very practical purposes, we can think of UTC as equivalent to GMT. The value millis is the same number that is returned from an invocation of System.currentTimeMillis. If you're interested in the difference between UTC and GMT, the documentation for the Date class is a good place to start.

10.1.2 Using a Network Time Server

The setTickCount method is an ideal way to set the real-time clock if you have a convenient means of acquiring the correct value of the millis parameter. One way to accomplish this is to get millis from System.currentTimeMillis on a host that already has the correct time and feed that value to setTickCount. Another way is to get the value from a network time server. If your TINI is on (or has access to) a network running a Time Protocol (RFC868)[1] server, you can connect to the server to read the current time.[2]

An RFC868 server listens for connections on "well-known port" number 37. When a connection is established, it returns the time as an unsigned 32-bit value and closes the connection. The returned time is the number of seconds since midnight, January 1, 1900 GMT. Ultimately, the number we're interested in is the number of milliseconds since midnight, January 1, 1970. From RFC868 we know the number of seconds between midnight, January 1, 1970 and midnight, January

---

1. RFC868 can be viewed at *http://www.faqs.org/rfcs/rfc868.html*
2. SNTP (Simple Network Time Protocol) is actually a much better protocol. We use Time Protocol here because of its simplicity. SNTP is specified in RFC2030 (see *http://www.faqs.org/rfcs/rfc2030.html*).

1, 1900 is 2,208,988,800. To convert the value received from the time server to a value that can be passed to `setTickCount`, we subtract from it the offset shown previously to get the total number of seconds since midnight, January 1, 1970. Finally, we multiply the result by 1000 for the unit conversion from seconds to milliseconds.

Listing 10.2 uses an RFC868 Time Protocol server to set the current date and time in TINI's RTC.

Listing 10.2   SetClock

```java
import java.io.IOException;
import java.io.DataInputStream;
import java.net.Socket;
import java.util.Date;

import com.dalsemi.system.Clock;
import com.dalsemi.system.TINIOS;

public class SetClock
{
    // Well known port for Time Protocol (RFC 868)
    static int TIME_PORT = 37;

    // Number of seconds between 00:00 1 Jan 1900 GMT and
    // 00:00 1 Jan 1970 GMT
    static long SECONDS_OFFSET = 2208988800L;

    public static void main(String[] args) {
        if (args.length != 1) {
            System.out.println("Usage: java TiniClock TIMESERVER");
            System.exit(1);
        }

        Socket s = null;
        try {
            System.out.println("Crusty date: " + new Date());

            // Establish a connection with the TIME server and read
            // 32 bit seconds count since 00:00 1 Jan 1900 GMT
            s = new Socket(args[0], TIME_PORT);
            DataInputStream din = new DataInputStream(
                                    s.getInputStream());

            // Compute # of seconds between now and 00:00 1 Jan 1970 GMT
            long time = (din.readInt() & 0xFFFFFFFFL) - SECONDS_OFFSET;

            Clock rtc = new Clock();
            // Commit the new date/time settings to the system clock
            rtc.setTickCount(time * 1000);
            // Set the local timezone
            TINIOS.setTimeZone("CST");
```

```
        System.out.println("Shiny new date: " + new Date());
    } catch (IOException ioe) {
        ioe.printStackTrace();
    } finally {
        try {
            s.close();
        } catch (IOException e) {}
    }
  }
}
```

SetClock takes the host name (wally, in this case) or IP address of the time server from the command line. It connects to the specified host and reads the 32-bit time value using the readInt method on a java.io.DataInputStream object. There is one somewhat subtle point here. Since the int primitive type is signed, the result returned from readInt must be promoted to a long and then truncated using the mask 0xFFFFFFFFL. This choice of a mask results in both the promotion of the value returned from readInt as well as removing the effect of the unwanted sign extension. The result is the true, unsigned 32-bit value returned by the time server represented within a long. Since longs are 64 bits in width, this leaves plenty of room to perform the final multiplication without the possibility of over-flow. Note that we could solve the problem more directly using the readLong method of DataInputStream. The time server returns only 4 bytes before closing the connection. The readLong method would attempt to read 8 bytes, and this would result in a java.io.IOException being thrown by the underlying socket.

It is easier to see the effect of this example by first setting a bogus date and time using the slush date command before running SetClock.

```
TINI /> date 010120250000 GMT
TINI /> date
Wed Jan 1 00:00:22 GMT 2025

TINI /> java SetClock.tini wally
Crusty date: Wed Jan 01 00:01:06 GMT 2025
Shiny new date: Wed Jan 31 16:33:09 CST 2001
```

SetClock uses the Date class to display the date and time before and after setting the RTC using setTickCount. Just for good measure, it also sets the local time zone before displaying the new date and time.

Finally, note that setting the clock is not something that an application must perform every time it is run. The clock is powered by a small lithium cell so that accurate time is maintained even in the absence of main power (V_{cc}). However, some applications may want to use a network time server to synchronize the clock with the network time during the initialization phase and perhaps periodically thereafter.

10.2   THE WATCHDOG

The watchdog timer provides a hardware reset of TINI's microcontroller to recover from fatal problems in software that prevent normal operation of the embedded system as a whole. This section presents the need for a watchdog and describes its use from a Java application.

10.2.1   Motivation for Using the Watchdog

Many embedded systems are deployed in remote locations and must run continuously without manual intervention. To achieve very reliable operation over long periods of time, an embedded system needs a mechanism for detecting and correcting fatal execution errors in the software that controls the system.

Unresponsive software can be caused by several distinct problems such as the following.

- Thread termination due to an unhandled exception
- Deadlocked threads
- A crash of the underlying OS
- Momentary hardware failures due to environmental stresses such as ESD (Electrostatic Discharge)

Of course application software should be written and tested to avoid these problems to the largest extent possible. However, for large applications executing under complex operating environments, like TINI, it is very difficult to guarantee flawless operation under all conditions. Also, there is no way for application or system-level software to guard against things like processor glitches, possibly caused by environmental stresses, that usually result in "runaway" code.

Whatever mechanism we use to protect against hanging applications, it can't be a purely software-based solution, since unreliable software operation is exactly what we're trying to protect against in the first place. The system software must be protected by a simple and reliable underlying hardware construct. For this reason, TINI's microcontroller supports a hardware-based timer known as the watchdog. The purpose of the watchdog is to guard against runaway code. The watchdog timer can be thought of as a countdown to a "hard" reset. If the timer ever expires, it produces an effect that is roughly equivalent to hitting the reset button on your PC. Using the watchdog timer is a harsh but effective way to ensure that your application does not "hang" indefinitely, leaving the system in an unresponsive and useless state.

The basic idea behind the operation of the watchdog is that periodically in your code you reinitialize or "feed" the watchdog, preventing a reset. If the code has become unresponsive to the point that it can't execute the critical sections of code that feed the watchdog, it is better to reset the entire system, returning it to a known state, than to continue executing "hung" code.

10.2.2 A Tail of Two Dogs

There are actually two different watchdog timers on TINI, one hardware based and one software based, that are used together to protect the entire embedded system, both the OS and the application(s), from runaway code. The hardware watchdog, completely managed by the operating system, has a limited range of time-out values that are determined by the processor clock. The largest possible time-out value of the hardware watchdog is less than three seconds. Three seconds is plenty of time for very small, dedicated embedded applications that have highly deterministic behavior and are written entirely in native code. In this case, feeding the watchdog is as simple and fast as writing to one of the processor's registers.

However, in a large, multi-threaded Java application, the amount of time that elapses between opportunities to feed the watchdog is nondeterministic and can be long. So a more flexible watchdog is required to allow for longer time-out values. The software watchdog provides arbitrarily large time-out values. The software watchdog is managed by the OS and is checked for expiration every time the task scheduler runs. By itself it would be sufficient to detect runaway application-level code, but it can't guard against a crash in the operating system. If the OS itself were to crash and the timer maintenance routine stopped getting called, the entire system could still hang indefinitely. For this reason, the hardware watchdog is used to ensure the integrity of the software watchdog. The software watchdog's timer maintenance routine feeds the hardware watchdog every time it is called by the task scheduler. During normal operation, a Java application feeds the software watchdog and the software watchdog feeds the hardware watchdog, keeping the system from resetting.

10.2.3 Using the Watchdog Timer

The com.dalsemi.system.TINIOS class provides these two methods for controlling the watchdog.

```
public static void setWatchdogTimeout(int mstimeout);
public static void feedWatchdog();
```

The setWatchdogTimeout method sets the watchdog timer to expire in the specified number of milliseconds. The watchdog timer can be disabled by invoking setWatchdogTimeout with a time-out value of 0. By default, the watchdog is disabled during bootup. Once setWatchdogTimeout has been invoked with a non-zero time-out, the watchdog timer begins. Finally, the feedWatchdog method is used to "knock back" the timer and prevent a system reset.

Even though it can be accessed by multiple applications, it should be used by only one application: the application that performs the lion's share of the system critical work. This is typically the application that is started after the OS boots.

Using the watchdog in your application is easy. The only trick is picking a good time-out value and choosing where and how often to feed it. Often an application has a main loop that runs periodically and performs some critical task. This is an excellent place to feed the watchdog. Other applications, such as Web servers, spend most of their time blocking with all threads sleeping, waiting for incoming network connections or some other asynchronous event. Applications that don't have a natural place to perform periodic maintenance can create a separate thread with the sole purpose of feeding the watchdog. This is not quite as effective as embedding the timer reset in critical code that must execute periodically and also adds the cost of an additional thread to the application. It is, however, a solid mechanism for recovering from a system-level crash.

Since the watchdog contributes nothing to the actual functionality of your application, you want the resources consumed by the watchdog to be as small as possible. This suggests the use of a large time-out value, typically on the order of several seconds. Also, it is important to feed the watchdog in intervals that are comfortably smaller than the time-out value. This avoids unnecessary resets due to race conditions caused by process and thread scheduling.

10.2.4 Example Use of the Watchdog Timer

Listing 10.3 illustrates the use of the watchdog timer.

Listing 10.3 Watchdog

```java
import java.io.IOException;
import com.dalsemi.system.TINIOS;

class Watchdog {
    boolean feedDog;
    int interval;

    // Create a thread for timer maintainence
    Thread feeder = new Thread(new Runnable() {
        public void run() {
            while (feedDog) {
                try {
                    Thread.sleep(interval);
                } catch (InterruptedException ie) {}
                System.out.println("Feeding the dog!");
                TINIOS.feedWatchdog();
            }
        }
    });
```

```
Watchdog(int timeout, int frequency) {
    // # of milliseconds between watchdog feedings
    interval = timeout / frequency;
    feedDog = true;
    feeder.start();
    // Set watchdog timeout value, this also starts the timer.
    TINIOS.setWatchdogTimeout(timeout);
}

public static void main(String[] args) throws IOException {
    // Set the timeout for 8 seconds and knock back the
    // timer 2 times during each timeout period (i.e. every
    // 4 seconds)
    Watchdog wd = new Watchdog(8000, 2);

    System.out.println("Hit <ENTER> and die!!!");
    int c = System.in.read();
    System.out.println("Shutting down Watchdog thread");
    // Allow Feeder thread to fall out of its run loop
    wd.feedDog = false;
    // Now we're just waiting to die!
    while (true) {
        System.out.println("Still breathing ...");
        try {
            Thread.sleep(2000);
        } catch (InterruptedException ie) {}
    }
}
}
```

Watchdog creates a thread to feed the watchdog, feeder, that keeps the system from resetting. The watchdog time-out is set to 8 seconds. As soon as the set-WatchdogTimeout method is invoked, the timer starts running. The timer mainte-nance thread resets the watchdog timer twice per time-out period. So every 4 seconds feeder wakes up, knocks back the watchdog, and goes back to sleep. As long as the feedDog boolean remains true, feeder will keep the system from resetting. The program's other thread of execution, the primordial thread, blocks waiting for user input. Once user input has been received, the primordial thread sets the feedDog boolean to false. The next time feeder wakes up, it detects that feedDog is false and falls out of the run loop. At this point, there is nothing run-ning in the system that can stop the watchdog timer from expiring. From that point, the system is 8 seconds from a hard reset.

Watchdog should be run from a serial session to view the boot progress mes-sages just shown. Also, since a watchdog reset is abrupt, the OS doesn't have any time to perform an orderly system shutdown, closing network connections and open files. So, before running Watchdog, be sure to exit any Telnet or FTP ses-sions, and kill all processes other than slush and the garbage collector. Here is a sample output of Watchdog.

```
TINI /> java Watchdog.tini
Hit <ENTER> and die!!!
Feeding the dog!
Feeding the dog!
Feeding the dog!
Shutting down Watchdog thread
Still breathing ...
Still breathing ...
Still breathing ...
Still breathing ...

----> TINI Boot <----
TINI OS 1.02
API Version 8009
```

Here we can see that the watchdog timer was knocked back three times before user input was received. So the application ran peacefully for about 12 seconds. At the point user input was received, the warning message "Shutting down Watchdog thread" was displayed, and the infinite loop in the primordial thread began executing. Somewhere between the fourth and fifth iteration of the "would be" infinite loop, the watchdog timer expired, rebooting the system.

10.2.5 Beware of Dog!

The watchdog is a very powerful and important tool in helping to ensure reliable operation for systems that use TINI technology. However, since a watchdog reset is a very abrupt action, it should be used only as a last resort to regain control of a completely unresponsive system. If an application is executing well enough to detect fatal errors, it should use the reboot method, provided in TINIOS, instead of forcing a watchdog reset. To avoid extraneous resets, use long time-out values, and feed the watchdog at least a couple of times per time-out interval.

10.3 THE EXTERNAL INTERRUPT

The external interrupt is so called because it is accessible to hardware not integrated into TINI's microcontroller. The external interrupt is exposed to peripheral devices as a port pin on the microcontroller. The external interrupt is exposed to the Java programmer through the small set of classes in the com.dalsemi.system package. These classes are used to configure the external interrupt and receive asynchronous notification from the system when an interrupt occurs. This section describes the important features and the correct use of the external interrupt classes.

10.3.1 Polling versus Interrupts

Polling is a pure software technique in which a thread of execution repeatedly asks all attached peripheral devices whether they have undergone a change in state that requires some action by the application software. If the answer is yes, the thread performs whatever action is required by the device, clearing the condition that caused the interrupt. If the answer is no, the thread will typically sleep for some small amount of time and ask again later.

Interrupts provide a much more efficient method of determining when a peripheral device requires attention. Instead of the application *asking* a peripheral whether it has data, the peripheral *tells* the application that it has data by interrupting it. Once the microcontroller detects the interrupt, it transfers execution control to a special software handler for the interrupt known as an ISR (Interrupt Service Routine). At this point, the ISR determines the source of the interrupt and what additional code, if any, is required to handle it.

The advantage of using interrupts is that no CPU cycles are burned unless one of the attached peripherals actually requires attention. This leaves the application free to go on about its business performing other, more useful, tasks.

10.3.2 Properties of the External Interrupt

The external interrupt pin is a "low true" pin. This is to say that the "active" state of the pin is a logic 0. The pin is pulled high (a logic 1) to its inactive state by a resistor internal to the microcontroller. To generate an interrupt, the peripheral drives this pin to a low level.

TINI's microcontroller provides three interrupt priority levels: low, high, and highest. The only interrupt that runs at the highest priority level is the "power fail" interrupt. The external interrupt is set by the OS during bootup to a high-priority interrupt. This implies that it will preempt the execution of code in either a normal (noninterrupting) state or code executing under a low-priority interrupt. This ensures that the ISR will receive quick notification of the interrupt.

10.3.3 Triggering the External Interrupt

The external interrupt can be configured to be either edge or level triggered. If edge triggering is selected, an interrupt is generated by a falling edge (a transition from a logic 1 to a logic 0) on the external interrupt pin. When using edge triggering, the interrupt is latched. This means that it is "remembered" by a memory element in the microcontroller, and the interrupt condition persists until it has been acknowledged by software. During the TINI OS boot process, the external interrupt is configured for edge triggering.

If level triggering is selected, the external interrupt pin must remain at a logic 0 until the microcontroller begins executing the low-level software routine that first handles interrupts. In other words, the fact that the interrupt occurred is not "remembered" by the microcontroller. So if the external interrupt pin returns to a logic 1 before the low-level ISR executes, it is as if the interrupt never occurred.

This results in loss of interrupts and a possible loss of synchronization between the processor and the peripheral generating the interrupts.

The triggering mechanism for the external interrupt can be configured from Java by invoking the following method on class `ExternalInterrupt`.

```
public static void setTrigger(boolean edgeTrigger,
                         ExternalInterruptEventListener owner)
    throws ExternalInterruptException
```

The `boolean` parameter `edge` is set to `true` for edge triggering and `false` for level triggering. The `owner` parameter is used by the system to provide a mutex (mutual exclusion) type semaphore. Once `setTriggering` is invoked by a process, that process is considered to be the owner of the interrupt. If another thread from the same process or a thread in a different process attempts to alter the triggering mode, an `ExternalInterruptException` is thrown. After the owning process terminates, the interrupt becomes unowned and the triggering mechanism can be altered by another process. Note that threads in other processes can still receive interrupt event notification. The triggering mode can be queried at any time by any thread using the `getTrigger` method.

```
public static boolean getTrigger()
```

The `getTrigger` method returns `true` for edge triggering and `false` for level triggering.

10.3.4   Receiving Notification of Interrupts

Notification of the occurrence of external interrupts is accomplished using an event listener model. `ExternalInterrupt` provides methods that allow an application to register and unregister for receiving interrupt notifications.

```
public void addEventListener(ExternalInterruptEventListener listener)
    throws TooManyListenersException
public void removeEventListener(ExternalInterruptEventListener listener)
```

Both methods require an instance of a class that implements the `ExternalInterruptEventListener` interface. `ExternalInterruptEventListener` defines the following method.

```
public void externalInterruptEvent(ExternalInterruptEvent ev)
```

This is the method that is invoked when an external interrupt has been received. The method is passed an `ExternalInterruptEvent` object. `ExternalInterruptEvent` extends `java.util.EventObject`. Currently, an `ExternalInterruptEvent` object encapsulates no information about the source of the interrupt. It is left to the application to communicate with the attached peripheral to determine additional information about the nature of the interrupt.

Applications can have multiple listeners for external interrupts. The first time addEventListener is successfully called, a daemon thread is created that immediately invokes a blocking native method. The native method puts the thread to sleep until an external interrupt occurs. When the interrupt occurs, the daemon thread is awakened by the system and returns from the native method. The thread then enumerates a vector of the event listeners and notifies them of the interrupt. Once the last listener invokes the removeEventListener method, the daemon thread is destroyed.

The program shown in Listing 10.4 listens for external interrupts. Every time an external interrupt occurs, it simply increments an event counter. For the sake of making the event causing the interrupts more concrete, a push-button switch was used to generate the interrupts.[3] To test the example one side of the switch is connected to the external interrupt pin[4] and the other side to ground. Recall that the external interrupt pin is pulled high to its inactive state internally. When the switch is closed, by depressing the push button, the external interrupt pin is pulled to ground, generating a falling edge that causes the interrupt.

Listing 10.4   PushButton

```
import java.util.TooManyListenersException;

import com.dalsemi.system.ExternalInterrupt;
import com.dalsemi.system.ExternalInterruptEvent;
import com.dalsemi.system.ExternalInterruptEventListener;

class PushButton implements ExternalInterruptEventListener {
    // Maintain a count of external interrupt events
    int count;
    ExternalInterrupt extInt;

    PushButton() throws TooManyListenersException {
        extInt = new ExternalInterrupt();
        extInt.addEventListener(this);
    }

    public void externalInterruptEvent(ExternalInterruptEvent ev) {
        ++count;
        System.out.println("Event count: " + count);
    }

    public static void main(String[] args)
```

---

3. This example ignores debounce problems altogether because it adds little to the discussion.
4. Pin 23 on the TINI Board Model 390.

```
        throws TooManyListenersException {
        PushButton pb = new PushButton();
        // Don't let the primordial thread die!
        try {
            Thread.sleep(Long.MAX_VALUE);
        } catch (InterruptedException ie) {}
    }
}
```

The `PushButton` class implements the `ExternalInterruptEventListener` interface and must provide an implementation of the `externalInterruptEvent` method. Every time an interrupt occurs, this method is invoked and it increments and displays the number of interrupts that have occurred since the listener was added.

After adding itself as a listener for external interrupts, the primordial thread itself has nothing left to do. So it puts itself to sleep for a practically infinite amount of time. This is roughly equivalent to invoking `Thread.suspend`, but it avoids using a deprecated method. We need to sleep forever as opposed to just exiting the main method because the notifier thread is a daemon thread and will exit when the last user thread exits. In this example, the only user thread is the primordial thread. If it exits, the application will terminate almost immediately after starting.

Every time the push button is depressed, the `externalInterruptEvent` method is invoked by the daemon notifier thread and the event count is incremented and displayed. This is the output from running `PushButton` as a background process from a Telnet session.

```
TINI /> java PushButton.tini &
Id:7 Event count: 1
Id:7 Event count: 2
Id:7 Event count: 3
Id:7 Event count: 4
Id:7 Event count: 5
Id:7 Event count: 6
```

The fact that the external interrupt is a shared system-wide resource can be seen by running another instance of `PushButton` in the background of the same Telnet session.

```
TINI /> java PushButton.tini &
Id:7 Event count: 7
Id:8 Event count: 1
Id:8 Event count: 2
Id:7 Event count: 8
Id:8 Event count: 3
Id:7 Event count: 9
```

Now there are two instances of the same application listening for the same external interrupts. Every time the push button is depressed, both processes increment and display their own internal event counter.

A closer look at the preceding output suggests an important point. The first two lines of output show that the first instance of PushButton received notification of the interrupt before the second instance. The next two lines of output show just the opposite: the second instance receives the first notification. The order in which event listeners are invoked is not guaranteed between different processes or different threads in the same process. The ordering depends on what process and/or thread is executing when the interrupt occurs. For all practical purposes, the ordering should be considered random.

10.3.5   Sharing a Common Interrupt Source

In the PushButton example, there was only one source for interrupts in the entire system: the push button. In a large embedded system, there may be multiple peripherals, each providing one or possibly more interrupt sources. This requires a mechanism for sharing the external interrupt.

An interrupt controller chip can be used to multiplex several different sources of interrupts into the same external interrupt pin. It is up to each listener to determine whether it is interested in the source of the interrupt. If so, it takes the appropriate action and acknowledges receipt of the interrupt in a fashion completely dependent on the hardware that generated the interrupt.

CHAPTER 11

Application Programming Tips

This chapter discusses techniques for profiling I/O performance, execution time, and memory use. These methods are employed to study the impact of I/O, memory, and code speed optimizations. It concludes with a discussion of how to harden an application for production deployment. All the suggestions and practices described in this chapter were written with TINI's runtime environment in mind. Some of these tips may be beneficial on other platforms, while others may not. In other words, your mileage may vary.

11.1 PERFORMANCE PROFILING

To avoid being vague about how a suggested optimization may improve application performance, most of the examples presented here will be timed before and after a specific optimization. This section describes the procedure used to time the performance of most of the code snippets in the following sections. It also provides some insight into issues that should be considered to accurately profile portions of your application.

The uptimeMillis method, defined in the com.dalsemi.system.TINIOS class, can be used for timing operations that execute over a period of a few milliseconds to several minutes with reasonable accuracy.

```
public static native final long uptimeMillis()
```

This method returns a `long` integer representing the number of milliseconds that have elapsed since the system was booted. It is maintained by the high-priority timer interrupt that drives system operations such as task scheduling. It is not tied to the real-time clock in any way, but it drifts only about 1 millisecond every second. The `currentTimeMillis` method, defined in `java.lang.System`, returns a long integer that represents the number of milliseconds that have elapsed since midnight, January 1, 1970 UTC. Its value is derived from reading the real-time clock and over long periods of time is very accurate. However, the smallest time interval granularity supported by TINI's real-time clock is 10 milliseconds, making it difficult to use `currentTimeMillis` to measure small intervals of time. Also, a lot of expensive arithmetic must be performed to compute the specified return value. In fact, it takes nearly 20 milliseconds per invocation of `currentTimeMillis` on a TINI Board model 390. Either method can be used for our purposes, but the execution times reported in this chapter are measured using `uptimeMillis` because of its relatively low overhead compared with `currentTimeMillis`.

To keep the overhead of profiling code to a dull roar, the timing measurements are taken in-line by capturing the OS tick count just before and just after the operation being timed. Additional method invocations are avoided. A sample code snippet is shown in Listing 11.1. With a granularity of approximately 1 millisecond returned by `uptimeMillis`, we should expect timing errors roughly within a +/– 2-millisecond range for two invocations of `uptimeMillis`.

Listing 11.1   Measuring elapsed time

```
import com.dalsemi.system.TINIOS;
...
class SomeClass {
    ...

    void someMethod() {
        ...
        long startTime = TINIOS.uptimeMillis();

        // Do stuff we're interested in timing
        ...
        long elapsed = TINIOS.uptimeMillis() - startTime;
        System.out.println("Time elapsed : " + elapsed);
    }
}
```

All source was compiled with javac distributed in JDK1.2.2. The time measurements were taken by executing the code snippets on a TINI Board Model 390 that runs at processor clock rate of 36.864[1] MHz. The TINI runtime version used

---

1.   The external crystal is actually 18.432 MHz, but the clock rate is doubled on the processor by a phase locked loop (PLL) to 36.864 MHz.

is v1.02, and all applications were launched from slush. No other processes were running. The numbers achieved when the applications are loaded directly into the flash ROM are about 3 to 4 percent faster. The performance of other TINI hardware implementations will of course vary depending largely on the processor clock rate. System loading caused by processing network and other interrupts can also cause noticeable timing variations.

Serious variations can occur when measuring operations that require only a small amount of time for execution. The variations can be caused by sudden changes in CPU load due to interrupts, from sources such as the Ethernet network controller, or just due to loss of execution because of either thread or process swapping. For this reason, the test environment should be reasonably well controlled. First, only one process should be actively executing. Other live processes, such as *init* (typically the shell) and *gc* (the garbage collector), are fine as long as they are dormant (not actively being scheduled). To avoid high percentage errors in measurement when measuring relatively quick operations, perform the operation a number of times, typically in a loop, and measure the entire time. Then divide the result by the number of loop iterations. If the overall execution time is aimed at several seconds, then any error due to interrupt latency under normal loads will be negligibly small.

11.2   EFFICIENT I/O

For most TINI applications, the first priority is efficiently moving data to and from system resources such as the serial port or Ethernet controller, as well as external application-specific hardware. TINI's runtime environment was written with this in mind. The native I/O infrastructure was carefully coded so that data can be moved quickly from application provided buffers (byte arrays) to system resources or attached circuitry. The most important thing a Java application must do to take advantage of this infrastructure is to move data between the application and native drivers quickly. This means moving data in reasonably large blocks as opposed to a single byte at a time. The process of moving data to and from streams, or other I/O mechanisms, a byte at a time will be loosely termed *byte-banging*.

11.2.1   Block Data Transfer versus Byte-Banging

Like other Java platforms, much of the I/O on TINI is stream based, including network, file system, and serial port communication. This means that moving data to and from an I/O resource usually boils down to invoking `read` and `write` methods on instances of subclasses of `java.io.InputStream` and `java.io.OutputStream`. Efficient I/O using streams can be achieved by utilizing these "block" `read` and `write` methods.

```
public int read(byte[] b, int off, int len) throws IOException
public void write(byte[] b, int off, int len) throws IOException
```

The default implementation of these methods provided in InputStream and
OutputStream is very inefficient. The write method, for example, simply
invokes the single byte write method iteratively len times to move len bytes of
data to the underlying resource. This makes sense because InputStream and
OutputStream are not tied to any concrete I/O resource and therefore are unable
to make any assumptions about the native interface provided for a specific
device or resource. However, subclasses of InputStream and OutputStream
override the read and write methods just shown. The subclass's implementation
maps directly to a native method call to a driver that takes the same parameters
and performs the requested I/O. The requested data transfer occurs at the
expense of only one, rather than len, context switches from the Java application
to the native runtime.

Listing 11.2 shows the worker thread of an echo server. The echo server
accepts connections from clients and creates an EchoWorker thread to manage
the connection. EchoWorker's constructor invokes the getInputStream and
getOutputStream methods on the socket to get the lowest level, and therefore
most efficient, streams available for reading data from and writing data to the
underlying connection. These are actually instances of SocketInputStream and
SocketOutputStream, which are private classes defined in the java.net package.
The run method waits for receive data. All data received is immediately
transmitted (or echoed) back to the sender. The run method will exit normally if
the echo client closes the connection or abruptly if an IOException occurs
during a network read or write operation. Inbound data from the client is read by
invoking the single-byte read method on the socket's input stream and written to
the client using the single-byte write method on the socket's output stream.

Listing 11.2   EchoWorker

```
...
private class EchoWorker implements Runnable {
    Socket s;
    InputStream sin;
    OutputStream sout;

    private EchoWorker(Socket s) throws IOException {
        this.s = s;
        sin = s.getInputStream();
        sout = s.getOutputStream();
    }

    public void run() {
        try {
```

```
        int count = 0;
        while (count != -1) {
            int c = sin.read();
            if (c != -1) {
                sout.write(c);
            }
        }
    } catch (IOException ioe) {
        System.out.println(ioe.getMessage());
        ioe.printStackTrace();
    } finally {
        try {
            s.close();
            sin.close();
            sout.close();
        } catch (IOException _) {}
    }
  }
}
```

To test the echo server, we'll need an echo client.[2] The echo client used here connects to the server and transmits a fixed amount of data to the server. It closes the connection after it has received all of the data it transmitted. The effective throughput of the server is measured by the client by dividing the number of bytes transmitted by the time elapsed between when the first byte is transmitted and the last byte is received. This is a measurement of the full-duplex[3] throughput of the server. The total number of bytes flowing between the client and server, ignoring network packet overhead, is twice the number of bytes transmitted by the client.

With the run method implemented as shown in Listing 11.2, the echo server achieves a total throughput of 110 bytes per second. We can see why the server is so slow by examining the series of events that occurs every time we invoke the write method on the SocketOutputStream. First, the write method invokes a native method to send the byte to the socket layer of the network stack. The native socket write routine copies the byte into a TCP output buffer. From there the byte makes its way down the network stack and finally is transmitted onto the network. In the read case, the data flow is reversed, but the cost per byte is about the same. Even if the overhead incurred by data processing in the network stack were negligible, the throughput would still be greatly limited just by the number of Java method invocations. We'll see in the next section that method invocations are fairly expensive.

---

2. The source code of the echo client and server used to generate the performance numbers that follow is included in the CD that accompanies this text.

3. Data is being simultaneously transmitted and received by both the client and server.

Listing 11.3 Modified run method

```
...
byte[] buf = new byte[4096];
...
public void run() {
    try {
        int count = 0;
        while (count != -1) {
            count = sin.read(buf, 0, buf.length);
            if (count > 0) {
                sout.write(buf, 0, count);
            }
        }
    } catch (IOException ioe) {
        ...
    }
}
```

If we change the run method to do block reads and writes, each method invocation can move multiple bytes at almost the same cost as moving a single byte. Listing 11.3 shows a modified run method. The new version creates a 4-kilobyte buffer that is used for both reads from and writes to the socket's streams. The read method that takes a byte array, an offset into the array, and a byte count is used to receive data from the client. It blocks until at least 1 byte of data is available to the stream. Once 1 or more bytes are available, they are copied into the caller-provided byte array. The number of bytes actually copied into the byte array is returned by read. All of the bytes read from the SocketInputStream are then written to the SocketOutputStream. The write operation is accomplished using the efficient write method that also takes a byte array, an offset into the array, and a length. The length supplied to write is identical to the number of bytes received by read.

If only 1 byte is available every time read is invoked, then the situation hasn't improved any. The read method will return the byte, and it will be echoed to the client. However, if the client is transmitting data at a rapid pace, there will usually be multiple bytes available on the input stream. In this example, data is being received over a TCP connection on an Ethernet network. This means the messages received by the network stack can contain as much as 1460^4 bytes of application data. Since there is no guarantee that an application will be ready to receive network data as soon as it's available, the network stack maintains fairly large buffers for receive and transmit data. TINI's network stack uses input buffers of 4 kilobytes in length—hence the size of buf chosen in Listing 11.3.

---

4. The maximum length of an unfragmented IP datagram encapsulated within an Ethernet frame is 1500 bytes. Accounting for a 20-byte IP header and a 20-byte TCP header, the resulting segment payload can be as large as 1460 bytes.

Running the new and improved version of `EchoServer` results in a total throughput of about 60,000 bytes per second. This is well over 500 times faster than the results obtained from the byte-banging version. This dramatic improvement underscores the point that the cost of moving a single byte at a time through a stream can be nearly as expensive as moving multiple bytes using byte arrays. If at all possible, an application should prorate the overhead of read and write operations by moving reasonably large blocks of data.

Byte-banging is appropriate, and actually a requirement, for some applications. The `TiniTerm` program, presented in Section 3.4, is a good example of an application that needs to move data in small, often single-byte, chunks. A terminal program appears more responsive to the user if it is not buffering the data before displaying it. As soon as a character is received by the terminal program, it should be echoed to the display. Also, data rates comparable to the 110 bytes per second achieved by the slow echo server are fine in the case of a terminal program because it's awfully tough to type more than 100 keystrokes in one second. However, the majority of TINI applications interface with hardware (as opposed to humans) that move data in bursts and often at the maximum rate supported by the communications channel. The `SerialToEthernet` example, presented in Section 3.5, was written to be able to move large amounts of data between a serial device and an Ethernet network. A throughput of only a few hundred bytes per second would render that application useless.

Since both the `EchoClient` and `EchoServer` programs used in this section are written in Java, it is a trivial matter to collect similar numbers for other platforms. When the byte-banging version of the echo server was run on a PIII Win2K machine, the server processed only about 1000 bytes per second. This is faster than the equivalent server running on TINI but still much slower than the efficient version of the echo server on TINI. This demonstrates that byte-banging isn't just inefficient on resource-constrained environments. It can be painfully slow on almost any platform.

In the echo client/server example, we focused on stream-based I/O, but this also applies to other forms of data transfer such as parallel I/O and 2-wire synchronous serial data transfer. The classes that expose these forms of I/O provide block `read` and `write` methods that accept a parameter list identical to those defined in `InputStream` and `OutputStream`. The performance differences between byte-banging and block moves are huge for both of these cases as well. If the `MemoryTester` application, developed in Section 8.3.2, used the single-byte `read` method on the `DataPort` object to read from and write to the external memory, the throughput would have been a few hundred bytes per second versus more than a hundred thousand bytes per second. In most cases, converting the I/O portions of an application to block moves from byte-banging will lead to throughput improvements of two to three orders of magnitude.

This section can be summarized as follows.

- Byte-banging: Bad, very bad!
- Moving data from stream to stream (or port to port, as the case may be) in reasonably large blocks: Good!

11.2.2   Buffered Streams

Under the right circumstances, the use of a `java.io.BufferedInputStream` or `java.io.BufferedOutputStream` can improve a program's performance, and when used for network I/O, they can also reduce the total amount of network traffic. As the names suggest, both provide buffering on top of another stream. The buffer is maintained internally as a byte array whose size can be specified during construction of the stream. The main idea is that most reads from or writes to the stream can occur directly to the internal buffer without incurring the overhead of native method invocations to transfer the data to or from the operating system. In the case of a `BufferedOutputStream`, for example, only when the internal buffer fills or the `flush` method is invoked is the underlying stream's `write` method called.

Using buffered streams does not always lead to greater efficiency. While buffering would improve the performance of the inefficient echo server from Listing 11.2, it would actually degrade the results produced by the modified version of the echo server in Listing 11.3. In this case, the buffered streams serve only to introduce another layer of data handling between the application and the network stack. In general, if an application already has a large block of data (that is, a buffer), it should probably use the stream that is the "closest to the metal" for greatest efficiency.

If your application consumes or produces data in small chunks, the use of buffered streams provides a large benefit. The `DataLogger` example, from Chapter 7, collected measurements that were represented as a couple of `double`s and a `long`. The measurements were transmitted to a network client using a `java.io.DataOutputStream` object attached to a socket. `DataOutputStream`'s `writeDouble` and `writeLong` methods each write 8 bytes of data to the underlying output stream. If that output stream were not buffered, each of these writes would copy the data directly to the native socket layer's write routine. The network stack would then be generating lots of small messages, transmitting most of the values in separate segments. By wrapping the `DataOutputStream` object in a `BufferedOutputStream`, the values written to the `DataOutputStream` are not copied to the network stack until the `BufferedOutputStream`'s internal buffer is full or its `flush` method is invoked. The result is that fewer network segments need to be generated because each segment contains more data. Network bandwidth is utilized more efficiently, and the overall application performance is improved.

11.3 MEMORY USAGE

As Java programmers we're used to enjoying the freedom of developing programs without considering how much memory we use or when we're using it. We torch memory with reckless abandon and let the garbage collector clean up the mess. For the most part, we would rather not concern ourselves with memory management issues at all, and there is certainly no requirement to do so when writing TINI applications. However, on TINI, we're working with heap sizes as small as a few hundred kilobytes versus a few hundred megabytes on a PC or workstation. A little consideration, especially during the design phase, of how your application behaves with respect to memory consumption can go a long way.

11.3.1 Object Creation

Object creation, initiated by the new operator, is expensive both in terms of memory and CPU consumption. All objects that are created are either arrays or class instances. When either is created, a malloc (memory allocation operation) is performed by the memory manager on behalf of the VM. Further adding to the cost of the malloc operation is the fact that malloc is effectively a "calloc" that clears all of the allocated memory to 0s. This is done so that all array elements, or instance fields, are properly initialized to their specified default values. The vast majority of the time required to create an array is spent performing the malloc operation. When a class instance is created, allocating the memory is just the first step. Next, the object's internal structure is initialized, and then its constructor and its superclasses's constructor (and so on) are all interpreted by the VM. The time this takes depends largely on what operations are performed by the individual constructors, but it can easily dwarf the amount of time required to allocate memory for the object. In some cases, the amount of object creation can be reduced by reusing previously created objects. Depending on the application, this may require care to avoid using stale information from an old object or possibly creating thread-safety problems.

11.3.2 Strings

Strings have a sneaky way of gobbling up lots of memory (and CPU in the process), but they are extremely useful. Every attempt has been made to make string operations efficient. For example, many of the methods in the String class are implemented as native methods. However, there isn't much that can be done about the amount of memory consumed by various methods in the String class. Methods like toUpperCase, toLowerCase, substring, and so forth all create and return new String objects. Imagine a scenario in which an array of strings is being parsed within a loop and in each iteration of the loop the string is compared to the lowercase version of a portion of some source string using a statement like the following.

```
if (s[i].equals(src.toLowerCase().substring(3, 6))) {
    ...
}
```

Two temporary strings are created. Each pass through the loop, chewing up both memory and time. In this case, the problem can be avoided by creating the string required for comparison outside of the loop and storing a reference to it in a local variable. The local reference can then be used for comparison within the loop.

String concatenation using the + operator is also expensive. The java compiler generates code that creates a `StringBuffer` object and uses its `append` method to copy the individual strings into the `StringBuffer`'s internal character array. The result is then converted back to a string by invoking `StringBuffer`'s `toString` method. The cost of string concatenation can be lowered by creating an appropriately sized `StringBuffer` directly. If the `StringBuffer` is created using the following constructor

```
public StringBuffer(int length)
```

with a capacity (the value of `length`) large enough to contain the final string, the `StringBuffer`'s internal character array will not have to be resized during concatenation (`append`) operations. This prevents creating new arrays as well as the array copy operations that would be required to copy the contents of the old buffer to the new buffer.

11.3.3   Profiling Memory Usage

There are a few things to keep in mind when analyzing your application's memory usage. First, because TINI is a multi-threaded, multi-process system, memory profiling is an inexact science. If you're analyzing a particular method executing within a particular thread, you may need to suspend other processes as well as other threads within the same process in case they are consuming memory as well. If your application, slush, and the garbage collector are the only processes running in the system, you shouldn't need to worry about the other processes. Slush won't use any memory unless you're interacting with a slush session. The only kernel process that could consume memory without direct cause from the application is the network stack's TCP process. When it establishes a connection with a remote peer, it allocates approximately 12 kilobytes of memory (for circular input and output buffers) from the garbage collected heap. Most other kernel processes use a fast memory manager that allocates data from a separate, small heap.

There are two methods that return the amount of free memory available in the garbage collected heap (Java heap). The `freeMemory` method that is defined in the `java.lang.Runtime` class

```
public long freeMemory()
```

and the `getFreeRAM` method defined in `com.dalsemi.system.TINIOS`.

```
public static final int getFreeRAM()
```

Both return the same value, but `getFreeRAM` is static and therefore doesn't require the creation of an object just for the sake of memory reporting.

If you're going to write the amount to the console using `System.out` or any `PrintStream` using a harmless-looking statement like the following

```
System.out.println("Free RAM:"+TINIOS.getFreeRAM());
```

be aware that just executing that statement consumes a noticeable amount of memory. To see this, you can execute the `MemReporter` example shown in Listing 11.4. It simply loops forever, displaying the amount of free memory.

Listing 11.4   MemReporter

```
import com.dalsemi.system.TINIOS;

class MemReporter {
    public static void main(String[] args) {
        while (true) {
            System.out.println("Free RAM:"+TINIOS.getFreeRAM());
        }
    }
}
```

Sample output from `MemReporter` is shown in Listing 11.5.

Listing 11.5   MemReporter output

```
TINI /> java MemReporter.tini &
...
Free RAM:312512
Free RAM:312224
Free RAM:311936
...
```

Each iteration consumes 288 bytes. The exact number of bytes consumed from iteration to iteration may vary by a small amount. Also, note that since the smallest chunk of memory allocated by the memory manager is 32 bytes, the difference between return values `getFreeRAM` from successive iterations will be a multiple of 32.

Let's take a look at where some of the memory is going. To manage the string concatenation, the compiler generates code to create a `StringBuffer`. The "Free RAM:" string is copied to the `StringBuffer`. Also, memory is consumed, converting the integer returned by `getFreeRAM` to a `String` using `Integer.toString`. The string representation of the free memory is then appended to the `StringBuffer`. Finally, the resulting `StringBuffer` is converted to a `String`. After the display string is fully cooked, it is written to the `PrintStream`. During that process the message string is first converted to a character array and then a byte array. All of these steps create objects, reducing the actual amount of free memory before it's even displayed. Of course, all of the memory consumed by the preceding statement quickly becomes garbage and will eventually be reclaimed.

To get a handle on where and how much memory your application is consuming, it helps to view the free memory without altering it. The `displayRAM` method shown in Listing 11.6 writes the current amount of free memory to `System.out` without consuming any memory.

Listing 11.6   displayRAM

```
...
private static final byte[] prompt = "Free RAM:".getBytes();
private static final byte[] lt =
    System.getProperty("line.separator").getBytes();

private static void displayRAM() {
    try {
        synchronized (prompt) {
            System.out.write(prompt);
            Debug.intDump(TINIOS.getFreeRAM());
            System.out.write(lt);
        }
    } catch (IOException ioe) {
        ioe.printStackTrace();
    }
}
```

It looks a little awkward, but it is effective. The memory for the fixed-text portion of the output is allocated only once when the class (static) initializers are run. Both the prompt and the line separator are maintained as byte arrays so that they can be used directly with `PrintStream`'s `write` method that takes a byte array as input. The static method `intDump`, defined in the class `com.dalsemi.system.Debug`, converts the integer to a printable form and writes the result to `System.out`. This replaces the memory-consuming method `Integer.toString`, used by `MemReporter`.

11.3.4 Garbage Collection

The garbage collector is launched in one of the following three ways:

- An application explicitly invokes System.gc().
- A new operation reduces the amount of free RAM to drop below a low-memory threshold (64 kilobytes).
- A Java process terminates.

On TINI, when an application invokes the gc method, it is treated as more than just a suggestion. If the garbage collector isn't already running on behalf of the application,[5] it will be launched immediately. It executes as an independent process as opposed to a separate thread executing within the same process. When the garbage collector runs, it will compete, on equal footing, with other processes for CPU time. This can cause a temporary degradation in your application's performance. For example, consider the typical case where only one Java process is actively competing for the CPU. When the garbage collector is idle, the Java process can utilize nearly 100 percent of the CPU. However, when the garbage collector is active, the Java process will share the CPU equally with the garbage collector. This reduces the Java process's maximum possible CPU utilization to 50 percent. After the garbage collector has completed its task, the gc process returns to an idle state in which it consumes no CPU. You can see this in action by letting the MemReporter example (Listing 11.4) run for a while. Once the free memory dips below 64 kilobytes, the garbage collector will start automatically and MemReporter's updates will slow. Once the garbage collector has finished, the updates will speed up again.

If the structure of your application is such that there exists a natural location to explicitly launch the garbage collector, then it may be possible to reduce the overall impact that garbage collection has on the application to a negligible level. Perhaps it periodically communicates with some device or network host, consuming memory in the process, and then goes quiet for long periods. During this quiet period your application can launch the garbage collector, allowing it to use most of the available CPU to quickly do its job and go back to sleep. The combination of reusing objects when appropriate and launching the garbage collector at opportune times can lead to a faster and more responsive application.

11.4 OTHER OPTIMIZATION TIPS

The controller at the heart of TINI's runtime environment is geared much more toward efficient I/O than quick execution of computationally intensive tasks.

---

5. The gc can collect garbage on multiple processes simultaneously.

Because of this, applications that perform a lot of data processing and analysis present performance challenges. In order to improve the performance of such applications and squeeze the most out of TINI's small controller, we'll spend just a little time under the hood of the JVM to see why certain operations are expensive. We'll discuss ways to exploit this knowledge for the sake of enhancing application performance in critical sections of code.

Most of the operations that are expensive on TINI execute in a negligible amount of time on your Hexium X, 2 Jillion Hz host development machine. Many coding inefficiencies can go completely unnoticed when running on a very fast machine. The tips presented here are geared for the TINI platform. Due to JiTs and other runtime optimizers, some of the following optimizations may not be nearly as effective when applied to other Java platforms. On TINI there is no JiT, no hotspot, and no runtime optimizations performed by the virtual machine. The techniques described here reduce the amount of work that must be undertaken by the bytecode interpreter and can therefore make a real difference to your application's overall performance.

11.4.1 Relative Cost of Common Operations

Before getting into specific optimizations, it is worth spending a little time exploring the cost, in terms of execution time, of common operations like accessing instance variables and invoking methods. Those listed below are ordered from most to least expensive.

- Class instance creation
- Array creation
- Method invocation
- Instance and class (static) variable access
- Array access[6]
- Local variable access

As discussed in Section 11.3, object creation is a very expensive operation, and creating class instances takes longer than creating new arrays. Method invocations, either static or instance, are also time consuming. They take about 5 to 10 times longer than storing or retrieving instance or static field values. The difference in execution speed of array access and field accesses isn't usually too dramatic. Finally, by comparison to the other operations listed, working with local variables is very fast. In certain cases, an application can save a lot of time by moving some

---

6. This assumes single-dimensional arrays. The use of multidimensional arrays is very expensive, both in terms of memory usage and access time.

of the slower operations from within loops that must execute quickly. We discuss a few possible ways to accomplish this in the following section.

11.4.2   Loop Optimizations

There may be occasions where your application will need to charge through an array in a loop performing some operation(s) on the individual array elements. The tips described in this section are designed to speed up performance of loops with modest to large iteration counts. The iteration count should be sufficient to prorate the overhead of single operations that are added outside of the loop with the goal of speeding operations within the loop.

For the purpose of illustration, we'll use a concrete, though highly contrived, example. The Bogus class, shown in Listing 11.7, contains the static method char-Counter that counts the number of occurrences of the specified character encapsulated within a String object. The main method concocts a test String that encapsulates a character array whose length is specified on the command line. The character array is initialized with a repeating sequence of incrementing lowercase ASCII characters (a–z). The string's length should be large enough to reduce the effect that short-duration transient spikes of system activity could have on the timing measurements.

Listing 11.7   Bogus

```
import com.dalsemi.system.TINIOS;

class Bogus {
    public static int charCounter(String s, char ch) {
        long startTime = TINIOS.uptimeMillis();
        int count = 0;
        for (int i = 0; i < s.length(); i++) {
            if (s.charAt(i) == ch) {
                ++count;
            }
        }
        long elapsed = TINIOS.uptimeMillis() - startTime;
        System.out.println("elapsed time: " + elapsed +
                            "ms for String of length " + s.length());
        return count;
    }

    public static void main(String[] args) {
        if (args.length != 1) {
            System.out.println("Usage: java Bogus.tini length");
            System.exit(1);
        }
        // Create a bogus String
        char[] ca = new char[Integer.parseInt(args[0])];
        for (int i = 0; i < ca.length; i++) {
```

```
            ca[i] = (char) ('a' + (i%26));
        }
        String s = new String(ca);
        System.out.println("number of a's="+charCounter(s, 'a'));
    }
}
```

All of the run times listed below apply to the time required for the char-Counter method's loop to process a test String of length 16384 (16 kilobytes). It will take charCounter plenty of time (on the order of several seconds) to slug its way through the entire string, leaving us with a reasonably accurate idea of just how effective the performance enhancements really are. Running the Bogus application as in Listing 11.7 produces an output similar to the following.

```
TINI /> java Bogus.tini 16384
elapsed time: 8564ms for String of length 16384
number of a's=631
```

It took about 8.6 seconds to count the number of a's contained within the String.

Now let's focus on charCounter's loop that computes the count and look for some possible performance improvements. We can start by looking at the for loop's conditional expression.

```
i < s.length()
```

Each iteration through the loop invokes the length method on the String object. We know from the previous section that method invocations are relatively expensive operations. Since strings are immutable, we know that their length will remain constant. To avoid this method invocation on every loop operation, we can cache the length in a local variable. So when the loop conditional is evaluated, the length is fetched quickly from the local variable rather than returned from a method. The modifications are shown in Listing 11.8.

Listing 11.8 Caching the length in a local variable

```
...
// Copy String length to local for faster access
int len = s.length();
for (int i = 0; i < len; i++) {
    if (s.charAt(i) == ch) {
        ++count;
    }
}
```

Executing Bogus again with these modifications reduces the execution time to 5997 milliseconds.

Next we can take a look inside the loop. Every iteration invokes the `charAt` method to determine the character value at the specified index. Again we can exploit the fact that strings are immutable to safely acquire a local copy of the character array and extract the characters directly from the array. The modifications are shown in Listing 11.9

Listing 11.9   Directly accessing character data

```
...
// Copy String length to local for faster access
int len = s.length();
// Get a local copy of char[]
char[] ca = new char[len];
s.getChars(0, len, ca, 0);
for (int i = 0; i < len; i++) {
    if (ca[i] == ch) {
        ++count;
    }
}
```

With this implementation, the execution time drops to 3248 milliseconds. Now there isn't much left to optimize away. No methods are invoked in the loop, the only array access is necessary, and all variables are local, as opposed to instance or static variables. We can still squeeze a few more CPU cycles out of the loop by optimizing the loop structure itself. To this point, a `for` loop has been used to iterate through the array elements. The loop expression compares two non-zero integer values to decide whether to terminate the loop. This comparison is accomplished by the JVM using one of a set (of six) Java opcodes that compare the top two integers on the operand stack and, depending on the result of the comparison, branch to a new location in the bytecode stream. Both integers are copied from a local variable to the top of the operand stack prior to the comparison. This all occurs reasonably quickly, but the comparison of an arbitrary integer with 0 is faster. There is a separate set of opcodes in which one of the operands (0) in the comparison is implied. This means that the VM only needs to copy the contents of one local variable to the top of the operand stack. If we convert our `for` loop to a `while` loop that just counts down to 0, we should see a small performance enhancement. The modifications are shown in Listing 11.10.

Listing 11.10   Using a faster loop

```
...
// Copy String length to local for faster access
int len = s.length();
// Get a local copy of char[]
char[] ca = new char[len];
s.getChars(0, len, ca, 0);
```

```
while (len > 0) {
    if (ca[--len] == ch) {
        ++count;
    }
}
```

This final tweak runs in a time of 2877 milliseconds. So from our starting point to now we've improved the method's performance by about 300 percent. It still isn't blazingly fast, but certainly the improvement is well worth the small amount of additional code.

The charCounter example was of course just used as a simple vehicle to discuss techniques for optimizing code within time-consuming loops. If we were actually interested in the functionality provided by the charCounter method, we might consider the implementation shown in Listing 11.11. At first glance, it seems reasonable that this approach would be more efficient than the original technique used in Listing 11.7 but somewhat less efficient than our fastest attempt shown in Listing 11.10.

Listing 11.11   Using indexOf

```
...
int count = 0;
int index = 0;
while (true) {
    index = s.indexOf(ch, index);
    if (index != -1) {
        ++count;
        ++index;
    } else {
        break;
    }
}
```

The results obtained using the above implementation of charCounter on the test string are in the neighborhood of 630 milliseconds. However, only the fact that indexOf is implemented as a native method on TINI makes it faster than Listing 11.10.

What wasn't mentioned in the previous discussion was the possible benefit of unrolling loops to further reduce the impact of the overhead of the loop structure. This isn't specific to TINI or Java. It is a time-honored tradition usually employed out of true desperation. Whether unrolling a loop is beneficial really depends on the time required testing for loop termination versus the time required for the sum of the operations performed inside the loop. If the loop structure is lean and mean when compared with the operations performed inside the loop, there is little practical benefit to unrolling the loop. On the other hand, if the loop terminator requires a large amount of time (perhaps due to necessary method invocations) compared to the time required to execute the code within the loop, it may be worthwhile.

In the previous example, we achieved substantial performance gains by replacing unnecessary method invocations with fast local variable accesses. Under certain circumstances we can also improve performance by caching class or instance fields in local variables. Accessing an instance variable is somewhat expensive because it requires the JVM to parse the object's internal structure and extract the specified field. Consider the array compare example shown in Listing 11.12. In this case the arrays a and b are private instance variables. If the arrays are of identical length, the isEqual method iterates through the elements of the array, checking for equality. If the array elements are unequal at any index, isEqual aborts immediately and returns false.

Listing 11.12   Array compare

```
...
private byte[] a;
private byte[] b;
...
private boolean isEqual() {
    if (a.length != b.length) {
        return false;
    }
    for (int i = 0; i < a.length; i++) {
        if (a[i] != b[i]) {
            return false;
        }
    }
    return true;
}
...
```

The worst-case execution time results when the arrays are identical. If isEqual is run on arrays 16 kilobytes in length with identical contents, it requires 7390 milliseconds to compare all of the elements. If we modify the method slightly and cache the array references, a and b, in local variables as shown in Listing 11.13, the resulting run time is 4431 milliseconds. In this case three instance variable accesses are replaced by local variable accesses for each loop iteration: two used in the comparison of the array elements and one used in extracting the array length.

Listing 11.13   Caching instance fields in local variables

```
...
byte[] a = this.a;
byte[] b = this.b;
for (int i = 0; i < a.length; i++) {
```

```
    if (a[i] != b[i]) {
        return false;
    }
}
...
```

The way the loop's conditional expression is constructed requires the JVM to interpret the `arraylength` opcode, fetching the length from the specified array for each iteration. This seems like a bit of a waste, since the array length is guaranteed to remain constant. Fetching the length of an array isn't a terribly slow operation but it is still faster to load a value from a local variable. In the code snippet in Listing 11.14, the array length is stored in the local variable `len`, which is then used in the loop's conditional expression.

Listing 11.14   Caching array length in a local variable

```
...
byte[] a = this.a;
byte[] b = this.b;
int len = a.length;
for (int i = 0; i < len; i++) {
    if (a[i] != b[i]) {
        return false;
    }
}
...
```

The resulting execution time is 4001 milliseconds. Finally, we can apply the same trick we used in the `charCounter` method in the previous example and restructure the loop so that the termination expression performs a comparison against 0. This change, shown in Listing 11.15, results in a run time of 3538 milliseconds, shaving an additional 363 milliseconds.

Listing 11.15   Using a faster loop

```
...
while (len > 0) {
    if (a[--len] != b[len]) {
        return false;
    }
}
...
```

11.4.3   Arithmetic Operations

Arithmetic operations on identical primitive types all take about the same amount of time, with the exception of multiplication and division (including the % operation that produces the remainder of an integer division). The fastest operations are those performed on the `int` primitive type. This is due to the fact that the smaller primitives like `byte` and `short` are widened to `int`s before an arithmetic operation is performed.

Whenever possible, integer (not just specifically the `int` data type) multiplication and division operations should be replaced by the equivalent shift operations. For example, you could replace the following statement

```
i /= 32;
```

with its mathematical equivalent[7] using the logical right shift operator.

```
i >>>= 5;
```

You can also improve the performance of mod (%) operations when the modulus is an even power of 2 by bit wise ANDing with the value of the modulus minus one. For example the following statement

```
i %= 32;
```

can be replaced with

```
i &= 0x1f// 31 decimal
```

The use of the shift operators, when possible, will be faster on most platforms, but the difference on TINI is far more striking. This is because the controller on which TINI is built does not have 32-bit ALU registers that can perform multiplication and division operations quickly in hardware. Instead, 32-bit multiplication or division requires many individual operations. The CPU does, however, offer some support for 32-bit shift operations, which results in shift operations on `int` primitives being much faster than multiplication or division.

By far the most time-consuming arithmetic operations are floating point calculations. Unlike your host development machine, TINI's controller does not contain a "built-in" floating point unit. So floating point operations must be carried out purely by a software floating point library. Surprisingly, using calculations on `double`s is faster than calculations on `float`s. This is because, on TINI, all `float`s are widened to `double`s before the calculation is performed. If your application needs to perform floating point arithmetic, it's probably best to use `double`s. One thing to keep in mind, however, is that `double`s are represented in 64 bits (8 bytes) and `float`s only 32 bits (4 bytes). So, for example, moving a double around using `DataInputStream` and `DataOutputStream` takes about twice as long.

---

7. It is assumed here that *i* is non-negative.

11.4.4 The ArrayUtils Class

While array accesses are not nearly as expensive as object creation or method invocations, they can still cause performance bottlenecks. One reason is that each array access requires bounds checking. To enhance the performance of array operations, the API provides a class named ArrayUtils in the com.dalsemi.system package. ArrayUtils consists entirely of static native methods geared toward speeding up common array operations. Because all of the methods in ArrayUtils are native, they are much faster than equivalent methods implemented in Java.

The arraycopy method, defined in the java.lang.System class, is implemented as a native method in most Java platforms (including TINI) and therefore has no analog in the ArrayUtils class. It allows the caller to quickly copy a portion of the contents of one array to another.

```
public static native void arraycopy(Object src, int src_position,
                                    Object dst, int dst_position, int length)
```

It copies data from a source array (src) to a destination (dst) array. When copying arrays of primitives, both of the arrays must be of identical type. The offsets into the source and destination arrays are src_position and dst_position, respectively. The total number of bytes copied is equal to the value specified by the length parameter.

The rest of the methods discussed in this section are defined in the com.dalsemi.system.ArrayUtils class.

The arrayCopyUnequal method takes a parameter list identical to that of arraycopy and performs a similar operation with a couple of exceptions.

```
public static native void arrayCopyUnequal(Object fromArray,
                                           int fromOffset,
                                           Object toArray, int toOffset,
                                           int length)
```

First, arrays of object references may not be copied using this method. The System.arraycopy method should be used for reference array copies. Next, and most important, arrays can be of different types. For example, a char array can be copied into a byte array and vice versa. If the primitive type of the source array (fromArray) is wider than the primitive type of the destination array (toArray), a truncating operation is performed on each element during the copy. For example, when copying from an int array to byte array, only the least significant byte of each integer in the int array will be copied to the byte array. If an int value of 0xffffff7f were extracted from a source int array, it would be truncated to 0x7f and stored in the byte array. If the primitive type of the toArray array is narrower than the primitive type of fromArray, then the most significant bytes of the elements copied to fromArray are set to 0. For example, if a short value of 0xff7f were extracted from a source `short` array, it equals 0x0000ff7f after a copy operation into an `int` array. In other words, the value is not sign extended.

The `arrayComp` method is a comparison analog to `arraycopy`.

```
public static native boolean arrayComp(Object array1, int offset1,
                               Object array2, int offset2, int length)
```

It compares two arrays from specified offsets (`offset1`, `offset2`). The number of bytes compared is specified by the `length` parameter. Both arrays (`array1`, `array2`) must be of identical type. If the array elements in the specified range are equal, `arrayComp` returns `true`. The `arrayComp` method is a general purpose and very fast version of the `isEqual` method we experimented with in Listing 11.12.

The `arrayFill` method that follows fills each element in the range specified by `fromIndex` and `toIndex` (inclusive) with the value specified by `fillValue`.

```
public static native void arrayFill(byte[] thisArray, int fromIndex,
                               int toIndex, byte fillValue)
```

The `getLong` and `setLong` methods store and retrieve a `long` primitive to and from a byte array.

```
public static native byte[] setLong(byte[] thisArray, int offset,
                               long value)
public static native long getLong(byte[] thisArray, int offset)
```

The `setLong` method returns a reference to the target array (`thisArray`). Corresponding `get*` and `set*` methods exist for the `short` and `int` primitive types as well. The byte ordering for all methods is big-endian. So for example the following statement

```
setInt(b, offset, val);
```

extracts bytes from the specified integer value and places them in the target array as shown here.

```
b[offset]   = (byte) (val>>>24);
b[offset+1] = (byte) (val>>>16);
b[offset+2] = (byte) (val>>>8);
b[offset+3] = (byte) (val>>>0);
```

Primitive values returned from the `get*` methods construct a return value by shifting the bytes into the target primitive in big-endian fashion. The most significant byte is located in the array element whose index is specified by `offset`.

```
int i = b[offset] << 24;
i = i | ((b[offset+1]<<16)&0xff0000);
i = i | ((b[offset+2]<<8)&0xff00);
i = i | ((b[offset+3]<<0)&0xff);
```

11.5 AN OPTIMIZATION STRATEGY

First, simply develop your application in a clean fashion without worrying too much about optimization. Otherwise, you may wind up writing awkward, hard to maintain code. After the application is functionally complete, focus on performance enhancements, if necessary. When you do get to the point of optimizing your code, go after the big targets first: I/O and memory usage. Use profiling techniques, such as those discussed in Section 11.1 and Section 11.3.3, to identify execution bottlenecks. After discovering where the bulk of the CPU cycles are being consumed, consider some of these techniques, discussed previously, summarized roughly in order of effectiveness.

- Identify the real performance bottlenecks. Then optimize only the code that must be fast.
- Optimize I/O by transferring relatively large blocks of data whenever possible. When your application must read and write small amounts of data to an underlying stream, use buffered streams. Use the `print` and `println` methods on `PrintStream` objects sparingly, since they are fairly abstract and consume memory when converting from character to byte arrays.
- Try reducing unnecessary memory usage. Reuse objects when feasible (that is, easy to do and thread-safe). Reducing unnecessary object creation will not only save memory, it will also speed code execution.
- Make judicious use of strings and be aware of their tendency to use memory. Consider using `StringBuffers`. This should allow some recycling of memory, and the `StringBuffer` can be easily converted to a `String` when necessary.
- For better performance within a tight loop try the loop optimization suggestions from Section 11.4.2. Avoid unnecessary method invocations and field accesses.
- If after a reasonable attempt at optimization you still need better performance, a native library may be required.

11.6 APPLICATION HARDENING

To this point in the chapter we've been discussing how to make your application faster and more responsive. Now we'll shift the focus to hardening the application. A production application must ultimately be able to deliver the uptime and reliability required of embedded network devices, as well as recover from unexpected events such as loss of power or runaway code.

11.6.1   TINI's Memory Technology and Data Persistence

First, it's important to understand the different types of memory technology used by TINI hardware and the purpose each serves so that you can make two important decisions.

- Where should your application be stored?
- Where should any other required persistent data be stored?

For the purposes of this discussion, persistent storage is defined as memory that retains its contents for long periods of time in the absence of primary power (V_{cc}). There are two distinct types of memory used by any TINI hardware implementation: flash ROM and static RAM (SRAM). The flash ROM is of course persistent and stores the bootstrap loader, the runtime environment, and the "flashed" Java application. Figure 1.6 shows how the different binary images are mapped into the flash ROM's memory space. The SRAM can also be made persistent using a small amount of additional circuitry and a lithium coin cell battery (see Figure 1.3). System configuration information such as static network parameters are stored in the SRAM along with the garbage collected heap and file system data.

If the SRAM is persistent, network parameters and file system data remain intact even in the absence of primary power. If the SRAM is volatile, critical system data must be stored in another memory device. The runtime environment makes provisions for storing network parameters in the flash ROM and restoring these parameters during the OS boot phase. Otherwise, the flash memory can't be used for arbitrary data storage. However, any hardware implementation may provide a separate persistent external memory device to store important data needed to bootstrap the system. This additional memory device can take the form of either a full parallel access memory with an address and data bus that is decoded in an unused portion of the system memory map (Figure 1.4) or a small serial memory such as an 1-Wire EEPROM. The TINI Board Model 390[8] for example, provides a small 1-Wire EEPROM (electrically erasable programmable read-only memory) chip to allow the application(s) to store up to 512 bytes of configuration data. The TBM390 also nonvolatilizes the SRAM, providing a total of three distinct types of persistent read/write memory.

Executing from Flash Memory.   During the application development phase, the persistent Java application is typically slush, or perhaps another shell, that

---

8.   Included on board revisions D and later

allows the developer to load, execute, and test her application. Slush can also be used in production because applications can be automatically launched by adding the appropriate line of text in the "/etc/.startup" file. This line is normally the same command used when launching your application from the command line. As a rule, however, the safest place for your application to live is in the flash ROM. This ensures the application binary image will withstand any damage that could be caused by heap corruption.[9] It also means that your application is automatically launched as the first Java process when the system is booted. This reduces the amount of time required for the application to begin executing from 11 seconds to about 3 seconds.

You can target your application for execution from the flash ROM by using the "–l" option on the TINIConvertor command line. This overrides the SRAM (file system) default execution target. The only change you may have to make to your application for it to execute properly from flash is to initialize the streams used for console I/O: System.in, System.out, and System.err. Use of the default serial port cannot be assumed by the system because there may be a picky serial device attached to the port that could get confused by unsolicited chatter when the system boots. If your application performs no console I/O, then it is not necessary to invoke either of the following methods.

A flashed application can enable console I/O on a serial port by invoking the setDefaultStreams method defined in the com.dalsemi.system.Debug class.

```
public static void setDefaultStreams(String port, int speed)
```

It takes a String, such as "serial0," specifying the serial port to be used for console I/O and the serial port baud rate. After setDefaultStreams has been invoked, System.in, System.out, and System.err will use the specified serial port for the actual data transfer.

```
public static void resetDefaultStreams()
```

The resetDefaultStreams method sets System.in to a NullInputStream and System.out and System.err to NullOutputStreams. Both "null" stream classes are defined in the com.dalsemi.comm package. This mutes all console I/O and allows the serial port to be used by the rest of the application. By invoking setDefaultStreams immediately after startup a flashed application can send console output and report progress during its startup phase. After its initialization is complete, it can invoke resetDefaultStreams to release the port for other, possibly more useful, serial communication.

---

9. If a corrupt heap is detected on bootup, the memory manager will clear the heap and re-initialize the file system, destroying your application. While this is an unlikely event, it can occur and should be guarded against for any production development.

11.6.2 Application Startup

The system boot flow was described in Section 1.4.5. We'll briefly review a small portion of the boot process and extend the startup discussion into the early phases of an application's initialization. Early in the boot process, the OS analyzes the contents of the SRAM, performing integrity checks on each of the following.

- Network parameters
- Heap
- File system

The network parameters are checked only if the network information was committed to the Flash ROM (see Section 5.2.1). If committed, the network information in the SRAM is compared to the contents of the flash ROM. If they differ, the flash version of the network data is copied to the SRAM. Next, the heap structures are checked for consistency. If the heap is found to be in a damaged state, it is reinitialized. Because the file system is contained in the heap, it will be destroyed and reinitialized in the event that the heap integrity check fails. If the integrity check succeeds, the file system structure is examined and any structural damage to the file system is repaired.

Detecting Boot-Up Problems.   The class `com.dalsemi.system.TINIOS` provides a method named `getBootState` that can be invoked to determine what, if any, recovery actions were performed by the operating system during the boot process.

```
public static native int getBootState()
```

It returns the boot state encoded as an integer value that is the bit-wise OR of zero or more of the following public constants defined in `TINIOS`.

```
NETWORK_CONFIGURATION_RESTORED
MASTER_ERASE_OCCURRED
HEAP_CLEAR_OCCURRED
FS_MODIFICATION_OCCURRED
```

If no recovery action was required during system boot, `getBootState` returns 0. Using this method, an application can determine whether it needs to initialize and/or restore any of its own persistent state. For example, it may need to load a configuration file from the network or an external memory device.

Forced Heap Initialization.   To force either the entire SRAM or just the file system to be reinitialized during system boot, an application can invoke the `blastHeapOnReboot` method in the `TINIOS` class.

```
public static final void blastHeapOnReboot(int blastType)
```

Invoking `blastHeapOnReboot` serves only as a trigger to reset the file system, and possibly the system configuration information, the next time the system boots. It does not have any immediate impact on the system. The `blastType` parameter can be either of the following public integer constants defined in `TINIOS`.

```
BLAST_HEAP
BLAST_ALL
```

The `BLAST_ALL` parameter should only be specified when the network commit/restore functionality has been enabled or when the application has network parameters stored in another persistent memory device. Resetting the heap happens automatically if the SRAM is not persistent. The `blastHeapOnReboot` method forces this action even if the SRAM is persistent, overriding the utility of the non-volatizing circuitry. It should only be used if it is necessary to guarantee that the heap is reinitialized during the boot process. This also assumes that the application can restore any necessary persistent system parameters and files.

To guard against heap corruption due to sudden loss of power, the memory manager maintains state in the system area of the SRAM. This state allows the memory manager to back out during system startup of an incomplete memory operation such as a "malloc" or a "free." Maintaining this state during normal execution imposes about a 30 percent overhead on memory management operations. This behavior can be disabled by invoking the `disablePowerFailRecovery` method in the TINIOS class.

```
public static final void disablePowerFailRecovery()
```

This result is faster memory operations and somewhat better performance for applications that perform lots of object creation. However, it should only be used in conjunction with `blastHeapOnReboot`. In this case, the heap's consistency at boot time isn't an issue because it will unconditionally be reinitialized.

Starting the Watchdog. For most applications the watchdog timer should be armed early in the initialization phase. The watchdog timer guards against a runaway or otherwise unresponsive system. Once armed, the timer must be reset periodically by the application or the system will automatically reboot. This is ideal, for example, at preventing the system from becoming permanently hung due to deadlocked threads. The watchdog's use is described thoroughly in Section 10.2.

11.6.3 Hardening Summary

For robust applications that can recover from otherwise fatal problems, keep the following tips in mind.

- Target your application for execution in the flash ROM.
- Use network commit/restore capabilities for static network parameters. This is not necessary if your application acquires network settings dynamically using DHCP.
- Check `getBootState` early in application execution, and, if necessary, take the appropriate recovery action.
- Use the watchdog to guard against runaway or unresponsive code.

All of these techniques can be used together to ensure that your application, and the embedded system it controls, can recover from unexpected problems gracefully. Combined, their implementation amounts to only a few lines of code and therefore they have only a negligible impact on the application's footprint and performance.

Almanac

LEGEND

The following is a very condensed summary of all of the classes defined in the TINI API, listed alphabetically. It also includes all useful 1-Wire API classes that are relavent to the TINI platform. The almanac is presented in the style introduced by Patrick Chan in the *Java Developers Almanac*.

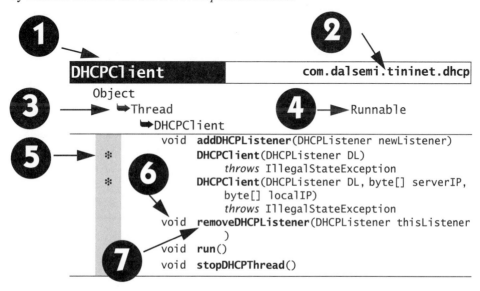

1. The name of the class.
2. The name of the package containing the class
3. The chain of superclasses. Each class is a subclass of the one above it.
4. The names of the interfaces implemented by each class.
5. A constructor. Other icons that may occur in this column are:
   - ○ abstract
   - ● final
   - ❏ static
   - ◼ static final
   - © protected
   - ✍ field
6. The return type of a method or the declared type of an instance variable.
7. The name of the class member. If it is a method, the parameter list and optional throws clause follows. Members are arranged alphabetically.

ADContainer	com.dalsemi.onewire.container
ADContainer	OneWireSensor

⬛	int	**ALARM_HIGH**
⬛	int	**ALARM_LOW**
	boolean	**canADMultiChannelRead**()
	void	**doADConvert**(boolean[] doConvert, byte[] state) *throws* com.dalsemi.onewire.adapter.OneWireIOException, com.dalsemi.onewire.OneWireException
	void	**doADConvert**(int channel, byte[] state) *throws* com.dalsemi.onewire.adapter.OneWireIOException, com.dalsemi.onewire.OneWireException
	double	**getADAlarm**(int channel, int alarmType, byte[] state) *throws* com.dalsemi.onewire.OneWireException
	boolean	**getADAlarmEnable**(int channel, int alarmType, byte[] state) *throws* com.dalsemi.onewire.OneWireException
	double	**getADRange**(int channel, byte[] state)
	double[]	**getADRanges**(int channel)
	double	**getADResolution**(int channel, byte[] state)
	double[]	**getADResolutions**(int channel, double range)
	double[]	**getADVoltage**(byte[] state) *throws* com.dalsemi.onewire.adapter.OneWireIOException, com.dalsemi.onewire.OneWireException
	double	**getADVoltage**(int channel, byte[] state) *throws* com.dalsemi.onewire.adapter.OneWireIOException, com.dalsemi.onewire.OneWireException
	int	**getNumberADChannels**()
	boolean	**hasADAlarmed**(int channel, int alarmType, byte[] state) *throws* com.dalsemi.onewire.OneWireException
	boolean	**hasADAlarms**()
	void	**setADAlarm**(int channel, int alarmType, double alarm, byte[] state) *throws* com.dalsemi.onewire.OneWireException

void	**setADAlarmEnable**(int channel, int alarmType, boolean alarmEnable, byte[] state) *throws* com.dalsemi.onewire.OneWireException
void	**setADRange**(int channel, double range, byte[] state)
void	**setADResolution**(int channel, double resolution, byte[] state)

Address com.dalsemi.onewire.utils

Object
   ⤷Address

❏	boolean	**isValid**(byte[] address)
❏	boolean	**isValid**(long address)
❏	boolean	**isValid**(String address)
❏	byte[]	**toByteArray**(long address)
❏	byte[]	**toByteArray**(String address)
❏	long	**toLong**(byte[] address)
❏	long	**toLong**(String address)
❏	String	**toString**(byte[] address)
❏	String	**toString**(long address)

ArrayUtils com.dalsemi.system

Object
   ⤷ArrayUtils

❏	boolean	**arrayComp**(Object array1, int offset1, Object array2, int offset2, int length)
❏	void	**arrayCopyUnequal**(Object fromArray, int fromOffset, Object toArray, int toOffset, int length)
❏	void	**arrayFill**(byte[] thisArray, int fromIndex, int toIndex, byte fillValue)
❏	int	**getInt**(byte[] thisArray, int offset)
❏	long	**getLong**(byte[] thisArray, int offset)
❏	short	**getShort**(byte[] thisArray, int offset)
❏	byte[]	**setInt**(byte[] thisArray, int offset, int value)
❏	byte[]	**setLong**(byte[] thisArray, int offset, long value)
❏	byte[]	**setShort**(byte[] thisArray, int offset, short value)

Bit

`com.dalsemi.onewire.utils`

Object
➥Bit

❑	int	**arrayReadBit**(int index, int offset, byte[] buf)
❑	void	**arrayWriteBit**(int state, int index, int offset, byte[] buf)
❋		**Bit**()

BitPort

`com.dalsemi.system`

Object
➥BitPort

❋		**BitPort**(byte bitname)
❋		**BitPort**(DataPort port)
	void	**clear**()
	void	**clear**(int bitpos) *throws* IllegalAddressException
◿■	byte	**ETH_EEDO**
◿■	byte	**ETH_EESK**
◿■	byte	**ETH_IOS0**
◿■	byte	**ETH_IOS1**
◿■	byte	**ETH_IOS2**
◿	int	**latchValue**
◿■	byte	**Port3Bit0**
◿■	byte	**Port3Bit1**
◿■	byte	**Port3Bit2**
◿■	byte	**Port3Bit3**
◿■	byte	**Port3Bit4**
◿■	byte	**Port3Bit5**
◿■	byte	**Port5Bit0**
◿■	byte	**Port5Bit1**
◿■	byte	**Port5Bit2**
◿■	byte	**Port5Bit3**
◿■	byte	**Port5Bit4**
◿■	byte	**Port5Bit5**
◿■	byte	**Port5Bit6**
◿■	byte	**Port5Bit7**
	int	**read**()
	int	**readBit**(int bitpos) *throws* IllegalAddressException
	int	**readLatch**()

	int	readLatch(int bitpos)
	void	set()
	void	set(int bitpos)
		throws IllegalAddressException

BytePort   com.dalsemi.system

Object
  ➡BytePort

✳		BytePort(byte portname)
✎■	byte	Port5
	int	read()
	void	write(int value)

CanBus   com.dalsemi.comm

Object
  ➡CanBus

	void	autoAnswerRemoteFrameRequest(int messageCenter, int ID, byte[] data) *throws* CanBusException
✳		CanBus(byte portnum) *throws* CanBusException
✎■	byte	CANBUS0
✎■	byte	CANBUS1
	void	close() *throws* CanBusException
	void	disableController() *throws* CanBusException
	void	disableMessageCenter(int messageCenter) *throws* CanBusException
	void	enableController() *throws* CanBusException
	void	enableControllerPassive() *throws* CanBusException
	void	enableMessageCenter(int messageCenter) *throws* CanBusException
	int	getRXErrorCount() *throws* CanBusException
	int	getTXErrorCount() *throws* CanBusException
	void	open() *throws* CanBusException
	void	receive(CanFrame frame) *throws* CanBusException
	int	receiveFramesAvailable() *throws* CanBusException
	boolean	receivePoll(CanFrame frame) *throws* CanBusException
	void	resetController() *throws* CanBusException
	void	sendDataFrame(int ID, boolean extendedID, byte[] data) *throws* CanBusException
	void	sendFrame(CanFrame frame) *throws* CanBusException

void	**sendRemoteFrameRequest**(int ID, boolean extendedID, byte[] data) *throws* CanBusException	
void	**set11BitGlobalIDMask**(int mask) *throws* CanBusException	
void	**set11BitMessageCenterArbitrationID**(int messageCenter, int ID) *throws* CanBusException	
void	**set29BitGlobalIDMask**(int mask) *throws* CanBusException	
void	**set29BitMessageCenter15IDMask**(int mask) *throws* CanBusException	
void	**set29BitMessageCenterArbitrationID**(int messageCenter, int ID) *throws* CanBusException	
void	**setBaudRatePrescaler**(int prescaler) *throws* CanBusException	
void	**setMessageCenterMessageIDMaskEnable**(int messageCenter, boolean maskEnable) *throws* CanBusException	
void	**setMessageCenterRXMode**(int messageCenter) *throws* CanBusException	
void	**setMessageCenterTXMode**(int messageCenter) *throws* CanBusException	
void	**setMessageCenterWriteOverEnable**(int messageCenter, boolean writeover) *throws* CanBusException	
void	**setReceiveQueueLimit**(int numframes) *throws* CanBusException	
void	**setSampleRate**(int sampleRate) *throws* CanBusException	
void	**setSiestaMode**() *throws* CanBusException	
void	**setSynchronizationJumpWidth**(int jumpWidth) *throws* CanBusException	
void	**setTransmitQueueLimit**(int numframes) *throws* CanBusException	
void	**setTSEG1**(int tseg1) *throws* CanBusException	
void	**setTSEG2**(int tseg2) *throws* CanBusException	

CanBusException
com.dalsemi.comm

```
Object
    ➡Throwable                          java.io.Serializable
        ➡Exception
            ➡CanBusException
```

✍▪	int	**ALLOCATION_ERROR**
✍▪	int	**BIT_ONE**
✍▪	int	**BIT_STUFF**
✍▪	int	**BIT_ZERO**
✳		**CanBusException**()
✳		**CanBusException**(String s, int reason)
✍▪	int	**CLOSE_NOTOWNER**
✍▪	int	**COUNT_EXCEEDED**

		int	CRC
		int	FORMAT
		int	getReason()
		int	NONE
		int	OPEN_ALREADYOPEN
		int	PORT_DISABLED
		int	PORT_NOTOPENED
		int	TRANSMIT_NO_ACK

CanFrame
com.dalsemi.comm

Object
    ➡CanFrame

✳			CanFrame()
✳			CanFrame(int ID, boolean extendedID, byte[] buf, int length)
		byte[]	data
		boolean	extendedID
		byte[]	getData()
		boolean	getExtendedID()
		int	getID()
		int	getLength()
		int	getMessageCenter()
		boolean	getRemoteFrameRequest()
		int	ID
		int	length
		int	messageCenter
		boolean	remoteFrameRequest
		void	setData(byte[] buf)
		void	setExtendedID(boolean extendedID)
		void	setID(int ID)
		void	setLength(int length)
		void	setMessageCenter(int MC)
		void	setRemoteFrameRequest(boolean RTR)

Clock
com.dalsemi.system

Object
    ➡Clock

❏		int	bcdToInt(int bcdVal)
❏		int	calculateDayOfWeek(int month, int date, int fullYear)
✳			Clock()
		boolean	get12Hour()
		int	getDate()
		int	getDay()

int	**getHour**()
int	**getHundredth**()
int	**getMinute**()
int	**getMonth**()
boolean	**getPm**()
void	**getRTC**()
int	**getSecond**()
long	**getTickCount**()
int	**getYear**()
byte	**intToBCD**(int intVal)
void	**set12Hour**(boolean is12Hour)
void	**setDate**(int date)
void	**setDay**(int day)
void	**setHour**(int hour)
void	**setHundredth**(int hundredth)
void	**setMinute**(int minute)
void	**setMonth**(int month)
void	**setPm**(boolean pm)
void	**setRTC**()
void	**setSecond**(int second)
void	**setTickCount**(long millis)
void	**setYear**(int year)

ClockContainer · com.dalsemi.onewire.container

ClockContainer · OneWireSensor

boolean	**canDisableClock**()
long	**getClock**(byte[] state)
long	**getClockAlarm**(byte[] state) *throws* com.dalsemi.onewire.OneWireExcept ion
long	**getClockResolution**()
boolean	**hasClockAlarm**()
boolean	**isClockAlarmEnabled**(byte[] state)
boolean	**isClockAlarming**(byte[] state)
boolean	**isClockRunning**(byte[] state)
void	**setClock**(long time, byte[] state)
void	**setClockAlarm**(long time, byte[] state) *throws* com.dalsemi.onewire.OneWireExcept ion
void	**setClockAlarmEnable**(boolean alarmEnable, byte[] state) *throws* com.dalsemi.onewire.OneWireExcept ion
void	**setClockRunEnable**(boolean runEnable, byte[] state) *throws* com.dalsemi.onewire.OneWireExcept ion

CommandAPDU

`com.dalsemi.onewire.container`

Object
    ➥CommandAPDU

✍■	int	**CLA**
✳		**CommandAPDU**(byte[] buffer)
✳		**CommandAPDU**(byte cla, byte ins, byte p1, byte p2)
✳		**CommandAPDU**(byte cla, byte ins, byte p1, byte p2, byte[] data)
✳		**CommandAPDU**(byte cla, byte ins, byte p1, byte p2, byte[] data, int le)
✳		**CommandAPDU**(byte cla, byte ins, byte p1, byte p2, int le)
●	byte[]	**getBuffer**()
●	byte	**getByte**(int index)
●	byte[]	**getBytes**()
	byte	**getCLA**()
	byte	**getINS**()
	int	**getLC**()
	int	**getLE**()
●	int	**getLength**()
	byte	**getP1**()
	byte	**getP2**()
✍■	int	**INS**
✍■	int	**LC**
✍■	int	**P1**
✍■	int	**P2**
●	void	**setByte**(int index, byte value)
	String	**toString**()

CommitException

`com.dalsemi.system`

Object
    ➥Throwable   `java.io.Serializable`
        ➥Exception
            ➥CommitException

✳	**CommitException**()
✳	**CommitException**(String error)

CRC16   com.dalsemi.onewire.utils

Object
   ➡CRC16

❏	int	**compute**(byte[] dataToCrc)
❏	int	**compute**(byte[] dataToCrc, int seed)
❏	int	**compute**(byte[] dataToCrc, int off, int len)
❏	int	**compute**(byte[] dataToCrc, int off, int len, int seed)
❏	int	**compute**(int dataToCrc)
❏	int	**compute**(int dataToCrc, int seed)

CRC8   com.dalsemi.onewire.utils

Object
   ➡CRC8

❏	int	**compute**(byte[] dataToCrc)
❏	int	**compute**(byte[] dataToCrc, int seed)
❏	int	**compute**(byte[] dataToCrc, int off, int len)
❏	int	**compute**(byte[] dataToCrc, int off, int len, int seed)
❏	int	**compute**(int dataToCRC)
❏	int	**compute**(int dataToCRC, int seed)

DataPort   com.dalsemi.system

Object
   ➡DataPort

✍	int	**address**
✳		**DataPort**()
✳		**DataPort**(int address)
	int	**getAddress**()
	boolean	**getFIFOMode**()
	int	**getStretchCycles**()
✍	int	**latchValue**
	int	**read**() *throws* IllegalAddressException
	int	**read**(byte[] arr, int off, int len) *throws* IllegalAddressException
	int	**readLatch**()
	void	**setAddress**(int address)
	void	**setFIFOMode**(boolean useFIFOAccess)
	void	**setStretchCycles**(byte stretch) *throws* IllegalArgumentException
✍■	byte	**STRETCH0**
✍■	byte	**STRETCH1**

⚐■	byte	**STRETCH10**
⚐■	byte	**STRETCH2**
⚐■	byte	**STRETCH3**
⚐■	byte	**STRETCH7**
⚐■	byte	**STRETCH8**
⚐■	byte	**STRETCH9**
⚐	byte	**stretchCycles**
⚐	boolean	**useFIFOAccess**
	void	**write**(byte[] arr, int off, int len)
		throws IllegalAddressException
	void	**write**(int value)
		throws IllegalAddressException

Debug · com.dalsemi.system

Object
   ➡Debug

▢	void	**debugDump**(byte[] arr, int length)
▢	void	**debugDump**(int b)
▢	void	**debugDump**(String out)
⚐▢	boolean	**defaultStreams**
▢	void	**dump**(byte[] arr, int length)
▢	void	**dump**(int b)
▢	void	**dump**(String out)
▢	void	**hexDump**(byte[] b)
▢	void	**hexDump**(byte[] b, int length)
▢	void	**hexDump**(int i)
▢	void	**hexDump**(java.io.PrintStream out, byte[] b)
▢	void	**hexDump**(java.io.PrintStream out, int i)
▢	void	**intDump**(int iVal)
▢	void	**resetDefaultStreams**()
▢	void	**setDefaultStreams**()
▢	void	**setDefaultStreams**(String port, int speed)
▢	void	**setNativeVerboseDebugSpew**(boolean verbose)

DebugOutputStream · com.dalsemi.comm

Object
   ➡java.io.OutputStream
      ➡DebugOutputStream

✳		**DebugOutputStream**()
	void	**write**(byte[] barr, int offset, int length)
		throws java.io.IOException
	void	**write**(int b) *throws* java.io.IOException

DefaultTINIShell · com.dalsemi.shell

```
Object
  ➥TINIShell
    ➥DefaultTINIShell
```

✻		**DefaultTINIShell**()
	void	**execute**(Object[] commandLine, server.SystemInputStream in, server.SystemPrintStream out, server.SystemPrintStream err, java.util.Hashtable env) *throws* Exception
	java.util.Hashtable	**getCurrentEnvironment**()
	byte	**getCurrentUID**()
	String	**getCurrentUserName**()
	String	**getFromCurrentEnvironment**(String key)
	String	**getName**()
	int	**getUIDByUserName**(String username)
	String	**getUserNameByUID**(byte uid)
	String	**getVersion**()
	int	**login**(String userName, String password)
	void	**logout**(Object info)

DHCPClient · com.dalsemi.tininet.dhcp

```
Object
  ➥Thread                    Runnable
    ➥DHCPClient
```

	void	**addDHCPListener**(DHCPListener newListener)
✻		**DHCPClient**(DHCPListener DL) *throws* IllegalStateException
✻		**DHCPClient**(DHCPListener DL, byte[] serverIP, byte[] localIP) *throws* IllegalStateException
	void	**removeDHCPListener**(DHCPListener thisListener)
	void	**run**()
	void	**stopDHCPThread**()

DHCPListener · com.dalsemi.tininet.dhcp

```
DHCPListener
```

	void	**ipError**(String error)
	void	**ipLeased**()
	void	**ipLost**()
	void	**ipRenewed**()

DNSClient

com.dalsemi.tininet.dns

```
Object
    ➥DNSClient
```

✳		DNSClient()
	String[]	getByIP(byte[] ip)
	String[]	getByIP(String ip)
	String[]	getByName(String name)
	void	setDNSTimeout(int timeout)
	void	setPrimaryDNS(String dns1)
	void	setSecondaryDNS(String dns2)

DSFile

com.dalsemi.fs

```
Object
    ➥java.io.File              java.io.Serializable,
Comparable
        ➥DSFile
```

▢	byte[]	buildAbsolutePath(String parent, String name)
	boolean	canExec()
✳		DSFile(java.io.File dir, String name)
✳		DSFile(String path)
✳		DSFile(String path, String name)
	int	executeFile() *throws* java.io.IOException
	int	executeFile(java.io.InputStream stdin, java.io.OutputStream stdout, java.io.OutputStream stderr, String[] args, boolean foreground, String processName) *throws* java.io.IOException
	int	executeFile(java.io.InputStream stdin, java.io.OutputStream stdout, java.io.OutputStream stderr, String[] args, String[] env, boolean foreground, String processName) *throws* java.io.IOException
	int	executeFile(java.io.InputStream stdin, java.io.OutputStream stdout, java.io.OutputStream stderr, String[] args, String[] env, boolean foreground, String processName, Process procObj) *throws* java.io.IOException
	int	getOtherPermissions() *throws* java.io.FileNotFoundException
	int	getUser() *throws* java.io.FileNotFoundException
	int	getUserPermissions() *throws* java.io.FileNotFoundException

	boolean	**listLong**(java.io.OutputStream out,
		boolean unixStyle)
		throws java.io.IOException
	void	**setOtherPermissions**(int perms)
		throws java.io.IOException
	void	**setUser**(byte uid) *throws* java.io.IOException
	void	**setUserPermissions**(int perms)
		throws java.io.IOException
	void	**touch**() *throws* java.io.IOException

DSPortAdapter   com.dalsemi.onewire.adapter

Object
   ➡DSPortAdapter

○	boolean	**adapterDetected**() *throws* OneWireIOException,
		com.dalsemi.onewire.OneWireException
○	boolean	**beginExclusive**(boolean blocking)
		throws com.dalsemi.onewire.OneWireExcept
		ion
	boolean	**canBreak**() *throws* OneWireIOException,
		com.dalsemi.onewire.OneWireException
	boolean	**canDeliverPower**() *throws* OneWireIOException,
		com.dalsemi.onewire.OneWireException
	boolean	**canDeliverSmartPower**()
		throws OneWireIOException,
		com.dalsemi.onewire.OneWireException
	boolean	**canFlex**() *throws* OneWireIOException,
		com.dalsemi.onewire.OneWireException
	boolean	**canHyperdrive**() *throws* OneWireIOException,
		com.dalsemi.onewire.OneWireException
	boolean	**canOverdrive**() *throws* OneWireIOException,
		com.dalsemi.onewire.OneWireException
	boolean	**canProgram**() *throws* OneWireIOException,
		com.dalsemi.onewire.OneWireException
⚠■	int	**CONDITION_AFTER_BIT**
⚠■	int	**CONDITION_AFTER_BYTE**
⚠■	int	**CONDITION_NOW**
○	void	**dataBlock**(byte[] dataBlock, int off,
		int len) *throws* OneWireIOException,
		com.dalsemi.onewire.OneWireException
⚠■	int	**DELIVERY_CURRENT_DETECT**
⚠■	int	**DELIVERY_EPROM**
⚠■	int	**DELIVERY_FOUR_SECONDS**
⚠■	int	**DELIVERY_HALF_SECOND**
⚠■	int	**DELIVERY_INFINITE**
⚠■	int	**DELIVERY_ONE_SECOND**
⚠■	int	**DELIVERY_SMART_DONE**
⚠■	int	**DELIVERY_TWO_SECONDS**
✳		**DSPortAdapter**()
○	void	**endExclusive**()

	void	**excludeFamily**(byte[] family)
	void	**excludeFamily**(int family)
○	boolean	**findFirstDevice**() *throws* OneWireIOException, com.dalsemi.onewire.OneWireException
○	boolean	**findNextDevice**() *throws* OneWireIOException, com.dalsemi.onewire.OneWireException
○	void	**freePort**() *throws* com.dalsemi.onewire.OneWireException
	String	**getAdapterAddress**() *throws* OneWireIOException, com.dalsemi.onewire.OneWireException
○	String	**getAdapterName**()
	String	**getAdapterVersion**() *throws* OneWireIOException, com.dalsemi.onewire.OneWireException
○	void	**getAddress**(byte[] address)
	long	**getAddressAsLong**()
	String	**getAddressAsString**()
	java.util.Enumeration	**getAllDeviceContainers**() *throws* OneWireIOException, com.dalsemi.onewire.OneWireException
○	boolean	**getBit**() *throws* OneWireIOException, com.dalsemi.onewire.OneWireException
○	void	**getBlock**(byte[] arr, int len) *throws* OneWireIOException, com.dalsemi.onewire.OneWireException
○	void	**getBlock**(byte[] arr, int off, int len) *throws* OneWireIOException, com.dalsemi.onewire.OneWireException
○	byte[]	**getBlock**(int len) *throws* OneWireIOException, com.dalsemi.onewire.OneWireException
○	int	**getByte**() *throws* OneWireIOException, com.dalsemi.onewire.OneWireException
○	String	**getClassVersion**()
	com.dalsemi.onewire.container.OneWireContainer	**getDeviceContainer**()
	com.dalsemi.onewire.container.OneWireContainer	**getDeviceContainer**(byte[] address)
	com.dalsemi.onewire.container.OneWireContainer	**getDeviceContainer**(long address)
	com.dalsemi.onewire.container.OneWireContainer	**getDeviceContainer**(String address)

	com.dalsemi.one-
	wire.con-
	tainer.OneWireCon
	tainer
		getFirstDeviceContainer()
		    throws OneWireIOException,
		    com.dalsemi.onewire.OneWireException

	com.dalsemi.one-
	wire.con-
	tainer.OneWireCon
	tainer
		getNextDeviceContainer()
		    throws OneWireIOException,
		    com.dalsemi.onewire.OneWireException

○	String	**getPortName**()
		    throws com.dalsemi.onewire.OneWireExcept
		    ion

○	java.util.Enumer- ation	**getPortNames**()
○	String	**getPortTypeDescription**()
	int	**getSpeed**()

	boolean	**isAlarming**(byte[] address)
		    throws OneWireIOException,
		    com.dalsemi.onewire.OneWireException

	boolean	**isAlarming**(long address)
		    throws OneWireIOException,
		    com.dalsemi.onewire.OneWireException

	boolean	**isAlarming**(String address)
		    throws OneWireIOException,
		    com.dalsemi.onewire.OneWireException

	boolean	**isPresent**(byte[] address)
		    throws OneWireIOException,
		    com.dalsemi.onewire.OneWireException

	boolean	**isPresent**(long address)
		    throws OneWireIOException,
		    com.dalsemi.onewire.OneWireException

	boolean	**isPresent**(String address)
		    throws OneWireIOException,
		    com.dalsemi.onewire.OneWireException

✍■	char	**LEVEL_BREAK**
✍■	char	**LEVEL_NORMAL**
✍■	char	**LEVEL_POWER_DELIVERY**
✍■	char	**LEVEL_PROGRAM**

○	void	**putBit**(boolean bitValue)
		    throws OneWireIOException,
		    com.dalsemi.onewire.OneWireException

○	void	**putByte**(int byteValue)
		    throws OneWireIOException,
		    com.dalsemi.onewire.OneWireException

	void	**registerOneWireContainerClass**(int family,
		    Class OneWireContainerClass)
		    throws com.dalsemi.onewire.OneWireExcept
		    ion

✍■	int	**RESET_ALARM**
✍■	int	**RESET_NOPRESENCE**
✍■	int	**RESET_PRESENCE**
✍■	int	**RESET_SHORT**

○	int	**reset**() *throws* OneWireIOException, com.dalsemi.onewire.OneWireException
	boolean	**select**(byte[] address) *throws* OneWireIOException, com.dalsemi.onewire.OneWireException
	boolean	**select**(long address) *throws* OneWireIOException, com.dalsemi.onewire.OneWireException
	boolean	**select**(String address) *throws* OneWireIOException, com.dalsemi.onewire.OneWireException
○	boolean	**selectPort**(String portName) *throws* OneWireIOException, com.dalsemi.onewire.OneWireException
○	void	**setNoResetSearch**()
	void	**setPowerDuration**(int timeFactor) *throws* OneWireIOException, com.dalsemi.onewire.OneWireException
	void	**setPowerNormal**() *throws* OneWireIOException, com.dalsemi.onewire.OneWireException
	void	**setProgramPulseDuration**(int timeFactor) *throws* OneWireIOException, com.dalsemi.onewire.OneWireException
○	void	**setSearchAllDevices**()
○	void	**setSearchOnlyAlarmingDevices**()
	void	**setSpeed**(int speed) *throws* OneWireIOException, com.dalsemi.onewire.OneWireException
⚠■	int	**SPEED_FLEX**
⚠■	int	**SPEED_HYPERDRIVE**
⚠■	int	**SPEED_OVERDRIVE**
⚠■	int	**SPEED_REGULAR**
	void	**startBreak**() *throws* OneWireIOException, com.dalsemi.onewire.OneWireException
	boolean	**startPowerDelivery**(int changeCondition) *throws* OneWireIOException, com.dalsemi.onewire.OneWireException
	boolean	**startProgramPulse**(int changeCondition) *throws* OneWireIOException, com.dalsemi.onewire.OneWireException
	void	**targetAllFamilies**()
	void	**targetFamily**(byte[] family)
	void	**targetFamily**(int family)

ExternalInterrupt   `com.dalsemi.system`

Object
  ➡ExternalInterrupt

	void	**addEventListener**(ExternalInterruptEventListener externalEventListener) *throws* java.util.TooManyListenersException
❋		**ExternalInterrupt**()
❑	boolean	**getTrigger**()
	void	**removeEventListener**(ExternalInterruptEventListener externalEventListener)
❑	void	**setTrigger**(boolean edgeTrigger, ExternalInterruptEventListener owner) *throws* ExternalInterruptException
⚏■	int	**TRIGGER_EDGE**
⚏■	int	**TRIGGER_LEVEL**

ExternalInterruptEvent   `com.dalsemi.system`

Object
  ➡java.util.EventObject   java.io.Serializable
    ➡ExternalInterruptEvent

❋	**ExternalInterruptEvent**(ExternalInterrupt externalInterrupt)

ExternalInterrupt-
EventListener   `com.dalsemi.system`

ExternalInterruptEventListener   java.util.EventListener

	void	**externalInterruptEvent**(ExternalInterruptEvent ev)

ExternalInterruptExcep-
tion   `com.dalsemi.system`

Object
  ➡Throwable   java.io.Serializable
    ➡Exception
      ➡ExternalInterruptException

❋	**ExternalInterruptException**()
❋	**ExternalInterruptException**(String error)

FTPServer — com.dalsemi.shell.server.ftp

```
Object
  ➥Thread                          Runnable
    ➥com.dalsemi.shell.server.Server
      ➥FTPServer
```

	void	**broadcast**(String sendThis)
✳		**FTPServer**() *throws* java.io.IOException
✳		**FTPServer**(int port)
		throws java.io.IOException
❑	String	**getConnectionMsgFile**()
❑	String	**getWelcomeMsgFile**()
❑	boolean	**isAnonymousAllowed**()
❑	boolean	**isRootAllowed**()
❑	String	**logAnon**()

FTPSession — com.dalsemi.shell.server.ftp

```
Object
  ➥Thread                          Runnable
    ➥com.dalsemi.shell.server.Session
      ➥FTPSession
```

	String	**getNextCommand**() *throws* java.io.IOException
	void	**login**() *throws* java.io.IOException

GetOpt — com.dalsemi.shell.server

```
Object
  ➥GetOpt
```

	int	**getopt**()
✳		**GetOpt**(String[] args, String opts)
	String	**optArgGet**()
◢▪	int	**optEOF**
◢▪	int	**optERR**

HTTPServer — com.dalsemi.tininet.http

```
Object
  ➥HTTPServer
```

◢▪	int	**DEFAULT_HTTP_PORT**
◢▪	int	**DELETE**
◢▪	int	**GET**
	String	**getHTTPRoot**()
	String	**getIndexPage**()

	String	**getLogFilename**()
	boolean	**getLogging**()
	int	**getPortNumber**()
✍■	int	**HEAD**
✍■	int	**HTTP_BAD_REQUEST**
✍■	int	**HTTP_CREATED**
✍■	int	**HTTP_FORBIDDEN**
✍■	int	**HTTP_INTERNAL_ERROR**
✍■	int	**HTTP_NOT_FOUND**
✍■	int	**HTTP_OK**
✍■	int	**HTTP_SERVER_ERROR**
✍■	int	**HTTP_UNAUTHORIZED**
✍■	int	**HTTP_UNSUPPORTED_TYPE**
✳		**HTTPServer**() *throws* HTTPServerException
✳		**HTTPServer**(int httpPort) *throws* HTTPServerException
✳		**HTTPServer**(int httpPort, boolean logEnabled) *throws* HTTPServerException
✍■	int	**OPTIONS**
✍■	int	**POST**
✍■	int	**PUT**
	int	**serviceRequests**() *throws* HTTPServerException
	int	**serviceRequests**(Object lock) *throws* HTTPServerException
❑	void	**setBitmapMimeType**(String newMimeType)
	void	**setHTTPRoot**(String httpRoot)
	void	**setIndexPage**(String indexPage)
	void	**setLogFilename**(String logFileName)
	void	**setLogging**(boolean logEnabled) *throws* HTTPServerException
	void	**setPortNumber**(int httpPort) *throws* HTTPServerException
✍■	int	**TRACE**
✍■	int	**TYPE_FULL_REQUEST**
✍■	int	**TYPE_FULL_RESPONSE**
✍■	int	**TYPE_SIMPLE_REQUEST**
✍■	int	**UNSUPPORTED**

HTTPServerException   com.dalsemi.tininet.http

```
Object
  ➡Throwable                          java.io.Serializable
    ➡Exception
      ➡RuntimeException
        ➡HTTPServerException
```

✳	**HTTPServerException**()
✳	**HTTPServerException**(String error)

I2CPort		com.dalsemi.system

Object
　➥I2CPort

	byte	clockDelay
	int	getStretchCycles()
✳		I2CPort()
✳		I2CPort(int SCLAddress, byte SCLMask, int SDAAddress, byte SDAMask)
	int	read(byte[] barr, int off, int len) *throws* IllegalAddressException
	int	SCLAddress
	byte	SCLMask
	int	SDAAddress
	byte	SDAMask
	void	setAddress(byte address)
	void	setClockDelay(byte delay)
	void	setStretchCycles(byte stretch) *throws* IllegalArgumentException
	byte	slaveAddress
	byte	STRETCH0
	byte	STRETCH1
	byte	STRETCH10
	byte	STRETCH2
	byte	STRETCH3
	byte	STRETCH7
	byte	STRETCH8
	byte	STRETCH9
	byte	stretchCycles
	int	write(byte[] barr, int off, int len) *throws* IllegalAddressException

IllegalAddressException		com.dalsemi.system

Object
　➥Throwable　　　　　　　　java.io.Serializable
　　➥Exception
　　　➥IllegalAddressException

✳	IllegalAddressException()
✳	IllegalAddressException(String s)

LCDOutputStream

Object
   ➚java.io.OutputStream
      ➚LCDOutputStream

	void	**close**() *throws* java.io.IOException
✳		**LCDOutputStream**(LCDPort lcd)
	void	**write**(byte[] barr, int offset, int len) *throws* java.io.IOException
	void	**write**(int ch) *throws* java.io.IOException

LCDPort

Object
   ➚LCDPort

	void	**close**() *throws* java.io.IOException
	int	**getOutputBufferSize**()
	java.io.Output-Stream	**getOutputStream**() *throws* java.io.IOException
✳		**LCDPort**(int portNum, int stream) *throws* java.io.IOException
	void	**open**()
❏	void	**sendControl**(int value)
❏	void	**sendData**(int value)
❏	void	**setAddress**(int address)
❏	void	**setLCDParams**(int paramNum, byte[] params, int length)
❏	void	**setNumberOfLines**(int num)
❏	void	**setShiftDirection**(boolean dir)
❏	void	**setShiftInterval**(int num_ms)
❏	void	**setShiftMode**(boolean on)
	void	**write**(byte[] arr) *throws* java.io.IOException
	void	**write**(byte[] arr, int offset, int len) *throws* java.io.IOException
	void	**write**(int ch) *throws* java.io.IOException

MemoryBank

MemoryBank

String	**getBankDescription**()
int	**getSize**()
int	**getStartPhysicalAddress**()
boolean	**isGeneralPurposeMemory**()
boolean	**isNonVolatile**()
boolean	**isReadOnly**()
boolean	**isReadWrite**()

boolean	**isWriteOnce**()
boolean	**needsPowerDelivery**()
boolean	**needsProgramPulse**()
void	**read**(int startAddr, boolean readContinue, byte[] readBuf, int offset, int len) *throws* com.dalsemi.onewire.adapter.OneWireIOException, com.dalsemi.onewire.OneWireException
void	**setWriteVerification**(boolean doReadVerf)
void	**write**(int startAddr, byte[] writeBuf, int offset, int len) *throws* com.dalsemi.onewire.adapter.OneWireIOException, com.dalsemi.onewire.OneWireException

NetworkMonitor   com.dalsemi.onewire.utils

Object
  ➡Thread   Runnable
    ➡NetworkMonitor

void	**addEventListener**(NetworkMonitorEventListener nme1)
boolean	**isMonitorRunning**()
void	**killMonitor**()
✳	**NetworkMonitor**(com.dalsemi.onewire.adapter.DSPortAdapter adapter)
void	**pauseMonitor**()
void	**removeEventListener**(NetworkMonitorEventListener nme1)
void	**resumeMonitor**()
void	**run**()

NetworkMonitorEvent   com.dalsemi.onewire.utils

Object
  ➡java.util.EventObject   java.io.Serializable
    ➡NetworkMonitorEvent

com.dalsemi.onewire.adapter.DSPortAdapter	**getAdapter**()
byte[]	**getAddress**()
long	**getAddressAsLong**()
String	**getAddressAsString**()

	com.dalsemi.one- wire.con- tainer.OneWireCon tainer	**getDeviceContainer**()
	OWPath	**getOWPath**()
✳		**NetworkMonitorEvent**(NetworkMonitor nm, com.dalsemi.onewire.adapter.DSPortAdapt er adapter, long address, OWPath path)

NetworkMonitorEventListener

com.dalsemi.onewire.utils

NetworkMonitorEventListener

	void	**networkArrival**(NetworkMonitorEvent nme)
	void	**networkDeparture**(NetworkMonitorEvent nme)
	void	**networkException**(Exception ex)

NullInputStream

com.dalsemi.comm

Object
  ➥java.io.InputStream
    ➥NullInputStream

✳		**NullInputStream**()
	int	**read**()

NullOutputStream

com.dalsemi.comm

Object
  ➥java.io.OutputStream
    ➥NullOutputStream

✳		**NullOutputStream**()
	void	**write**(byte[] barr, int offset, int length)
	void	**write**(int b)

OneWireAccessProvider

com.dalsemi.onewire

Object
  ➥OneWireAccessProvider

❑	java.util.Enumer- ation	**enumerateAllAdapters**()

❏	adapter.DSPort-
	Adapter
		getAdapter(String adapterName,
		    String portName)
		    throws adapter.OneWireIOException, One-
		    WireException

❏	adapter.DSPort-
	Adapter
		getDefaultAdapter()
		    throws adapter.OneWireIOException, One-
		    WireException

❏	String	**getProperty**(String propName)

OneWireContainer`com.dalsemi.onewire.container`

```
Object
   ➥OneWireContainer
```

	void	**doSpeed**()
		    throws com.dalsemi.onewire.adapter.OneWi
		    reIOException, com.dalsemi.onewire.One-
		    WireException

	com.dalsemi.one- wire.adapter.DSPo rtAdapter	**getAdapter**()
	byte[]	**getAddress**()
	long	**getAddressAsLong**()
	String	**getAddressAsString**()
	String	**getAlternateNames**()
	String	**getDescription**()
	int	**getMaxSpeed**()
	java.util.Enumer- ation	**getMemoryBanks**()
	String	**getName**()

	boolean	**isAlarming**()
		    throws com.dalsemi.onewire.adapter.OneWi
		    reIOException, com.dalsemi.onewire.One-
		    WireException

	boolean	**isPresent**()
		    throws com.dalsemi.onewire.adapter.OneWi
		    reIOException, com.dalsemi.onewire.One-
		    WireException

✳		**OneWireContainer**()

✳		**OneWireContainer**(com.dalsemi.onewire.adapter
		    .DSPortAdapter sourceAdapter,
		    byte[] newAddress)

✳		**OneWireContainer**(com.dalsemi.onewire.adapter
		    .DSPortAdapter sourceAdapter,
		    long newAddress)

✳		**OneWireContainer**(com.dalsemi.onewire.adapter
		    .DSPortAdapter sourceAdapter,
		    String newAddress)

	void	**setSpeed**(int newSpeed, boolean fallBack)

void	**setupContainer**(com.dalsemi.onewire.adapter.D SPortAdapter sourceAdapter, byte[] newAddress)
void	**setupContainer**(com.dalsemi.onewire.adapter.D SPortAdapter sourceAdapter, long newAddress)
void	**setupContainer**(com.dalsemi.onewire.adapter.D SPortAdapter sourceAdapter, String newAddress)

OneWireContainer01

com.dalsemi.onewire.container

Object
  ➥OneWireContainer
    ➥OneWireContainer01

String	**getAlternateNames**()
String	**getDescription**()
String	**getName**()
*	**OneWireContainer01**()
*	**OneWireContainer01**(com.dalsemi.onewire.adapt er.DSPortAdapter sourceAdapter, byte[] newAddress)
*	**OneWireContainer01**(com.dalsemi.onewire.adapt er.DSPortAdapter sourceAdapter, long newAddress)
*	**OneWireContainer01**(com.dalsemi.onewire.adapt er.DSPortAdapter sourceAdapter, String newAddress)

OneWireContainer02

com.dalsemi.onewire.container

Object
  ➥OneWireContainer
    ➥OneWireContainer02

void	**copyScratchpad**(int key, byte[] passwd, int blockNum) *throws* com.dalsemi.onewire.adapter.OneWi reIOException, com.dalsemi.onewire.One- WireException, IllegalArgumentException
String	**getAlternateNames**()
String	**getDescription**()
String	**getName**()
*	**OneWireContainer02**()
*	**OneWireContainer02**(com.dalsemi.onewire.adapt er.DSPortAdapter sourceAdapter, byte[] newAddress)
*	**OneWireContainer02**(com.dalsemi.onewire.adapt er.DSPortAdapter sourceAdapter, long newAddress)

<table>
<tr><td>✻</td><td></td><td>OneWireContainer02(com.dalsemi.onewire.adapt
er.DSPortAdapter sourceAdapter,
String newAddress)</td></tr>
<tr><td></td><td>byte[]</td><td>readScratchpad()
throws com.dalsemi.onewire.adapter.OneWi
reIOException, com.dalsemi.onewire.One-
WireException</td></tr>
<tr><td></td><td>void</td><td>readSubkey(byte[] data, int key,
byte[] passwd)
throws com.dalsemi.onewire.adapter.OneWi
reIOException, com.dalsemi.onewire.One-
WireException, IllegalArgumentException</td></tr>
<tr><td></td><td>byte[]</td><td>readSubkey(int key, byte[] passwd)
throws com.dalsemi.onewire.adapter.OneWi
reIOException, com.dalsemi.onewire.One-
WireException, IllegalArgumentException</td></tr>
<tr><td></td><td>void</td><td>writePassword(int key, byte[] oldName,
byte[] newName, byte[] newPasswd)
throws com.dalsemi.onewire.adapter.OneWi
reIOException, com.dalsemi.onewire.One-
WireException, IllegalArgumentException</td></tr>
<tr><td></td><td>void</td><td>writeScratchpad(int addr, byte[] data)
throws com.dalsemi.onewire.adapter.OneWi
reIOException, com.dalsemi.onewire.One-
WireException, IllegalArgumentException</td></tr>
<tr><td></td><td>void</td><td>writeSubkey(int key, int addr,
byte[] passwd, byte[] data)
throws com.dalsemi.onewire.adapter.OneWi
reIOException, com.dalsemi.onewire.One-
WireException, IllegalArgumentException</td></tr>
</table>

OneWireContainer04   com.dalsemi.onewire.container

```
Object
  ➡OneWireContainer
      ➡OneWireContainer04          ClockContainer
```

boolean	**canDisableClock**()
boolean	**canReadAfterExpire**(byte[] state)
String	**getAlternateNames**()
long	**getClock**(byte[] state)
long	**getClockAlarm**(byte[] state) <i>throws</i> com.dalsemi.onewire.OneWireExcept ion
long	**getClockResolution**()
long	**getCycleCounter**(byte[] state)
long	**getCycleCounterAlarm**(byte[] state)
String	**getDescription**()
long	**getIntervalTimer**(byte[] state)
long	**getIntervalTimerAlarm**(byte[] state)
java.util.Enumer- ation	**getMemoryBanks**()

String	**getName**()
boolean	**hasClockAlarm**()
boolean	**isAutomaticDelayLong**(byte[] state)
boolean	**isClockAlarmEnabled**(byte[] state)
boolean	**isClockAlarming**(byte[] state)
boolean	**isClockRunning**(byte[] state)
boolean	**isClockWriteProtected**(byte[] state)
boolean	**isCycleCounterAlarmEnabled**(byte[] state)
boolean	**isCycleCounterAlarming**(byte[] state)
boolean	**isCycleCounterWriteProtected**(byte[] state)
boolean	**isIntervalTimerAlarmEnabled**(byte[] state)
boolean	**isIntervalTimerAlarming**(byte[] state)
boolean	**isIntervalTimerAutomatic**(byte[] state)
boolean	**isIntervalTimerStopped**(byte[] state)
boolean	**isIntervalTimerWriteProtected**(byte[] state)
❋	**OneWireContainer04**()
❋	**OneWireContainer04**(com.dalsemi.onewire.adapt er.DSPortAdapter sourceAdapter, byte[] newAddress)
❋	**OneWireContainer04**(com.dalsemi.onewire.adapt er.DSPortAdapter sourceAdapter, long newAddress)
❋	**OneWireContainer04**(com.dalsemi.onewire.adapt er.DSPortAdapter sourceAdapter, String newAddress)
byte[]	**readDevice**() *throws* com.dalsemi.onewire.adapter.OneWi reIOException, com.dalsemi.onewire.One- WireException
void	**setAutomaticDelayLong**(boolean delayLong, byte[] state)
void	**setClock**(long time, byte[] state)
void	**setClockAlarm**(long time, byte[] state) *throws* com.dalsemi.onewire.OneWireExcept ion
void	**setClockAlarmEnable**(boolean alarmEnable, byte[] state) *throws* com.dalsemi.onewire.OneWireExcept ion
void	**setClockRunEnable**(boolean runEnable, byte[] state) *throws* com.dalsemi.onewire.OneWireExcept ion
void	**setCycleCounter**(long cycles, byte[] state)
void	**setCycleCounterAlarm**(long cycles, byte[] state)
void	**setCycleCounterAlarmEnable**(boolean alarmEnab le, byte[] state)
void	**setIntervalTimer**(long time, byte[] state)

void	**setIntervalTimerAlarm**(long time, byte[] state)
void	**setIntervalTimerAlarmEnable**(boolean alarmEna ble, byte[] state)
void	**setIntervalTimerAutomatic**(boolean autoTimer, byte[] state)
void	**setIntervalTimerRunState**(boolean runState, byte[] state)
void	**setReadAfterExpire**(boolean readAfter, byte[] state)
void	**writeDevice**(byte[] state) *throws* com.dalsemi.onewire.adapter.OneWi reIOException, com.dalsemi.onewire.One-WireException
void	**writeProtectClock**(byte[] state)
void	**writeProtectCycleCounter**(byte[] state)
void	**writeProtectIntervalTimer**(byte[] state)

OneWireContainer05   com.dalsemi.onewire.container

Object
  ➡OneWireContainer
    ➡OneWireContainer05   SwitchContainer

void	**clearActivity**() *throws* com.dalsemi.onewire.OneWireExcept ion
String	**getAlternateNames**()
String	**getDescription**()
boolean	**getLatchState**(int channel, byte[] state)
boolean	**getLevel**(int channel, byte[] state)
String	**getName**()
int	**getNumberChannels**(byte[] state)
boolean	**getSensedActivity**(int channel, byte[] state) *throws* com.dalsemi.onewire.OneWireExcept ion
boolean	**hasActivitySensing**()
boolean	**hasLevelSensing**()
boolean	**hasSmartOn**()
boolean	**isHighSideSwitch**()
✳	**OneWireContainer05**()
✳	**OneWireContainer05**(com.dalsemi.onewire.adapt er.DSPortAdapter sourceAdapter, byte[] newAddress)
✳	**OneWireContainer05**(com.dalsemi.onewire.adapt er.DSPortAdapter sourceAdapter, long newAddress)
✳	**OneWireContainer05**(com.dalsemi.onewire.adapt er.DSPortAdapter sourceAdapter, String newAddress)
boolean	**onlySingleChannelOn**()

byte[]	**readDevice**()
	throws com.dalsemi.onewire.adapter.OneWi reIOException, com.dalsemi.onewire.One-WireException
void	**setLatchState**(int channel, boolean latchState, boolean doSmart, byte[] state)
void	**writeDevice**(byte[] state)
	throws com.dalsemi.onewire.adapter.OneWi reIOException, com.dalsemi.onewire.One-WireException

OneWireContainer06   `com.dalsemi.onewire.container`

Object
  ➡OneWireContainer
    ➡OneWireContainer06

String	**getDescription**()
java.util.Enumer-ation	**getMemoryBanks**()
String	**getName**()
✳	**OneWireContainer06**()
✳	**OneWireContainer06**(com.dalsemi.onewire.adapt er.DSPortAdapter sourceAdapter, byte[] newAddress)
✳	**OneWireContainer06**(com.dalsemi.onewire.adapt er.DSPortAdapter sourceAdapter, long newAddress)
✳	**OneWireContainer06**(com.dalsemi.onewire.adapt er.DSPortAdapter sourceAdapter, String newAddress)

OneWireContainer08   `com.dalsemi.onewire.container`

Object
  ➡OneWireContainer
    ➡OneWireContainer08

String	**getDescription**()
java.util.Enumer-ation	**getMemoryBanks**()
String	**getName**()
✳	**OneWireContainer08**()
✳	**OneWireContainer08**(com.dalsemi.onewire.adapt er.DSPortAdapter sourceAdapter, byte[] newAddress)
✳	**OneWireContainer08**(com.dalsemi.onewire.adapt er.DSPortAdapter sourceAdapter, long newAddress)
✳	**OneWireContainer08**(com.dalsemi.onewire.adapt er.DSPortAdapter sourceAdapter, String newAddress)

OneWireContainer09   `com.dalsemi.onewire.container`

```
Object
  ➥OneWireContainer
      ➥OneWireContainer09
```

	String	**getAlternateNames**()
	String	**getDescription**()
	int	**getMaxSpeed**()
	java.util.Enumeration	**getMemoryBanks**()
	String	**getName**()
✳		**OneWireContainer09**()
✳		**OneWireContainer09**(com.dalsemi.onewire.adapter.DSPortAdapter sourceAdapter, byte[] newAddress)
✳		**OneWireContainer09**(com.dalsemi.onewire.adapter.DSPortAdapter sourceAdapter, long newAddress)
✳		**OneWireContainer09**(com.dalsemi.onewire.adapter.DSPortAdapter sourceAdapter, String newAddress)

OneWireContainer0A   `com.dalsemi.onewire.container`

```
Object
  ➥OneWireContainer
      ➥OneWireContainer0A
```

	String	**getDescription**()
	int	**getMaxSpeed**()
	java.util.Enumeration	**getMemoryBanks**()
	String	**getName**()
✳		**OneWireContainer0A**()
✳		**OneWireContainer0A**(com.dalsemi.onewire.adapter.DSPortAdapter sourceAdapter, byte[] newAddress)
✳		**OneWireContainer0A**(com.dalsemi.onewire.adapter.DSPortAdapter sourceAdapter, long newAddress)
✳		**OneWireContainer0A**(com.dalsemi.onewire.adapter.DSPortAdapter sourceAdapter, String newAddress)

OneWireContainer0B   `com.dalsemi.onewire.container`

```
Object
 ➡OneWireContainer
    ➡OneWireContainer0B
```

String	**getAlternateNames**()
String	**getDescription**()
java.util.Enumeration	**getMemoryBanks**()
String	**getName**()
✻	**OneWireContainer0B**()
✻	**OneWireContainer0B**(com.dalsemi.onewire.adapter.DSPortAdapter sourceAdapter, byte[] newAddress)
✻	**OneWireContainer0B**(com.dalsemi.onewire.adapter.DSPortAdapter sourceAdapter, long newAddress)
✻	**OneWireContainer0B**(com.dalsemi.onewire.adapter.DSPortAdapter sourceAdapter, String newAddress)

OneWireContainer0C   `com.dalsemi.onewire.container`

```
Object
 ➡OneWireContainer
    ➡OneWireContainer0C
```

String	**getDescription**()
int	**getMaxSpeed**()
java.util.Enumeration	**getMemoryBanks**()
String	**getName**()
✻	**OneWireContainer0C**()
✻	**OneWireContainer0C**(com.dalsemi.onewire.adapter.DSPortAdapter sourceAdapter, byte[] newAddress)
✻	**OneWireContainer0C**(com.dalsemi.onewire.adapter.DSPortAdapter sourceAdapter, long newAddress)
✻	**OneWireContainer0C**(com.dalsemi.onewire.adapter.DSPortAdapter sourceAdapter, String newAddress)

OneWireContainer0F · com.dalsemi.onewire.container

```
Object
  ➥OneWireContainer
      ➥OneWireContainer0F
```

	String	**getAlternateNames**()
	String	**getDescription**()
	int	**getMaxSpeed**()
	java.util.Enumeration	**getMemoryBanks**()
	String	**getName**()
✳		**OneWireContainer0F**()
✳		**OneWireContainer0F**(com.dalsemi.onewire.adapter.DSPortAdapter sourceAdapter, byte[] newAddress)
✳		**OneWireContainer0F**(com.dalsemi.onewire.adapter.DSPortAdapter sourceAdapter, long newAddress)
✳		**OneWireContainer0F**(com.dalsemi.onewire.adapter.DSPortAdapter sourceAdapter, String newAddress)

OneWireContainer10 · com.dalsemi.onewire.container

```
Object
  ➥OneWireContainer
      ➥OneWireContainer10          TemperatureContainer
```

❑	double	**convertToCelsius**(double fahrenheitTemperature)
❑	double	**convertToFahrenheit**(double celsiusTemperature)
	void	**doTemperatureConvert**(byte[] state) *throws* com.dalsemi.onewire.adapter.OneWireIOException, com.dalsemi.onewire.OneWireException
	String	**getAlternateNames**()
	String	**getDescription**()
	double	**getMaxTemperature**()
	double	**getMinTemperature**()
	String	**getName**()
	double	**getTemperature**(byte[] state) *throws* com.dalsemi.onewire.adapter.OneWireIOException
	double	**getTemperatureAlarm**(int alarmType, byte[] state)
	double	**getTemperatureAlarmResolution**()
	double	**getTemperatureResolution**(byte[] state)
	double[]	**getTemperatureResolutions**()
	boolean	**hasSelectableTemperatureResolution**()

	boolean	**hasTemperatureAlarms**()
✳		**OneWireContainer10**()
✳		**OneWireContainer10**(com.dalsemi.onewire.adapt er.DSPortAdapter sourceAdapter, byte[] newAddress)
✳		**OneWireContainer10**(com.dalsemi.onewire.adapt er.DSPortAdapter sourceAdapter, long newAddress)
✳		**OneWireContainer10**(com.dalsemi.onewire.adapt er.DSPortAdapter sourceAdapter, String newAddress)
	byte[]	**readDevice**() *throws* com.dalsemi.onewire.adapter.OneWi reIOException, com.dalsemi.onewire.One- WireException
⚠■	double	**RESOLUTION_MAXIMUM**
⚠■	double	**RESOLUTION_NORMAL**
	void	**setTemperatureAlarm**(int alarmType, double alarmValue, byte[] state)
	void	**setTemperatureResolution**(double resolution, byte[] state)
	void	**writeDevice**(byte[] state) *throws* com.dalsemi.onewire.adapter.OneWi reIOException, com.dalsemi.onewire.One- WireException

OneWireContainer12   com.dalsemi.onewire.container

Object
　➡OneWireContainer
　　➡OneWireContainer12   SwitchContainer

⚠■	byte	**CHANNEL_A_ONLY**
⚠■	byte	**CHANNEL_B_ONLY**
⚠■	byte	**CHANNEL_BOTH**
⚠■	byte	**CHANNEL_NONE**
	byte[]	**channelAccess**(byte[] inbuffer, boolean toggleRW, boolean readInitially, int CRCMode, int channelMode, boolean clearActivity, boolean interleave) *throws* com.dalsemi.onewire.OneWireExcept ion, com.dalsemi.onewire.adapter.One- WireIOException
	void	**clearActivity**()
⚠■	byte	**CRC_DISABLE**
⚠■	byte	**CRC_EVERY_32_BYTES**
⚠■	byte	**CRC_EVERY_8_BYTES**
⚠■	byte	**CRC_EVERY_BYTE**
⚠■	byte	**DONT_CHANGE**
	String	**getAlternateNames**()

	String	**getDescription**()
	boolean	**getLatchState**(int channel, byte[] state)
	boolean	**getLevel**(int channel, byte[] state)
	java.util.Enumer- ation	**getMemoryBanks**()
	String	**getName**()
	int	**getNumberChannels**(byte[] state)
	boolean	**getSensedActivity**(int channel, byte[] state)
	boolean	**hasActivitySensing**()
	boolean	**hasLevelSensing**()
	boolean	**hasSmartOn**()
	boolean	**isHighSideSwitch**()
	boolean	**isPowerSupplied**(byte[] state)
✻		**OneWireContainer12**()
✻		**OneWireContainer12**(com.dalsemi.onewire.adapter.DSPortAdapter sourceAdapter, byte[] newAddress)
✻		**OneWireContainer12**(com.dalsemi.onewire.adapter.DSPortAdapter sourceAdapter, long newAddress)
✻		**OneWireContainer12**(com.dalsemi.onewire.adapter.DSPortAdapter sourceAdapter, String newAddress)
	boolean	**onlySingleChannelOn**()
✐■	byte	**POLARITY_ONE**
✐■	byte	**POLARITY_ZERO**
	byte[]	**readDevice**() *throws* com.dalsemi.onewire.adapter.OneWireIOException, com.dalsemi.onewire.OneWireException
	void	**setLatchState**(int channel, boolean latchState, boolean doSmart, byte[] state)
	void	**setSearchConditions**(byte channel, byte source, byte polarity, byte[] state)
	void	**setSpeedCheck**(boolean doSpeedCheck)
✐■	byte	**SOURCE_ACTIVITY_LATCH**
✐■	byte	**SOURCE_FLIP_FLOP**
✐■	byte	**SOURCE_PIO**
	void	**writeDevice**(byte[] state) *throws* com.dalsemi.onewire.adapter.OneWireIOException, com.dalsemi.onewire.OneWireException

OneWireContainer13   `com.dalsemi.onewire.container`

```
Object
  ➥OneWireContainer
      ➥OneWireContainer13
```

String	**getAlternateNames**()
String	**getDescription**()
java.util.Enumeration	**getMemoryBanks**()
String	**getName**()
✳	**OneWireContainer13**()
✳	**OneWireContainer13**(com.dalsemi.onewire.adapter.DSPortAdapter sourceAdapter, byte[] newAddress)
✳	**OneWireContainer13**(com.dalsemi.onewire.adapter.DSPortAdapter sourceAdapter, long newAddress)
✳	**OneWireContainer13**(com.dalsemi.onewire.adapter.DSPortAdapter sourceAdapter, String newAddress)

OneWireContainer14   `com.dalsemi.onewire.container`

```
Object
  ➥OneWireContainer
      ➥OneWireContainer14
```

String	**getAlternateNames**()
String	**getDescription**()
java.util.Enumeration	**getMemoryBanks**()
String	**getName**()
✳	**OneWireContainer14**()
✳	**OneWireContainer14**(com.dalsemi.onewire.adapter.DSPortAdapter sourceAdapter, byte[] newAddress)
✳	**OneWireContainer14**(com.dalsemi.onewire.adapter.DSPortAdapter sourceAdapter, long newAddress)
✳	**OneWireContainer14**(com.dalsemi.onewire.adapter.DSPortAdapter sourceAdapter, String newAddress)

OneWireContainer16 — com.dalsemi.onewire.container

Object
→OneWireContainer
→OneWireContainer16

int	**AID_LENGTH_OFFSET**
int	**AID_LENGTH_SIZE**
int	**AID_NAME_OFFSET**
int	**AID_SIZE**
int	**APDU_PACKET_LENGTH**
int	**APPLET_FILE_HEADER_SIZE**
ResponseAPDU	**deleteAppletByAID**(String aid) *throws* com.dalsemi.onewire.OneWireException, com.dalsemi.onewire.adapter.OneWireIOException, IllegalArgumentException
ResponseAPDU	**deleteAppletByNumber**(int index) *throws* com.dalsemi.onewire.OneWireException, com.dalsemi.onewire.adapter.OneWireIOException, IllegalArgumentException
ResponseAPDU	**deleteSelectedApplet**() *throws* com.dalsemi.onewire.OneWireException, com.dalsemi.onewire.adapter.OneWireIOException, IllegalArgumentException
ResponseAPDU	**getAIDByNumber**(int index) *throws* com.dalsemi.onewire.OneWireException, com.dalsemi.onewire.adapter.OneWireIOException, IllegalArgumentException
String	**getAlternateNames**()
ResponseAPDU	**getAppletGCMode**() *throws* com.dalsemi.onewire.OneWireException, com.dalsemi.onewire.adapter.OneWireIOException, IllegalArgumentException
ResponseAPDU	**getATR**() *throws* com.dalsemi.onewire.OneWireException, com.dalsemi.onewire.adapter.OneWireIOException, IllegalArgumentException
CommandAPDU	**getCommandAPDUInfo**()
ResponseAPDU	**getCommandPINMode**() *throws* com.dalsemi.onewire.OneWireException, com.dalsemi.onewire.adapter.OneWireIOException, IllegalArgumentException

ResponseAPDU	**getCommitBufferSize**()
	throws com.dalsemi.onewire.OneWireExcept ion, com.dalsemi.onewire.adapter.One- WireIOException, IllegalArgumentExcep tion
String	**getDescription**()
ResponseAPDU	**getEphemeralGCMode**()
	throws com.dalsemi.onewire.OneWireExcept ion, com.dalsemi.onewire.adapter.One- WireIOException, IllegalArgumentExcep tion
ResponseAPDU	**getErrorReportingMode**()
	throws com.dalsemi.onewire.OneWireExcept ion, com.dalsemi.onewire.adapter.One- WireIOException, IllegalArgumentExcep tion
ResponseAPDU	**getExceptionMode**()
	throws com.dalsemi.onewire.OneWireExcept ion, com.dalsemi.onewire.adapter.One- WireIOException, IllegalArgumentExcep tion
ResponseAPDU	**getFirmwareVersionString**()
	throws com.dalsemi.onewire.OneWireExcept ion, com.dalsemi.onewire.adapter.One- WireIOException, IllegalArgumentExcep tion
ResponseAPDU	**getFreeRAM**()
	throws com.dalsemi.onewire.OneWireExcept ion, com.dalsemi.onewire.adapter.One- WireIOException, IllegalArgumentExcep tion
ResponseAPDU	**getLastError**()
	throws com.dalsemi.onewire.OneWireExcept ion, com.dalsemi.onewire.adapter.One- WireIOException, IllegalArgumentExcep tion
int	**getLoadPacketSize**()
ResponseAPDU	**getLoadPINMode**()
	throws com.dalsemi.onewire.OneWireExcept ion, com.dalsemi.onewire.adapter.One- WireIOException, IllegalArgumentExcep tion
int	**getMaxSpeed**()
String	**getName**()
ResponseAPDU	**getPORCount**()
	throws com.dalsemi.onewire.OneWireExcept ion, com.dalsemi.onewire.adapter.One- WireIOException, IllegalArgumentExcep tion

ResponseAPDU	**getRandomBytes**(int numBytes) *throws* com.dalsemi.onewire.OneWireExcept ion, com.dalsemi.onewire.adapter.One- WireIOException, IllegalArgumentExcep- tion
ResponseAPDU	**getRealTimeClock**() *throws* com.dalsemi.onewire.OneWireExcept ion, com.dalsemi.onewire.adapter.One- WireIOException, IllegalArgumentExcep- tion
ResponseAPDU	**getResponseAPDUInfo**()
ResponseAPDU	**getRestoreMode**() *throws* com.dalsemi.onewire.OneWireExcept ion, com.dalsemi.onewire.adapter.One- WireIOException, IllegalArgumentExcep- tion
int	**getRunTime**()
ResponseAPDU	**loadApplet**(String fileName, String directoryName, String aid) *throws* com.dalsemi.onewire.OneWireExcept ion, com.dalsemi.onewire.adapter.One- WireIOException, IllegalArgumentExcep- tion, java.io.FileNotFoundException, java.io.IOException
ResponseAPDU	**masterErase**() *throws* com.dalsemi.onewire.OneWireExcept ion, com.dalsemi.onewire.adapter.One- WireIOException, IllegalArgumentExcep- tion
	OneWireContainer16()
	OneWireContainer16(com.dalsemi.onewire.adapt er.DSPortAdapter sourceAdapter, byte[] newAddress)
	OneWireContainer16(com.dalsemi.onewire.adapt er.DSPortAdapter sourceAdapter, long newAddress)
	OneWireContainer16(com.dalsemi.onewire.adapt er.DSPortAdapter sourceAdapter, String newAddress)
int	**PASSWORD_LENGTH_SIZE**
int	**PASSWORD_SIZE**
ResponseAPDU	**process**(CommandAPDU capdu) *throws* com.dalsemi.onewire.OneWireExcept ion, com.dalsemi.onewire.adapter.One- WireIOException, IllegalArgumentExcep- tion
ResponseAPDU	**select**(String aid) *throws* com.dalsemi.onewire.OneWireExcept ion, com.dalsemi.onewire.adapter.One- WireIOException, IllegalArgumentExcep- tion

ResponseAPDU	**sendAPDU**(CommandAPDU capdu, int runTime) *throws* com.dalsemi.onewire.OneWireExcept ion, com.dalsemi.onewire.adapter.One-WireIOException, IllegalArgumentExcep tion
ResponseAPDU	**setAppletGCMode**(int mode) *throws* com.dalsemi.onewire.OneWireExcept ion, com.dalsemi.onewire.adapter.One-WireIOException, IllegalArgumentExcep tion
ResponseAPDU	**setCommandPINMode**(int mode) *throws* com.dalsemi.onewire.OneWireExcept ion, com.dalsemi.onewire.adapter.One-WireIOException, IllegalArgumentExcep tion
ResponseAPDU	**setCommitBufferSize**(int size) *throws* com.dalsemi.onewire.OneWireExcept ion, com.dalsemi.onewire.adapter.One-WireIOException, IllegalArgumentExcep tion
ResponseAPDU	**setCommonPIN**(String newPIN) *throws* com.dalsemi.onewire.OneWireExcept ion, com.dalsemi.onewire.adapter.One-WireIOException, IllegalArgumentExcep tion
ResponseAPDU	**setEphemeralGCMode**(int mode) *throws* com.dalsemi.onewire.OneWireExcept ion, com.dalsemi.onewire.adapter.One-WireIOException, IllegalArgumentExcep tion
ResponseAPDU	**setErrorReportingMode**(int mode) *throws* com.dalsemi.onewire.OneWireExcept ion, com.dalsemi.onewire.adapter.One-WireIOException, IllegalArgumentExcep tion
ResponseAPDU	**setExceptionMode**(int mode) *throws* com.dalsemi.onewire.OneWireExcept ion, com.dalsemi.onewire.adapter.One-WireIOException, IllegalArgumentExcep tion
boolean	**setLoadPacketSize**(int size)
ResponseAPDU	**setLoadPINMode**(int mode) *throws* com.dalsemi.onewire.OneWireExcept ion, com.dalsemi.onewire.adapter.One-WireIOException, IllegalArgumentExcep tion
void	**setPIN**(String passwd)
ResponseAPDU	**setRestoreMode**(int mode) *throws* com.dalsemi.onewire.OneWireExcept ion, com.dalsemi.onewire.adapter.One-WireIOException, IllegalArgumentExcep tion
void	**setRunTime**(int newRunTime) *throws* IllegalArgumentException

	void	setupContainer(com.dalsemi.onewire.adapter.D SPortAdapter sourceAdapter, byte[] newAddress)
	void	setupContainer(com.dalsemi.onewire.adapter.D SPortAdapter sourceAdapter, long newAddress)
	void	setupContainer(com.dalsemi.onewire.adapter.D SPortAdapter sourceAdapter, String newAddress)
	void	setupJibComm(com.dalsemi.onewire.adapter.DSP ortAdapter sourceAdapter, byte[] newAddress)

OneWireContainer18	**com.dalsemi.onewire.container**

Object
  ➥OneWireContainer
    ➥OneWireContainer18

	byte	AUTH_HOST
	boolean	bindSecretToiButton(int page, byte[] bind_data, byte[] bind_code, int secret_number) *throws* com.dalsemi.onewire.adapter.OneWi reIOException, com.dalsemi.onewire.One-WireException
	byte	COMPUTE_CHALLENGE
	byte	COMPUTE_FIRST_SECRET
	byte	COMPUTE_NEXT_SECRET
	byte	COMPUTE_SHA
	byte	COPY_SCRATCHPAD
	boolean	copyScratchPad() *throws* com.dalsemi.onewire.adapter.OneWi reIOException, com.dalsemi.onewire.One-WireException
	byte	ERASE_SCRATCHPAD
	boolean	eraseScratchPad(int page) *throws* com.dalsemi.onewire.adapter.OneWi reIOException, com.dalsemi.onewire.One-WireException
String		getAlternateNames()
String		getDescription()
int		getMaxSpeed()
java.util.Enumer-ation		getMemoryBanks()
String		getName()
	boolean	installMasterSecret(int page, byte[] secret, int secret_number) *throws* com.dalsemi.onewire.adapter.OneWi reIOException, com.dalsemi.onewire.One-WireException
	byte	MATCH_SCRATCHPAD

	boolean	**matchScratchPad**(byte[] mac)
		throws com.dalsemi.onewire.adapter.OneWireIOException, com.dalsemi.onewire.OneWireException
✳		**OneWireContainer18**()
✳		**OneWireContainer18**(com.dalsemi.onewire.adapter.DSPortAdapter sourceAdapter, byte[] newAddress)
✳		**OneWireContainer18**(com.dalsemi.onewire.adapter.DSPortAdapter sourceAdapter, long newAddress)
✳		**OneWireContainer18**(com.dalsemi.onewire.adapter.DSPortAdapter sourceAdapter, String newAddress)
✍■	byte	**READ_AUTHENTICATED_PAGE**
✍■	byte	**READ_MEMORY**
✍■	byte	**READ_SCRATCHPAD**
	boolean	**readAuthenticatedPage**(int pageNum, byte[] data, int start)
		throws com.dalsemi.onewire.adapter.OneWireIOException, com.dalsemi.onewire.OneWireException
	void	**readMemoryPage**(int pageNum, byte[] data, int start)
		throws com.dalsemi.onewire.adapter.OneWireIOException, com.dalsemi.onewire.OneWireException
	int	**readScratchPad**(byte[] data, int start)
		throws com.dalsemi.onewire.adapter.OneWireIOException, com.dalsemi.onewire.OneWireException
✍■	byte	**RESUME**
	void	**setSpeedCheck**(boolean doSpeedCheck)
	void	**setupContainer**(com.dalsemi.onewire.adapter.DSPortAdapter sourceAdapter, byte[] newAddress)
	boolean	**SHAFunction**(byte function)
		throws com.dalsemi.onewire.adapter.OneWireIOException, com.dalsemi.onewire.OneWireException
	boolean	**SHAFunction**(byte function, int T)
		throws com.dalsemi.onewire.adapter.OneWireIOException, com.dalsemi.onewire.OneWireException
✍■	byte	**SIGN_DATA_PAGE**
	void	**useResume**(boolean set)
✍■	byte	**VALIDATE_DATA_PAGE**
	boolean	**waitForSuccessfulFinish**()
		throws com.dalsemi.onewire.adapter.OneWireIOException, com.dalsemi.onewire.OneWireException

▲■	byte	**WRITE_SCRATCHPAD**
	boolean	**writeDataPage**(int page_number, byte[] page_data) *throws* com.dalsemi.onewire.adapter.OneWireIOException, com.dalsemi.onewire.OneWireException
	boolean	**writeScratchPad**(int targetPage, int targetPageOffset, byte[] inputbuffer, int start, int length) *throws* com.dalsemi.onewire.adapter.OneWireIOException, com.dalsemi.onewire.OneWireException

OneWireContainer1A   com.dalsemi.onewire.container

Object
  ➡OneWireContainer
    ➡OneWireContainer1A

	String	**getAlternateNames**()
	String	**getDescription**()
	int	**getMaxSpeed**()
	java.util.Enumeration	**getMemoryBanks**()
	String	**getName**()
✳		**OneWireContainer1A**()
✳		**OneWireContainer1A**(com.dalsemi.onewire.adapter.DSPortAdapter sourceAdapter, byte[] newAddress)
✳		**OneWireContainer1A**(com.dalsemi.onewire.adapter.DSPortAdapter sourceAdapter, long newAddress)
✳		**OneWireContainer1A**(com.dalsemi.onewire.adapter.DSPortAdapter sourceAdapter, String newAddress)

OneWireContainer1D   com.dalsemi.onewire.container

Object
  ➡OneWireContainer
    ➡OneWireContainer1D

	String	**getDescription**()
	int	**getMaxSpeed**()
	java.util.Enumeration	**getMemoryBanks**()
	String	**getName**()
✳		**OneWireContainer1D**()
✳		**OneWireContainer1D**(com.dalsemi.onewire.adapter.DSPortAdapter sourceAdapter, byte[] newAddress)

✳		**OneWireContainer1D**(com.dalsemi.onewire.adapt er.DSPortAdapter sourceAdapter, long newAddress)
✳		**OneWireContainer1D**(com.dalsemi.onewire.adapt er.DSPortAdapter sourceAdapter, String newAddress)
	long	**readCounter**(int counterPage) *throws* com.dalsemi.onewire.adapter.OneWi reIOException, com.dalsemi.onewire.One- WireException

OneWireContainer1F com.dalsemi.onewire.container

Object
➥OneWireContainer
   ➥OneWireContainer1F SwitchContainer

✍▪	int	**CHANNEL_AUX**
✍▪	int	**CHANNEL_MAIN**
	void	**clearActivity**() *throws* com.dalsemi.onewire.OneWireExcept ion
	void	**dischargeLines**(int time) *throws* com.dalsemi.onewire.adapter.OneWi reIOException, com.dalsemi.onewire.One- WireException
	String	**getAlternateNames**()
	int	**getControlChannelAssociation**(byte[] state)
	int	**getControlData**(byte[] state)
	String	**getDescription**()
	boolean	**getLastSmartOnDeviceDetect**()
	boolean	**getLatchState**(int channel, byte[] state)
	boolean	**getLevel**(int channel, byte[] state) *throws* com.dalsemi.onewire.OneWireExcept ion
	String	**getName**()
	int	**getNumberChannels**(byte[] state)
	boolean	**getSensedActivity**(int channel, byte[] state) *throws* com.dalsemi.onewire.OneWireExcept ion
	boolean	**hasActivitySensing**()
	boolean	**hasLevelSensing**()
	boolean	**hasSmartOn**()
	boolean	**isHighSideSwitch**()
	boolean	**isModeAuto**(byte[] state)
✳		**OneWireContainer1F**()
✳		**OneWireContainer1F**(com.dalsemi.onewire.adapt er.DSPortAdapter sourceAdapter, byte[] newAddress)

✳		**OneWireContainer1F**(com.dalsemi.onewire.adapt er.DSPortAdapter sourceAdapter, long newAddress)
✳		**OneWireContainer1F**(com.dalsemi.onewire.adapt er.DSPortAdapter sourceAdapter, String newAddress)
	boolean	**onlySingleChannelOn**()
	byte[]	**readDevice**() *throws* com.dalsemi.onewire.adapter.OneWi reIOException, com.dalsemi.onewire.One- WireException
	void	**setControlChannelAssociation**(int channel, byte[] state) *throws* com.dalsemi.onewire.OneWireExcept ion
	void	**setControlData**(boolean data, byte[] state) *throws* com.dalsemi.onewire.OneWireExcept ion
	void	**setLatchState**(int channel, boolean latchState, boolean doSmart, byte[] state)
	void	**setModeAuto**(boolean makeAuto, byte[] state)
	void	**setSpeedCheck**(boolean doSpeedCheck)
	void	**writeDevice**(byte[] state) *throws* com.dalsemi.onewire.adapter.OneWi reIOException, com.dalsemi.onewire.One- WireException

OneWireContainer20   com.dalsemi.onewire.container

```
Object
  ➡OneWireContainer
    ➡OneWireContainer20          ADContainer
```

✎■	int	**ALARM_OFFSET**
✎■	int	**BITMAP_OFFSET**
	boolean	**canADMultiChannelRead**()
✎■	int	**CHANNELA**
✎■	int	**CHANNELB**
✎■	int	**CHANNELC**
✎■	int	**CHANNELD**
	void	**doADConvert**(boolean[] doConvert, byte[] state) *throws* com.dalsemi.onewire.adapter.OneWi reIOException, com.dalsemi.onewire.One- WireException
	void	**doADConvert**(boolean[] doConvert, int[] preset, byte[] state) *throws* com.dalsemi.onewire.adapter.OneWi reIOException, com.dalsemi.onewire.One- WireException

void	**doADConvert**(int channel, byte[] state)
		throws com.dalsemi.onewire.adapter.OneWireIOException, com.dalsemi.onewire.OneWireException
void	**doADConvert**(int channel, int preset, byte[] state)
		throws com.dalsemi.onewire.adapter.OneWireIOException, com.dalsemi.onewire.OneWireException, IllegalArgumentException
⚠■ int	**EXPOWER_OFFSET**
double	**getADAlarm**(int channel, int alarmType, byte[] state)
boolean	**getADAlarmEnable**(int channel, int alarmType, byte[] state)
double	**getADRange**(int channel, byte[] state)
double[]	**getADRanges**(int channel)
double	**getADResolution**(int channel, byte[] state)
double[]	**getADResolutions**(int channel, double range)
double[]	**getADVoltage**(byte[] state)
		throws com.dalsemi.onewire.adapter.OneWireIOException, com.dalsemi.onewire.OneWireException
double	**getADVoltage**(int channel, byte[] state)
		throws com.dalsemi.onewire.adapter.OneWireIOException, com.dalsemi.onewire.OneWireException
String	**getAlternateNames**()
String	**getDescription**()
boolean	**getDevicePOR**(byte[] state)
int	**getMaxSpeed**()
java.util.Enumeration	**getMemoryBanks**()
String	**getName**()
int	**getNumberADChannels**()
boolean	**getOutputState**(int channel, byte[] state)
		throws IllegalArgumentException
boolean	**hasADAlarmed**(int channel, int alarmType, byte[] state)
boolean	**hasADAlarms**()
❏ double	**interpretVoltage**(long rawVoltage, double range)
boolean	**isOutputEnabled**(int channel, byte[] state)
		throws IllegalArgumentException
boolean	**isPowerExternal**(byte[] state)
⚠■ int	**NO_PRESET**
⚠■ int	**NUM_CHANNELS**
❋	**OneWireContainer20**()
❋	**OneWireContainer20**(com.dalsemi.onewire.adapter.DSPortAdapter sourceAdapter, byte[] newAddress)

✳		**OneWireContainer20**(com.dalsemi.onewire.adapt er.DSPortAdapter sourceAdapter, long newAddress)
✳		**OneWireContainer20**(com.dalsemi.onewire.adapt er.DSPortAdapter sourceAdapter, String newAddress)
⚠■	int	**PRESET_TO_ONES**
⚠■	int	**PRESET_TO_ZEROS**
	byte[]	**readDevice**() *throws* com.dalsemi.onewire.adapter.OneWi reIOException, com.dalsemi.onewire.One- WireException
	void	**setADAlarm**(int channel, int alarmType, double alarm, byte[] state)
	void	**setADAlarmEnable**(int channel, int alarmType, boolean alarmEnable, byte[] state)
	void	**setADRange**(int channel, double range, byte[] state)
	void	**setADResolution**(int channel, double resolution, byte[] state)
	void	**setOutput**(int channel, boolean outputEnable, boolean outputState, byte[] state)
	void	**setPower**(boolean external, byte[] state)
❏	int	**voltageToInt**(double voltage, double range)
	void	**writeDevice**(byte[] state) *throws* com.dalsemi.onewire.adapter.OneWi reIOException, com.dalsemi.onewire.One- WireException

OneWireContainer21   com.dalsemi.onewire.container

Object
  ➡OneWireContainer
    ➡OneWireContainer21   TemperatureContainer,
ClockContainer

	boolean	**canDisableClock**()
	void	**clearMemory**() *throws* com.dalsemi.onewire.adapter.OneWi reIOException, com.dalsemi.onewire.One- WireException
⚠■	int	**CONTROL_REGISTER**
	double	**decodeTemperature**(byte tempByte)
	void	**disableMission**() *throws* com.dalsemi.onewire.adapter.OneWi reIOException, com.dalsemi.onewire.One- WireException
	void	**doTemperatureConvert**(byte[] state) *throws* com.dalsemi.onewire.adapter.OneWi reIOException, com.dalsemi.onewire.One- WireException

void	**enableMission**(int sampleRate)
	throws com.dalsemi.onewire.adapter.OneWi reIOException, com.dalsemi.onewire.One-WireException
byte	**encodeTemperature**(double temperature)
byte[]	**getAlarmHistory**(byte alarmBit)
	throws com.dalsemi.onewire.adapter.OneWi reIOException, com.dalsemi.onewire.One-WireException
boolean	**getAlarmStatus**(byte alarmBit, byte[] state)
java.util.Calen-dar	**getAlarmTime**(byte[] state)
String	**getAlternateNames**()
long	**getClock**(byte[] state)
long	**getClockAlarm**(byte[] state)
long	**getClockResolution**()
String	**getDescription**()
int	**getDeviceSamplesCounter**(byte[] state)
long	**getFirstLogOffset**(byte[] state)
boolean	**getFlag**(int register, byte bitMask)
	throws com.dalsemi.onewire.adapter.OneWi reIOException, com.dalsemi.onewire.One-WireException
boolean	**getFlag**(int register, byte bitMask, byte[] state)
int	**getMaxSpeed**()
double	**getMaxTemperature**()
java.util.Enumer-ation	**getMemoryBanks**()
double	**getMinTemperature**()
int	**getMissionSamplesCounter**(byte[] state)
java.util.Calen-dar	**getMissionTimeStamp**(byte[] state)
String	**getName**()
int	**getSampleRate**(byte[] state)
double	**getTemperature**(byte[] state)
double	**getTemperatureAlarm**(int alarmType, byte[] state)
double	**getTemperatureAlarmResolution**()
int[]	**getTemperatureHistogram**()
	throws com.dalsemi.onewire.adapter.OneWi reIOException, com.dalsemi.onewire.One-WireException
byte[]	**getTemperatureLog**(byte[] state)
	throws com.dalsemi.onewire.adapter.OneWi reIOException, com.dalsemi.onewire.One-WireException
double	**getTemperatureResolution**(byte[] state)
double[]	**getTemperatureResolutions**()
boolean	**hasClockAlarm**()

boolean	**hasSelectableTemperatureResolution**()
boolean	**hasTemperatureAlarms**()
boolean	**isClockAlarmEnabled**(byte[] state)
boolean	**isClockAlarming**(byte[] state)
boolean	**isClockRunning**(byte[] state)
byte	**MEMORY_CLEAR_ENABLE_FLAG**
byte	**MEMORY_CLEARED_FLAG**
byte	**MISSION_ENABLE_FLAG**
byte	**MISSION_IN_PROGRESS_FLAG**
byte	**ONCE_PER_DAY**
byte	**ONCE_PER_HOUR**
byte	**ONCE_PER_MINUTE**
byte	**ONCE_PER_SECOND**
byte	**ONCE_PER_WEEK**
	OneWireContainer21()
	OneWireContainer21(com.dalsemi.onewire.adapter.DSPortAdapter sourceAdapter, byte[] newAddress)
	OneWireContainer21(com.dalsemi.onewire.adapter.DSPortAdapter sourceAdapter, long newAddress)
	OneWireContainer21(com.dalsemi.onewire.adapter.DSPortAdapter sourceAdapter, String newAddress)
byte	**OSCILLATOR_ENABLE_FLAG**
byte	**readByte**(int memAddr) *throws* com.dalsemi.onewire.adapter.OneWireIOException, com.dalsemi.onewire.OneWireException
byte[]	**readDevice**() *throws* com.dalsemi.onewire.adapter.OneWireIOException, com.dalsemi.onewire.OneWireException
byte	**ROLLOVER_ENABLE_FLAG**
byte	**SAMPLE_IN_PROGRESS_FLAG**
void	**setClock**(long time, byte[] state)
void	**setClockAlarm**(int hours, int minutes, int seconds, int day, int alarmFrequency, byte[] state)
void	**setClockAlarm**(long time, byte[] state) *throws* com.dalsemi.onewire.OneWireException
void	**setClockAlarmEnable**(boolean alarmEnable, byte[] state)
void	**setClockRunEnable**(boolean runEnable, byte[] state)

void	**setFlag**(int register, byte bitMask,	
		boolean flagValue)
		throws com.dalsemi.onewire.adapter.OneWi
		reIOException, com.dalsemi.onewire.One-
		WireException
void	**setFlag**(int register, byte bitMask,	
		boolean flagValue, byte[] state)
void	**setMissionStartDelay**(int missionStartDelay,	
		byte[] state)
void	**setSpeedCheck**(boolean doSpeedCheck)	
void	**setTemperatureAlarm**(int alarmType,	
		double alarmValue, byte[] state)
void	**setTemperatureResolution**(double resolution,	
		byte[] state)
		throws com.dalsemi.onewire.OneWireExcept
		ion
int	**STATUS_REGISTER**	
byte	**TEMP_CORE_BUSY_FLAG**	
byte	**TEMP_HIGH_SEARCH_FLAG**	
byte	**TEMP_LOW_SEARCH_FLAG**	
byte	**TEMPERATURE_HIGH_ALARM**	
byte	**TEMPERATURE_HIGH_FLAG**	
byte	**TEMPERATURE_LOW_ALARM**	
byte	**TEMPERATURE_LOW_FLAG**	
byte	**TIMER_ALARM**	
byte	**TIMER_ALARM_FLAG**	
byte	**TIMER_ALARM_SEARCH_FLAG**	
void	**writeByte**(int memAddr, byte source)	
		throws com.dalsemi.onewire.adapter.OneWi
		reIOException, com.dalsemi.onewire.One-
		WireException
void	**writeDevice**(byte[] state)	
		throws com.dalsemi.onewire.adapter.OneWi
		reIOException, com.dalsemi.onewire.One-
		WireException

OneWireContainer23   com.dalsemi.onewire.container

Object
  ➡OneWireContainer
    ➡OneWireContainer23

String	**getAlternateNames**()
String	**getDescription**()
int	**getMaxSpeed**()
java.util.Enumer- ation	**getMemoryBanks**()
String	**getName**()
	OneWireContainer23()

✳		OneWireContainer23(com.dalsemi.onewire.adapter.DSPortAdapter sourceAdapter, byte[] newAddress)
✳		OneWireContainer23(com.dalsemi.onewire.adapter.DSPortAdapter sourceAdapter, long newAddress)
✳		OneWireContainer23(com.dalsemi.onewire.adapter.DSPortAdapter sourceAdapter, String newAddress)

OneWireContainer26   com.dalsemi.onewire.container

Object
   ➥OneWireContainer
      ➥OneWireContainer26   ADContainer, Temperature-
Container, ClockContainer

✍▪	byte	**AD_FLAG**
✍▪	byte	**ADB_FLAG**
✍▪	byte	**CA_FLAG**
	void	**calibrateCurrentADC**() *throws* com.dalsemi.onewire.adapter.OneWireIOException, com.dalsemi.onewire.OneWireException, IllegalArgumentException
	boolean	**canADMultiChannelRead**()
	boolean	**canDisableClock**()
✍▪	int	**CHANNEL_VAD**
✍▪	int	**CHANNEL_VDD**
	void	**doADConvert**(boolean[] doConvert, byte[] state) *throws* com.dalsemi.onewire.adapter.OneWireIOException, com.dalsemi.onewire.OneWireException
	void	**doADConvert**(int channel, byte[] state) *throws* com.dalsemi.onewire.adapter.OneWireIOException, com.dalsemi.onewire.OneWireException
	void	**doTemperatureConvert**(byte[] state) *throws* com.dalsemi.onewire.adapter.OneWireIOException, com.dalsemi.onewire.OneWireException
✍▪	byte	**EE_FLAG**
	double	**getADAlarm**(int channel, int alarmType, byte[] state) *throws* com.dalsemi.onewire.OneWireException
	boolean	**getADAlarmEnable**(int channel, int alarmType, byte[] state) *throws* com.dalsemi.onewire.OneWireException
	double	**getADRange**(int channel, byte[] state)
	double[]	**getADRanges**(int channel)

double	**getADResolution**(int channel, byte[] state)
double[]	**getADResolutions**(int channel, double range)
double[]	**getADVoltage**(byte[] state)
	throws com.dalsemi.onewire.adapter.OneWireIOException, com.dalsemi.onewire.OneWireException
double	**getADVoltage**(int channel, byte[] state)
	throws com.dalsemi.onewire.adapter.OneWireIOException, com.dalsemi.onewire.OneWireException
String	**getAlternateNames**()
int	**getCCA**()
	throws com.dalsemi.onewire.adapter.OneWireIOException, com.dalsemi.onewire.OneWireException, IllegalArgumentException
long	**getClock**(byte[] state)
long	**getClockAlarm**(byte[] state)
	throws com.dalsemi.onewire.OneWireException
long	**getClockResolution**()
double	**getCurrent**(byte[] state)
int	**getDCA**()
	throws com.dalsemi.onewire.adapter.OneWireIOException, com.dalsemi.onewire.OneWireException, IllegalArgumentException
String	**getDescription**()
long	**getDisconnectTime**(byte[] state)
long	**getEndOfChargeTime**(byte[] state)
boolean	**getFlag**(byte flagToGet)
	throws com.dalsemi.onewire.adapter.OneWireIOException, com.dalsemi.onewire.OneWireException, IllegalArgumentException
int	**getICA**()
	throws com.dalsemi.onewire.adapter.OneWireIOException, com.dalsemi.onewire.OneWireException, IllegalArgumentException
double	**getMaxTemperature**()
double	**getMinTemperature**()
String	**getName**()
int	**getNumberADChannels**()
double	**getRemainingCapacity**()
	throws com.dalsemi.onewire.adapter.OneWireIOException, com.dalsemi.onewire.OneWireException, IllegalArgumentException
double	**getSenseResistor**()
double	**getTemperature**(byte[] state)
double	**getTemperatureAlarm**(int alarmType, byte[] state)
	throws com.dalsemi.onewire.OneWireException

	double	**getTemperatureAlarmResolution**() *throws* com.dalsemi.onewire.OneWireExcept ion
	double	**getTemperatureResolution**(byte[] state)
	double[]	**getTemperatureResolutions**()
	boolean	**hasADAlarmed**(int channel, int alarmType, byte[] state) *throws* com.dalsemi.onewire.OneWireExcept ion
	boolean	**hasADAlarms**()
	boolean	**hasClockAlarm**()
	boolean	**hasSelectableTemperatureResolution**()
	boolean	**hasTemperatureAlarms**()
⚠■	byte	**IAD_FLAG**
	boolean	**isCharging**(byte[] state) *throws* com.dalsemi.onewire.adapter.OneWi reIOException, com.dalsemi.onewire.One- WireException, IllegalArgumentException
	boolean	**isClockAlarmEnabled**(byte[] state)
	boolean	**isClockAlarming**(byte[] state)
	boolean	**isClockRunning**(byte[] state)
⚠■	byte	**NVB_FLAG**
❋		**OneWireContainer26**()
❋		**OneWireContainer26**(com.dalsemi.onewire.adapt er.DSPortAdapter sourceAdapter, byte[] newAddress)
❋		**OneWireContainer26**(com.dalsemi.onewire.adapt er.DSPortAdapter sourceAdapter, long newAddress)
❋		**OneWireContainer26**(com.dalsemi.onewire.adapt er.DSPortAdapter sourceAdapter, String newAddress)
	byte[]	**readDevice**() *throws* com.dalsemi.onewire.adapter.OneWi reIOException, com.dalsemi.onewire.One- WireException
	byte[]	**readPage**(int page) *throws* com.dalsemi.onewire.adapter.OneWi reIOException, com.dalsemi.onewire.One- WireException, IllegalArgumentException
	void	**setADAlarm**(int channel, int alarmType, double alarm, byte[] state) *throws* com.dalsemi.onewire.OneWireExcept ion
	void	**setADAlarmEnable**(int channel, int alarmType, boolean alarmEnable, byte[] state) *throws* com.dalsemi.onewire.OneWireExcept ion
	void	**setADRange**(int channel, double range, byte[] state)
	void	**setADResolution**(int channel, double resolution, byte[] state)

```
void  setCCA(int ccaValue)
          throws com.dalsemi.onewire.adapter.OneWi
          reIOException, com.dalsemi.onewire.One-
          WireException, IllegalArgumentException
void  setClock(long time, byte[] state)
void  setClockAlarm(long time, byte[] state)
          throws com.dalsemi.onewire.OneWireExcept
          ion
void  setClockAlarmEnable(boolean alarmEnable,
          byte[] state)
          throws com.dalsemi.onewire.OneWireExcept
          ion
void  setClockRunEnable(boolean runEnable,
          byte[] state)
          throws com.dalsemi.onewire.OneWireExcept
          ion
void  setDCA(int dcaValue)
          throws com.dalsemi.onewire.adapter.OneWi
          reIOException, com.dalsemi.onewire.One-
          WireException, IllegalArgumentException
void  setFlag(byte flagToSet, boolean flagValue)
          throws com.dalsemi.onewire.adapter.OneWi
          reIOException, com.dalsemi.onewire.One-
          WireException, IllegalArgumentException
void  setICA(int icaValue)
          throws com.dalsemi.onewire.adapter.OneWi
          reIOException, com.dalsemi.onewire.One-
          WireException, IllegalArgumentException
void  setSenseResistor(double resistance)
void  setSpeedCheck(boolean doSpeedCheck)
void  setTemperatureAlarm(int alarmType,
          double alarmValue, byte[] state)
          throws com.dalsemi.onewire.OneWireExcept
          ion, com.dalsemi.onewire.adapter.One-
          WireIOException
void  setTemperatureResolution(double resolution,
          byte[] state)
          throws com.dalsemi.onewire.OneWireExcept
          ion, com.dalsemi.onewire.adapter.One-
          WireIOException
void  setThreshold(byte thresholdValue)
          throws com.dalsemi.onewire.adapter.OneWi
          reIOException, com.dalsemi.onewire.One-
          WireException
```

🖉■	byte	**TB_FLAG**
	void	**writeDevice**(byte[] state)
		throws com.dalsemi.onewire.adapter.OneWireIOException, com.dalsemi.onewire.OneWireException
	void	**writePage**(int page, byte[] source, int offset)
		throws com.dalsemi.onewire.adapter.OneWireIOException, com.dalsemi.onewire.OneWireException

OneWireContainer28   com.dalsemi.onewire.container

```
Object
   ➡OneWireContainer
      ➡OneWireContainer28          TemperatureContainer
```

🖉■	byte	**CONVERT_TEMPERATURE_COMMAND**
	float	**convertToFahrenheit**(float celsiusTemperature)
🖉■	byte	**COPY_SCRATCHPAD_COMMAND**
	void	**copyScratchpad**()
		throws com.dalsemi.onewire.adapter.OneWireIOException, com.dalsemi.onewire.OneWireException
	void	**doTemperatureConvert**(byte[] state)
		throws com.dalsemi.onewire.adapter.OneWireIOException, com.dalsemi.onewire.OneWireException
	String	**getAlternateNames**()
	String	**getDescription**()
	double	**getMaxTemperature**()
	double	**getMinTemperature**()
	String	**getName**()
	double	**getTemperature**(byte[] state)
		throws com.dalsemi.onewire.adapter.OneWireIOException
	double	**getTemperatureAlarm**(int alarmType, byte[] state)
	double	**getTemperatureAlarmResolution**()
	double	**getTemperatureResolution**(byte[] state)
	double[]	**getTemperatureResolutions**()
	boolean	**hasSelectableTemperatureResolution**()
	boolean	**hasTemperatureAlarms**()
	boolean	**isExternalPowerSupplied**()
		throws com.dalsemi.onewire.adapter.OneWireIOException, com.dalsemi.onewire.OneWireException
✳		**OneWireContainer28**()

✱		**OneWireContainer28**(com.dalsemi.onewire.adapt er.DSPortAdapter sourceAdapter, byte[] newAddress)
✱		**OneWireContainer28**(com.dalsemi.onewire.adapt er.DSPortAdapter sourceAdapter, long newAddress)
✱		**OneWireContainer28**(com.dalsemi.onewire.adapt er.DSPortAdapter sourceAdapter, String newAddress)
⚠■	byte	**READ_POWER_SUPPLY_COMMAND**
⚠■	byte	**READ_SCRATCHPAD_COMMAND**
	byte[]	**readDevice**() *throws* com.dalsemi.onewire.adapter.OneWi reIOException, com.dalsemi.onewire.One-WireException
	byte[]	**readScratchpad**() *throws* com.dalsemi.onewire.adapter.OneWi reIOException, com.dalsemi.onewire.One-WireException
⚠■	byte	**RECALL_E2MEMORY_COMMAND**
	byte[]	**recallE2**() *throws* com.dalsemi.onewire.adapter.OneWi reIOException, com.dalsemi.onewire.One-WireException
⚠■	byte	**RESOLUTION_10_BIT**
⚠■	byte	**RESOLUTION_11_BIT**
⚠■	byte	**RESOLUTION_12_BIT**
⚠■	byte	**RESOLUTION_9_BIT**
	void	**setTemperatureAlarm**(int alarmType, double alarmValue, byte[] state) *throws* com.dalsemi.onewire.OneWireExcept ion, com.dalsemi.onewire.adapter.One-WireIOException
	void	**setTemperatureResolution**(double resolution, byte[] state) *throws* com.dalsemi.onewire.OneWireExcept ion
⚠■	byte	**WRITE_SCRATCHPAD_COMMAND**
	void	**writeDevice**(byte[] state) *throws* com.dalsemi.onewire.adapter.OneWi reIOException, com.dalsemi.onewire.One-WireException
	void	**writeScratchpad**(byte[] data) *throws* com.dalsemi.onewire.adapter.OneWi reIOException, com.dalsemi.onewire.One-WireException

OneWireContainer2C	com.dalsemi.onewire.container

Object
➡OneWireContainer
   ➡OneWireContainer2C   PotentiometerContainer

int	**decrement**()
	throws com.dalsemi.onewire.adapter.OneWireIOException, com.dalsemi.onewire.OneWireException
int	**decrement**(boolean reselect)
	throws com.dalsemi.onewire.adapter.OneWireIOException, com.dalsemi.onewire.OneWireException
String	**getAlternateNames**()
int	**getCurrentWiperNumber**(byte[] state)
String	**getDescription**()
int	**getMaxSpeed**()
String	**getName**()
int	**getWiperPosition**()
	throws com.dalsemi.onewire.adapter.OneWireIOException, com.dalsemi.onewire.OneWireException
int	**increment**()
	throws com.dalsemi.onewire.adapter.OneWireIOException, com.dalsemi.onewire.OneWireException
int	**increment**(boolean reselect)
	throws com.dalsemi.onewire.adapter.OneWireIOException, com.dalsemi.onewire.OneWireException
boolean	**isChargePumpOn**(byte[] state)
boolean	**isLinear**(byte[] state)
int	**numberOfPotentiometers**(byte[] state)
int	**numberOfWiperSettings**(byte[] state)
❊	**OneWireContainer2C**()
❊	**OneWireContainer2C**(com.dalsemi.onewire.adapter.DSPortAdapter sourceAdapter, byte[] newAddress)
❊	**OneWireContainer2C**(com.dalsemi.onewire.adapter.DSPortAdapter sourceAdapter, long newAddress)
❊	**OneWireContainer2C**(com.dalsemi.onewire.adapter.DSPortAdapter sourceAdapter, String newAddress)
int	**potentiometerResistance**(byte[] state)
byte[]	**readDevice**()
	throws com.dalsemi.onewire.adapter.OneWireIOException, com.dalsemi.onewire.OneWireException

	void	**setChargePump**(boolean charge_pump_on, byte[] state)
	void	**setCurrentWiperNumber**(int wiper_number, byte[] state)
	boolean	**setWiperPosition**(int position) *throws* com.dalsemi.onewire.adapter.OneWireIOException, com.dalsemi.onewire.OneWireException
	boolean	**wiperSettingsAreVolatile**(byte[] state)
	void	**writeDevice**(byte[] state) *throws* com.dalsemi.onewire.adapter.OneWireIOException, com.dalsemi.onewire.OneWireException

OneWireContainer30   com.dalsemi.onewire.container

```
Object
  ➥OneWireContainer
      ➥OneWireContainer30            ADContainer, Temperature-
Container
```

	boolean	**canADMultiChannelRead**()
✐■	byte	**CC_PIN_STATE_FLAG**
✐■	byte	**CHARGE_ENABLE_FLAG**
✐■	byte	**CHARGE_OVERCURRENT_FLAG**
	void	**clearConditions**() *throws* com.dalsemi.onewire.adapter.OneWireIOException, com.dalsemi.onewire.OneWireException
✐■	byte	**DC_PIN_STATE_FLAG**
✐■	byte	**DISCHARGE_ENABLE_FLAG**
✐■	byte	**DISCHARGE_OVERCURRENT_FLAG**
	void	**doADConvert**(boolean[] doConvert, byte[] state) *throws* com.dalsemi.onewire.adapter.OneWireIOException, com.dalsemi.onewire.OneWireException
	void	**doADConvert**(int channel, byte[] state) *throws* com.dalsemi.onewire.adapter.OneWireIOException, com.dalsemi.onewire.OneWireException
	void	**doTemperatureConvert**(byte[] state) *throws* com.dalsemi.onewire.adapter.OneWireIOException, com.dalsemi.onewire.OneWireException
✐■	byte	**EEPROM_BLOCK_0_LOCK_FLAG**
✐■	byte	**EEPROM_BLOCK_1_LOCK_FLAG**
✐■	byte	**EEPROM_COPY_FLAG**
✐■	byte	**EEPROM_LOCK_ENABLE_FLAG**
✐■	byte	**EEPROM_REGISTER**

double	**getADAlarm**(int channel, int alarmType, byte[] state) *throws* com.dalsemi.onewire.OneWireExcept ion
boolean	**getADAlarmEnable**(int channel, int alarmType, byte[] state) *throws* com.dalsemi.onewire.OneWireExcept ion
double	**getADRange**(int channel, byte[] state)
double[]	**getADRanges**(int channel)
double	**getADResolution**(int channel, byte[] state)
double[]	**getADResolutions**(int channel, double range)
double[]	**getADVoltage**(byte[] state) *throws* com.dalsemi.onewire.adapter.OneWi reIOException, com.dalsemi.onewire.One-WireException
double	**getADVoltage**(int channel, byte[] state) *throws* com.dalsemi.onewire.adapter.OneWi reIOException, com.dalsemi.onewire.One-WireException
String	**getAlternateNames**()
double	**getCurrent**(byte[] state) *throws* com.dalsemi.onewire.adapter.OneWi reIOException, com.dalsemi.onewire.One-WireException
String	**getDescription**()
boolean	**getFlag**(int memAddr, byte flagToGet) *throws* com.dalsemi.onewire.adapter.OneWi reIOException, com.dalsemi.onewire.One-WireException
boolean	**getLatchState**() *throws* com.dalsemi.onewire.adapter.OneWi reIOException, com.dalsemi.onewire.One-WireException
double	**getMaxTemperature**()
double	**getMinTemperature**()
String	**getName**()
int	**getNumberADChannels**()
double	**getRemainingCapacity**(byte[] state) *throws* com.dalsemi.onewire.adapter.OneWi reIOException, com.dalsemi.onewire.One-WireException
double	**getTemperature**(byte[] state)
double	**getTemperatureAlarm**(int alarmType, byte[] state) *throws* com.dalsemi.onewire.OneWireExcept ion
double	**getTemperatureAlarmResolution**() *throws* com.dalsemi.onewire.OneWireExcept ion
double	**getTemperatureResolution**(byte[] state)
double[]	**getTemperatureResolutions**()

boolean	**hasADAlarmed**(int channel, int alarmType,	
		byte[] state)
		throws com.dalsemi.onewire.OneWireExcept
		ion
boolean	**hasADAlarms**()	
boolean	**hasSelectableTemperatureResolution**()	
boolean	**hasTemperatureAlarms**()	
void	**lockBlock**(int blockNumber)	
		throws com.dalsemi.onewire.adapter.OneWi
		reIOException, com.dalsemi.onewire.One-
		WireException
	OneWireContainer30()	
	OneWireContainer30(com.dalsemi.onewire.adapt	
		er.DSPortAdapter sourceAdapter,
		byte[] newAddress)
	OneWireContainer30(com.dalsemi.onewire.adapt	
		er.DSPortAdapter sourceAdapter,
		long newAddress)
	OneWireContainer30(com.dalsemi.onewire.adapt	
		er.DSPortAdapter sourceAdapter,
		String newAddress)
byte	**OVERVOLTAGE_FLAG**	
byte	**PIO_PIN_SENSE_AND_CONTROL_FLAG**	
byte	**PROTECTION_REGISTER**	
byte	**PS_PIN_STATE_FLAG**	
byte	**READ_NET_ADDRESS_OPCODE_FLAG**	
byte	**readByte**(int memAddr)	
		throws com.dalsemi.onewire.adapter.OneWi
		reIOException, com.dalsemi.onewire.One-
		WireException
void	**readBytes**(int memAddr, byte[] buffer,	
		int start, int len)
		throws com.dalsemi.onewire.adapter.OneWi
		reIOException, com.dalsemi.onewire.One-
		WireException
byte[]	**readDevice**()	
		throws com.dalsemi.onewire.adapter.OneWi
		reIOException, com.dalsemi.onewire.One-
		WireException
byte[]	**readEEPROMBlock**(int blockNumber)	
		throws com.dalsemi.onewire.adapter.OneWi
		reIOException, com.dalsemi.onewire.One-
		WireException
void	**setADAlarm**(int channel, int alarmType,	
		double alarm, byte[] state)
		throws com.dalsemi.onewire.OneWireExcept
		ion
void	**setADAlarmEnable**(int channel, int alarmType,	
		boolean alarmEnable, byte[] state)
		throws com.dalsemi.onewire.OneWireExcept
		ion

void	**setADRange**(int channel, double range, byte[] state)	
void	**setADResolution**(int channel, double resolution, byte[] state)	
void	**setFlag**(int memAddr, byte flagToSet, boolean flagValue)	
	throws com.dalsemi.onewire.adapter.OneWireIOException, com.dalsemi.onewire.OneWireException	
void	**setLatchState**(boolean on)	
	throws com.dalsemi.onewire.adapter.OneWireIOException, com.dalsemi.onewire.OneWireException	
void	**setRemainingCapacity**(double remainingCapacity)	
	throws com.dalsemi.onewire.adapter.OneWireIOException, com.dalsemi.onewire.OneWireException	
void	**setResistorExternal**(double Rsens)	
void	**setResistorInternal**()	
void	**setTemperatureAlarm**(int alarmType, double alarmValue, byte[] state)	
	throws com.dalsemi.onewire.OneWireException, com.dalsemi.onewire.adapter.OneWireIOException	
void	**setTemperatureResolution**(double resolution, byte[] state)	
	throws com.dalsemi.onewire.OneWireException, com.dalsemi.onewire.adapter.OneWireIOException	
byte	**SLEEP_MODE_ENABLE_FLAG**	
byte	**SPECIAL_FEATURE_REGISTER**	
byte	**STATUS_REGISTER**	
byte	**UNDERVOLTAGE_FLAG**	
void	**writeByte**(int memAddr, byte data)	
	throws com.dalsemi.onewire.adapter.OneWireIOException, com.dalsemi.onewire.OneWireException	
void	**writeDevice**(byte[] state)	
	throws com.dalsemi.onewire.adapter.OneWireIOException, com.dalsemi.onewire.OneWireException	
void	**writeEEPROMBlock**(int blockNumber, byte[] data)	
	throws com.dalsemi.onewire.adapter.OneWireIOException, com.dalsemi.onewire.OneWireException	

OneWireContainer33   `com.dalsemi.onewire.container`

```
Object
   ➡OneWireContainer
      ➡OneWireContainer33
```

void	**computeNextSecret**(int addr, byte[] nextsecret, byte[] partialsecret, byte[] mac) *throws* com.dalsemi.onewire.adapter.OneWireIOException, com.dalsemi.onewire.OneWireException
String	**getAlternateNames**()
void	**getChallenge**(byte[] get)
String	**getDescription**()
int	**getMaxSpeed**()
java.util.Enumeration	**getMemoryBanks**()
String	**getName**()
void	**getSecret**(byte[] get)
boolean	**isContainerSecretSet**() *throws* com.dalsemi.onewire.adapter.OneWireIOException, com.dalsemi.onewire.OneWireException
boolean	**isMACValid**(int addr, byte[] SerNum, byte[] memory, byte[] mac, byte[] challenge, byte[] secret) *throws* com.dalsemi.onewire.OneWireException, com.dalsemi.onewire.adapter.OneWireIOException
boolean	**isPageOneEPROMmode**() *throws* com.dalsemi.onewire.adapter.OneWireIOException, com.dalsemi.onewire.OneWireException
boolean	**isSecretWriteProtected**() *throws* com.dalsemi.onewire.adapter.OneWireIOException, com.dalsemi.onewire.OneWireException
boolean	**isWriteProtectAllSet**() *throws* com.dalsemi.onewire.adapter.OneWireIOException, com.dalsemi.onewire.OneWireException
boolean	**isWriteProtectPageZeroSet**() *throws* com.dalsemi.onewire.adapter.OneWireIOException, com.dalsemi.onewire.OneWireException
boolean	**loadFirstSecret**(byte[] data) *throws* com.dalsemi.onewire.adapter.OneWireIOException, com.dalsemi.onewire.OneWireException
	OneWireContainer33()

✱	**OneWireContainer33**(com.dalsemi.onewire.adapter.DSPortAdapter sourceAdapter, byte[] newAddress)
✱	**OneWireContainer33**(com.dalsemi.onewire.adapter.DSPortAdapter sourceAdapter, long newAddress)
✱	**OneWireContainer33**(com.dalsemi.onewire.adapter.DSPortAdapter sourceAdapter, String newAddress)
void	**setChallenge**(byte[] challengeset)
void	**setContainerSecret**(byte[] secretset)
void	**setEPROMModePageOne**() *throws* com.dalsemi.onewire.adapter.OneWireIOException, com.dalsemi.onewire.OneWireException
void	**setupContainer**(com.dalsemi.onewire.adapter.DSPortAdapter sourceAdapter, byte[] newAddress)
void	**setupContainer**(com.dalsemi.onewire.adapter.DSPortAdapter sourceAdapter, long newAddress)
void	**setupContainer**(com.dalsemi.onewire.adapter.DSPortAdapter sourceAdapter, String newAddress)
void	**writeProtectAll**() *throws* com.dalsemi.onewire.adapter.OneWireIOException, com.dalsemi.onewire.OneWireException
void	**writeProtectPageZero**() *throws* com.dalsemi.onewire.adapter.OneWireIOException, com.dalsemi.onewire.OneWireException
void	**writeProtectSecret**() *throws* com.dalsemi.onewire.adapter.OneWireIOException, com.dalsemi.onewire.OneWireException

OneWireException · com.dalsemi.onewire

```
Object
  ➥Throwable                    java.io.Serializable
    ➥Exception
      ➥OneWireException
```

✱	**OneWireException**()
✱	**OneWireException**(String desc)

OneWireIOException · com.dalsemi.onewire.adapter

```
Object
  ➥Throwable                    java.io.Serializable
```

➥Exception
    ➥com.dalsemi.onewire.OneWireException
       ➥OneWireIOException

✳	**OneWireIOException**()
✳	**OneWireIOException**(String desc)

OneWireMonitor · com.dalsemi.onewire.utils

Object
  ➥Thread   Runnable
    ➥OneWireMonitor

	void	**addEventListener**(OneWireMonitorEventListener owmel)
	void	**killMonitor**()
✳		**OneWireMonitor**(com.dalsemi.onewire.adapter.DSPortAdapter adapter)
	void	**removeEventListener**(OneWireMonitorEventListener owmel)
	void	**run**()

OneWireMonitorEvent · com.dalsemi.onewire.utils

Object
  ➥java.util.EventObject   java.io.Serializable
    ➥OneWireMonitorEvent

	com.dalsemi.one-wire.adapter.DSPortAdapter	**getAdapter**()
	byte[]	**getAddress**()
	long	**getAddressAsLong**()
	String	**getAddressAsString**()
	com.dalsemi.one-wire.con-tainer.OneWireContainer	**getDeviceContainer**()
✳		**OneWireMonitorEvent**(OneWireMonitor owm, com.dalsemi.onewire.adapter.DSPortAdapter adapter, long address)

OneWireMonitorEventListener · com.dalsemi.onewire.utils

OneWireMonitorEventListener

	void	**oneWireArrival**(OneWireMonitorEvent owme)
	void	**oneWireDeparture**(OneWireMonitorEvent owme)

OneWireSensor	com.dalsemi.onewire.container

OneWireSensor

byte[]	**readDevice**()
	throws com.dalsemi.onewire.adapter.OneWi reIOException, com.dalsemi.onewire.One- WireException
void	**writeDevice**(byte[] state)
	throws com.dalsemi.onewire.adapter.OneWi reIOException, com.dalsemi.onewire.One- WireException

OTPMemoryBank	com.dalsemi.onewire.container

OTPMemoryBank   PagedMemoryBank

boolean	**canLockPage**()
boolean	**canLockRedirectPage**()
boolean	**canRedirectPage**()
int	**getRedirectedPage**(int page)
	throws com.dalsemi.onewire.adapter.OneWi reIOException, com.dalsemi.onewire.One- WireException
boolean	**isPageLocked**(int page)
	throws com.dalsemi.onewire.adapter.OneWi reIOException, com.dalsemi.onewire.One- WireException
int	**isPageRedirected**(int page)
	throws com.dalsemi.onewire.adapter.OneWi reIOException, com.dalsemi.onewire.One- WireException
boolean	**isRedirectPageLocked**(int page)
	throws com.dalsemi.onewire.adapter.OneWi reIOException, com.dalsemi.onewire.One- WireException
void	**lockPage**(int page)
	throws com.dalsemi.onewire.adapter.OneWi reIOException, com.dalsemi.onewire.One- WireException
void	**lockRedirectPage**(int page)
	throws com.dalsemi.onewire.adapter.OneWi reIOException, com.dalsemi.onewire.One- WireException
void	**redirectPage**(int page, int newPage)
	throws com.dalsemi.onewire.adapter.OneWi reIOException, com.dalsemi.onewire.One- WireException

OWFile	com.dalsemi.onewire.utils

```
Object
    ➥OWFile
```

boolean	**canRead**()
boolean	**canWrite**()
void	**close**() *throws* java.io.IOException
int	**compareTo**(Object o)
int	**compareTo**(OWFile pathname)
boolean	**createNewFile**() *throws* java.io.IOException
boolean	**delete**()
boolean	**equals**(Object obj)
boolean	**exists**()
void	**format**() *throws* java.io.IOException
OWFile	**getAbsoluteFile**()
String	**getAbsolutePath**()
OWFile	**getCanonicalFile**() *throws* java.io.IOException
String	**getCanonicalPath**() *throws* java.io.IOException
OWFileDescriptor	**getFD**() *throws* java.io.IOException
int	**getFreeMemory**() *throws* java.io.IOException
int	**getLocalPage**(int page)
com.dalsemi.onewire.container.PagedMemor yBank	**getMemoryBankForPage**(int page)
String	**getName**()
com.dalsemi.onewire.container.OneWireCon tainer	**getOneWireContainer**()
int[]	**getPageList**() *throws* java.io.IOException
String	**getParent**()
OWFile	**getParentFile**()
String	**getPath**()
int	**hashCode**()
boolean	**isAbsolute**()
boolean	**isDirectory**()
boolean	**isFile**()
boolean	**isHidden**()
long	**lastModified**()
long	**length**()
String[]	**list**()
OWFile[]	**listFiles**()
OWFile[]	**listRoots**(com.dalsemi.onewire.container.OneW ireContainer owc)
boolean	**mkdir**()

	boolean	**mkdirs**()
✳		**OWFile**(com.dalsemi.onewire.container.OneWire Container owd, String pathname)
✳		**OWFile**(com.dalsemi.onewire.container.OneWire Container owd, String parent, String child)
✳		**OWFile**(OWFile parent, String child)
⬛	String	**pathSeparator**
⬛	char	**pathSeparatorChar**
	boolean	**renameTo**(OWFile dest)
⬛	String	**separator**
⬛	char	**separatorChar**
	boolean	**setLastModified**(long time)
	boolean	**setReadOnly**()
	String	**toString**()

OWFileDescriptor   com.dalsemi.onewire.utils

Object
➡OWFileDescriptor

✳		**OWFileDescriptor**()
	void	**sync**() *throws* java.io.SyncFailedException
	boolean	**valid**()

OWFileInputStream   com.dalsemi.onewire.utils

Object
➡java.io.InputStream
  ➡OWFileInputStream

	int	**available**() *throws* java.io.IOException
	void	**close**() *throws* java.io.IOException
	void	**finalize**() *throws* java.io.IOException
●	OWFileDescriptor	**getFD**() *throws* java.io.IOException
	void	**mark**(int readlimit)
	boolean	**markSupported**()
✳		**OWFileInputStream**(com.dalsemi.onewire.contai ner.OneWireContainer owd, String name) *throws* java.io.FileNotFoundException
✳		**OWFileInputStream**(OWFile file) *throws* java.io.FileNotFoundException
✳		**OWFileInputStream**(OWFileDescriptor fdObj)
	int	**read**() *throws* java.io.IOException
	int	**read**(byte[] b) *throws* java.io.IOException
	int	**read**(byte[] b, int off, int len) *throws* java.io.IOException
	void	**reset**() *throws* java.io.IOException
	long	**skip**(long n) *throws* java.io.IOException

OWFileOutputStream   `com.dalsemi.onewire.utils`

```
Object
  ➥java.io.OutputStream
      ➥OWFileOutputStream
```

	void	**close**() *throws* java.io.IOException
	void	**finalize**() *throws* java.io.IOException
	OWFileDescriptor	**getFD**() *throws* java.io.IOException
✱		**OWFileOutputStream**(com.dalsemi.onewire.conta iner.OneWireContainer owd, String name) *throws* java.io.FileNotFoundException
✱		**OWFileOutputStream**(com.dalsemi.onewire.conta iner.OneWireContainer owd, String name, boolean append) *throws* java.io.FileNotFoundException
✱		**OWFileOutputStream**(OWFile file) *throws* java.io.FileNotFoundException
✱		**OWFileOutputStream**(OWFileDescriptor fdObj)
	void	**write**(byte[] b) *throws* java.io.IOException
	void	**write**(byte[] b, int off, int len) *throws* java.io.IOException
	void	**write**(int b) *throws* java.io.IOException

OWPath   `com.dalsemi.onewire.utils`

```
Object
  ➥OWPath
```

	void	**add**(com.dalsemi.onewire.container.OneWireCon tainer owc, int channel)
	void	**close**() *throws* com.dalsemi.onewire.OneWireExcept ion, com.dalsemi.onewire.adapter.One-WireIOException
	void	**copy**(OWPath currentOWPath)
	boolean	**equals**(OWPath compareOWPath)
	java.util.Enumer-ation	**getAllOWPathElements**()
	void	**open**() *throws* com.dalsemi.onewire.OneWireExcept ion, com.dalsemi.onewire.adapter.One-WireIOException
✱		**OWPath**(com.dalsemi.onewire.adapter.DSPortAda pter adapter)
✱		**OWPath**(com.dalsemi.onewire.adapter.DSPortAda pter adapter, OWPath currentOWPath)
	String	**toString**()

OWPathElement — com.dalsemi.onewire.utils

```
Object
  ➥OWPathElement
```

int	**getChannel**()
com.dalsemi.one- wire.con- tainer.OneWireCon tainer	**getContainer**()
❊	**OWPathElement**(com.dalsemi.onewire.container. OneWireContainer owcInstance, int channelNumber)

PagedMemoryBank — com.dalsemi.onewire.container

PagedMemoryBank   MemoryBank

String	**getExtraInfoDescription**()
int	**getExtraInfoLength**()
int	**getMaxPacketDataLength**()
int	**getNumberPages**()
int	**getPageLength**()
boolean	**hasExtraInfo**()
boolean	**hasPageAutoCRC**()
boolean	**haveExtraInfo**()
void	**readPage**(int page, boolean readContinue, byte[] readBuf, int offset) *throws* com.dalsemi.onewire.adapter.OneWi reIOException, com.dalsemi.onewire.One- WireException
void	**readPage**(int page, boolean readContinue, byte[] readBuf, int offset, byte[] extraInfo) *throws* com.dalsemi.onewire.adapter.OneWi reIOException, com.dalsemi.onewire.One- WireException
void	**readPageCRC**(int page, boolean readContinue, byte[] readBuf, int offset) *throws* com.dalsemi.onewire.adapter.OneWi reIOException, com.dalsemi.onewire.One- WireException
void	**readPageCRC**(int page, boolean readContinue, byte[] readBuf, int offset, byte[] extraInfo) *throws* com.dalsemi.onewire.adapter.OneWi reIOException, com.dalsemi.onewire.One- WireException

	int	**readPagePacket**(int page,
		boolean readContinue, byte[] readBuf,
		int offset)
		throws com.dalsemi.onewire.adapter.OneWi
		reIOException, com.dalsemi.onewire.One-
		WireException
	int	**readPagePacket**(int page,
		boolean readContinue, byte[] readBuf,
		int offset, byte[] extraInfo)
		throws com.dalsemi.onewire.adapter.OneWi
		reIOException, com.dalsemi.onewire.One-
		WireException
	void	**writePagePacket**(int page, byte[] writeBuf,
		int offset, int len)
		throws com.dalsemi.onewire.adapter.OneWi
		reIOException, com.dalsemi.onewire.One-
		WireException

Ping   `com.dalsemi.tininet.icmp`

Object
   ➡Ping

	byte	**DEFAULT_TTL**
	boolean	**pingNode**(java.net.InetAddress addr)
	long	**pingNode**(java.net.InetAddress addr,
		byte ttl, byte[] response)
	int	**pingNode**(java.net.InetAddress addr,
		int count)

PotentiometerContainer   `com.dalsemi.onewire.container`

PotentiometerContainer   OneWireSensor

	int	**decrement**()
		throws com.dalsemi.onewire.adapter.OneWi
		reIOException, com.dalsemi.onewire.One-
		WireException
	int	**decrement**(boolean reselect)
		throws com.dalsemi.onewire.adapter.OneWi
		reIOException, com.dalsemi.onewire.One-
		WireException
	int	**getCurrentWiperNumber**(byte[] state)
	int	**getWiperPosition**()
		throws com.dalsemi.onewire.adapter.OneWi
		reIOException, com.dalsemi.onewire.One-
		WireException
	int	**increment**()
		throws com.dalsemi.onewire.adapter.OneWi
		reIOException, com.dalsemi.onewire.One-
		WireException

int	**increment**(boolean reselect)
	throws com.dalsemi.onewire.adapter.OneWi
	reIOException, com.dalsemi.onewire.One-
	WireException
boolean	**isChargePumpOn**(byte[] state)
boolean	**isLinear**(byte[] state)
int	**numberOfPotentiometers**(byte[] state)
int	**numberOfWiperSettings**(byte[] state)
int	**potentiometerResistance**(byte[] state)
void	**setChargePump**(boolean charge_pump_on,
	byte[] state)
void	**setCurrentWiperNumber**(int wiper_number,
	byte[] state)
boolean	**setWiperPosition**(int position)
	throws com.dalsemi.onewire.adapter.OneWi
	reIOException, com.dalsemi.onewire.One-
	WireException
boolean	**wiperSettingsAreVolatile**(byte[] state)

PPP	**com.dalsemi.tininet.ppp**

Object
   ➡Thread   Runnable
      ➡PPP

void	**addEventListener**(PPPEventListener eventListe
	ner)
	throws java.util.TooManyListenersExcepti
	on
void	**addInterface**(String name)
void	**authenticate**(boolean value)
void	**close**()
void	**down**()
void	**freeInterfaceWrapper**()
int	**getACCM**()
boolean	**getAuthenticate**()
boolean	**getDefaultInterface**()
byte[]	**getLocalAddress**()
int	**getMaxConfig**()
int	**getMaxFailure**()
int	**getMaxTerminate**()
boolean	**getPassive**()
String	**getPeerID**()
String	**getPeerPassword**()
byte[]	**getRemoteAddress**()
int	**getRestartPeriod**()
int	**getTransmitter**(byte index)
int	**getUsernamePassword**(int option,
	byte[] value)

	boolean	**getXonXoffEscape**()
	void	**open**()
✎■	byte	**PEER_ID**
✎■	byte	**PEER_PASSWORD**
✳		**PPP**()
	void	**removeEventListener**(PPPEventListener eventListener)
	void	**removeInterface**(String name)
●	void	**run**()
	void	**setACCM**(int newACCM)
	void	**setAuthenticate**(boolean value)
	void	**setDefaultInterface**(boolean value)
	void	**setLocalAddress**(byte[] address)
	void	**setMaxConfig**(int count) *throws* PPPException
	void	**setMaxFailure**(int count) *throws* PPPException
	void	**setMaxTerminate**(int count) *throws* PPPException
	void	**setPassive**(boolean value)
	void	**setPassword**(String password) *throws* PPPException
	void	**setRemoteAddress**(byte[] address)
	void	**setRestartPeriod**(int timeout) *throws* PPPException
	void	**setUsername**(String userName) *throws* PPPException
	void	**setXonXoffEscape**(boolean value)
	void	**stopPPPThread**()
	void	**up**(javax.comm.SerialPort sp)

PPPEvent   com.dalsemi.tininet.ppp

Object
    ➥java.util.EventObject   java.io.Serializable
        ➥PPPEvent

✎■	int	**ADDR**
✎■	int	**AUTH**
✎■	int	**AUTHENTICATION_REQUEST**
✎■	int	**CLOSED**
	int	**getEventType**()
	int	**getLastError**()
✎■	int	**NONE**
✎■	int	**REJECT**
✎■	int	**STARTING**
✎■	int	**STOPPED**
✎■	int	**TIME**
✎■	int	**UP**

PPPEventListener | com.dalsemi.tininet.ppp

PPPEventListener | java.util.EventListener

| | void | **pppEvent**(PPPEvent ev) |

PPPException | com.dalsemi.tininet.ppp

Object
  ➡Throwable   java.io.Serializable
    ➡Exception
      ➡PPPException

| ✳ | | **PPPException**() |
| ✳ | | **PPPException**(String s) |

ResponseAPDU | com.dalsemi.onewire.container

Object
  ➡ResponseAPDU

●	byte	**getByte**(int index)
●	byte[]	**getBytes**()
●	byte[]	**getData**()
●	int	**getLength**()
●	int	**getSW**()
●	byte	**getSW1**()
●	byte	**getSW2**()
✳		**ResponseAPDU**(byte[] buffer)
	String	**toString**()

Security | com.dalsemi.system

Object
  ➡Security

| ❏ | int | **getRandom**() |
| ❏ | byte[] | **hashMessage**(byte[] MsgStr) |

SerialInputStream | com.dalsemi.comm

Object
  ➡java.io.InputStream
    ➡SerialInputStream

| | int | **available**() *throws* java.io.IOException |
| | void | **close**() *throws* java.io.IOException |

```
int  read() throws java.io.IOException
int  read(byte[] barr, int offset, int len)
        throws java.io.IOException
void  unread(byte b) throws java.io.IOException
```

SerialOutputStream   com.dalsemi.comm

```
Object
 ➡java.io.OutputStream
    ➡SerialOutputStream
```

```
void  close() throws java.io.IOException
 *     SerialOutputStream(InternalSerialPort sp)
void  write(byte[] barr, int offset, int len)
        throws java.io.IOException
void  write(int ch) throws java.io.IOException
```

SerialServer   com.dalsemi.shell.server.serial

```
Object
 ➡Thread                          Runnable
    ➡com.dalsemi.shell.server.Server
       ➡SerialServer
```

```
void  broadcast(String sendThis)
void  closeAllPorts() throws java.io.IOException
 *     SerialServer(String portName, int speed,
           int dataBits, int stopBits, int parity)
           throws Exception
```

SerialSession   com.dalsemi.shell.server.serial

```
Object
 ➡Thread                          Runnable
    ➡com.dalsemi.shell.server.Session
       ➡SerialSession
```

```
String  getNextCommand() throws java.io.IOException
  void  login() throws java.io.IOException
  void  updatePrompt(String withThis)
```

Server   com.dalsemi.shell.server

```
Object
 ➡Thread                          Runnable
    ➡Server
```

```
   void  broadcast(String sendThis)
String[]  getConnectedUsers()
```

	void	**run**()
	void	**sessionEnded**(Session session)
	void	**shutDown**() *throws* java.io.IOException

Session   com.dalsemi.shell.server

```
Object
  ➡Thread                    Runnable
      ➡Session
```

	void	**addToHistory**(String str)
	void	**broadcast**(String sendThis)
✍☐	String	**CURRENT_COMMAND**
✍☐	String	**CURRENT_DIRECTORY**
●	void	**endSession**()
●	void	**forceEndSession**()
	java.util.Hash-table	**getEnvironment**()
	java.io.Print-Stream	**getErrStream**()
	String	**getFromEnvironment**(String key)
	String	**getHistoryNumber**(int number)
	String	**getNextCommand**() *throws* java.io.IOException
	java.io.Print-Stream	**getOutputStream**()
☐	Object[]	**getParams**(String str)
	String	**getUserName**()
	boolean	**inCommand**()
	void	**printHistory**(java.io.PrintStream out)
✍☐	String	**PROMPT**
●	void	**run**()
	String	**stepDownHistory**()
	String	**stepUpHistory**()
	boolean	**su**(String userName, String password)
	void	**updatePrompt**(String withThis)
✍☐	String	**welcomeMessage**

SHAiButton   com.dalsemi.onewire.container

```
Object
  ➡SHAiButton
```

	int	**answerChallenge**(byte[] challenge, byte[] mac, byte[] pagedata) *throws* com.dalsemi.onewire.adapter.OneWireIOException, com.dalsemi.onewire.OneWireException
✍■	int	**AUTHENTICATION_FAILED_ERROR**
✍■	int	**BIND_SECRET_ERROR**

	int	CRC_ERROR
	int	ERASE_SCRATCHPAD_ERROR
boolean		**generateChallenge**(int page_number, int offset, byte[] ch) *throws* com.dalsemi.onewire.adapter.OneWireIOException, com.dalsemi.onewire.OneWireException
byte[]		**getBindCode**()
byte[]		**getBindData**()
int		**getLastError**()
int		**getUserFileExtension**()
String		**getUserFileName**()
boolean		**isCoprocessor**()
	int	NO_COPROCESSOR_ERROR
	int	NO_ERROR
	int	NO_USER_ERROR
	int	READ_AUTHENTICATED_ERROR
	int	READ_MEMORY_PAGE_ERROR
	int	READ_SCRATCHPAD_ERROR
int		**readFile**(int start_page, byte[] page) *throws* com.dalsemi.onewire.adapter.OneWireIOException, com.dalsemi.onewire.OneWireException
void		**setAuthenticationPageNumber**(int pg)
void		**setBindCode**(byte[] buf, int offset)
void		**setBindData**(byte[] buf, int offset)
void		**setFilename**(byte[] buf, int start)
void		**setiButton**(OneWireContainer18 ibc)
void		**setInitialSignature**(byte[] sig_ini, int start)
void		**setSigningChallenge**(byte[] ch, int start)
void		**setSigningPageNumber**(int pg)
boolean		**setUser**(int file_page_number)
void		**setWorkspacePageNumber**(int pg)
	int	SHA_FUNCTION_ERROR
		SHAiButton()
		SHAiButton(OneWireContainer18 ibc)
boolean		**signDataFile**(SHAiButton user, int newbalance, int write_cycle_counter, byte[] pagedata) *throws* com.dalsemi.onewire.adapter.OneWireIOException, com.dalsemi.onewire.OneWireException
String		**toString**()
	int	VERIFICATION_FAILED_ERROR

		int	**verifyAuthentication**(SHAiButton user, byte[] pagedata) *throws* com.dalsemi.onewire.OneWireExcept ion, com.dalsemi.onewire.adapter.One-WireIOException
		boolean	**verifyUserMoney**(byte[] userpage, SHAiButton user, int wcc) *throws* com.dalsemi.onewire.adapter.OneWi reIOException, com.dalsemi.onewire.One-WireException
✍■		int	**WRITE_MEMORY_PAGE_ERROR**
✍■		int	**WRITE_SCRATCHPAD_ERROR**

SwitchContainer   com.dalsemi.onewire.container

SwitchContainer   OneWireSensor

		void	**clearActivity**() *throws* com.dalsemi.onewire.OneWireExcept ion
		boolean	**getLatchState**(int channel, byte[] state)
		boolean	**getLevel**(int channel, byte[] state) *throws* com.dalsemi.onewire.OneWireExcept ion
		int	**getNumberChannels**(byte[] state)
		boolean	**getSensedActivity**(int channel, byte[] state) *throws* com.dalsemi.onewire.OneWireExcept ion
		boolean	**hasActivitySensing**()
		boolean	**hasLevelSensing**()
		boolean	**hasSmartOn**()
		boolean	**isHighSideSwitch**()
		boolean	**onlySingleChannelOn**()
		void	**setLatchState**(int channel, boolean latchState, boolean doSmart, byte[] state)

SystemInputStream   com.dalsemi.shell.server

Object
  ➡java.io.InputStream
    ➡SystemInputStream

●		int	**available**() *throws* java.io.IOException
		boolean	**errorOccurred**()
✍		String	**fileInName**
	java.io.Input-Stream		**getRootStream**()
●		int	**read**() *throws* java.io.IOException
		int	**read**(byte[] buff, int off, int len) *throws* java.io.IOException
		String	**readLine**()

	void	**setEcho**(boolean echo)
	void	**setEchoStream**(java.io.PrintStream echo)
	void	**setRawMode**(boolean rawMode)
	void	**setRootStream**(java.io.InputStream newIn)
	void	**setSession**(Session session)
✳		**SystemInputStream**(java.io.InputStream in, java.io.PrintStream out)
✳		**SystemInputStream**(java.io.InputStream in, java.io.PrintStream out, String fileInName)

SystemPrintStream `com.dalsemi.shell.server`

```
Object
  ➥java.io.OutputStream
     ➥java.io.FilterOutputStream
        ➥java.io.PrintStream
           ➥SystemPrintStream
```

✍	boolean	**append**
	boolean	**checkError**()
✍	String	**fileOutName**
	java.io.Output-Stream	**getRootOutputStream**()
	void	**print**(boolean b)
	void	**print**(char c)
	void	**print**(char[] s)
	void	**print**(double d)
	void	**print**(float f)
	void	**print**(int i)
	void	**print**(long l)
	void	**print**(Object obj)
	void	**print**(String s)
	void	**println**()
	void	**println**(boolean x)
	void	**println**(char x)
	void	**println**(char[] x)
	void	**println**(double x)
	void	**println**(float x)
	void	**println**(int x)
	void	**println**(long x)
	void	**println**(Object x)
	void	**println**(String x)
	void	**setRootStream**(java.io.OutputStream root)
	void	**setSession**(Session s)
✍	boolean	**shieldsUp**
✳		**SystemPrintStream**(java.io.OutputStream root)

✳		**SystemPrintStream**(java.io.OutputStream out, boolean autoFlush)
✳		**SystemPrintStream**(java.io.OutputStream root, String fileOutName, boolean append)
	void	**write**(byte[] buf, int off, int len)
	void	**write**(int b)

TelnetServer   `com.dalsemi.shell.server.telnet`

Object
➥Thread   Runnable
　➥com.dalsemi.shell.server.Server
　　➥TelnetServer

❑	String	**getWelcomeFile**()
❑	boolean	**isRootAllowed**()
✳		**TelnetServer**() *throws* java.io.IOException
✳		**TelnetServer**(int port) *throws* java.io.IOException

TelnetSession   `com.dalsemi.shell.server.telnet`

Object
➥Thread   Runnable
　➥com.dalsemi.shell.server.Session
　　➥TelnetSession

	void	**login**() *throws* java.io.IOException
	void	**updatePrompt**(String withThis)

TemperatureContainer   `com.dalsemi.onewire.container`

TemperatureContainer   OneWireSensor

✎▪	int	**ALARM_HIGH**
✎▪	int	**ALARM_LOW**
	void	**doTemperatureConvert**(byte[] state) *throws* com.dalsemi.onewire.adapter.OneWireIOException, com.dalsemi.onewire.OneWireException
	double	**getMaxTemperature**()
	double	**getMinTemperature**()
	double	**getTemperature**(byte[] state) *throws* com.dalsemi.onewire.adapter.OneWireIOException
	double	**getTemperatureAlarm**(int alarmType, byte[] state) *throws* com.dalsemi.onewire.OneWireException
	double	**getTemperatureAlarmResolution**() *throws* com.dalsemi.onewire.OneWireException

double	**getTemperatureResolution**(byte[] state)
double[]	**getTemperatureResolutions**()
boolean	**hasSelectableTemperatureResolution**()
boolean	**hasTemperatureAlarms**()
void	**setTemperatureAlarm**(int alarmType, double alarmValue, byte[] state) *throws* com.dalsemi.onewire.OneWireException
void	**setTemperatureResolution**(double resolution, byte[] state) *throws* com.dalsemi.onewire.OneWireException

TINIExternalAdapter   `com.dalsemi.onewire.adapter`

Object
➥DSPortAdapter
  ➥TINIAdapter
    ➥TINIExternalAdapter

boolean	**canDeliverPower**() *throws* OneWireIOException, com.dalsemi.onewire.OneWireException
boolean	**canFlex**() *throws* OneWireIOException, com.dalsemi.onewire.OneWireException
boolean	**canHyperdrive**() *throws* OneWireIOException, com.dalsemi.onewire.OneWireException
boolean	**canOverdrive**() *throws* OneWireIOException, com.dalsemi.onewire.OneWireException
String	**getAdapterName**()
String	**getClassVersion**()
String	**getPortName**() *throws* com.dalsemi.onewire.OneWireException
java.util.Enumer-ation	**getPortNames**()
String	**getPortTypeDescription**()
boolean	**selectPort**(String portName) *throws* OneWireIOException, com.dalsemi.onewire.OneWireException
void	**setProgramPulseDuration**(int timeFactor) *throws* OneWireIOException, com.dalsemi.onewire.OneWireException
boolean	**startProgramPulse**(int changeCondition) *throws* OneWireIOException, com.dalsemi.onewire.OneWireException
❋	**TINIExternalAdapter**()

TINIInternalAdapter		**com.dalsemi.onewire.adapter**

Object
➥DSPortAdapter
　➥TINIAdapter
　　➥TINIInternalAdapter

	boolean	**canDeliverPower**() *throws* OneWireIOException, com.dalsemi.onewire.OneWireException
	boolean	**canFlex**() *throws* OneWireIOException, com.dalsemi.onewire.OneWireException
	boolean	**canHyperdrive**() *throws* OneWireIOException, com.dalsemi.onewire.OneWireException
	boolean	**canOverdrive**() *throws* OneWireIOException, com.dalsemi.onewire.OneWireException
	String	**getAdapterName**()
	String	**getClassVersion**()
	String	**getPortName**() *throws* com.dalsemi.onewire.OneWireException
	java.util.Enumeration	**getPortNames**()
	String	**getPortTypeDescription**()
	boolean	**selectPort**(String portName) *throws* OneWireIOException, com.dalsemi.onewire.OneWireException
✳		**TINIInternalAdapter**()

TININet		**com.dalsemi.tininet**

Object
➥TININet

❏	void	**addInterfaceEntry**(byte[] name, byte[] ipAddr, byte[] subnet, byte[] gateway, byte flags, byte type, int transmitter)
❏	void	**commitNetworkState**() *throws* com.dalsemi.system.CommitException
⬛	int	**COMMITTED**
❏	byte[]	**createIPFromString**(String fromThis)
❏	String	**createIPString**(byte[] fromThis)
❏	void	**disableNetworkRestore**()
⬛	int	**ETH_STATUS_LINK**
⬛	int	**ETH_STATUS_RX**
⬛	int	**ETH_STATUS_TX**
❏	byte[]	**getARPCacheTable**()
❏	byte[]	**getConnectionTable**()
❏	String	**getDHCPServerIP**()

❑	void	**getDHCPServerIP**(byte[] address)
❑	int	**getDNSTimeout**()
❑	String	**getDomainname**()
❑	String	**getEthernetAddress**()
❑	void	**getEthernetAddress**(byte[] address)
❑	int	**getEthernetStatus**()
❑	String	**getGatewayIP**()
❑	void	**getGatewayIP**(byte[] address)
❑	String	**getGatewayIP**(String interfaceName)
❑	void	**getGatewayIP**(String interfaceName, byte[] address)
❑	String	**getHostname**()
❑	boolean	**getInterfaceInfo**(int interfaceNum, byte[] data)
❑	String	**getIPAddress**()
❑	void	**getIPAddress**(byte[] address)
❑	String	**getIPAddress**(String interfaceName)
❑	void	**getIPAddress**(String interfaceName, byte[] address)
❑	String	**getMailhost**()
❑	int	**getNetworkCommitState**()
❑	String	**getPrimaryDNS**()
❑	int	**getProxyPort**()
❑	String	**getProxyServer**()
❑	String	**getSecondaryDNS**()
❑	String	**getSubnetMask**()
❑	void	**getSubnetMask**(byte[] address)
❑	String	**getSubnetMask**(String interfaceName)
❑	void	**getSubnetMask**(String interfaceName, byte[] address)
❑	void	**removeInterfaceEntry**(byte[] name)
✍■	int	**RESTORE_DISABLED**
❑	boolean	**setDefaultInterface**(byte[] name)
❑	boolean	**setDHCPServerIP**(String dhcpServer)
❑	boolean	**setDNSTimeout**(int dnsTimeout)
❑	boolean	**setDomainname**(String domain)
❑	boolean	**setGatewayIP**(byte[] gateway)
❑	boolean	**setGatewayIP**(String gateway)
❑	boolean	**setGatewayIP**(String interfaceName, byte[] gateway)
❑	boolean	**setGatewayIP**(String interfaceName, String gateway)
❑	boolean	**setHostname**(String host)
❑	boolean	**setIPAddress**(byte[] localIP)
❑	boolean	**setIPAddress**(String localIP)
❑	boolean	**setIPAddress**(String interfaceName, byte[] localIP)

❏	boolean	**setIPAddress**(String interfaceName, String localIP)	
❏	boolean	**setMailhost**(String mailhost)	
❏	boolean	**setOptions**(byte[] dhcp, byte[] ip, byte[] gateway, byte[] subnet, byte[] dns1, byte[] dns2, byte[] domain, byte[] mailhost)	
❏	boolean	**setPrimaryDNS**(String primaryDNS)	
❏	boolean	**setProxyPort**(int proxyPort)	
❏	boolean	**setProxyServer**(String proxyServer)	
❏	boolean	**setSecondaryDNS**(String secondDNS)	
❏	boolean	**setSubnetMask**(byte[] subnetMask)	
❏	boolean	**setSubnetMask**(String subnetMask)	
❏	boolean	**setSubnetMask**(String interfaceName, byte[] subnetMask)	
❏	boolean	**setSubnetMask**(String interfaceName, String subnetMask)	
✳		**TININet**()	
✍▪	int	**UNCOMMITTED**	
❏	void	**update**()	

TINIOS			com.dalsemi.system

Object
    ➡TINIOS

✍▪	int	**BLAST_ALL**
✍▪	int	**BLAST_HEAP**
▪	void	**blastHeapOnReboot**(int blastType)
▪	void	**disablePowerFailRecovery**()
▪	void	**enableSerialPort1**()
▪	void	**enableSerialPort1**(boolean enable)
❏	void	**execute**(Object[] commandLine, com.dalsemi.shell.server.SystemInputStream in, com.dalsemi.shell.server.SystemPrintStream out, com.dalsemi.shell.server.SystemPrintStream err, java.util.Hashtable env) *throws* Exception
❏	void	**feedWatchdog**()
✍▪	int	**FS_MODIFICATION_OCCURRED**
❏	int	**getBootState**()
❏	java.util.Hashtable	**getCurrentEnvironment**()
❏	byte	**getCurrentUID**()
❏	String	**getCurrentUserName**()
❏	int	**getExternalSerialPortAddress**(int portNum)
❏	boolean	**getExternalSerialPortEnable**(int portNum)

❑	boolean	**getExternalSerialPortSearchEnable**()
■	int	**getFreeRAM**()
❑	String	**getFromCurrentEnvironment**(String key)
❑	int	**getLCDAddress**()
❑	int	**getOwnerIDByTaskID**(int taskid)
❑	boolean	**getRecoveryHash**(byte[] recoveryHash)
❑	boolean	**getRTSCTSFlowControlEnable**(int portNumber)
■	boolean	**getSerialBootMessagesState**()
❑	com.dalsemi.shell .TINIShell	**getShell**()
❑	String	**getShellName**()
❑	String	**getShellVersion**()
❑	java.util.Hash-table	**getSystemEnvironment**()
❑	int	**getTaskID**()
❑	String[]	**getTaskTable**()
❑	int[]	**getTaskTableIDs**()
❑	String	**getTimeZone**()
❑	String	**getTINIHWVersion**()
❑	String	**getTINIOSFirmwareVersion**()
■	String	**getTINISerialNumber**()
❑	int	**getUIDByUserName**(String username)
❑	String	**getUserNameByUID**(byte uid)
✍■	int	**HEAP_CLEAR_OCCURRED**
❑	boolean	**isAdmin**(byte uid)
❑	boolean	**isConsoleOutputEnabled**()
❑	boolean	**isCurrentTaskInit**()
❑	boolean	**isCurrentUserAdmin**()
❑	boolean	**isTaskRunning**(int taskid)
❑	void	**killTask**(int taskID)
❑	void	**lockInitProcesses**()
❑	int	**login**(String userName, String password)
❑	void	**logout**(Object info)
✍■	int	**MASTER_ERASE_OCCURRED**
✍■	int	**NETWORK_CONFIGURATION_RESTORED**
■	void	**reboot**()
❑	void	**setConsoleOutputEnabled**(boolean set)
■	void	**setDebugMessagesState**(boolean on)
❑	void	**setExternalSerialPortAddress**(int portNum, int address)
❑	void	**setExternalSerialPortEnable**(int portNum, boolean enable)
❑	void	**setExternalSerialPortSearchEnable**(boolean enable)
❑	void	**setIrDAClockPinState**(boolean on)
❑	void	**setLCDAddress**(int address)
❑	void	**setRecoveryHash**(byte[] recoveryHash)

❏	boolean	**setRTSCTSFlowControlEnable**(int portNumber, boolean enable) *throws* javax.comm.UnsupportedCommOperati onException
■	void	**setSerialBootMessagesState**(boolean on)
❏	void	**setShell**(com.dalsemi.shell.TINIShell newShel l) *throws* SecurityException
❏	void	**setTimeZone**(String zone) *throws* IllegalArgumentException
❏	void	**setWatchdogTimeout**(int mstimeout)
■	void	**sleepProcess**(int ms)
■	long	**uptimeMillis**()

TINIShell   `com.dalsemi.shell`

Object
   ➡TINIShell

⚠■	byte	**adminUID**
○	void	**execute**(Object[] commandLine, server.SystemInputStream in, server.SystemPrintStream out, server.SystemPrintStream err, java.util.Hashtable env) *throws* Exception
○	java.util.Hash-table	**getCurrentEnvironment**()
○	byte	**getCurrentUID**()
○	String	**getCurrentUserName**()
○	String	**getFromCurrentEnvironment**(String key)
○	String	**getName**()
	java.util.Hash-table	**getSystemEnvironment**()
○	int	**getUIDByUserName**(String username)
○	String	**getUserNameByUID**(byte uid)
○	String	**getVersion**()
	boolean	**isAdmin**(byte uid)
	boolean	**isCurrentUserAdmin**()
○	int	**login**(String userName, String password)
○	void	**logout**(Object info)
✳		**TINIShell**()

Index

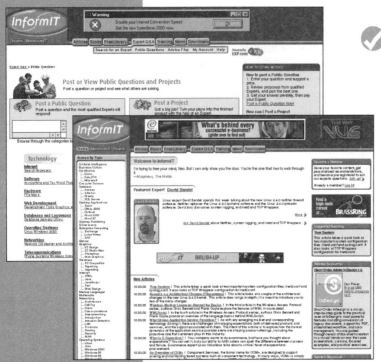

Register
Your Book
at www.aw.com/cseng/register

You may be eligible to receive:

- Advance notice of forthcoming editions of the book
- Related book recommendations
- Chapter excerpts and supplements of forthcoming titles
- Information about special contests and promotions throughout the year
- Notices and reminders about author appearances, tradeshows, and online chats with special guests

Contact us

If you are interested in writing a book or reviewing manuscripts prior to publication, please write to us at:

Editorial Department
Addison-Wesley Professional
75 Arlington Street, Suite 300
Boston, MA 02116 USA
Email: AWPro@aw.com

Visit us on the Web: http://www.aw.com/cseng

CD-ROM Warranty

Addison-Wesley warrants the enclosed disc to be free of defects in materials and faulty workmanship under normal use for a period of ninety days after purchase. If a defect is discovered in the disc during this warranty period, a replacement disc can be obtained at no charge by sending the defective disc, postage prepaid, with proof of purchase to:

Editorial Department
Addison-Wesley Professional
Pearson Technology Group
75 Arlington Street, Suite 300
Boston, MA 02116
Email: AWPro@awl.com

Addison-Wesley and Dallas Semiconductor Corporation make no warranty or representation, either expressed or implied, with respect to this software, its quality, performance, merchantability, or fitness for a particular purpose. In no event will Dallas Semiconductor Corporation or Addison-Wesley, its distributors, or dealers be liable for direct, indirect, special, incidental, or consequential damages arising out of the use or inability to use the software. The exclusion of implied royalties is not permitted in some states. Therefore, the above exclusion may not apply to you. This warranty provides you with specific legal rights. There may be other rights that you may have that vary from state to state. The contents of this CD-ROM are intended for non-commercial use only.

More information and updates are available at:
http://www.awl.com/cseng/titles/0-201-72218-6